REMEMBERING LUCILE

REMEMBERING LUCILE

A VIRGINIA FAMILY'S RISE FROM SLAVERY
AND A LEGACY FORGED A MILE HIGH

Polly E. Bugros McLean

University Press of Colorado

Boulder

Published by University Press of Colorado
245 Century Circle, Suite 202
Louisville, Colorado 80027

 The University Press of Colorado is a proud member
of the Association of American University Presses.

The University Press of Colorado is a cooperative publishing enterprise supported, in part, by Adams State University, Colorado State University, Fort Lewis College, Metropolitan State University of Denver, Regis University, University of Colorado, University of Northern Colorado, Utah State University, and Western State Colorado University.

∞ This paper meets the requirements of the ANSI/NISO Z39.48-1992 (Permanence of Paper).

ISBN: 978-1-60732-824-7 (cloth)
ISBN: 978-1-64642-195-4 (paper)
ISBN: 978-1-60732-825-4 (ebook)
DOI: https://doi.org/10.5876/9781607328254

Library of Congress Cataloging-in-Publication Data

Names: McLean, Polly E. Bugros (Polly Elise Bugros), author.
Title: Remembering Lucile : a Virginia family's rise from slavery and a legacy forged a mile high / Polly E. Bugros McLean.
Description: Louisville, Colorado : University Press of Colorado, [2018] | Includes bibliographical references and index.
Names: McLean, Polly E. Bugros (Polly Elise Bugros), author.
Title: Remembering Lucile : a Virginia family's rise from slavery and a legacy forged a mile high / Polly E. Bugros McLean.
Description: Louisville, Colorado : University Press of Colorado, [2018] | Includes bibliographical references and index.
Identifiers: LCCN 2018033990| ISBN 9781607328247 (cloth) | ISBN 9781646421954 (paperback) | ISBN 9781607328254 (ebook)
Subjects: LCSH: Jones, Lucile Berkeley Buchanan, 1884–1989—Biography. | University of Colorado Boulder—Students—Biography. | Children of freedmen—Biography.
Classification: LCC E185.97.J66 M35 2018 | DDC 378.0092 [B] —dc23
LC record available at https://lccn.loc.gov/2018033990.

Cover art from the Buchanan Archives.

To the conservers & guardians
and all those who have a story to tell

and to my mother, Christina Ignecia

Contents

Acknowledgments

A brief conversation with Wendy Hall, a librarian at Boulder's Carnegie Library for Local History, about a *Rocky Mountain News* article detailing Lucile Berkeley Buchanan Jones's connection to the University of Colorado sparked my journey. Intrigued by our discussion, and unbeknownst to me, Wendy took charge and spoke with Janice Prater, a genealogist at the Western History/Genealogy Department (WH/GD) at Denver Public Library, who faxed me information about Lucile's family in Denver with the tag line "Just to Whet Your Appetite." And that it did. So much so that the fifth floor of the WH/GD soon became my second home. Orchestrating my every move was James Jeffrey, a West Virginian transplant with an unabashed southern charm, who would spice my discoveries with yet another challenge. To the excellent library crew (those past and present) at the WH/GD who helped shape this book in various ways—Wendle Cox, Coi Drummond-Gehrig, Bruce Hanson, Hannah Parris, James Rogers, Ariana Ross, and Brian Tremdath: I thank you for fulfilling all my requests.

To those who work tirelessly to keep Black history alive in Colorado—Charleszine "Terry" Nelson, Senior Special Collection and Community Resource Manager of Denver's Blair-Caldwell African American Research Library: I thank you for your sisterly love and unwavering help. Denver's Black Genealogy Search Group, the African American Historical & Genealogical Society of Colorado Springs, and the Black American West Museum & Heritage Center, Jefferson County Black History Preservation Society and the wonderful Black women who are continuing to enrich Colorado's Black history—Iris Agard Hawkins, Annie Mabry, Lynda F. Dickson, Candice McKnight, and Clementine Washington Pigford: thank you for laying the groundwork for me to follow.

Special thanks to those who make up my local and national support system for their patience, advice, prodding, enthusiasm, and belief that Lucile and her family's story was worth telling. My sister friends, jewels of distinction—the late Joanne Arnold; Safiya Bandele; Joanne Belknap; Kathleen Curry; Lynn Gilbert; Deborah Hollis, who connected me with archivists around the country; Joan Johnson; Mary Fishback, author and library assistant at the Thomas Balch Library in Leesburg, Virginia; Patricia N. Limerick; Jodell Larimer; Kelty Logan; Linda McDowell; Dayna Mathews; Catrice Montgomery, a Buchanan descendent who shared her stories; Connie Orians; Sallye McKee; and Ardyth Sohn, who kept me centered. There were others who heard Lucile's story and stepped in to help without my asking—archivist Holly A. Smith from Spelman College, Debbie Stevenson, and Debbie Heglin.

A very special thanks to the Virginians who graciously let me into their lives and work—the late Teckla Cox; Stephen Hammond, whose grandmother was a friend of Lucile's; Lori Kimball, director of programming and education at Oatlands Historic House and Gardens; David Prokop, who was instrumental in saving the Evergreen Manor House, where Lucile's mother spent time as a slave; Mary Louise Berkeley Stoy, the great-granddaughter of Edmund Berkeley; John Fishback, the former Loudoun County Historic Records Manager, who gave me my first document on Lucile's grandfather; Donald L. Wilson, archivist extraordinaire, from the Ruth E. Lloyd Information Center for Genealogy and Local History (RELIC) in Manassas, who does not include the word "no" in his vocabulary; and local historians and authors Wynne Saffer, Eugene M. Scheel, and Ronald Ray Turner.

To all the conservators and guardians at Tuskegee University Archives; Arkansas Baptist College; Arkansas State Archives; the Newberry Library in Chicago; the University of Chicago; the Chicago Public Schools archives; Fairmount Cemetery; Harold Washington Library Center; Tennessee State Library and Archives; Winston-Salem State University; the Alumni Association archives at Columbia University in New York City; the Penrose Library at the University of Denver; the Church of the Holy Redeemer in Denver; the Stephen H. Hart Library & Research Center in Denver; the Michener Library at the University of Northern Colorado;

the University of Colorado Special Collections; Archives & Preservation and its dedicated staff, David Hays (my go-to archivist for CU's history), Sean Babbs, Philip Gaddis, Susan Guinn-Chipman, and Jennifer Sanchez; the University of Colorado Alumni Center; CU Heritage Center; the Carnegie Library for Local History, Marti Anderson and Hope Arculin; the University of Colorado's Center for Western History; the National Personnel Records Center in Missouri; and to all of you and those whom I may have forgotten: THANKS.

My deepest gratitude to some of my former doctoral students. A special shout-out to Keyana Simone for her courage to confront the greater and lesser challenges of life. She shepherded me on my first research trip tracking Lucile's deceased sisters in Los Angeles. It was a thrill observing her in the field as she charged up the steps at their former home to check out the open picture window, only to charge down after being greeted by a raven in a cage. A second shout-out to David Wallace, who helped collect and organize information at multiple stops in my journey. It was especially great to have him visit the Oatlands Plantation with me in Leesburg. A final shout-out to Ashmi Desai and Megan Hurson for their support with fact checking and getting clearances.

I would also like to thank the University of Colorado Undergraduate Research Opportunity Program (UROP) for a grant that provided support for two undergraduate students to learn archival research by assisting me at the plantations in Virginia and in the city of Chicago. And thanks to the staff in the CU's Office of Diversity, Equity, and Community Engagement and to Jeri Bonnes, Office of the Registrar, for their thoughtfulness and professional help.

To a brilliant group of individuals who played any number of roles and have been reliable advocates and listeners, connecting me with local residents, helping with research, and providing feedback over the years—Eric Arthur, Mara Boyd, Eben Carsey, Kelly Davidson, Tegan Davis, Lisa Dicksteen, Lucy Garrett, Emma Goodman, Bethany Hilyard, Rachel Laux, Ancil Liddelow, Sarah McCall, Murray Meetze, Kenneth McVey, Steve Moss, Kelly Orians, Paige Padilla, Jeffrey B. Perry, Kristina Schoonover, Dylan Sallee (my tech fixer), Debbie Stevenson, Katy Stira, Floyd Thompson, Brad Watts, Thomas Windham, and Jan Whitt, who connected me to the former managing editor of the *Waco Tribune-Herald*, who traveled with me to Bandera, Texas, on an amazing learning experience. (Thanks, Barbara.)

I wish to thank a unique group of people for their endless support, kindness, and devotion to Lucile and her family and who luckily knew her and/or her brother Fenton—Viola Garlington, Ernestine Gavin, Larry Harris, Donna Teviotdale, and Doris Smith, an angel of great proportion. To the family of Lucile's caregiver—Audrey Theisen (helper extraordinaire), Margie Heldenbrand, and Allan and

Wendell Dick: I have benefitted greatly from your generosity and invaluable assistance in letting me into Lucile's life.

I extend a heartfelt thanks to the University Press of Colorado / Utah State University Press under the direction of Darrin Pratt, who saw the vision in bringing Lucile's story out of obscurity and into the historical mainstream. It is with deep gratitude I recognize some of the most fabulous, talented, people—Laura Furney, Dan Pratt, Beth Svinarich, and Charlotte Steinhardt—for having the patience, faith, and serenity to guide me through the editorial process, believing in my passion, and providing insightful comments and suggestions. Let me not forget Jessica d'Arbonne, who went on to other challenges, for getting me started.

With pleasure and appreciation, I want to thank my mother, Christina Ignecia, the first Miss Trinidad, a woman who courageously crossed the border and to whom this book is dedicated. My sons—Che Kwame and Omar Raj: thank you for the encouragement and countless cups of coffee. I am so happy you have been in my corner, providing advice, copyediting, and suggestions; traveling with me; and keeping me centered. My love for you will live forever.

Prologue
Her Voice Can Be Heard

Just as a tree without roots is dead, a people without history or culture becomes a dead people.
— MALCOLM X

If historians of the American West and of the African American experience
have ignored the contributions of western blacks, they have been especially
negligent in chronicling the presence of black women on the western frontier.
— GLENDA RILEY

Lucile Berkeley Buchanan Jones never sought the spotlight or public recognition. Instead, she chose a life as hushed as falling autumn leaves. As I began to unravel the woman she was, I developed a passionate curiosity about the remarkable life she led. Born in a barn to emancipated slaves from Virginia near the South Platte River in Denver, Colorado, on June 13, 1884, toward the end of the Victorian era, she would die on November 13, 1989, as the Decade of Greed and the "Me" Generation came to a close.

Through ten-and-a-half decades, Lucile rejected, with prejudice, the traditional domestic roles set aside for Black women, and instead chose a career path that would require courage in the face of pernicious Jim Crow laws. She was confronted with the visceral reality of lynch mob violence when on the evening of June 19, 1913, less than a mile from where she lived in Hot Springs, Arkansas, a mob lynched twenty-one-year-old William Norman. His body was riddled with bullets, his corpse burned and left at the site as Whites continued to celebrate his death the next day, sifting through the ashes and collecting bones as souvenirs.[1] Like the fictional character Forrest Gump, in the 1994 film of the same name, Lucile witnessed spectacular and inspiring moments in US history. In 1893 she celebrated the hard work of Colorado's Black and White suffragettes, as the women of Colorado received the right to vote through popular referendum twenty-seven years before national women's suffrage. A year later, she witnessed Denver's Black suffragist Elizabeth Piper Ensley rallying Black women to the polls.

In 1924, while in Kansas City, she attended the inaugural Negro League World Series between the National Negro League champions, the Kansas City Monarchs, and the Eastern Colored League champions, the Hilldale Daisies of Darby, Pennsylvania. In 1933, when Thomas Andrew Dorsey—credited as "the father of gospel music"[2] and who wrote such popular songs as "Peace in the Valley" and "Take My Hand, Precious Lord"—organized the National Convention of Gospel Choirs and Choruses in Chicago, where Lucile served as the organization's first recording secretary.

She was fluent in German, a language she began studying in Colorado in 1905, and also read Latin. In the 1920s, while teaching at the all-Black Lincoln High School in Kansas City, Missouri, she created the school's first student newspaper, the *Observer*, as well as the World Affairs Club. A complex woman, Lucile maintained a long-distance courtship for seven years with John Dotha Jones, a man she would eventually marry. After enduring emotional abuse and abandonment, she divorced him in 1940 and never looked back. After burying her beloved brother, Fenton, in 1963, Lucile was determined to maintain the family's house in Denver where her independence only grew. To that end, she hired a neighbor, Herman Dick, to help take care of her basic needs. This arrangement lasted until 1986,[3] the year the City and County of Denver unceremoniously ripped Lucile from her home, only to place her in a nursing home without notice and consent.

FACING THE UNEXPECTED

I learned of Lucile Berkeley Buchanan Jones in September 2001, by way of a course I taught on Historical and Contemporary Issues of African American Women for the Women's Studies program (currently Women & Gender Studies) at the University of Colorado, Boulder. The course usually examines the varying roles Black women played in shaping US history. This time, I wanted to set higher academic expectations by getting students outside the classroom to find primary sources so they could critically examine the history of Black women in Boulder, a predominantly White community tucked away in the foothills of the Rocky Mountains.

When discussing this assignment with colleagues, I endured many jokes about the dearth of Black women, both at the university and in Boulder County. Comments ranged from "You mean the four of you?" to "Where are you going to find them?" Most people simply laughed. Things looked less promising on the first day of class. My students (fifteen Whites, four Blacks, and one Latina) knew that Boulder had a very small Black population and wanted to expand the assignment to include Denver, located about twenty-nine miles southeast of Boulder, where they knew for certain they could find Black women. Still, even as I began to doubt the wisdom of the assignment, I dug in and refused to broaden the scope. Considering the movement of Blacks to the West after Reconstruction and the hard-rock mining activities in the nearby mountain communities of Gold Hill, Nederland, Jamestown, and Ward, my instincts and experience led me to believe that Black women likely played important roles at various junctures and, in varying ways, in Boulder County's long history.

GUARDIANS OF THE HISTORY

In preparing my class for the assignment, I visited several local archives looking for evidence of Black women and their contributions. I first visited the Boulder campus's Heritage Center, located on the third floor of Old Main—the university's first building, completed in 1876. Operated by the Alumni Association, the Heritage Center is the repository of the accomplishments of the university's renowned, mostly White, alumni—bandleader Glenn Miller; author, screenwriter, and Academy Award winner Dalton Trumbo; US Supreme Court Justice Byron White; the 1958 Miss America pageant winner, Marilyn Van Derbur; and Aurora 7 astronaut M. Scott Carpenter, to name a few.

As of 2001, despite the many accomplished Black alumni, the Heritage Center only celebrated three: Dr. Ruth Cave Flowers (1924), a highly achieving educator and lawyer recognized as the university's first Black graduate; David Bolen (1950), a track star and the university's first Olympic athlete, who went on to become the US ambassador to the German Democratic Republic, Botswana, Lesotho, and Swaziland; and John Wooten (1959), one of the first Black football players recruited to the university and an NFL veteran.

On a subsequent visit to the Heritage Center, the director gave me a copy of an article that appeared in the *Rocky Mountain News* on June 14, 1993. The headline read: "She was CU's first Black female grad: A pioneer buried without a headstone."[4] The story explicitly heralded Lucile as the university's first Black female graduate. I asked whether anyone at the Heritage Center or at the university's archives had checked into the veracity of the claim. In both cases, I was told "no." How then did this educational achievement come about? Does this story have any historical basis?

As someone skeptical about labels—the "first" as an example—I began to think beyond the label to the unending tension between memory and history that was created some eighty-three years ago. As Pierre Nora puts it, "History is the reconstruction, always problematic and incomplete, of what is no longer; it's an intellectual and secular production that calls for analysis and criticism. Memory is a perpetually actual phenomenon, a bond tying us to the eternal present; history is a representation of the past."[5] Hence, history is ever changing as new phenomenon is discovered that may indeed clash with memory. What was Lucile's cultural and social memory concerning the university and the city of Boulder? What memory remained for the small number of Black students in a racial climate that may have labeled them as Other? How were they able to address the passive or active racism that they faced every day? The few Black students who attended the university in the first two decades of the twentieth century were from Denver and other Colorado cities. Their connection to Boulder's Black community was temporary. Their presence at the university blurred. Once graduated they were wiped off the historical screen. Lucile would be one such example.

However, what the university and the White press missed, the weekly African American newspaper the *Denver Star* covered and celebrated. Their Boulder News column on December 29, 1917, states, "Miss Alice Norton [a freshman], who is attending the State University, will return to her home at Fort Logan, Saturday, to spend her two weeks' vacation. Miss Lucile Buchanan [a junior], also a student at the university, will visit her parents in Denver during her vacation." The *Denver Star* confirms that in 1917, Lucile was a student at the university.

Why had Lucile's achievement been ignored? I knew these types of "oversights" are far from exceptional at universities and colleges across the United States. All too often institutions rush to crown the first Black "whatever" without corroborating evidence or asking the right questions. Although historical and cultural preservation efforts are complex, power-laden processes, deliberate decisions are all too often made as to what will be remembered and what will be forgotten.

What was most surprising is that in the 1993 *Rocky Mountain News* article, Kathy McClurg, a spokesperson for the university, states, "We will correct the mistake in our records and publications, wherever it appears." Eight years later, the university had yet to correct the record. It seemed Lucile's place in the university's history was sealed and that she had been, wittingly or unwittingly, left out.

SETTLING THE DEBATE AND A COMMUNITY'S GUILT

But who was Lucile Berkeley Buchanan? Several well-meaning colleagues at the university often reminded me that Lucile was "not like a Rosa Parks." The cultural icon associated with the 1955 Montgomery, Alabama, bus boycott. What many do not realize is that we all stand on the shoulders of trailblazers who went before us, making it easier for us to follow. Rosa Parks stood on the shoulders of all who refused before to yield their seats on segregated public transportation in Montgomery, Alabama—Aurelia Browder, Susie McDonald, Claudette Colvin, Jo Ann Gibson Robinson, Mary Louise Smith—and the women who preceded those in Montgomery who challenged Jim Crow segregation laws on public transportation and were arrested—Elizabeth Jennings Graham (New York City in 1854); Charlotte Brown (San Francisco, 1863); Pauli Murray and Adelene McBean (Durham, North Carolina, 1940); Irene Morgan (Gloucester County, Virginia, 1944), Maggie Lena Walker (Richmond, Virginia, 1904), and the other women who remain mostly unheralded.

Most could not get beyond the fact that seemingly ordinary people could do extraordinary things while never making it into the historical record. Still, the university's oversight puzzled me, especially in light of the 1993 newspaper article. A colleague and an alumna of the university, Dr. Joanne Arnold, lightheartedly reminded me that Lucile had not bequeathed anything to the university. Thus, fixing the error was not a priority.

Early in my search, I discovered several pieces of evidence corroborating the fact that beginning in the fall of 1916, Lucile was a student at the university. The university had listed Lucile in the *Directory of Students and Faculty, 1916–1917*, noting that she lived at 821 Mapleton Avenue in a turn-of-the century home, in the Mapleton Hill Historic District. The following year the *Directory* showed her living at 1304 Pine Street, currently the outdoor parking lot of the Hotel Boulderado.

With these first pieces of evidence, I began to draw some initial impressions about Lucile. Whether by choice, convenience, or necessity, she did not live within the confines of the "Little Rectangle," also known as the "Goss-Grove Ghetto," a four-block area between Nineteenth and Twenty-third Streets and Goss and Water (today Canyon) Streets, which housed Boulder's largest Black community from the end of the nineteenth century until the 1940s. Shortly after her graduation in 1918, the 1922 edition of the *University of Colorado Directory of Officers and Graduates, from 1877 to 1921* listed Lucile's address as Slater State Normal in Winston-Salem, a historically Black teacher-training institution in North Carolina. Perhaps the most definitive evidence was a copy of Lucile's official transcript from the Registrar's Office, which confirmed that the university conferred an AB (Artium Baccalaureatus) degree on Lucile on June 5, 1918.

One might think that securing Lucile's place in the university's history would be an easy task, but that was not the case. As word about my research began to spread, I encountered questions typical in an academic environment about my research methodologies. But the question from the office of former University of Colorado president Elizabeth Hoffman, while preparing to give a talk to Denver's Black community highlighting the "first" Black student during Black History Month, was most surprising: "Are you sure your research is correct?"[6]

I kept asking myself, do I really want to do this? But what most people didn't know is that my attraction to Lucile's story had nothing to do with being "FIRST." The problem with identifying the first Black graduate at a university that opened in 1877 is that race and ethnic designations were not kept until the mid-1940s and not all graduates were featured in the university's yearbooks, thereby leaving the door open for an ever-changing story. Dismissing the "first" designation, it was the sub-title of the story in the *Rocky Mountain News* that piqued my curiosity: *A pioneer buried without a headstone.* I thought of the numerous towns and cities across the United States whose Black bodies had been buried unceremoniously in unmarked graves. Not to mention the practice of burying slaves in unmarked graves. The question left to be settled is, How did a pioneering Colorado woman end up in an unmarked grave in the latter half of the twentieth century?

FEELING IN THE DARK

Quite accidentally, I fell into what became known as the "Lucile Project." But for those who became involved with the project, there wasn't anything acciden-tal about it. To them, it seemed that Lucile was being "channeled" through me. Mostly, I found the suggestions of "channeling" absurd, and I chuckled every time I heard from family, friends, and especially my research assistants that Lucile had selected me to be her conduit for her story. Yet a series of uncanny coincidences allowed me to whimsically entertain the idea that fate may have had a hand in bringing Lucile and me together, making it impossible to deny the role of chance in the world. These coincidences made me think of Carl Jung's theory of synchro-nicity, which suggests that although coincidences cannot be explained by cause and effect, there is a relationship between coinciding events that goes beyond mere chance.[7]

To start, Lucile and I shared a connection to the university. She was the first Black woman to graduate from the University of Colorado and the first to major in German. I am the first Black woman to earn tenure at the University of Colorado on the Boulder campus and the first Black woman there to head an academic unit (Women and Gender Studies, 2003–7).

More connections—some obvious, some obscure—surfaced. Five years into the project I discovered that Lucile's husband, John Dotha Jones, and I shared the same alma mater, Columbia University in New York City. Next, I learned that Lucile's driver/aide Herman Dick's wife, Ester, was born in Trinidad, Colorado.[8] I was born on the Caribbean island of Trinidad.

When Lucile died in 1989, she was buried in an unmarked grave at Denver's Fairmount Cemetery. Fred Walsen,[9] the Samaritan who placed Lucile's name on the tombstone at her burial site in 1998, is a 1939 alumnus of the College of Journalism at the University of Colorado—the same program of study that first hired me as a faculty member.[10] As more whimsical coincidences surfaced, colleagues and students continued to tease me about inadvertently awakening Lucile's spirit.

REFLECTING ON THE RESEARCH AND THE CHALLENGES

My research began under the wisdom and guidance of the father of Black history, Carter G. Woodson, who said, "Those who have no record of what their forebears have accomplished lose the inspiration which comes from the teaching of biography and history."[11] Drawing on personal experiences, I reflected on my own story and the influence of my forebears, strong Black and Latina women who never feared telling their story or articulating their voice, in spite of the personal or political consequences they faced. Thus, I came into this research from a Black feminist and testimonio (first-person narrative) perspective, guided by qualitative research and critical paradigms constructed within the process of self-reflexivity.

Self-reflexivity is characterized by the willingness of the researcher to learn about oneself, one's research purpose, and one's relationship with the social world.[12] Certainly, this alternative epistemology runs counter to the idea of a "value-free" framework based on neo-positivism ideas of objective reality and empiricism. As bell hooks states, "Hearing each other's voices, individual thoughts, and sometimes associating these voices with personal experience make us more acutely aware of each other."[13]

Thus, from the beginning of my research I was acutely aware of Lucile's life on the margins of society (no matter how much she may have struggled to redefine or explain herself to others). I wondered how she worked to defy misconceptions that were held by the majority culture by refusing to be shamed, silenced, or stereotyped. How much did W.E.B. Du Bois's thinking on "double consciousness" and Patricia Hill Collins's "outsider-within" affect Lucile in 1916 as a student at the University of Colorado? A century later, as a Black faculty member on the same campus, I would ask the same question: How is my voice being challenged through the "outsider-within" orthodoxy?

As the project progressed, I found it increasingly difficult to remain outside the research, whether exploring diaries, love letters, city directories, Sanborn maps of Denver, census data, birth and death certificates, marriage records, draft registration cards from the Civil War through World War II, cemetery records, photos, school transcripts, receipts, or visual recordings. While some of my research may be viewed as orderly and quantifiable, I could not dismiss the inaccuracies caused by human error. For example, the enumerator of the 1885 Colorado State Census lists Lucile and her family as "White." I had to be aware of the unpredictability of the data and the complexities and inaccuracies that presented themselves.

I also felt this research in a personal way. I cringed whenever I was told Lucile was "not like a Rosa Parks," as if all Black women had to be measured by one cultural icon, or when I was told that slavery was *different*, implying better, in one part of Virginia versus another. Therefore, I had to filter my insights through their meaning-making as a way to improve the quality of the information I was discovering.

Consequently, I supplemented library, archival, and online databases with my observations and interviews conducted in the field: visiting the Big House and walking through the grounds of plantations where Lucile's parents and relatives toiled; visiting homes where Lucile lived and the sites that once marked the schools where she taught; conducting interviews across race, class, age, and gender lines; examining her personal accessories; and visiting the home of Lucile's last two living relatives soon after they committed suicide.

This end of the research led me to feel as if I was on an archaeological dig, entering dark spaces, not always sure what I would discover. It was particularly significant to enter these dark spaces, which often bore her footprints. I saw this process as a rite of passage as I attempted to find meaning in the many cities she called home and from the discoveries I made trekking across ten states (Alabama, Arkansas, California, Illinois, Missouri, Nevada, New York, North Carolina, Texas, and Virginia) in search of Lucile's story.

Along the way, I encountered unique challenges. Tracking potential interviewees was a slow and painstaking process, where in most cases I was racing against time. Frequently, by the time I located a source, the person had died fairly recently. In other cases, the failing memories of potential research participants left me questioning the role of memory in the construction of Lucile's history. Some potential interviewees refused to participate while others were apologetic, explaining to me that they never thought Lucile was important or they would have asked more questions about her. Others said, "We just didn't know, and we didn't believe what she told us." Linda Moore, one of the last nurses to care for Lucile, remembered seeing her parents' emancipation papers and taking them to her church in Denver to show the minister and congregants. However, because of her failing memory, she could not recall what happened to the papers after Lucile died.

One of the challenges of writing about a non-celebrity is that you do not have one main repository of the person's papers, which forced me to hunt for materials about Lucile in obscure places and, in many cases, hoping I would gain access to the material. South African writer John Matshikiza once said, "You have to work harder to interest people in the unknown figures of history than you do to interest them in Dave Beckham or J. Y. Stalin."[14] Unlike Matshikiza, I did not have to work hard to interest people in Lucile's story. But I must admit that I thought recovering Lucile's life would be easier if she were famous or notorious. This turned out not to be the case at all.

For the last four years of Lucile's life, attorney Robert L. Steenrod Jr., the public administrator for the City and County of Denver, was tasked with managing her assets and finances while she lived in a nursing home. My many calls to secure an interview with Steenrod and to get copies of the public records in his possession proved futile. I then solicited the help of Michael Carrigan, an attorney and a member of the university's Board of Regents, hoping that Steenrod would respond to a professional colleague. Carrigan was also unsuccessful. I returned to the court in hopes of finding another alternative. Luckily, a staff member with a degree in history took an interest in Lucile's story, and within two days of my visit I had Lucile's court records.[15]

Bits and pieces of her material possessions were dispersed among several people. It took an astonishing eight years to gain access to what was left of her personal and family memorabilia, photos, letters, shoes, clothing, graduation cap and gown, and other artifacts from one of the previous owners of Lucile's home. For several years, the only people helping me reconstruct Lucile's story were those who knew her as an elder in the Barnum neighborhood in Denver, who knew her through their parents, or who came to know her during the last years of her life. Even with their compassion and love for her, the retelling of what they remembered of Lucile was at times clouded, leaving me with layers of interpretation. Reconstructing Lucile's life history would require me to do what sociologist Erving Goffman suggests—not give any weight to what people say but try instead to triangulate what they say with events and hard data.[16]

My research became a team effort. There were countless people I met along the journey who contributed to the reconstruction of Lucile's story. Throughout the project I forged connections with people across racial and class divides, from Colorado to Virginia and various points in-between. Some were the guardians of history, others were reclaiming their own history from distortions and omissions, and some lived on the periphery of society warning me about the do's and don'ts, but they all opened their doors to me, sharing their own historical journeys, and keeping me informed of new discoveries through online exchanges.

The "Lucile Project" became a deeply personal exploration into the life of a forgotten Black woman. As I began to delve into her life, searching for the internal and external forces that shaped Lucile and her family, I became convinced that I had set out to remedy historical amnesia by rescuing a pioneering Black family from obscurity. As a result, I entered into the area of social history, which is concerned with the life and experiences of ordinary people rather than privileged elites.[17] Even though I managed to maintain a certain detachment, I kept hearing the words of Western historian Shirley A. Leckie, who so eloquently said, "All biography is, in part, autobiographical."[18]

Getting at Lucile's story made me acutely aware of the challenges of telling history and telling life stories. Hearing stories about her and reading what she left behind was inspiring. Yet, I longed for an unrehearsed performance piece of her life story that would give voice to the text I was writing. How would she recount her own memories? After eight years of searching for a performative example, I was introduced to Lucile through a seven-minute videotape that was recorded in Denver by Larry Harris and his wife, Doris, in the summer of 1987, when Lucile was 103 years of age.

The video opens with Lucile patiently sitting in a wheelchair in front of the Stovall Care Center, the senior nursing home where she lived. She is smartly dressed, with a white turban hat, a pink and light green floral-patterned dress covering an emerald green blouse, and a small black purse cradled in her lap. The next shot cuts to her sister Laura's gray granite grave marker at Denver's Fairmount Cemetery. I was told by Doris that Lucile was quite familiar with the cemetery since she had an old tradition of Memorial Day visits to decorate family graves with peonies.[19] Next to Laura's plot the camera pans to Lucile's granite grave marker, which she had purchased for herself as a final resting place thirty-four years earlier. The camera then takes a panoramic view of the monuments in the vicinity before revealing her parents' and siblings' grave sites. before zooming to Lucile sitting in the front seat of a white Buick Skylark parked on the cemetery grounds with the door ajar. Her face is expressive. Her eyebrows add emphasis, jerking sharply up and down, as she begins engaging in conversation with Doris and Larry.

Although she is blind, her eyes are not at a fixed point. She has a commanding voice that demands attention—she is self-assured in her articulation. As a former teacher, she understands the value of effective classroom management, which she uses as a criteria to judge the nursing home staff and their failure to discipline a resident who she reports as "prowling around and steal[ing] my things." She argues: "They don't discipline her. They don't try to correct her. They just make excuses." Continuing in her teacher role, she asks Larry if he knew any Harrises in New York, a direct reference to her deceased ex-husband's family. She then describes some of the historical events in her maternal family's life, including the family's relationship to Edmund Berkeley (her mother's slave owner and father) and that he was responsible for selecting a husband for her mother and that they were married in the Big House on the grounds of the old plantation. Furthermore, she reveals that Berkeley bought the property where her family's home was located in Denver, and that she was named after her mother's (White) half-sister.

Unable to stand on her own, her body hunched over, she is helped by Doris to her parents' upright headstone, completely shrouded by an evergreen shrub planted some years ago to serve as a memorial to her family's resting place and as a living metaphor for the immortal soul and to the plantation of the same name (Evergreen) where her mother was born.

Lucile gently reaches out to the shrub, occasionally sniffing her hand as she attempts to break off a piece. "It's hard for me to take one out," she said. Doris breaks off a short twig and places it in her hand. After gently touching and sniffing the twig, she places it in her purse to take back to the nursing home. This video, which I was able to obtain almost eight years into the project, took me into Lucile's world, where she continues to display her sharp intellect. An inviting feeling came over me, which made my search for Lucile even more relevant.

Lucile's life, and that of her family, is a portrait of how a family born in slavery survived the Civil War and what one historian has so aptly labeled the "Nadir" of racism in the United States (1890–1920) as Blacks were victimized in everything from housing, transportation, and employment to participation in electoral politics and anti-Black violence. And while Colorado Blacks were not subjected to the anti-Black violence that was pronounced in the southern states, racial disparities still existed as Lucile was denied a teaching position in 1905 in the Denver public school system because of the assumption that White parents would not be comfortable with a Black teacher. She thumbed her nose at Colorado and went to Little Rock, Arkansas, where she launched her teaching career.

I often wondered how Lucile's family learned to triumph, shape political discourse, create a social life, gain respectability, suffer in silence, and take on or escape the racial disparities confronting Blacks in the American West? As a member of the first generation born after slavery, what ideological premises helped to forge Lucile's character, solidarity, and a sense of civic duty with the plight of the Black masses? Her life and her story is, after all, a story of the United States. A story worth remembering.

REMEMBERING LUCILE

1

Inquiry and Epiphany

Pursue some path, however narrow and crooked, in
which you can walk with love and reverence.
— HENRY DAVID THOREAU

Four days after the attacks of 9/11, I paid my first visit to the Buchanan family's
former home at 227 Raleigh Street, situated in a neighborhood with a mix of white-
and blue-collar residents of Latino and European heritage in southwest Denver.
The homes are modest ranchers, with a handful of split-level and two-story dwellings. The vast majority of the exteriors are painted white, with few bright accents.
Most of the homes are reminiscent of those built in the post–World War II years.
Driving through the neighborhood, I watched several residents busily arranging
yard sales and pull-starting lawn mowers.

THE HOUSE ON THE HILL

A well-aged chain-link fence surrounded the two-story red brick house situated
on a small hillside. An old, white, weather-beaten, slightly rusted mailbox bearing
the number 227 hung to the right of the gate. To the left of the gate, near the curb,
stood a massive American elm tree with several dead branches. I opened the gate
and climbed the stairs to the front door. A "Beware of Dog" sign,[1] hung adjacent to
a black plaque with the name J. L. Price in brass, greeted me. The only life was the

FIGURE 1.1. *227 Raleigh Street, Denver. The Buchanan family home from the late 1880s until 1987, ca. 2003. Author's collection.*

old spruce that stood in the desolate front yard. The "Beware of Dog" sign made me apprehensive; and the appearance of the house itself, which seemed out of place among the more modern, well-kept homes in the neighborhood, added to my discomfort. The house appeared to hold many secrets. With much trepidation, I climbed the four steps onto the peeling silver-gray wood porch.

I rang the bell, and a middle-aged White man in his early sixties opened the door. He introduced himself as Jim Price. I introduced myself and told him I was interested in a Black woman who had once lived in the house. He immediately knew whom I was referring to and suggested that I speak to Joe Rodriquez, the next-door neighbor, who had known Lucile. Before I left, he showed me a photo-montage of a young Black woman mounted in a silver-painted rectangular wood frame. He identified the woman as Mrs. Jones (Lucile) and told me that the former home owners, Larry and Doris Harris, had left it behind.

The woman in the picture wore a white crepe de chine and lace dress. Her hair was set in the beautiful Marcel wave style popular in the 1920s. She sat posed on a bench with a bouquet of white roses and a rolled parchment that appeared to be a diploma. The dress and hairstyle appeared to date from the second decade of the 1900s, when Lucile graduated from the University of Colorado. Although we had just met, Price offered me the picture on loan. I was exuberant. Even though Price had never met Lucile, I accepted his assurance that I was holding a picture of her.

About six years after that visit I located Evelyn Napper, Lucile's ninety-three-year-old niece, who identified the woman in the photograph as Carol Jarrett, another of Lucile's nieces, now deceased, at her graduation from North Denver High School in 1927. Six years into the project, I had no authentic photograph of Lucile except for a photocopy of the one that appeared in the *Rocky Mountain News* story.

OH, WHAT TENACITY

Joe Rodriquez, Lucile's former next-door neighbor, remembered her fondly. His house on Raleigh Street sits on one of the five lots Lucile's family once owned. According to Rodriquez, Lucile built the house he lives in for her niece Carol, who chose instead to live in Los Angeles. Rodriquez remembered Lucile's strength, fierce independence, tenacity, and resolve, especially in her fight with the city of Denver to save the American elm tree her father planted years ago in front of the family's home. He remembered Lucile constantly nursing the tree. "To keep moisture in, she placed grass shavings around its base." According to Rodriquez, "She defended the tree until her death."

The American elm stands as a reminder of a once vital part of Denver's urban forest. In 1905, as Lucile's father was putting the final touches on the family home, Mayor Robert Speer initiated a free giveaway of elm and maple trees for planting along parkways and city streets. Tragically, in 1948 Dutch elm disease hit Denver hard. Beginning in 1968 through the early 1970s, the city's Forestry Division conducted an aggressive drive to eradicate the disease by removing thousands of trees.[2] Lucile's tree was on their hit list.

Lucile, in her mid-eighties and losing her sight, insisted that her elm was healthy and worth saving. According to Rodriquez, she launched a major assault on the city, successfully blocking the attempts to cut it down. "I think if she didn't get her way, she probably would have chained herself to the tree," Rodriquez said.

The tree was part of Lucile's heritage. Planted by her father, James, it was part of the scenic beauty of the house, part of the history of Denver. Tended for years, the elm soon provided shade from the summer heat. Its magnificent limbs spanned the sidewalk and overhung the street. Rodriquez remarked that Lucile told him she remembered the elm when it was "a little bitty tree."

Not long after winning her tree fight with the city, given her advancing age and deteriorating physical condition, Lucile realized she could no longer care for the tree. She turned to Rodriquez for help. Since the elm stands on the border of their adjoining properties, he agreed if she would also give him the property on which it stood. True to her nature, Lucile adamantly objected to this suggestion and firmly told Rodriquez, as he fondly recalled, "All you get is the tree." Her decision not to grant Rodriquez's wish did not deter him from taking care of the tree, even as he advanced in age.[3] This magnificent American elm, now well over a hundred years old, continues to stand as a reminder of Lucile's cunning and tenacity.

THE FIRST PATH

I left my first meeting with Price and Rodriquez intent on finding the couple from whom Price had bought the home, Larry and Doris Harris. I considered them vital primary sources in the re-creation of Lucile's life, especially since the *Rocky Mountain News* article on Lucile's interment in an unmarked grave reported that they visited her at Stovall Care Center, the nursing home where she spent her final years. The article also noted that the Harrises had, on several occasions, brought Lucile back to her former home at 227 Raleigh Street.

Price told me that Larry used the professional name Charlie McDaniels, as a country and western singer. Rodriquez remembered that Doris once worked at a restaurant on Eighth Avenue and that Larry worked a series of odd jobs, including selling home siding. Telephone directories and internet searches proved futile. I began to pursue the country-singing angle by contacting every local country and western establishment from Denver to Fort Collins and beyond. This also proved futile. Later, I learned that Larry's stage name was actually Carlin Harris. Who knows where the name Charlie McDaniels had come from?

A break came on September 28, 2002, when I attended the Colorado Council of Genealogical Societies' Rocky Mountain Regional Conference in Denver, and someone suggested that I hire genealogy family detective Kathleen Hinckley to locate Larry and Doris Harris. I gave Hinckley their names and the 227 Raleigh Street address. Twenty-four hours and fifty dollars later, I had the current addresses and phone numbers for both Doris and Larry, now divorced. Doris had remarried and lived with her husband, David Smith, in Kiowa, Colorado. Larry lived on a ranch in Lampasas, Texas.

I contacted Doris, who, with great compassion, shared aspects of her unusual relationship with Lucile, which began soon after she bought Lucile's house. She mentioned that her ex-husband had a videotape of Lucile and suggested that I contact him directly. On Monday, September 30, 2002, I made my first of several contacts.

Responding the same day, Larry reported he had two steamer trunks filled with Lucile's clothes (including her wedding dress and shoes), hundreds of family photos, large portraits, her mother's rocking chair, and an armoire Lucile reportedly said her parents had brought from Virginia in 1882. In addition, Larry said he had her high school diploma, some letters, and other memorabilia. Most important, Larry confirmed he had a videotape of Lucile talking about her history that he shot at Denver's Fairmount Cemetery. Indeed, Larry had a treasure trove of archival documents that would breathe life into the "Lucile Project." In addition, Larry claimed to have information about the construction of Lucile's family's home, about their day trips to Golden and Idaho Springs, and on Lucile's husband's dramatic death in a duel.

I would spend almost a decade ascertaining the veracity of Larry's claims about the family's history and the accuracy of the stories he recalled Lucile telling him. For now, my search for Lucile took me to Kiowa, about thirty miles southeast of Denver, to the home of Doris Smith.

STORIES LEFT BEHIND

Named for one of America's first peoples, Kiowa is a small ranching and farming community that, according to the 2000 Census, is home to 581 residents, of whom 549 are White and two are Black.[4] Driving east toward Kiowa along Highway 88, I was struck by spectacular views of plush green fields dotted with spacious homes and horses grazing in wide-open pastures.

My research assistant, Keyana Simone, and I met Doris at the Homestead Café, one of the town's two restaurants. She spoke about Lucile with passion and shared her memories unconditionally. After lunch, we went to Doris's home. The fifteen-minute drive took us from paved to gravel roads on streets named after Native American tribes to numbered county and private roads. Doris's ranch-style home sits on seven acres bordering Colorado's Black Forest. She and her husband had multiple vegetable plots, honeybee hives, and piles of chopped firewood to heat the home's wood-burning fireplace. When I asked her about living a pioneering life, she chuckled, reminding me that she has electricity, indoor plumbing, and running water.

After passing time at Doris's kitchen table talking at length about Lucile's life, Doris abruptly left and quickly returned with a large framed photograph of an attractive young woman of mixed ethnic heritage whom she identified as Lucile, which she gave me. I had my doubts, though. Something about the young woman's dress and hairstyle spoke of an earlier era, before Lucile was born.[5]

Doris then showed Keyana and me the English-language books that had once belonged to Lucile. To protect them and retain their value, Doris kept the books in three walnut bookcases with glass doors. The bookcases and books were part of the inventory Doris and Larry purchased with Lucile's house in 1987. We knew that Lucile was literate in German and Latin, but Doris, who understood neither of those languages, confessed that she had given most of Lucile's foreign-language books to Goodwill.

Lucile's collection included a six-volume set of encyclopedias, a 1910 collection titled *Memoirs of the Court of Europe*, and a fifty-volume set of the *Harvard Classics*, compiled and edited by Charles William Elliot, the twenty-first president of Harvard University. There were also 173 other books, including college and high school textbooks that Lucile may have been required to read or might have used in her teaching, such as Washington Irving's 1809 *Knickerbocker's History of New York, Complete*; J. P. Gordy's *New Psychology*, published in 1895; Wilbur F. Gordy's 1908 *A History of the United States for School*; a ten-volume *Mental Efficiency Series*, published in 1915; and Russell Judd's *The American Educational System*, published in 1940. And there was a 1912 copy of German author Kaethe Schirmacher's *The Modern Woman's Rights Movement: A Historical Survey* and an 1867 copy of *Berlin and Sans-Souci; or Frederick the Great and His Friends* by the famous German historical romance novelist Luise Mühlbach. She was a fan of the Persian astronomer, mathematician, and philosopher Omar Khayyam, owning two brown leather-bound copies of the *Rubaiyat*, one of which was given to her as a Christmas gift by "E" (her sister Edith).

Her collection also included Ronald S. Crain's 1932 *A Collection of English Poems, 1600–1800* and an 1922 book of Longfellow poetry, a gift from her female students at Lincoln High School in Kansas City. She seemed to gravitate toward the poems of Percy Bysshe Shelley, William Blake, John Keats, and Lord Byron, the quintessential English romantic poets of the nineteenth century, who may have helped her as she fell in and out of love.

Lucile was a serious reader—a bookhound. I wondered whether her passion for reading related to her parents' twenty years in slavery, where they were not allowed to have books and teaching them to read and write was prohibited under the law. Lucile's books told me that she read for information, enlightenment, practical advice, and pleasure. Although she read history and women's suffrage literature, she also seemed to favor poetry and novels.

AND THEN THERE WAS PAUL LAURENCE DUNBAR

Lucile also paid attention to the leading Black literature of the day. When she came home from Hot Springs, Arkansas, for a visit on December 29, 1911, she gave her father, James, a signed copy of W.E.B. Du Bois's *Souls of Black Folk*, with the inscription "To Papa from Lucy, Wishing you many happy returns of the day." She also kept an 1849 edition of Frederick Douglass's *Narrative of the Life of Frederick Douglass, an American Slave*. She purchased a twenty-five-cent copy of a 1941 *Chicago Defender* publication *KYRA Booklet* (*Know Your Race Achievers*), whose aim was "to perpetuate the memory of the great men and women of the Race whose achievement should serve as an inspiration to Negroes everywhere."

And then there was Paul Laurence Dunbar, the first Black poet and writer to gain national prominence with both Black and White audiences. In her collection, lovingly stored in Doris's home, I found Dunbar's third novel, *The Fanatics* (1901), which attempts to show the origins of northern White prejudice and the resulting ghettoization of Blacks in the North.[6]

Lucile's introduction to the work of the twenty-seven-year-old Dunbar likely came when he paid a brief visit to Denver in the fall of 1899. She would have been fifteen years old then. Suffering from tuberculosis, Dunbar came at his doctor's behest because Denver's climate was considered beneficial to people suffering from upper respiratory diseases. While in Denver, he seized the opportunity to work as a freelance poet and essayist for the *Denver Post*. By the time he arrived, on September 12, 1899, the town was abuzz with Dunbar fever. While local papers kept the public abreast of his every move and hung on his impressions and interpretations of the West, local White socialites clamored to have him read his poetry in their living rooms.

A leading Denver citizen, William C. Daniels, the millionaire co-owner of Denver's largest department store, Daniels and Fisher,[7] took a special liking to

Dunbar. Dunbar's later writings made it clear that he felt uncomfortable with the favors Daniels showered on him and took steps to sever their relationship. Eventually, however, Dunbar found ways to handle his discomfort and ultimately found his friendship with Daniels so tremendously rewarding that he dedicated his second novel, *The Love of Landry,* published in 1900, to Daniels with the inscription "My friend MAJOR WILLIAM COOKE DANIELS, In memory of some pleasant days spent over this little story."

As much as Dunbar appreciated the accolades from Denver's citizens, he was stunned by the beauty of the city itself, which he described in a letter written to a friend as a city filled "with great rolling illimitable plains, and bleak mountains standing up like hoary sentinels guarding the land." Blending his keen observations with his poetic acumen, he wrote, "The city where so many hopes are blighted, where so many dreams come true, where so many fortunes go up and so many lives go down. Denver, over which nature broods with mystic calm, and through which humanity struggles with hot strenuous life."[8]

Dunbar's visit might have been a topic of discussion in the Buchanan household. Lucile's brother-in-law Elias Jarrett worked as the butler at the Daniels home at 1555 Sherman Avenue, where Dunbar was a frequent guest. Elias had earned a position of trust, securing privileges that gave him insider knowledge of Dunbar and his whereabouts. Elias's relationship with Daniels also earned him such a degree of respect that years later Daniels consented to have Adarose toiletries that Elias's wife, Hattie (Lucile's oldest sister), created sold at his department store.[9]

Seeing Lucile's books gave me some insights into who she was and the topics she cared about and provided me with one more window into her character. However, the inscriptions she wrote in a number of books would lead me on several more journeys and provide even greater insight into Lucile Berkeley Buchanan.

- At Ark [Arkansas] Baptist College, "Lucile Berkeley Buchanan."
- Sept. 1, 1915, Lucile Buchanan, Chicago University, Chicago, Ill.
- Lucile Buchanan, University of Chicago, 1915
- Lucile B. Buchanan, Denver University 1920
- Lucile B. Buchanan, Lincoln H.S. (Kansas City, Missouri)
- Property of Chicago Board of Education, Douglas School, Lucile B. Jones, 1928. (Chicago)
- Lucile B. Jones, 4758 So. Park Ave. (Chicago)
- Lucy B. Jones, University of Chicago, 1937.

Others were clearly gifts, bearing the signatures of those who had given them.

- Miss Lucile Buchanan Compliments of Mr. and Mrs. S. H. Tarbet, June 6, 1914. May this day mark the beginning of a useful career.
- To Miss Lucile from Francis Galloway, Chicago, IL, Dec. 25, 1915
- Miss Lucile Buchanan from Seniors and Juniors
- Miss Josie Beard, Miss Sarah Graham, Miss Vers Kanegay, Miss Beatrice Hughes, Kansas City, Missouri 1922

In time, I learned that by 1914, Lucile was teaching at Arkansas Baptist College, a historically Black college and university in Little Rock. In the fall of 1915, during the peak of the first Great Migration of Blacks from the South, she moved to Chicago and enrolled in undergraduate courses at the University of Chicago (UChicago). She spent Christmas there with her lifelong friend Frances Galloway, a music teacher who, on December 25, 1915, gave her William Henry Carson's third novel, *Tito*, published in 1903. The April 18, 1903, edition of the *New York Times Review of Books* called it a "story full of excitement." In 1922 the juniors and seniors she taught at Lincoln High School in Kansas City, Missouri, gave her a gift of Longfellow's poetry.

Through reading the inscriptions from her personal library, I found her married name, Jones, in use from 1928 and 1937, the only details about her marriage that I had at this point. Her inscriptions during the late 1920s and the 1930s indicated that she had worked and lived in the Bronzeville neighborhood of Chicago, known in the early twentieth century as the "Black Metropolis," and had taken graduate courses at UChicago.

While the visit to Doris rendered some important answers, I still had questions that would remain unanswered for some time. Two years passed, and I wasn't any closer to gaining access to the hundreds of archival materials Larry Harris allegedly had. Larry seemed to understand the importance of the information I needed and had conveyed his willingness to cooperate, yet his actions were those of a self-righteous gatekeeper restricting my access to what he owned that had once belonged to Lucile.

To break Larry's stalling tactics, I invited him to give a talk on Lucile at the university's Hazel Gates Cottage on April 16, 2005. I carefully orchestrated this event with a student audience who by now was bent on helping me to establish an endowed scholarship named for Lucile. While this event was intended to gain Larry's trust and support for the "Lucile Project," I also invited Doris in hopes that she would serve as a point-counterpoint to Larry's assertions about Lucile and her parents that he made in the *Rocky Mountain News* article.

My hunch paid off on two levels. Doris enlarged the discussion by providing unique examples of what she had learned about Lucile's life—her commanding presence, confident assertiveness, the discomfort caused by her hair loss, her love for her father, James, and her knack for insightful one-liners. While Larry spent much time reiterating the information that appeared in the news article, he did bring six 18 × 20 late nineteenth- and early twentieth-century portrait photographs of family members, a 1910 family portrait, and—after four years of relentless searching—my first photo of Lucile from her 1905 State Normal School graduation. As I held these photos in my hand, I felt great respect and reverence. And over the years I smiled a lot at these photos in times of both joy and sadness as I chronicled Lucile's and her family's lives.

THE SECRETS OF AN OLD FLAT TOP STEAMER TRUNK

In August 2007, Keyana and I made a second trip to see Doris and to look at the contents of an old olive-green Flat Top Steamer Trunk, a popular style of trunks from the late 1870s to around 1920, which Larry had recently delivered to her. Built for long trips, particularly on steam trains, boats, and stagecoaches, this trunk had traveled great distances before landing in Doris's garage in Kiowa. A carved label on the right side told me that the trunk originally belonged to Lucile's oldest sister, Hattie Jarrett. Surprisingly, the trunk, which was possibly over a hundred years old, was in good shape. However, a musty odor greeted us as we gently removed the layers of inner tray compartments, each revealing clues to Lucile's life.

The contents included forty-four pictures of Whites (primarily babies and young children) who lived in the Barnum neighborhood where Lucile grew up. There were thirty-seven photographs of African Americans, of which thirteen were identified mostly by first names. I began to piece together a picture of people whom Lucile (or her family or both) knew and were associated with.

One photograph was that of Dr. Justina Laurena Warren Ford, the first African American woman physician licensed to practice in Colorado. Ford, who specialized in obstetrics, helped to deliver Lucile's two nieces, Carol Marjorie Jarrett in 1906 and Evelyn Lucile Parker in 1914. There was also a postcard displaying an exterior and an interior shot of Zion Baptist Church and an upper-body shot of Dr. Ford and her husband, the Rev. John E. Ford, who served as pastor from 1899 to 1906. And there was one of the Rev. George W. Dupree, who also served as pastor of Zion in 1884.

Through the prism of these photographs, I could look into the past and try to make sense of the relationships—often across racial lines—Lucile's family had with Colorado's early citizens. They became a storyboard of sorts, helping me uncover whether racial boundaries were less pronounced at the turn of the twentieth century in Denver compared with other Western cities where Blacks settled.

FIGURE 1.2. *Dr. Justina Ford, her husband Rev. John E. Ford, and the Zion Baptist Church, ca. early 1990s. Buchanan Archives.*

The steamer trunk also held thirty Christmas and Easter cards Lucile saved from 1910 to the mid-1960s from friends in Chicago, including Gladis Storm Berry, a librarian who taught French and Latin in the Chicago public schools. She also kept communiqués from Denverites, such as Dorothy Alyce Deneal Lewis, a long-standing member of Zion Baptist Church, who sent Lucile condolences in 1921 upon hearing of the death of her mother, Sarah. The trunk also contained several private letters that were a particularly fascinating blend of formalized and non-formalized greetings and salutations, transmissions of gossip, apologies, and flowery romantic words from a suitor in Hot Springs, Arkansas, in 1914.

There were several items of clothing, including an expensive ivory-colored machine- and hand-sewn matte-satin woman's dress similar to Victorian era–style wedding gowns of the 1870s,[10] around the time Lucile's mother wed in Virginia. The dress was elaborately adorned with handmade ruffled lace around the neckline and tiny pearl beads around the cuff of the short-waist, fitted Basque bodice.

The trunk also held Lucile's mortarboard and gown that she wore to her graduations from Colorado State Normal School (University of Northern Colorado) and the University of Colorado. Lastly, in her collection were three pairs of shoes in excellent condition. The most intriguing was a limited edition of a 1920s champagne-colored satin Mary Jane ankle-strap button shoe purchased at the Louvre Boot Shop in Kansas City, Missouri.

More importantly, the trunk held more evidence of Lucile's possible marriage. Tucked neatly among her belongings was a 1925 *Maroon and Gold* yearbook from Columbian Heights High School in Winston-Salem, North Carolina, where on the first page was a headshot of a well-dressed, rather serious Black man with intense gray eyes. The dedication below the photo read, "To our beloved Principal John D. Jones who has worked so earnestly and efficiently in the interest of the students of Columbian Heights High School, we, the Class of '25, respectfully dedicate this book." Elsewhere in the trunk was an unframed picture of the same Mr. Jones.

DANCING WITH LARRY

Between 2007 and 2010, I had sporadic contacts with Larry in an effort to obtain a copy of the videotape he had made of Lucile and the remaining photographs to which he often referred. I sent an email on Sunday, January 10, 2010, requesting the materials and asking when it would be convenient to visit him in Bandera, Texas, where he now lived with his new wife, Jana. After months of negotiations, made possible with Jana's support, I finally headed off to Bandera on April 30, 2010.

My journey began in Fredericksburg, Texas, where I met up with Barbara Elmore, a veteran journalist who agreed to travel with me to Bandera. Having Barbara along was a suggestion from a colleague with Texas roots who felt that as a Black woman, I needed an insider as I tackled Bandera—the "Cowboy Capital of the World," where cowboys and bikers reign side by side. Armed with GPS, we began driving through the Texas Hill Country on a two-lane blacktop. Fields of native wildflowers—from bluebonnets to Indian paintbrushes and Mexican hats—dotted the landscape, and packs of motorcycle riders swarmed the roadway, all en route to Bandera.

When Barbara and I arrived, Larry showed us a small box that contained a hodgepodge of items: three 36 inch × 17 inch Italian tapestry wall hangings depicting privileged Victorian-era Europeans in various home and garden settings; a 1948 ivory-colored electric Westclox wall clock that had apparently hung in Lucile's kitchen; a framed poem by the American poet Nan Terrell Reed, "To You, Mother," surrounded by an illustration copyrighted in 1920 and a sheet of negatives consisting mainly of exterior shots of the house at 227 Raleigh Street that Larry had taken sometime around 1988. There was also one black-and-white 8 × 10 photograph of Lucile and a badly damaged 12 inch × 20 inch oil painting of the Spanish-American War, its frame held together by four Shattuck Stretcher Keys. The most significant item he presented me with was the seven-minute video of Lucile at Fairmount Cemetery visiting the grave sites of her parents; her sisters Laura, Hannah, and Edith; and her brother Fenton and her finding her own grave marker next to Laura's. At long last, I had footage of Lucile.

As I came to the end of my eight-year research journey with Larry, I still had many unanswered questions and mounds of conflicting information to sift through and reconcile. More and more, as I assembled the fragments of Lucile's story, I recognized the intricacies, strategies, and challenges of writing a biography of someone who was deceased. Having had to rely upon a single gatekeeper to fill in historical gaps was frustrating, to say the least.

Often, in my dealings with primary sources like Larry, I remembered the insight of Shirley A. Leckie, who said that in the case of women or people of color (and Lucile bore both labels), primary sources are inadequate for the task of answering important questions about a person's life, so biographers must make creative use of whatever is available.[11] This was particularly useful as I went about trying to separate fact from fiction and determine what was real memory and what had been altered by time in everything Lucile may have told Larry so very long ago.

For example, in the *Rocky Mountain News* article published following Lucile's death, Larry raised the idea that the racial identity of Lucile's parents was a factor that drove them to Colorado. He said that her mother being "part White" and her father "Black" didn't sit well in Virginia because "at that time mixed marriages were not well-received in Virginia." Granted, Virginia's anti-miscegenation laws prohibited interracial marriages, but the prohibition was between Whites and Blacks and did not cover marriages between Mulattoes like Lucile's mother, Sarah, and Blacks. At times, I was uncertain whether the reporter had been hearing Lucile's voice or Larry's.

In the same news article, Larry is quoted as saying that Lucile's parents' arrival in Colorado in 1866 had been prompted by a job offer made by P. T. Barnum, who hired them to come to Denver to manage his property. Initial research revealed, however, that Lucile's mother would have been about twelve years old and her father about seventeen when they allegedly arrived in Denver in 1866.

In addition, Barnum's circus was in Virginia during 1876 and 1877. In 1876, Lucile's mother, Sarah, was pregnant and would soon give birth to her third daughter, Hannah. Barnum returned to Virginia in 1877, a year before he bought the property in Denver where the Buchanans would eventually reside.

At this point, I had only rudimentary notions of Lucile's life. While I understood the value of the snippets of information I had received from Larry and the *Rocky Mountain News* article, I had to evaluate each one's accuracy and authenticity with a hint of skepticism. And then I had to deal with a new set of research challenges.

TIME AND TRUTH

One major challenge I faced had to do with relational ethics. Sociologist Carolyn Ellis states, "Relational ethics requires researchers to act from our hearts and minds, to acknowledge our interpersonal bonds to others, and initiate and maintain conversations."[12] As part of relational ethics, "We seek to deal with the reality and practice of changing relationships with our research participants over time. If our participants become our friends, what are our ethical responsibilities toward them? What are our ethical responsibilities toward intimate others who are implicated in the stories we write about ourselves? How can we act in a humane, non-exploitive way, while being mindful of our role as researchers?"[13]

Here I am, writing about the life of a person now dead. My ethical responsibilities did not disappear because Lucile could not give me permission to write her story, to offer her views, or to correct inaccuracies that might have crept into the memories of those I interviewed. On whose authority could I speak for Lucile, her family, and the other dead who were the subjects of my research? Sociologist

Nick Couldry suggests that we must understand the difference between speaking "about" others and how we "speak personally" are inextricably linked.[14]

I also had to come to grips with family members and friends who became part of the narrative. What personal biases might color the information shared with me? How do I raise contentious issues discovered in my research without creating conflict with key informants? How do I explain Lucile being abandoned by her last living relatives? Although I was very clear about my role and responsibilities in researching Lucile's life, I noticed that as I became close to participants with whom I was building bridges, the boundaries between myself as a professional researcher and those with whom I interacted were beginning to blur. When it came to Larry, for example, I acknowledged that at times my only option was patience. However, as much as he had power over when and what he chose to divulge and share about Lucile, I also had power over what I chose to write about him and our interactions.

One thing that became clear from the *Rocky Mountain News* article is that Virginia held the key to unraveling much of the mystery behind Lucile's parents' early life. They had, after all, been born into slavery in Loudoun and Prince William Counties in the mid-1800s, and four of her siblings were born there during Reconstruction.

Clearly, I had to go to Virginia to understand the environmental influences that shaped her parents' lives as slaves and as freed people following emancipation. Who were their masters and mistresses? What kind of community did slaves build on the plantations where they were born and lived? In what way did Lucile's parents' slavery and post-slavery experiences influence them and their children? How did Edmund Berkeley, Lucile's White grandfather, reconcile his public role as a slaveholder with his private life in which he fathered Lucile's mother, Sarah? And how did Lucile's parents' life in Virginia affect the one they would eventually build in Colorado? How did they transition from bondage to middle-class status? To understand her life's course, I had to understand her family's roots and the impact they had on her transition from birth to adulthood. Virginia, therefore, became the next logical step in my search for Lucile.

2

Born in Slavery

THE MASTER, THE MISTRESS, AND THEIR CHATTEL

You have seen how a man was made a slave;
You shall now see how a slave was made a man.
— FREDERICK DOUGLASS

Three generations of Lucile's paternal ancestors lived and died as the property of George Carter and his heirs at the Oatlands Plantation in Loudoun County, Virginia. Arriving at Oatlands toward the end of the eighteenth century, when Carter already owned at least seventeen slaves, Lucile's ancestors—who used the surname Buchanan at that time—lived under the same roof as or near other slave families, forming what Thomas Bender described as a "network of social relations marked by mutuality and emotional bonds."[1]

Today, what remains of this former 3,400-acre great plantation, nestled in the farmlands and rolling hills of Northern Virginia, is a 261-acre National Trust for Historic Preservation and part of the National Historic Landmarks Program designated by the US secretary of the interior as a nationally historic place representing an outstanding aspect of US history and culture.[2]

REFLECTING ON THE MODERN-DAY PLANTATION

At Oatlands, as at many of America's former plantations that survived the Civil War, there exists a peculiar mix of selective nostalgia characterized by the development

FIGURE 2.1. *Oatlands Plantation Lane and Big House (Mansion). Courtesy, National Trust for Historic Preservation.*

of "plantation tourism." Here, visitors of varying ethnic groups can walk back in time without being burdened with a critical perspective of the dehumanizing nature of slavery as they experience the architectural significance of the antebellum buildings and celebrate an array of seasonally themed public and private events, including weddings, corporate retreats, holiday teas, and a variety of other activities on the beautifully manicured grounds.

I went to Oatlands for the first time in the summer of 2005. It was my first visit to a plantation. I turned off the James Monroe Memorial Highway and onto the lengthy stone driveway called Oatlands Plantation Lane for what I assumed would at least be a thought-provoking and probably an emotionally jarring experience. Almost immediately, an anachronistic sense of dread fell upon me as I realized that over 140 years ago, chattel slaves walked, ran, laughed, and labored in any number of directions over the landscape before me. Their blood, sweat, and tears were part of the soil that nourished the dignified European larch and English oak trees George Carter, Oatlands's first slaveholder, apparently planted back in the eighteenth century.[3]

Today one arrives first at a red brick walkway, where visitors can purchase "special bricks" for $150 with an inscription of their choice added. Oatlands offers its visitors a choice of two gift shops: the Carriage House, located in a former stable built in the post-slavery era by its third owners, William and Edith Eustis, and the Potting Shed Shop, a marvelously restored greenhouse built in 1810 by George Carter, during which time Lucile's second cousin, Martin Van Buren Buchanan, trained as a gardener and labored during the antebellum period.

Elizabeth Simon, the house manager, greeted me and led me on a brief, unofficial tour of the multi-story Greek Revival mansion, providing me with access to the archives tucked away in the basement. Even though she made a passing reference to house slaves, I could not help but notice how sanitized Oatlands was and how the vestiges of slavery were rendered almost invisible. Oatlands is not unique in this regard. David L. Butler's fieldwork on southern plantations in 2001 found the harsh reality of slavery either removed or marginalized at the plantations he visited. He states, "Most of them [plantations], in their tour narratives, did not even utter the words 'slave' or 'slavery,' far less establish their connections with the landscape in such features as slave graveyards and former slave cabins. Nor, for that matter, did they mention their contribution to the total antebellum plantocratic infrastructure."[4]

In the summer of 2008, I took my third and final field research trip to Oatlands. During this visit, I decided to take the "official" tour. At the entrance to the mansion, I waited with the other visitors for the tour to begin. As the only Black person on the tour, I sensed that my presence brought on some unease among my fellow tourists. While I tried to make eye contact and smile, people avoided me. The genial overtures of southern hospitality that I had grown accustomed to were noticeably absent. The White visitors, it seemed, came to admire the opulence of such a magnificent structure, which sat on beautiful, wide-ranging grounds, while ignoring the contentious aspects of a past in which the plantation was home to both the enslaved and their enslavers. I was there to understand precisely the parts of that past they planned to ignore—and my presence made that harder for them from the first moment. Sitting on the master's veranda, surrounded by the huge round Corinthian columns that supported the portico, I came prepared to walk through the front door of the master's house, acutely aware that while the ancestors of my fellow tourists might have been invited in, it's unlikely that Carter's slaves walked through this door.

Although most of the architecture built over two centuries ago had been carefully preserved, nearly all of the family's furniture and furnishings were long gone. Only a sideboard from the Carter dynasty remained. The majority of the furnishings and lavish decor date back to 1903, when a powerful and privileged Washington couple, William and Edith Eustis, bought the mansion and sixty acres. The opulence was everywhere, especially in the majestic sweeping staircases on either side of the entryway, the era's most coveted architectural feature and a status symbol for a plantation home.

A majority of the information provided by the tour guide centered on the Eustis's wealth, lifestyle, furnishings, and their close relationship with Presidents Franklin D. Roosevelt and Harry S. Truman, among other powerful political and social figures of their time. During the forty-minute tour, discussion of the generations of Africans who toiled under the yoke of slavery and the slaves who built and labored at Oatlands was limited to a few dry facts: 17 slaves from Virginia's Northern Neck helped build the mansion; Robert Carter III (aka Councilor Carter) freed the plantation's 500 slaves; 80 slaves fled with the Union Army during the Civil War. It was as though no human beings owned by other human beings entered the back door of the mansion (aka Big House) to clean, cook, serve, empty the chamber pot, or entertain the master. A visitor would never imagine that slave wet nurses had slept on the second floor at the foot of the bed in the nursery or in the hallway outside the nursery door.

The mansion was a picture-perfect memory of something that never existed. I was reminded of what John Michael Vlach argues in *The Planter's Prospect: Privilege and Slavery in Plantation Paintings* that "by rendering slaveholding estates in a manner that either hid or diminished the presence of African Americans, those paintings functioned as documents of denial. Such paintings offered a soothing propaganda that both confirmed and justified the social dominance of the planter class."[5]

A discussion of plantation life that focuses only on the master, the mistress, and their children obscures the real facts behind the practice and culture of slavery in the United States. It dilutes to invisibility the statements of power encoded in all plantation landscapes. The plantation, as Charles Ball, a slave from Maryland, observed, "was the master's empire, his labourers are his subjects, and revolt and violence, instead of abridging his power, are followed by inevitable and horrible punishment. The laws of the land do not, indeed, authorize the master to take life, but they do not forbid him to wear it out by excessive toil."[6]

In Loudoun County, Oatlands had been an empire unto itself. Here, slavery loomed large and was firmly entrenched in the commercial production of wheat and other small grains for both domestic and international markets. Carter further diversified his plantation by raising sheep for their wool, having a vineyard for wine, and building a mill complex on nearby Goose Creek for the grinding of grain, milling of timber, and pressing of flax seed to produce oil cake.[7] Within this plantation complex, relationships were forged among Whites, free Blacks, and the slaves who greatly outnumbered them both. Seeing no end to their life in bondage, the Buchanans labored in a system that marked them as property without rights but responsible for keeping the economic engine of capitalism flourishing. Thus, they were as much a part of Oatlands as the wealthy Whites who owned the buildings and the land on which they toiled.

Nonetheless, an even-handed and neutral historical overview of the plantation is essential. Using a core-periphery paradigm, the physical and figurative plantation and the planter class were functionally tied together at the core, with the enslaved at the periphery. The core had certain requirements, which the periphery supplied. This core-periphery relationship experience undergirded slave life at Oatlands. It is also what helped the Buchanans forge the attitudes they would need for success, develop the strengths and strategies they would need to combat seemingly insurmountable obstacles, and allow them to feel equal to their White neighbors when they finally arrived in Colorado.

THE MASTER SPEAKS

On August 16, 1796, Robert "Councilor" Carter III divided his 70,000 acres of land, consisting of seventeen plantations spread over five Virginia counties, among his nine surviving children: seven daughters (Pricilla, Sarah Fairfax, Elizabeth Landon, Anne Tasker, Sophia, Harriot Lucy, and Julia) and two sons (John Tasker and George). He included the proviso that while "he was still alive each child would pay him a yearly fee of one hundred dollars."[8] Nineteen-year-old George Carter, the younger son, inherited about 3,400 acres of farmland, which included the 1,000-acre Goose Creek tract that was part of the Leo Plantation in Loudoun County.[9] This is where he built Oatlands and where Lucile's paternal lineage began toward the end of the eighteenth century.

In addition to the yearly fee he had to pay his father, two other stipulations did not sit well with George. The first required him to honor the leases his father gave to the free Blacks living on his land, especially at Leo Plantation, which had the largest population of free Blacks living on small farms.[10] The second and probably the most taxing requirement was his father's "Deed of Gift," which directed the manumit of approximately 452 slaves throughout his seventeen plantations. Thereby, giving away a large part of his inheritance.[11]

From these actions and the deed, it would appear that Robert Carter III had moral doubts about the institution of slavery and exposed his children to his unorthodox ownership practices that resulted from those doubts. According to author Andrew Levy, George's father instituted a number of radical approaches to managing his human property, such as worshipping in the same church as many of his slaves and prohibiting the flogging of runaways. He valued their expertise, and he rarely whipped his slaves or allowed them to be whipped by others. His slaves also enjoyed many uncommon freedoms; they were able to teach their children their own trades, and families were kept together on the same plantations. He often accepted their version of events in a dispute with an overseer or other Whites.[12]

FIGURE 2.2. *George Carter, 1777–1846, and Elizabeth O. Carter, 1797–1885. Courtesy, National Trust for Historic Preservation.*

It is unclear how much his father's ideas about slavery rubbed off on George. Although George frowned on his father's manumission policy and bought slaves to replace those he had lost, he nonetheless continued the tradition of keeping families together, which made good business sense if nothing else. While slaves were never far from George's control, his actions resulted in maintaining core family groups like the Buchanans. On such a large plantation, these decisions may have led these families to experience more freedom in their private lives, which allowed them to build stronger, more monogamous family structures than those whose owners denied their slaves even these small signals of their humanity.

George, a confirmed bachelor for much of his adult life, married a thirty-nine-year-old widow, Elizabeth Osborne Grayson Lewis, at age fifty-eight on November 12, 1835. The Reverend George Adie of Shelburne Parish performed the ceremony at Elizabeth's residence in Clifton, near Upperville, Virginia.[13] His neighbors and friends must have asked why this very wealthy Virginian broke with the tradition of early marriage. In fact, his life was surrounded by gossip and speculation, both while he lived and for many years after his death. Adding to the intrigue surrounding his late marriage, John Randolph Barden, the director of the Maine State Law and Legislative Reference Library, wrote that George's sexual appetite was being satisfied by the Black females he owned. Accordingly, George's female slaves were not only a source of labor but also a source for meeting his sexual desires, a fact known to George's agents and family, although their reactions varied. "Girls are more frequently for sale than Boys," prompted a salacious agent in 1805, adding "would you object to a very likely one—a virgin—of about 14 or 15."[14]

Perhaps the most embarrassing questions about his scandalous lifestyle came in a letter his younger sister Sophia wrote to him on June 17, 1816, asking about his sexual exploits with slave women. In his response, the thirty-nine-year-old Carter did everything to assure her that the rumors were slanderous gossip. The number of Mulatto children on the plantation, he argued, was not a result of his indiscretions with slave women: "The injury I have sustained arising from the malicious Slanders which appear from your letter you have pleased to give a willing ear to, I forgive & forget—My habits like most men are vicious & corrupt—but in this I comfort myself in knowing I have no mulatto children—it is a Sin, I am only answerable for, to my God."[15] While it is nearly impossible to say for certain what George's sexual predilections toward his slaves were, it is safe to say that he was in a position that if he chose to exploit his chattel for his sexual satisfaction, he had the authority to do so.

THE MASTER'S LEGACY AND HIS HUMAN CHATTEL

When George died in 1846, his fifty-year-old widow, Elizabeth, inherited the family business and became the mistress of Oatlands. At this time, she owned two generations of Lucile's paternal family. According to the US Slave Schedule for 1850, Elizabeth—with eighty-five slaves—was the largest slaveholder in Loudoun. She continued to maintain this position, and by 1860 her slave population had grown to 128.[16] Not surprisingly, George's will documents a co-residential family structure consisting of married slaves and their families, including their future progeny, who were considered slaves at birth, for example, Charles, his wife and children, their offspring, and Joe Rust (Russ) and his wife and children. George also acknowledged female-headed households, their children, and future progeny—Louisa and her children, John, George, Joshua, and Nancy. Listing mothers without fathers could have been influenced by a number of factors, including widowhood, sale of the spouse, children of the White slaveholder/overseer, abroad marriages (where a spouse lived at another plantation), or the fact that the female was considered the recognized parent since her slave status determined the status of any children she bore.

Several of George's slaves were also listed with surnames—Alanda and Gerard Day, Fanny Canes, Tom Carpenter, and Gerrud Smith.[17] It's surmised that slaves with surnames were more common in Virginia than elsewhere.[18] When George advertised for Billy, a slave who had run away in 1809, he said, "BILLY, sometimes calls himself William Jordan Augustas." Similarly, in another runaway slave ad, this one for Isaac, George indicates that Isaac's chosen surname is "Clerk,"[19] clearly demonstrating that in the early nineteenth century, at least at Oatlands, some slaves exercised their own agency when it came to the use of surnames. There were other surnames that slaves either assumed or had when they arrived at Oatlands—Gleed, Valentine, Bryant, Hughes, Turner, Moore, Barnes, Stewart, and Buchanan. These slave families formed the core workforce during the antebellum years, with some continuing to work at Oatlands or at newly created farms emerging out of Oatlands in the postbellum years.

From July 1860 through October 1872, Carter's widow, Elizabeth, kept a 247-page diary of her daily observations and activities at Oatlands and later Bellefield, one of her residences in Upperville, where she lived for about nine years during the Civil War and in the early years of Reconstruction.[20] Her diary reveals how she managed her life and her properties, including her slaves. Most of the themes in the diary are not very different from those in other nineteenth-century southern women's diaries. There are references to family and friendships, community, recreation, work, the political stakes, economic issues, slavery (the enslaved and freedmen and women), and the Civil War and its aftermath.[21]

She wrote about the daily drama of taking care of her family's financial needs, health, and sustenance, as well as providing nursemaids from her female slave stock when they fell ill. She recorded her transactions with the Bank of Baltimore, established in 1795, and with the Burke and Herbert Bank, established in 1852 in Alexandria, Virginia. Also included are other financial and related transactions, such as paying for goods and services, weather conditions, planting and harvesting crops, killing livestock and preserving meat, and getting the wheat to market. She also detailed her social life, including dinners and teas with family and friends, and her forced dealings with Union troops, and her willing work for the Confederacy. Her diary portrays a shrewd, brazen, no-nonsense, independent woman, a Confederate sympathizer who readily engaged in public life and who could be both callous and conciliatory, especially regarding female slaves who occasionally challenged her authority.[22]

On October 20, 1861, about six months into the war, Elizabeth learned that the fighting had reached Dranesville, twenty-three miles from Oatlands. Her diary from that date shows her immediately "packing up here + moving." Her son George, a courier for several confederate generals between Leesburg and Manassas, stopped by shortly after they left: "I found my Mother and the ladies had left the house taking all the pictures hanging on the walls and all valuables the furniture that could be moved with the books such as beds, mattrasses [sic] and everything that could be carried off in wagons—Instead of finding my Mother at home, the Mansion was used as headquarters by Genl' Evans."[23]

With most of her belongings, including a few of her most trusted slaves who had served her well in the Big House, Elizabeth took up residence at Bellefield, leaving her English-born gardener, John W. Gillespie, and her overseer, Robert Costello, in charge of Oatlands. When her son George became ill and was discharged from the battlefield in the fall of 1862, he went first to Bellefield to recuperate and then to Oatlands where, "under his mother's direction, he looked after her interest."[24]

As the plantation's mistress, Elizabeth understood how to wield power and exert authority when needed. Schooled in working in the public sphere, she naturally took an active role in legitimizing and assisting the Confederacy, in both traditional and nontraditional ways. As one of the more affluent women in the county, she organized several of her contemporaries to provide the Evergreen Guards (Company C of the Eighth Virginia Volunteer Infantry) with clothing, uniforms, and food. Company C was under the leadership of Edmund Berkeley of neighboring Prince William County, where Lucile's mother was enslaved. While Elizabeth, and her family and friends, provided clothing, she needed the help of her slaves to feed the soldiers.

With the war intensifying, Elizabeth lent her support to the men of the Forty-third Battalion of the Virginia Cavalry, known as Mosby's Partisan Rangers.[25] As a morale booster, she hosted the Rangers as overnight guests—providing a temporary safe haven that included beds and hot food while keeping her in the thick of things as she got firsthand news of Confederate defeats and triumphs. As for her slaves, their relationships with the Rangers were not necessarily conflict-free. For example, on March 31, 1865, a mere two-and-a-half weeks before the war ended and a month after the establishment of the Freedmen's Bureau, Charles McBlair, a Mosby Ranger staying at Bellefield, shot one of her slaves, Jacob (aka Jake), and wounded him. The shooting enraged one of the female slaves, who openly confronted Elizabeth about the injustice, making little impact on her mistress, who wrote in her diary on April 1, 1885, "Fann very insolent to me because Jacob had been shot by Charles McBlair."

Entries in Elizabeth's diary about the slaves on whom she relied on in her private sphere and those with whom she struggled are significant. Early in her diary, she hinted at frustrating conflicts with sassy female slaves who challenged her authority, an act she considered "impudence." Elizabeth became frustrated. She often chose to sell off the most impudent. One of these impudent women was Lucile's great aunt; on January 2, 1861, Elizabeth reported sending "Nancy to jail for improper conduct to her master [Elizabeth] and the overseer [Robert Costello]." Then, on January 19, she sold Nancy to George Kerst, a farmer from Union Township in Berks County, Pennsylvania.

FIGHTING FOR MY FREEDOM

From the beginning of the Civil War, slaves took advantage of the often-chaotic circumstances at Oatlands and Bellefield to run away, taking horses to help them on their journey. On November 16, 1864, Elizabeth's diary notes: "Tom and Lewis stole a horse belonging to Mr. Lufborough + went to Washington to the Yanks/ They went from Oatlands."

Elizabeth reluctantly recognized that the desire for "freedom" was at the heart of their actions. In fact, not all left secretly. On May 21, 1865, "Wallice [sic] walked off sayin he was free + was goin for wages." And on August 11, 1865, "Louisa + her five took there [sic] departure for freedom."

In contrast, she exulted when a former slave returned. Take Hannah. After twice visiting her husband, Chilton, a former Oatlands slave, in Alexandria, Elizabeth alleged that with his encouragement she returned to Oatlands, noting in her diary on October 25, 1866, "Hannah came from Alexandria/Perfectly charmed to get back to Mistress + her old home."

Emancipated slaves like Hannah found themselves in destitute conditions in urban areas such as Alexandria and were not prepared for living mostly in over-crowded camps where "Black refugees had difficulty securing adequate housing, food, clothing and medicine, which sometime[s] resulted in starvation, disease and death."[26] And while camps provided education and offered the newly freed lessons about freedom and equal rights, "thousands remained dependent upon government aid and were unable to secure an independent livelihood."[27]

General Orders from the military made it clear that Blacks must find work; if they did not, "the destitute rations will not be issued to any persons whatever, who are unable to labor, unless they can show that they have made efforts and found it impossible to obtain work . . . All colored persons living in the country, are informed that it is much better for them to remain there than to come to the already overstocked city, and they will not be permitted to come here for work or subsistence unless they cannot obtain them where they are."[28]

Slaves' optimistic dreams were met with frightening realities. Freed Blacks were often homeless, with few possessions, often unable to find work, and thus unable to purchase sufficient food even when it was available. Then diseases such as smallpox, against which they had no immunity and access to treatment, took their toll. Many became dependent on the federal government for survival.

In the face of all this, many emancipated slaves returned to the only secure place they had ever known. While Elizabeth responded with a coming-home celebration to justify her own importance and the vindicated southern idea that Blacks "preferred" slavery because they were unable to make it on their own, I read Hannah's action as both proof of the difficulties facing freed people, especially women, and reflective of the idiom "better the devil you know than the devil you don't."

Between sixty and eighty-one slaves remained at Oatlands during the war or returned defeated, in search of lodging and a place to work. Marietta Minnigerode Andrews wrote, "Sixty helpless Negroes came back at one time, after having run away with the Yankees, and settled down again at Oatlands, living on Uncle Carter [Elizabeth's son George], raising enormous families, working or not working as they pleased, that being their understanding of 'freedom.' . . . To this day their descendants live on the place, to the third and fourth generations."[29]

A handwritten note from George Carter II to his brother Benjamin tells a different story. George noted that the war caused a financial crisis, which made it difficult to supply "the needs of the many servants" who had remained at Oatlands. Horses were slaughtered for meat, and he went into debt buying corn and clothes for the servants. Most of the abled-bodied men were gone, leaving behind about eighty-one "demoralized" slaves (mainly women, children, and the elderly) who were not able to raise sufficient crops to feed themselves. George ended his letter by noting that when the war ended, the eighty-one slaves still on the plantation "had been comfortably cared for."[30]

While it is open to speculation as to how George defined comfort, the disparities between Elizabeth's and her son George's perceptions of the situation during the war were often dramatic. Where George reported hunger and want, Elizabeth's diary reported a great deal of planting, harvesting, slaughtering of livestock for sale and consumption, and purchasing of food, brandy, and whiskey. She also reported receiving goods in return for livestock confiscated by the Confederacy, as noted in her entry on January 3, 1865: "Chinn delivered three hundred yards of cotton for cattle taken by government." From her entries, it would be safe to infer that Elizabeth, with the help of her son George and other brokers, provided goods and services to the Confederacy. Since the Carters depended on their slaves to do the brunt of the work required to create those goods, it is safe to say that slaves at both Oatlands and Bellefield toiled for the Confederacy under Elizabeth's watchful eyes.

With the loss of her human property following the conclusion of the Civil War, Elizabeth Carter's monetary worth dropped drastically from her reported personal estate (which included her slaves) in the 1860 US Federal Census of $250,000 to a mere $870 by the 1870 Census.[31] The 1870 Census also shows that seventy-three-year-old Elizabeth, who once reported owning $150,000 worth of real estate, now owned properties worth $6,212. Elizabeth's diary shows an attempt to maintain Oatlands and its lifestyle and luxuries with some of her former slaves working for wages: on February 26, 1866, "Paid Sophia five dollars for her work wages," and on March 22, 1870, "Paid Amelia fifty cts for a day's work." Now strapped for cash, an aging Elizabeth began renting some of her properties (e.g., the mill and the Burnt House) before turning over the operation of Oatlands to her son George and his wife, Katherine, who established a girls' school followed by a summer boarding house.[32]

In 1870 Elizabeth's immediate household was completely Black. It included three families of emancipated slaves: Jacob (aka Jake) Howard, the gardener, and his wife and children; Eva Moten, the dairywoman, and her granddaughter; and two housekeepers, Hannah Warner and Hannah Fisher. When the 1880 Census[33] was taken, Elizabeth, now eighty-three, lived with her niece, Ann Fitzhugh, and her four children. Blacks in her household still included the vestiges of former slaves (Hannah Warner, Edmund Parker, Frances Moten) and the children of former slaves (Edward Gaskin).

THE BUCHANANS OF OATLANDS

What happened to the Buchanans and the vast majority of other Oatlands slaves after the war? Samuel J. Barrows, who toured Virginia and several southern states in 1891, suggests that "the Negro and his descendants remain pretty much in the places where they lived when the war closed. Three courses were open to him as a free man: first, to rent his own labor; second, to rent and work the land of his former master; third, to buy and work a farm for himself."[34] Barrows's observations could very well apply to the Buchanans as they continued to live in the shadow of their old lives with a new caveat thrown in—Virginia's Vagrancy Act of 1866, which made it illegal to be unemployed, forcing Blacks back into slavery.

There is another way to look at how freed men and women coped with their newfound freedom and its responsibilities. After emancipation in 1863, as well as during the Civil War, Black men and women walked away from Oatlands showing no loyalty to Elizabeth. Faced with bleak economic conditions and without an extended family for support, some returned to Loudoun County, often working near or at Oatlands. A few who actively outsmarted Elizabeth during slavery continued to use her to their advantage, meeting her expectations but strictly on their own terms. Many performed the stereotypical Sambo or Mammy roles, only to turn them off when she was not around.[35] Moreover, many of the emancipated slaves from Oatlands were bent on finding ways to reap the benefits accorded free citizens in Loudoun.

It is difficult to pinpoint the exact moment when Lucile's paternal family came to Oatlands or to know precisely how they fared during slavery. With the exception of a few pieces of oral history passed down through thirteen generations, they left no descriptions of their life that could be termed ethnographically valuable. However, it is known that they were one of the plantation's core enslaved families, with several generations of them continuing to live and work on or near the former plantation during the Reconstruction period (roughly 1865–77) and into the Progressive era (1890s–1920s).

At times, it was quite a challenge to document the lives of Lucile's forebears. Since most Blacks were enslaved and considered three-fifths of a person, there are no records of their names from the first enumeration in 1790. However, beginning in 1790 through 1840, slave owners were required to list the number of slaves within a cluster by age (e.g., Slaves—Male 36 through 54 or Female 36 through 54). In 1850 and 1860 the clustering system was abandoned for an enumeration system wherein the slave owner listed each individual slave by age (often approximate), sex, color (Black or Mulatto), whether the slave was a fugitive, number manumitted, and whether deaf, blind, insane, or idiotic.[36]

At a small farm it could be easier to locate a specific person without a name, but doing so was difficult at a large plantation such as Oatlands. For example, the 1850 Census lists six Black males thirty years of age, six Black females ten years of age, and nine females thirty-five years of age.

Even with these limitations, using the 1870 Census proved to be easier than I expected. For one, it is the first Federal Census to list African Americans by their first and last names. Consequently, I could now corroborate my findings with birth, death, and marriage records, the Will Book of George Carter, and Elizabeth Carter's diary by examining the various spellings for the name "Buchanan."

Lucile's paternal ancestry begins to show up in George Carter's Will Book dated May 20, 1842, and includes three males identified with the surname Buchanan in the 1870 Census: Lucile's great-uncles George (b. 1815) and Robert (b. 1821) and her future grandfather Fenton (b. 1820). The fourth Buchanan male in Carter's Will Book is Andrew. When Robert Buchanan died on March 21, 1885, the Loudoun County Death Register, 1853–96, lists his parents as Andrew and Fannie Buchanan (Lucile's paternal great-grandparents). Fannie (aka Fanny) also shows up in Carter's Will Book in 1842 and in Elizabeth's Diary from March 17,

1862, through April 11, 1869, with the final notation, "Paid Fanny ten dollars on her wages for 1869."

The one Buchanan whose life took a different path is Lucile's great aunt Nancy. As mentioned earlier, Nancy's fate takes an unusual turn in that Elizabeth sends her to jail for impudence on January 2, 1861, and seventeen days later she is sold to a farmer in Pennsylvania. The next time we see Nancy is in the 1880 Census listed as Nancy Stewart and living with her niece Elizabeth Valentine, Robert Buchanan's daughter. Elizabeth reports her death on February 13, 1896.[37]

Although difficult to pinpoint whether Nancy had children, the children of the three brothers (Fenton, George, and Robert) would be the third generation born during slavery at Oatlands and included Virginia (1842), Martin (1844),[38] Hannah (1845), Frances (1848), James Fenton—Lucile's future father (1850), Helen (1851), Thornton (1852), Elizabeth (1853), Julia (1854), Travers (1854), Sinah R. (1855), Mahala (1857), Mary (1859), Susan (1861), and Luther (1863).

On the plantation, some of the Buchanans worked as artisans. Andrew and his son George were blacksmiths. Fenton, Robert, and James, as well as many of the Buchanan women, worked as field hands. However, Catrice Montgomery, the family genealogist, notes that Buchanan women also worked as cooks and maids during Reconstruction under the Carters and continued through the mid-1960s, when the Eustises owned the property.[39] These factors make it very likely that Buchanan women were among those serving in the Big House during slavery.

When the Civil War fighting reached Loudoun County, the Buchanan family had two choices: leave the plantation, either on their own volition or with the Union forces fleeing to federal lines, or remain at Oatlands. But for one Buchanan, the choice to leave was made in 1863, a year that had special significance for Blacks. First, the Emancipation Proclamation was issued on January 1, 1863. This life-altering event was followed by a March 21 editorial by prominent abolitionist and former slave Frederick Douglass, which urged Black men to "fly to arms, and smite with death the power that would bury the government and your liberty in the same grave" by joining the Union Army. The editorial was reprinted in newspapers throughout the North and made into broadsides placed in many public locations.[40]

Then, on May 22, the Union War Department authorized the formation of the Bureau of Colored Troops to facilitate the entry of Black soldiers into the Union Army. Even though Lucile's second cousin Martin Van Buren Buchanan was born free because of his mother, Mahala Jackson's, free status, his father and all of his paternal relatives were enslaved. Hence, his father's bondage certainly weighed heavily on him when he left Oatlands to enlist. Martin's decision may have been predicated on additional enticements as well. On March 3, 1863, the US Congress passed the Enrollment Act,[41] instituting America's first draft for all able-bodied White males between ages twenty and thirty-five and all freed Black men in the same age range. Exemptions could be achieved by paying a $300 computation fee or finding a substitute draftee.

Martin's enrollment records indicate that he served as a substitute for a man named Tracey Harris. Little is known about Harris, but author Eugene C. Murdock notes that while initially Black men could only serve as substitutes for other Black men, this restriction was sometimes ignored during the last months of the war.[42] Then, beginning in May 1861, Congress approved a legalized federal bounty (a fee granted for enlistment) of $100 for all volunteers or regulars enlisting for three years and serving at least two years or to the end of the war, with the bounty paid at discharge only.

After taking the oath of allegiance to the United States on Wednesday, September 30, 1863, Martin joined Company G, Second Regiment, US Colored Infantry, as a private for a period of three years. He would be one of the 178,895 US Colored Troops who served during the Civil War. His enlistment provides yet another example of a Black man taking the initiative to chart his own course, even though as a volunteer he was treated very differently from his White counterparts. For example, the base pay for White privates was $13 per month and free uniforms, while Blacks received $10 per month from which a $3 deduction was taken to pay for their uniforms."[43] Not until June 15, 1864, did Congress vote to require equal pay. However, only Blacks free at the beginning of the war were eligible. The difference in pay remained in force for all other Black soldiers until March 3, 1865.[44] Even though Martin's records indicate that he was free "on or before April 19, 1861" (coinciding with the attack on Fort Sumter), he would continue to be hemmed in by the same bigotry he had set out to fight against and would not see his pay increase until eighteen months after his enlistment.

On October 10, 1863, four weeks and one day after his swearing in, Martin dispatched to Arlington, where they were headquartered. On November 1, 1863, two months into his enlistment, Martin was promoted to corporal, and his unit was ordered to the Gulf in New Orleans, Louisiana, a month later, then to Key West, Florida, on February 13, 1864. About a month before heading to Key West, the Company's Muster Roll for November–December 1863 states, "Reduced to Ranks from Corp. Stoppage 1 Bayonet." Stoppage is explained on the Muster Roll as "$_____100 for _____." Black recruits frequently received "inferior firearms and equipment."[45] It is highly likely that Martin received a damaged bayonet. Whatever the reason for the "stoppage" of his bayonet, the soldier was ultimately responsible for the condition of his bayonet.

From May 5 through August 21, 1864, Martin and his unit participated in attacks on Confederate fortifications at Tampa along Florida's west coast, including raids from Fort Myers to Bayport and from Cedar Key to St. Andrew's Bay. Again, misfortune struck, as Martin's service record indicates that his bayonet developed mechanical failure in January 1865. This was probably quite taxing and may even have broken young Martin's spirit. Less than a month later, on February 3, 1865, he was on detached service as a guard on the schooner *Matchless*, a mahogany-hulled, two-mast schooner built at Key West, Florida, in 1859 and used as a slaver before the Civil War.[46] Martin's regiment mustered out on January 5, 1866.[47]

Little is known of Martin's whereabouts for the next fourteen years. But by 1880 Martin had returned to Loudoun to work at Oatlands in the same gardens he had labored in as a free Black. Martin's life there was far from dull. On one of her visits to Oatlands during the postbellum era, Marietta Minnigerode Andrews describes an unexpected encounter with Martin and her grandmother's maid, Martha: "One evening at dusk I had gone into the lower garden for just one more of the luscious Bartlett pears which fell there on the ground, when the deep sound of a man's voice chilled the very blood in my veins—had he—could he be? No, it was Martin the colored gardener, and presently on a cooing tone, which I nevertheless recognized as the voice of my dear Martha came this apocryphal utterance—'Do dat agin, sweet Martin—I likes it.' It was from Martha that I learned that *a man* has something to do with everything."[48]

Lucile's grandfather Fenton also left Oatlands during the Civil War, along with her grandmother Hannah and their four children—Frances, James (Lucile's future father), Julia, and Mary. They, like many other slaves, went to Alexandria, Virginia, which was under Union control. Alexandria had become a safety zone for slaves, referred to as Contraband,[49] who were escaping involuntary servitude during the Civil War. With the issuance of the Emancipation Proclamation, freedmen and women were converging on Alexandria in greater numbers. According to Margaret Richardson, "When they arrived in Alexandria, some freedmen and women found employment and the opportunity for a new life. They worked as nurses, bakers, laborers, stevedores (loading/unloading ships at port), painters, woodcutters, cooks, gravediggers, railroad workers, and personal servants. Some were provided with schools, hospitals, and housing; some even fought in the war."[50]

Fenton and Hannah were more than likely searching for employment. With little more than what they were wearing and some food for the long journey, they took off on the forty-five-mile trek to Alexandria, exercising much caution so as not to be captured. Once there, they secured housing in a relatively new barracks at 24 Prince Street. Living conditions were deplorable. Julia Ann Wilbur, an abolitionist and member of the Rochester, New York, Ladies' Anti-Slavery Society, who lived in Alexandria during the Civil War, described the conditions: In the old Slave pen there are several rooms. In the small room (a brick floor I discovered through the dirt) with one window were 20 women and children, many of them sick, a little fire wh[ich] they were huddled around, c[oul]d not all get to it at once, and they were wrapped in their old rags."[51]

Either Hannah was pregnant or she became pregnant shortly after arriving in Alexandria. In either case, in March 1864 Hannah gave birth to a daughter named Sina Ann. Poverty, sickness, and disease were rampant and took their toll on the new inhabitants, particularly the children. On June 29, 1864, at age three months and nineteen days, Sina Ann died at the Prince Street Barracks. Hannah and Fenton buried her at the newly established Freedmen's Cemetery at the corner of South Washington and Church Streets, which opened that same year.[52]

In addition to the high infant mortality rate, diseases hit the adult population hard, with smallpox and influenza topping the list of killers. Not long after the death of Sina Ann, thirty-five-year-old Hannah took ill and died on February 1, 1865. She is also buried in the Freedmen's Cemetery. There is no evidence as to how long following Hannah's death Fenton and the children remained in Alexandria, but by August 31, 1870, they were back in Loudoun County, where Fenton and James were working as laborers, possibly for the Carters or other farmers in the area.

The Buchanans, like other slaves on the plantation, appear to have worn the mask of invisibility by learning the cultural codes necessary for survival. At Oatlands, they lived and worked in two geographically detached spaces. One was the slave quarters, where they were able to forge lifelong bonds, plan social, recreational, and spiritual activities, and learn the resilience and adaptation skills required to outmaneuver the Carters and the exploitive situation under which they lived. Positioned within the material and social landscape situated well above their own world, made up of enormous material wealth and opulence and including immense self-indulgence, existed the master's world in which they worked, always separate and unequal.

I am not suggesting that the Buchanans were never physically or emotionally abused, rented out, sold (take Nancy for example), or indentured as apprentices. Five years after the Civil War, the 1870 Federal Census points to several young Buchanans who appear to have been cut off from the main family at Oatlands, working as laborers for former slaveholders in the northern and eastern parts of Loudoun County and in the neighboring county of Fauquier. By 1880 many of these young people were reunited with their immediate families and were living and working in Loudoun County or the District of Columbia.

FIGURE 2.3. *Fenton Mercer Buchanan, Lucile's Paternal Grandfather, ca. 1880s. Buchanan Archives.*

Like most slaves, the Buchanans seem to have understood the reciprocal relationships that some slaves were able to build with their owners and the small benefits that accrued. Given the ongoing relationship the Buchanans seemed to have had with the Carters during Reconstruction and in the years following, it is not far-fetched to assume that many of them understood and benefited from the positive things offered by some members of the Carter family to those slaves with whom they became close.

While enslaved, the Buchanans were able to mingle with approximately 422 free Blacks in Loudoun County, sharing spiritual, recreational, and social activities, particularly on Sundays, when slaves were often given a day off. As Elizabeth notes on Sunday July 3, 1864, "The hands finished harvest. Then went off and staid [sic] five days without permission." During Reconstruction, she notes on May 21, 1866, "Negroes all gon to a large picnick a [sic] Upperville." And then on October 6, 1866, "The Negroes had a picknic [sic] in the grove at Llangolan," a neighboring plantation. As a result of these close interactions, it was common for free Blacks to marry slaves in Virginia.[53] For example, Lucile's uncle Robert and Mahala Jackson, a free woman during the antebellum era, jumped the broom around 1843, even though their marriage was not protected by Virginia law.

Although the Buchanans left behind no records to chart their experiences at Oatlands, documents left by the planter class provide a snapshot of the slave culture and how slaves exercised their voices and humanity. Elizabeth's diary is studded with comments like this: On December 3, 1867, "Fan most impertinent + with a theat [sic] that she would bring me to justice," and on July 10, 1869, "Susan got very mad with me + send John for Ben to come up + take her home because I told her she aught to mend Ben's cloathes [sic]," giving us access to the voices that were unable to speak for themselves and making them more real to us as self-reflecting subjects. George Carter's runaway slave advertisements also demonstrate that slaves as a group not only rebelled against bondage as a concept but were individuals in their own right who chose not only to run away (and take on the attendant risk) but who also chose to assert their individuality by taking on surnames. George's will adds further evidence of multi-layered family structures within the slave class through his acknowledgment of two-parent households, single-parent households headed by men or women, monogamous relationships, extended families, and married slave families with surnames intact.

Lucile's father, as a member of the third generation of Buchanan slaves at Oatlands, typified the type of stability they enjoyed and passed on, with each generation teaching the next what they would need to know to survive and how to navigate the boundaries and rules within a White privilege culture. As a result of many years of living beside but not with their White overlords, they came to understand Whites and White culture far more clearly than most Whites imagined. In some cases, even more than Whites understood themselves.

This knowledge, gained through the slave grapevine and stories passed on, taught them to outsmart George, Elizabeth, and their progeny. They fell in love, jumped the broom, had children, nursed the elderly and the sick, buried their dead, and built a family structure that by 2017 had survived from Lucile's great uncle Robert for fourteen generations.[54] This understanding and application of strategies for survival would take the Buchanans to the Western frontier as they sought to renegotiate and re-create their lives as free people and build the economic stability, cultural practices and relationships required to thrive in the American West.

3

The Berkeleys, a Slave Named
Harriet Bishop, and Her Daughter, Sarah

In some parts of America, the European and the Negro
races are so crossed by one another that it is rare to meet
with a man who is entirely black, or entirely white.
—ALEXIS DE TOCQUEVILLE, *DEMOCRACY IN AMERICA*, 1837

Having completed my initial fieldwork at Oatlands in the summer of 2005, I headed to the Evergreen Plantation in Haymarket, Prince William County, Virginia, in search of Lucile's maternal ancestry. My interest in Evergreen was spurred by Lucile's middle name, Berkeley, as well as where her mother, Sarah, had been born and her mother's family had spent a good part of their lives enslaved.

Like the Carters of Oatlands, the Berkeley family ranked amongst the prominent Virginia Tidewater aristocracy, commonly known as the "First Families of Virginia." Evergreen lay within Carter Burwell's 2,000-acre portion of Robert "King" Carter's Bull Run Tract. By 1822 Lewis Berkeley, a Burwell descendent, had carved out a 1,064-acre plantation on which Evergreen was built.[1] Located at the foot of the Bull Run Mountains in northwestern Prince William County, Evergreen is situated about five miles from the town of Haymarket and about fourteen miles from Oatlands Plantation. Lucile's maternal family comes into the story around the time the plantation passed from Lewis Berkeley to his twenty-three-year-old son Edmund, on July 4, 1845.

FACING THE MODERN-DAY PLANTATION

Though impressive, Evergreen lacked the majesty of Oatlands. No grand driveway lined with English oak and European larch led to Evergreen's "Big House." As I arrived, I was greeted by an American flag waving proudly at the front gate of the aged two-and-a-half story, gable-roofed white building dotted with peeling stucco. Built circa 1827, the house, a Greek Revival style dominant in the antebellum era, is all that has survived of the original plantation. Six columns support the open back porch, which runs the length of the house.

Evergreen's major modern-day attraction is the Evergreen Country Club, a private eighteen-hole golf course. A banner across the club's website reads, "A Breathtaking Backdrop to a Charmed Way of Life."[2] Like Oatlands, the Evergreen Country Club frequently hosts weddings and other engagements.

The day I arrived, staff were busily preparing for that day's wedding of a Black couple. I wondered how the couple reconciled the location's history on the site where they would take their marriage vows. Blacks were horrifically exploited under the yoke of slavery and were prohibited from marrying. I could not come to grips with whether the marriage was a victory or an erasure of both the reality of the history of slavery and the paradox of the economic exploitation of that history as well as the land on which it was built.

As at Oatlands, I found it difficult to comprehend the transformation of Evergreen into a golf course and wedding venue. Another plantation history of chattel slavery had been blotted out, leaving the "Charmed Way of Life" memorialized through a lens clouded with distortions. As an ethnographer engaged in historical research, I soon realized I was having what Rosanna Hertz refers to as ongoing conversations about my experiences "while simultaneously living in the moment."[3] Through self-interrogation, I often looked to my own life in the process of trying to create meaning from Lucile's ancestors' family life and the memories of those I interviewed in the current century.

THE BERKELEYS OF EVERGREEN

Like George and Elizabeth Carter of Oatlands Plantation, the Berkeleys were among the 5 percent of slaveholders wealthy enough to own twenty or more slaves. At twenty-two years of age, Edmund Berkeley broke with tradition by choosing a bride outside of Virginia's Tidewater aristocracy, Mary Lawson Williams, whom he met at the College of William and Mary. Mary hailed from Knoxville, Tennessee, the daughter of Thomas Lanier Williams, a Tennessee state senator

FIGURE 3.1. *Edmund Berkeley (1824–1915), ca. 1890s. Courtesy, Mary Berkeley and Evergreen Manor House, ca. 1937, Prints and Photographic Division VA-833, Library of Congress, Washington, DC.*

and US Supreme Court justice and an ancestor of famed American playwright Thomas Lanier "Tennessee" Williams.

On the occasion of her wedding to Edmund in Knoxville on January 21, 1845, Mary's father offered her a choice between two types of property as a wedding gift: real estate or slaves and their importuning. Eighteen-year-old Mary easily chose the human property, which would be invaluable as she made the transition to her new home in Virginia. By choosing slaves, she followed a tradition her father had begun by giving slaves to her three older sisters.[4] The new couple made the trip from Knoxville to Evergreen, the women and children in wagons and the men walking.[5] Harriet (Lucile's maternal grandmother) also accompanied Mary as a young slave girl, approximately eight years of age. Among the other slaves accompanying Mary was forty-three-year-old Celia and a fifteen-year-old male named White.[6] These three slaves shared the common surname Bishop, and of the three, White would be the first one to be legally identified as such. In the 1870 Census, taken shortly after the Civil War, Celia is identified as a Bishop who was born in Tennessee. These three slaves appear to have been a family unit, and it is from them that Lucile's maternal family is descended.

The landscape of Evergreen was emblematic of what author John Michael Vlach describes as the "plantation landscape ensemble." For Vlach, all plantation architecture defined its relationship to the Big House: "Big House slave quarters were either set behind or to the side of the planter's residence or flanked the roadway to

TABLE 3.1. Largest slaveholders in Haymarket, Prince William County, 1850–60

Slaveholder	Profession	# of Slaves 1850	Real Estate Value 1850	# of Slaves 1860	Real Estate Value/Personal Estate Value 1860
Edmund Berkeley	Farmer	33	$19,000	53	$45,000/$50,000
Alfred Ball	Farmer	39	$40,500	32	$7,000/$22,6000
Jesse Ewell	Physician	15	NA	28	$5,250/$17,332
Willis Foley	Farmer	16	$4,000	23	$12,750/$11,180
Frederic Foote	Farmer	22	$40,000	19	$40,000/$24,250
Benoni E. Harrison	Farmer	26	$10,200	32	$17,500/$35,400
Robert M. Lewis	Farmer	10	NA	20	$10,400/$14,528
Charles B. Stuart	Farmer	23	NA	22	$19,500/$15,955

Source: Ancestry.com. *1850 US Federal Census—Slave Schedules* [database online]. Provo, UT: Ancestry.com Operations, Inc., 2004; Ancestry.com. *1860 US Federal Census—Slave Schedules* [database online]. Provo, UT: Ancestry.com Operations, Inc., 2010.

the Big House, impressing visitors with the number of slaves owned before they even arrived at the Big House."[7] This seems to have been true for Evergreen, as fifteen small slave cabins were once located on "Quarters Lane (the mile-long road in front of the [Big] house)."[8]

In addition, Evergreen had a large meat house, a carriage house, a springhouse, an icehouse, a corn house, and an overseer's house made of stone and called "Mountain Rest."[9] Between Mountain Rest and the Big House sat a large double cabin with two large stone chimneys, home to some of the slaves too old for hard work who were given a little piece of land to till.[10]

Evergreen had a large number of slaves in comparison to other Prince William County plantations. According to the 1850 US Federal Census Slave Schedules, only the widow, Sarah Carter Ball, owned more slaves than Edmund. In the 1860 Slave Schedules, Edmund was not only Prince William County's largest slaveholder; he also had the largest holdings of land and personal property in the village of Haymarket (table 3.1).

At this time, the Slave Schedules indicated that Edmund's slave property had increased to a total of fifty-three, of which twenty-two were six years of age and under.[11] That year's Slave Schedules also show most of the births clustered in a three-year span in the mid-1850s. In the ten years since the 1850 Census, Edmund's personal household grew as well. Mary had given birth to four additional children, bringing the total to six. Also living at the plantation was Susannah M. Goode, a twenty-year-old teacher from Maryland, who ran a private school for Edmund's children and the children from nearby farms and plantations.

LIFE AT EVERGREEN: THE MASTER SPEAKS

Unlike the single diary Elizabeth Carter kept, Edmund kept several diaries from the antebellum era through the early twentieth century (titled *Edmund Berkeley's Evergreen Farm Day Book*).[12] In the entries from April 15, 1851, through August 31, 1855, Edmund recorded his daily business transactions: the challenges of managing a large plantation; his relations with family, friends, tenants, and business associates; money transactions; day-to-day dealings with his slaves, and the intricacies of social and cultural life among the White planter class. What is most interesting about Edmund's diaries are his notations on Lucile's family—her mother, Sarah, her grandmother Harriet, her great-grandmother Celia, and her uncle White.

During the antebellum era, Evergreen and the other plantations in which Edmund had an interest were organized around a grain economy based on wheat, corn, and related milling activities, in addition to raising, slaughtering, and selling cattle, sheep, and swine. The plantation's economy dictated how slaves organized their time, work schedules, families, and community life. Edmund demanded that his slaves follow strict pre-set routines. In his day book he notes, "Dec. 01, 1853—Thursday, came home and found things getting on pretty well, the hands [slaves] had been getting in and housing corn and hauling stone, went to Aldie [another Berkeley farm in Loudoun County] found all well."[13] Following a trip to Weaverville, he writes that "things at home had progressed tolerably well during my absence, hands had been fencing and commenced ploughing."[14]

Strict adherence to routine helped maximize profits and enhanced the containment of chattel property, typical on large-scale plantations. As Stephanie M.H. Camp observes, "Planters presided over controlled and controlling landscapes dictating the movements of their slaves into the fields or yards and back to the quarters, with carefully considered breaks and holidays."[15]

At Evergreen, under close supervision of their overseer, slaves worked in small units at various agricultural sites: Stone house field, Pettys lot, Carters Green, Graham Tract, Waterloo, and the North and East Tracts. Edmund also sent slaves to help at his mother's and brother's farms and rented out their services to his neighbors as a source of additional income. He gave a few male slaves latitude to move outside the boundaries of the plantation by sending them on errands. These privileged few—Billy Queen, Billy Lewis, and White Bishop (Lucile's maternal great-uncle)—acted on Edmund's behalf and were responsible for watching out for his interests. It is also possible that one of these men served as the head slave driver, responsible for setting the schedule, maintaining the work pace, and enforcing the plantation's rules.

Edmund clearly understood the culturally set limits and standards of decency by which his slaves (reluctantly) knew he had to abide. Therefore, he could not fail to give them Sundays and religious holidays off, and when he failed to do so, he knew he had to compensate them monetarily. Ultimately, however, the plantation economy was not stable, and promises made often did not materialize until months later, if at all. Interestingly, Edmund behaved similarly toward the Whites he did business with on a regular basis, promising to pay for goods and services at a future date or giving them partial payment.

Occasionally, a few of Edmund's slaves were given the opportunity to engage in their own entrepreneurial activities through the sale of crops, poultry, goods, and service to Edmund. For example, on August 13, 1855, Edmund purchased fifteen chickens for his mother from Lucile's uncle White for $1.87½.[16] Edmund on occasion even borrowed money from or bartered with his slaves: "May 8, 1851—Borrowed 50 cents from old Rachel to pay Creel" and "bought Jenny a pair of shoes for $1.12 ½ [half] to be paid for in chickens."[17] He also loaned them money on occasion: "Dec 26, 1853, Lent Billy Lewis 62½ cents."[18]

When slaves disrupted the plantation's business through verbal or non-verbal action, Edmund did not hesitate to punish them for any "impudence" or other infraction, whether real or imagined. As Frederick Douglass wrote, the word *impudence* "may mean almost anything, or nothing at all, just according to the caprice of the master or overseer, at the moment. This offence may be committed in various ways; in the tone of an answer; in answering at all; in not answering; in the expression of countenance; in the motion of the head; in the gait, manner and bearing of the slave."[19]

To address his displeasure with his slave property, Edmund frequently used whipping, either delegating the responsibility to his overseer, William Powell, or doing it himself. In 1853 Edmund wrote, "July 18, 1853, Harry ran off from Mr. Powell who was trying to whip him." "September 10, 1853—Had to give Jenny and Juno a severe whipping for quarreling." "January 30, 1854—Bob was impudent and ran off."[20] "April 28, 1855—Saturday, planting corn, had to have Nelson whipped for impudence."[21] Impudence resulted in a miserable fate, subject to the whims and proclivities of the master. Nonetheless, fear did not stop slaves from pushing the boundaries, confident in their ability to survive on their wits.

HARRIET AND HER DAUGHTER, SARAH

In this master-slave culture, at the foot of the Bull Run Mountains, a slave named Harriet gave birth to a daughter, which Edmund recorded in his day book on September 29, 1853. He registered her birth in October 1853, during the tax assessor's annual household visit. Harriet's daughter, Lucile's mother-to-be, was named Sarah.

By the time Sarah was born, attitudes toward the birthing of the children of enslaved women had undergone changes brought on by increased professionalism among medical doctors, especially in the area of midwifery, and the need to grow a productive labor force. The latter was essential since in 1808 the US Congress effectively stopped the importation of slaves. Growing the labor force now rested on the shoulders of enslaved women—their bodies were not their own. According to historian Marie Jenkins Schwartz, this new service, supplied by the slave master and performed by White males, clashed with the time-honored birthing and healing practice in the slave community, which elder enslaved women performed and which was rooted in traditional herbal medicine.[22] Edmund engaged two local county doctors, Thomas M. Boyle from Aldie and Jesse Ewell, his friend, to take care of his family, his parents, and his slaves. Between January 18 and December 1, 1858, Ewell made seventeen visits to Evergreen, twelve of which were to provide medical care to nine of Edmund's slaves (table 3.2).

In at least three cases, Ewell provided obstetric services at night, since pregnant slaves were not permitted to take time away from work during the day and were often forced to work until the last minute before giving birth. In April 1858 Harriet received obstetric services subsequent to the birth of her daughter, Sarah.

There is little recorded information providing specifics as to the medical condition of these slaves or of Ewell's diagnoses and treatments. It appears that his main course of treatment was prescribing pills, for which he collected between $0.25 and $0.50 each. The only identifiable medications were aperients, a type of laxative, and carminative tincture, which was used for treating worms.

Examining the fee structure, Schwartz suggests that doctors did not always anticipate receiving the same fees for attending to slave women as they did for attending to women in the slaveholders' family.[23] Ewell's bill, however, suggests a different approach: his fee per visit was $2.00, whether he was attending to Mary Berkeley or the Berkeley slaves.

TRAIL OF DISCOVERIES

On December 26, 1854, when Sarah was about fifteen months old, Edmund recorded in his day book, "married Harriet to Mr. Clark's man Thomas."[24] Thomas belonged to John Clark (aka Joel C. Clark), a sixty-eight-year-old farmer who lived in close proximity to the Berkeleys. Marriages often occurred during a "break in

TABLE 3.2. Physician's bill for Edmund Berkeley's slaves and family, January 18–December 1, 1858

Slave	Berkeley Family	Condition	Prescription/Cost	Cost of Visit
Moses		Unknown	Powder and Medicine/25¢	$2.00
Peter		Unknown		$2.00 incl. medicine
Old Harriet and Jenny		Unknown	4 doz. Aperinet Pills/50¢	
Miss Louisa		Unknown	6 oz Carminative Tincture 50¢	
Rachel (Night visit)		Obstetric and subsequent visits		$6.00
Susan		Unknown		$2.00 incl. medicine
Jessie		Unknown		$6.00 (3 separate visits)
Emily		Obstetric		$6.00 (multiple visits)
	Mary Berkeley	Unknown	Pills and Morphine/25¢	
Jenny (Night visit)		Obstetric		$10.00 (2 visits)
	Mary Berkeley	Unknown	Spirits of Lavender/25¢	
Harriet (Night visit)		Obstetric		$6.00
	Mary Berkeley	Obstetric		$2.00
	Edmund Berkeley	Unknown	2 doz. Pills/50¢	
	Mary Berkeley	Obstetric	1 doz, Anodyne Pills, Vial Paragoric, 4 doz. Aperient Pills/$1.00	$10.00 for calls a week
	Mary Berkeley			$2.00
Susan and colored children		Unknown	4 doz. Pills/50¢	$2.00

Source: WPA Records of Prince William County, Virginia, compiled by W. R. Hobbs, Teresa A. Kelley, and Sallie C. Pusey (Westminster, MD: Willow Bend Books, 2001), 725; "Diaries and Correspondence from the Evergreen Attic," *Evergreen Report*, 4.

the agricultural work at the end of the harvest in December or January and in the lay-by period of July."[25] While there were at least seven eligible males at Evergreen who could have married Harriet, Edmund selected a male from another plantation and solemnized the marriage himself on his plantation. The only known account of Edmund fathering a child, with a slave named Harriet, comes from the oral history passed on from Harriet's daughter, Sarah, to her children in Colorado; the question remains as to why Edmund decided to marry off Harriet. Why this forced pairing on a nearby plantation?

Thomas and Harriet had the most common type of slave marriage, an abroad marriage, in which marital partners continued to live and work at separate plantations. Within a year of their marriage, Thomas and Harriet had their first child, Hugh (b. 1855). Their second child, a daughter named Juda (later changed to Julia), was born in April 1858 at Evergreen (see table 3.2); a third child, a son named Jarit, was born in 1860; and Harriet, her mother's namesake, arrived in 1861.

Harriet Bishop Churchill (aka Churchwell or Churchman), Sarah's mother and Lucile's maternal grandmother, died sometime between the birth of her fifth child, in 1861, and 1863. There is no notation of exactly when she died or what caused her death. Thomas, now a widower with several young children, married Isabel in 1864 (a year following emancipation). The 1870 Census shows three of Harriet's four children, Julia, Jarit, and Harriet, living with their father and stepmother, Isabel, in Gainsville, Virginia. Harriet and Thomas's oldest son, Hugh (Churchman), was working as a farm laborer for John W. Power in Leesburg, Virginia.[26]

The lingering question of Sarah's paternity remained. All official records identify her with the surname Bishop, which had been in her maternal family for several generations. When Sarah married James Buchanan in 1872, the marriage certificate lists Bishop as her maiden name and Harriet as her mother. The space for her father's name remains blank.

While slave owners rarely acknowledged offspring they created with slave women and the offsprings' paternity did nothing to protect them from being sold, Sarah's upbringing tells a different story. Her maternal family arrived at Evergreen in 1845 as part of Edmund's wife's dowry and remained intact for multiple generations. Celia, her daughter Harriet and son White, and Harriet's daughter, Sarah, are all included in a list of slaves living at either Evergreen or Goose Pond Plantations at the beginning of the Civil War. In the June 1, 1860, Slave Schedules, Sarah is listed as a six-year-old Mulatto. And while slavery tore apart many or most families, the Bishops remained within the private sphere of the Berkeleys' influence and trust, which likely protected them from this particularly wrenching aspect of chattel slavery.

In Sarah's case, she is kept close to Edmund's land properties or with a relative. Once the Civil War began, she appeared to have taken up residence at another property he owned, quite possibly living with her mother or with other slave family members. When the 1870 Census was taken, Sarah was living at Stoke, a farm located between Bull Run and Blue Ridge Mountains in Aldie, Virginia, continuing her life as a domestic servant to Edmund's sister Molly Berkeley (her aunt) and her husband, Richard Cox.

In an interview videotaped in 1987 at the gravesite of her parents,[27] Lucile, a spry elder at 103 years old, states unequivocally that her mother's father was Edmund Berkeley of Evergreen Plantation. I often thought that Lucile, who was a stickler for detail, led the effort among her siblings to claim Edmund Berkeley as their mother's father and thus their grandfather. When Lucile and her brother Fenton applied for Social Security cards in 1939 and 1963, respectively, they both listed their mother's full name before marriage as Sarah Berkeley. When Sadie Bishop Reed, Lucile's sister, died on March 14, 1969, in Riverside, California, the California Death Index listed her mother's maiden name as Berkeley. The 1963 funeral registry book for Lucile's brother Fenton lists Edward Berkeley as his grandfather—pointedly, the only grandfather listed. In addition, Sarah's racial designation in the 1860 Slave Schedules and the 1870 and 1880 US Censuses was Mulatto, which meant that one of her parents was either White or Mulatto.

CARRYING ON THE BERKELEY TRADITION: THE BLACK SIDE

As I searched for Lucile, it became clear that the Black side of Lucile's family did not shy away from the deep secret that governed the White side of the family. Lucile, the bearer of the Berkeley name, took her heritage seriously. Along the way to adulthood, Lucy unofficially changed her name to Lucile. Lucy was the name of one of Edmund's acknowledged White daughters, her aunt. By giving Lucy the middle name "Berkeley," Sarah was also following the tradition she and her husband, James, were exposed to in Virginia on both sides of the Black and White divide: naming a child for a parent, a grandparent, or someone the parents admired.[28] This action, and information gathered though oral histories, suggests that Edmund was more than simply admired; he was, according to Lucile, "my mother's father."

While I can only surmise what Sarah's life and experiences were like as a slave at Evergreen, it is probably safe to assume that in many ways her life followed a predictable pattern as a house slave. First, as a young child she played in the Big House with Edmund's legitimate children. Lewis was her age, Edmund's daughter Mary

FIGURE 3.2. *Sarah Bishop, Lucile's mother, ca. 1870s. Buchanan Archives.*

about a year younger, and Lucy three years younger. Likely, they were all raised together, with Sarah as a companion to any or all of the Berkeleys' young children.

Once she reached age six or younger, depending on her size and physical maturity, Sarah would have begun to learn the domestic skills necessary for her position in plantation life. This included carrying water, weeding, sweeping, tending infants, milking, gathering eggs, and churning butter, eventually graduating to doing laundry and cooking.[29] As a Mulatto and a member of the next generation of domestics, Sarah held a privileged position on the plantation. *The Negro in*

Virginia, compiled by workers of the Writers' Program, explains that "left-handed marriages" were described as numerous in Virginia, and bronze replicas of master were often assigned to house duty to save them from 'common' labor in the field."[30]

Sarah, a Mulatto of exquisite beauty, was brought into the Berkeley household. Accordingly, "Some mulatto house girls possessed a somber beauty as intriguing to men as it was disturbing to women."[31] How did Mary Berkeley respond to Sarah? There is no evidence to suggest indifference or animosity. Sarah, who had been brought into the Big House as a young child, was groomed to exhibit certain character traits such as neatness, physical grace, positive attitude, goodness, diligence, patience, dependability, devotion, probity, and loyalty—the skills necessary to placate the woman of the house, Mary Berkeley.[32]

Sarah's racial mixture certainly gave her other advantages. As Harper notes, "Throughout the slave period both Whites and Blacks felt that mulattoes were superior in intelligence to pure Blacks."[33] On plantations, slaves were acutely aware that variations in skin color, hair texture, and facial features meant preferential treatment over their darker-skinned counterparts with more African features.[34] This colorism further reinforced the division of labor, in which lighter-skinned slaves worked under less intensive conditions as domestics, cooks, servants to the children, wet nurses, hairdressers, seamstresses, and butlers in the owners' homes. These lighter-skinned slaves were often better fed and clothed and were held to different standards. Conversely, darker-skinned slaves worked in the fields, cultivating the land and growing and harvesting the crops under all weather conditions.[35]

With their monetary worth significantly reduced through the loss of their slave property, life for slaveholders changed radically at the end of the Civil War. While Edmund and his family continued to live at Evergreen, the real estate value of the plantation dropped, from $45,000 in 1860 to $12,100 in 1870. Edmund's personal estate decreased from $55,000 to $2,361 over the same time period.[36] Like the Carters, most of Edmund's losses in his personal estate stemmed from a decrease in human property. The number of Blacks at Evergreen had dwindled, from fifty at its peak to five: sixty-eight-year-old Celia Bishop (Lucile's grandmother), eleven-year-old Virginia Boyd, Eliza Tolaru, a forty-three-year-old domestic servant, and Eliza's two children. Ten years later Edmund had three Black workers: Eliza Brooks, a forty-two-year-old servant; Silvia McKenny, a nineteen-old washerwoman; and William Carter, a fifty-six-year-old farm laborer. By the time the 1900 Census was conducted, seventy-six-year-old Edmund was widowed and living with his forty-one-year-old single daughter, Lucy; his seventy-two-year-old brother, Norborne; and three Blacks: Mary Coram, a thirty-six-year old servant, and her two children, with her eight-year-old listed as a servant.

Letters written by the formerly enslaved to a former slaveholder are rare, especially those written thirty-three years after the abolition of slavery. As a free woman and long after she had created a life for herself, Sarah wrote a letter to Edmund dated, March 17, 1898, and postmarked from "Barnam [sic] Colo."

Mr. Berkeley, Dear Sir:

As I haven't heard from any of you for so long, that I thought that I would write and find out how you all were or where you were. Tell me all about the family and whose [sic] at the old place. I should like to step my feet on Evergreen once more, but I don't expect I ever will, as my health is getting bad, I've had a real hard sick spell, and the doctor says it is from hard work, my constitution is run down. You see I've had to work very hard since I've been out here, and you know that I never knew what hard work were [sic], and as I am in need, I am forced to ask you to send me a little money ever so little would help me ever so much, remember me to Miss Fannie and her family. Ask Miss Lucy to send me her picture, if she has one to spare; Tell her as I am not able to do so much, I can sit and look at it and think of the good times we have had. I will say goodbye and am in hope this will find you all well. Yours ever, Sarah, please write and let me know how you all are anyway, direct your letter to Barnam [sic], Colo, Barnam [sic] P.O.

While the letter does not discuss any familial relationship between Sarah and Edmund, it does suggest a level of intimacy and affection not common between master and slave. It is also interesting that not only did Edmund keep Sarah's letter in the day book he maintained from January 1, 1897, through January 14, 1906, but it was the only letter in the day book, which contains 2,934 daily entries.

Her letter suggests that not all of her experiences at Evergreen were unpleasant. She longed to return. In fact, her life in Colorado seems to have been more difficult than the life she led as a slave. As a house slave, she was valued and treated preferentially. Edmund was in the business of buying and selling slaves for profit, and a beautiful light-skinned Mulatto would have commanded a higher price, yet Sarah was never sold. In fact, the only move she made was from Edmund's plantations to his sister Molly's home. In both places, he could keep in close contact with her. Many light-skinned Blacks were allowed to work in the homes of their owners because they were the owners' illegitimate children. By keeping them close by, slave owners were able to compensate for the guilt they often felt for having had children with slave women. By allowing their biracial children to work in the house under better conditions, slave owners could ease their guilty consciences knowing they were treating these children, their children, better than they did slaves who were not their offspring.[37] In her letter, Sarah asks Edmund for financial assistance, a request that reveals the nature of their unusually close relationship and the idea that he might feel some paternal obligation to her.[38]

It appears from the letter that Sarah had close relationships with two of Edmund's daughters, Fannie (Frances) and Lucy. She writes, "Remember me to Miss Fannie and her family," knowing as she writes the letter that Frances is married with several children. She makes a point to ask him to have Lucy (who lived with Edmund) send her a picture, indirectly reminding him of the good times they had, indicating the type of relationship that comes from growing up with friends. Her use of "Miss" before their forenames and referring to Edmund as "Mr. Berkeley" is exemplary of the deference expected in that era rather than of the distance such nomenclature might indicate today.[39] The phrase "As I haven't heard from you for so long" also suggests prior contact between Edmund and Sarah, further supporting the idea that they shared a bond that slavery did not destroy and that they remained interested in each other's lives long after she left Virginia sixteen years prior.

As I read the letter, I wondered whether Sarah was manipulating Edmund to gain favors, such as the money she requested, or whether it was possibly a manifestation of the Stockholm syndrome. But further re-reading revealed no evidence that Sarah was running a con; nor could I seriously entertain the idea of Stockholm syndrome without evidence. The letter clearly demonstrated a close relationship—one she recalled fondly, prompting her to write a personal and affectionate letter to her father and former owner requesting financial assistance. Edmund, who was meticulous in recording financial transactions and dealings with family, friends, and business associates in his diaries, was silent. There is no way of knowing whether the letter garnered a response or what that response might have been.

Closely held secrets among the master and his wife, their children, and his female slaves were not uncommon. Leslie W. Lewis writes about secrets within the slave community that were often about the slaveholding family, particularly the master. Thus, the dialectic within the slave community transformed slaveholders from subjects to objects of discourse—especially their sexual liaisons with enslaved women. Likewise, women on the slaveholders' side—wives, daughters, and sisters—also kept secrets about their sexual trysts with male slaves.[40]

While secrets prevailed, denial also loomed large, as Mulatto children were seldom acknowledged as the offspring of White slaveholders. Even though Edmund was a pillar of Virginia's aristocracy and a leader in his community, credited for helping to initiate a peaceful transition following the Civil War and always with a pocketful of candy for neighborhood children, he was still a product of a hegemonic master culture that found it acceptable to inflict pain on his human chattel and unacceptable to acknowledge the offspring of his sexual relations.

South Carolinian author Mary Boykin Chesnut presents her take on Mulatto children: "This is *only* what I see: like the patriarchs of old, our men live all in one house with their wives and their concubines, and the Mulattoes one sees in every family exactly resemble the white children and every lady tells you who is the father of all the Mulatto children in everybody's household, but those in her own, she seems to think drop from the clouds, or pretends so to think."[41]

Denial increasingly hardened among the descendants of slave owners. I first met a descendent of the Berkeleys (by marriage) at the Thomas Balch Library in Leesburg, Virginia, in 2003. I suggested to this charming southern woman the possibility of Edmund's paternity of Sarah, an idea she adamantly shot down. I was met with a flat "NO, NO." She just as quickly softened her position when a local White male historian and author, who overheard our conversation, reminded her that miscegenation was a reality of southern life.

Over the years, I longed to meet a more direct descendent of Edmund. My wish came true in the summer of 2011, when Edmund's great-great granddaughter Mary Louise Berkeley Stoy graciously agreed to meet. David Prokop, the chair of the Evergreen Manor House Preservation Committee, arranged the meeting at the Evergreen Country Club. We sat on the balcony overlooking the Manor House, where Edmund lived and on the grounds of the plantation where Sarah was enslaved. This time I came totally prepared. I began to describe my interest in the Berkeley name and laid out several pieces of evidence regarding Sarah's paternity, including photographs of her in which the family resemblance is uncanny. While I did not expect to receive a resounding "yes," I felt that Mary truly listened. David, upon seeing a photograph of Sarah, commented on the resemblance between her and Edmund, especially their facial structures.

As I sat with Mary on that cool August evening, sipping coffee on the grounds of a former plantation, I could not help but recall Dr. Martin Luther King Jr.'s "I Have a Dream" speech, delivered forty-eight years earlier on a hot day in August 1963, that "one day on the red hills of Georgia, the sons of former slaves and the sons of former slave owners will be able to sit down together at the table of brotherhood."

Harriet, the small community of slaves at Evergreen, the Bishops, and the Berkeleys all knew and protected the secret of Sarah's paternity. It was a secret James Fenton Buchanan would have known when he married his beloved Sarah, since the secrets of master-slave sexual liaisons were sometimes shared in the community among male slaves. It was the actions of the Buchanans and the Bishops immediately following emancipation, their efforts to breathe full meaning into their newly acquired freedom, as well as to understand their rights of belonging to a community that treated them as less than human.

4

Slavery's Chain Done Broke at Last

For some slaves, the first step out of bondage is to
learn to see their lives with new eyes.

— KEVIN BALES

With the chain of chattel slavery broken, newly emancipated slaves seized the opportunity to flee from the places that had brought them countless humiliation and pain, vowing never to return. However, many opted to stay, at least temporarily, to work as paid labor on the remnants of plantations or farms that had been sold or rented to Whites. It was not unusual in Loudoun County for emancipated slaves to remain as part of the new labor force, even though many plantations were in ruins or abandoned, houses burned and gutted, tools wrecked, and livestock decimated. These "stayers" likely sought opportunities for themselves as freed men and women, hoping they could reap the benefits of the new social order as free citizens in Loudoun, working as landowners or tenant farmers.

In addition, there were a number of systems organized and developed by Blacks that helped forge stable communities in areas they already knew. For instance, beginning in 1840, slaves and free people of color lived in an area "east of Catoctin Mountain known as Negro Mountain." Over time, the Negro Mountain Blacks established the community's first Black churches between 1862 and 1868, and between 1865 and 1867 they built the first Black schools in Middleburg, Hillsboro, Leesburg, and Waterford.[1] These actions, taken at the start of the transition from slavery to freedom, showed that Blacks wanted to get off the plantation system but also wanted to become part of Virginia society, given the remarkable things they began to accomplish for themselves.

THE BUCHANANS OF LOUDOUN COUNTY

At the time slavery ended, Lucile's paternal family had managed to remain in Virginia pretty much intact. The 1870 US Census recorded twenty-four freed Blacks with the surname Buchanan in Loudoun County. Of them, twelve lived near the village of Aldie, ten lived in the nearby county seat of Leesburg, and two resided in the village of Pleasant Valley. In addition, there were three Buchanan males, ranging in age from fourteen to twenty-eight and related to the main branch in Loudoun, who lived in neighboring Fauquier County. Among those in Loudoun were three brothers—George, Fenton, and Robert Buchanan—emancipated slaves from Oatlands Plantation; their wives and children, and some blood and non-blood relatives. George and Fenton were among those who lived near Aldie within proximity of their former plantation, whereas Robert lived about twelve miles away in Leesburg, Virginia.[2]

The decision to remain at Oatlands or in its vicinity raises a number of questions and speculations about the Buchanans' motivations. Were the Carters such benevolent slave owners that their freed slaves felt indebted to the family? Over a century later, Phillip Buchanan, Robert Buchanan's great-great-grandson, suggested that "there had to have been a friendly relationship" with the slave owners.[3]

With the southern economy in shambles, did they imagine that they would have the opportunity to purchase land or that it might be offered to them for "services rendered"? Carter's daughter-in-law, Kate Powell Carter, suggests in her diary a motive that might have led the Buchanans to consider such possibilities: "One of the stories they [Union troops] circulated here was that if they conquered us, the lands were to be taken from the rich and divided between the poor people and the servants."[4] Furthermore, the Freedmen's Bureau distributed a circular in May 1865, which many former slaves interpreted as proof that they were entitled to their former masters' property and support regardless of whether they worked. To clarify this policy, they issued another circular stating that "former masters have the right to refuse them anything that he might deny to a perfect stranger, and is no more bound to feed, clothe, or protect them than if he had never been their master. They may remain with him if he and they both desire it and agree on the terms, in which case, each party is equally bound by the contract."[5]

Certainly, one can surmise that with three generations of masters and enslaved living on the same plantation, broad social interaction existed, whether on the fields, in the gardens, or in the Big House. But this was far from an equal relationship. The groups occupied separate spheres, with one living at the core and the other on the periphery of society. Historian Franklin Frazier reminds us that "despite the 'human' relations which developed between Negroes and Whites on the plantation where a paternalistic type of control developed, the Negro was, nevertheless, an article of commerce or an animate tool, according to Aristotle's definition of a slave."[6]

In addition, George and Elizabeth Carter may have believed it was to their economic advantage to mollify slaves by giving them incentives to remain on the plantation and not run away. While some of the Buchanans stayed and worked for the Carters during Reconstruction and in its aftermath, still othersworked for non-slave–holding yeoman farmers, or for themselves, others left Loudoun County to seek a new destiny elsewhere.

As newly freed Blacks, Fenton and his son, James, transitioned from field hands under slavery to farm laborers, the lowest position among the agricultural occupations. In 1870 Fenton, a forty-five-year-old widower and single father, lived with his three daughters—twenty-two-year-old Frances, sixteen-year-old Julia, and eleven-year-old Mary—and his twenty-year-old son James. Living with the Buchanans were seventy-six-year-old Nellie Evenlin; her son, thirty-six-year-old Parker Evenlin; and his five-year-old daughter, Mary Evenlin. The census lists Nellie as "keeping house," a category for women who took care of the house for their own families or for themselves and had no other gainful occupation.

Fenton's oldest brother (and Lucile's great-uncle), George Buchanan, lived close by with his wife, Frances, and their three children: seven-year-old Luther, three-year-old George, and eight-month-old Ella, also known as Elinora. As one of seven blacksmiths in the village, his household also included his twenty-year-old apprentice, Arthur Watson; Arthur's brother, thirteen-year-old Llewellyn; and eighteen-year-old Laura Thomas, a housekeeper.[7] Arthur Watson, who was about fifteen when chattel slavery was abolished, would marry Fenton's oldest daughter Frances (Lucile's aunt) in 1870.

Lucile's other great-uncle, Robert Buchanan, a fifty-year-old farmer, lived in Leesburg with his wife, Mahala, their twenty-five-year-old daughter, Virginia, her one-year-old daughter, Fannie, and his mother-in-law, Hannah Jackson. Two young children lived with them as well, a four-year-old and a two-year-old, both named John Ball.

Five years after the Civil War, Robert had acquired $100 in real estate property and owned personal property worth about $150. It is unclear whether his farm received payment for services rendered to the Carters or whether he purchased the property from them. During this period, land sold for between $2 and $3 an acre. Robert's farmland stretched between thirty and fifty acres.[8]

The emancipation of George, Fenton, Robert, their spouses, and their children, along with 4 million other slaves, stripped the planters of their labor force, most of their wealth, and their political authority. Impoverished by the war, without slave labor to work the plantations, and often too poor to hire wage laborers, former slave owners were glad to sell pieces of their land to anyone who had the money. Some freed people rented from their former owners, only to purchase the property a decade or two later. Other times, landowners subdivided acreage and sold lots. For freed slaves, land ownership became essential for economic independence and freedom.[9] Even though during the late 1860s and early 1870s Blacks acquired perhaps 80,000 to 100,000 acres of land in Virginia, most Blacks were landless and therefore penniless. Without land, Blacks were forced into unfair "wage fixing combinations and worked for the inadequate pay of five dollars a month. Some found themselves in a state of extreme destitution."[10]

An article in the June 29, 1865, edition of the *New York Herald* describes Virginia's desolation after the Civil War. While mostly discussing counties bordering Loudoun, the descriptions could very well have applied to Loudoun's fields—the pride of White farmers—which were now ruined, with ditches filled up and corn houses and barns in shambles as well. Much of the once majestic forests of oak, hickory, chestnut, and pine had disappeared, replaced with the rude huts and cabins built and then abandoned by the armies of both sides. Instead of fallen nuts and berries from the trees, "the ground was covered with old canteens, worn-out knapsacks, odd shoes, bread boxes, the inevitable 'hard tack' [a cracker-like staple rationed to troops], bayonet scabbards, occasional ten-pound Parrott shells, and everywhere 'little Minies,'" a type of bullet used by troops of both flags.[11]

PICKING UP THE PIECES

After the end of the Civil War, a communal approach to Black households took shape as numerous extended family groupings—long-lost sisters, cousins, children, aunts, uncles, husbands, wives, and in-laws—found each other. Newly freed Blacks also expanded the notion of family by taking friends, orphans, and the elderly into their homes, providing opportunities for mutual aid, friendship, sympathy, solace, and moral support. This interdependence became the basis of the future Buchanan family structure, with family constituting a system of blood and fictive (non-blood) kin bound together through reciprocal support and a strong sense of caring and responsibility. The Buchanans had a diverse, multi-layered family structure consisting of two-parent households, single male and female-headed households, and an extended structure of older parents, in-laws, grand-children, non-familial members, live-in employees, and children without their own biological families.

The eighteenth-century practice of naming children after parents or grandpar-ents provides additional information about Lucile's family's household. Her pater-nal grandfather, Fenton Mercer, named his son James Fenton, and James Fenton named his only son Fenton Mercer. Historian Mechal Sobel contends that Blacks had begun to follow a "White" Virginian pattern of naming children for grandpar-ents and sons after fathers.[12] It's just as likely that they were following an almost identical West African naming tradition in which a father gave his own name as a middle name to his son.[13]

As a form of hero worship, slaves, free Blacks, and Whites[14] in Loudoun County named their children after a local celebrity, Charles Fenton Mercer, a prominent attorney and a politician who established the village of Aldie in 1804. Charles's celebrity status was elevated even more when he became a founding member of the American Colonization Society and vice president of the Virginia Colonization Society,[15] aimed at repatriating free Blacks to Liberia. The names Fenton and Mercer, therefore, become popular in Loudoun across racial and privilege lines during slavery and in the post-Reconstruction era.

Although there was an accepted practice of naming children after grandparents, aunts, brothers, or sisters in an effort to tie the child to the family group, many of these names were also common among Whites. It has been suggested over time that slaves adopted their masters' names or the names of the masters' progeny. Cultural anthropologist Denise Oliver-Velez challenges this line of thinking, sug-gesting that during slavery, the practices for choosing children's first and second names were more complex than simply duplicating the names of slaveholders or their progeny. She theorizes that these names were instead a form of "strategic flattery" by slaves attempting to manipulate their owners and, by using a form of psychology, attempted to manipulate their owners by naming their own children in their honor. According to Oliver-Velez, "You name your child after the master or mistress or allow them the privilege of naming your child in hopes that the child would [be] less likely to be auctioned off."[16]

Surnames were even more complex. Slaveholders rarely allowed slaves to have surnames, but this did not stop slaves from adopting them. Beginning with the issuance of the Emancipation Proclamation in 1863 and culminating with the end of the Civil War in 1865 and the passage of the Thirteenth Amendment abolishing slavery, newly freed Blacks began to take surnames for legal purposes as well as to proclaim their new identity. A number of factors were considered when choosing a surname. For some, declaring their new name was simply a matter of announcing it, since during slavery many had secretly adopted a surname, which they never revealed to their owners. Others, who feared that their emancipation could be taken away, moved quickly to adopt a surname disconnected from any relationship to their previous circumstances. Some freed slaves took the name of the county in which they were residing as their surname, signaling the geographic location of origination while at the same time providing some generational continuity. Sometimes, those who had been sold away from their families took on the names of their previous owners, as they thought it might be easier for long-lost relatives to find them under a familiar name.[17]

Emancipated slaves also invented surnames to describe their new identities, such as Freeman and Newman, or they adopted names of former American presidents, such as Washington, Lincoln, Jefferson, Grant, and Buchanan. For historian Leon Litwack, "The names assumed or revealed after emancipation reflected a new beginning—and an essential step toward achieving the self-respect, the personal dignity, and the independence which slavery had compromised."[18]

IT'S TIME TO JUMP THE BROOM

Plantation owners had little concern for, and often outright antipathy toward, their slaves' familial relationships. Slave marriages were never legally sanctioned, and thus never secure; nor did they protect those in them from being sold separately. Husbands, their wives, and their offspring were routinely separated and sold at the discretion of the master or mistress. So it might be an unusual circumstance that George Carter's Last Will and Testament describes (and possibly honors) some family connections among slaves and mentions co-residential and two-parent units. The Buchanans seem to have benefited from the family structures that developed on the plantation, in that at least three generations lived at Oatlands with other enslaved families—all of whom had long historical, cultural, emotional, and familial ties to each other and to the family of the plantation owners. During the antebellum era, men and women of these slave families who were prevented from legally marrying secretly engaged in a tradition known as "jumping the broom" as the only way to solemnize their marriages.

Two-parent households, as well as married couples (though illegal), were more common at Oatlands than elsewhere, thereby suggesting a slightly more favorable family environment in the slave quarters. While slaves at Oatlands were not immune to all family disruptions, their familial experiences suggest the presence of greater kinship and community ties that continued into freedom, as many of the Buchanan children who were born into slavery moved to either legalize their marriages or enter into marriages with spouses they had grown up with on the plantation. Examples include the Barnes, Gleeds, Valentines, Smiths, and Gaskins (table 4.1).

Among the emancipated slaves who formed marriage bonds with the Buchanans was John (Jack) Gleed, who was born in 1830 at Oatlands. He had a peculiar and enduring relationship with the Buchanan family. In 1870 Gleed and his wife, Lucinda, were Robert Buchanan's next-door neighbors. The census lists John's occupation as a farm laborer with $250 in real estate property. Robert's household consisted of himself and his oldest daughter, twenty-five-year-old Virginia (Ginnie). Following Lucinda's death, forty-five-year-old John married Virginia on March 11, 1875. During that marriage he continued buying and selling small parcels of land, sometimes at a loss. He is credited with founding the village of Gleedsville[19] and co-founding, in 1890, Mt. Olive Methodist Episcopalian Church in Loudoun County. A year after Virginia's death in 1888, he married her younger sister Mahala, twenty years his junior. The 1900 census shows sixty-nine-year-old John in Leesburg living with his brother-in-law, Martin Van Buren Buchanan (Lucile's second cousin), and his family, and he is listed as a carpenter.

Beginning in the late 1870s and early 1880s, the younger generation of Buchanans had developed greater stability and begun to make plans for the future. While some migrated out of Virginia, many more stayed behind. Those who stayed in Virginia were thinking of land ownership as a means of establishing their autonomy as well as their economic independence. Thus, in 1883 Sinah and Nancy Buckhannon (another spelling for Buchanan) bought twelve acres of land from Hampton R. Brown near what would later be called Buchanan's Gap for $800, each paying $400.[20] Two years later Lucile's uncle George and his wife, Frances, bought land close by, and in 1888 they sold their eleven acres to their twenty-five-year-old son Luther and his first wife, Eva (or Eave), Buckhannon. Luther built a stone house near the pass, and partly because of this building, Buchanan's Gap was named for him. In 1906, now widowed, Luther married Alice Crawford. The marriage lasted about four years. In the 1920s, after working as a coachman for Henry Fairfax at Oak Hill, Luther took a job as a laborer with a meat-packing company, and he and his third wife, Irene, left Loudoun for Richmond, Virginia.

TABLE 4.1. Marriage patterns among former Buchanan slaves from Oatlands

Date of Marriage License	Groom and Age	Bride and Age	Groom's Parents	Bride's Parents
10/20/1870	Arthur Watson (21)	Frances (22)	Unah and Frances Watson	Fenton and Hannah Buckhanan
12/28/1871	James Gaskin (27)	Hannah (26)	James and Amy Gaskins	Robert and Mahala Buchanan
11/14/1872	James Fenton (22)	Sarah (19)	Hannah and Fenton Buchanan	Harriet Bishop Edmund Berkeley
4/9/1874	Hiram Valentine (22)	Elizabeth (21)	Alfred and Ann Valentine	Robert and Mahala Buchanan
4/11/1874	Arthur Smith (36)	Julia (23)	Jesse and Amanda Smith	Joseph and Amanda Buchanan
3/11/1875	Jack/John Gleed (35)	Virginia/Ginnie (33)	Richard and Clara Gleed	Robert and Mahala Buchanan
11/14/1878	Thornton S. Buchanan (25)	Mary (19)	George and Leah Buchanan	William and Elizabeth Godfrey
10/19/1879	Stephen Hall (22)	Mary (20)	Alfred and Amy Hall	Fenton and Hannah Buchanan
1/8/1880	William Willis (27)	Julia (23)	Tony and Tabia Willis	Fenton and Hannah Buchanan
1880 (?)	Fenton M. Buchanan (55)	Amy/Annie (40)	Andrew and Fannie Buchanan	Unknown
1880	Travers D. Buchanan (26)	Maryetta (25)	George and Leah Buchanan	Peter and Chaney Chillis
12/17/1889	John/Jack Gleed (51)	Mahala A. Buchanan (31)	Richard and Clara Gleed	Robert and Mahala Buchanan
10/7/1891	John Barnes (55)	Susan Buchanan (30)	John and Mary Barnes	Robert and Mahala Buchanan
1892	Martin Van Buren Buchanan (47)	Amelia Ann (26)	Robert and Mahala Buchanan	Spencer Massey and Lucy Johnson
4/11/1893	George W. Johnson (22)	Nancie/Nannie S. (19)	Sandy and Letha Johnson	Hiram and Elizabeth (nee Buchanan) Valentine

Source: Marriage Register, Loudoun County Clerk's Office, Book 2, 1865–79; Book 3, *Marriages between Oatlands Former Slave Families*. Some of this information can be found in Patricia B. Duncan and Elizabeth R. Frain, *Loudoun County, Virginia Marriages after 1850*, vol. 1: *1851–1880* (Westminster, MD: Willow Bend Books, 2000). Buchanan was also spelled Buckman, Buckanon, Buchner, Buckner, Buckhansor, Buckhannan, Buckannan, and Buchannan.

THE BISHOPS OF PRINCE WILLIAM COUNTY

In contrast, Lucile's mother, Sarah Bishop, transitioned from one Berkeley house-hold to another. By 1870 she had moved from Evergreen, the plantation of her father and former slave owner, Edmund Berkeley, in Prince William County, Virginia, to Aldie in Loudoun County, putting herself within close proximity of her future husband, James Buchanan. Now seventeen years old, Sarah lived and worked as a domestic at Stoke, the home of her aunt, Molly Cox, Edmund's sister.

As a result of living on the same plantation for several generations, the Buchanans benefited from an immediate and larger extended family support net-work. However, Sarah's family structure and life were altogether different. She was the product of a slave mother and a White master; raised in the Big House, she came into close contact with her father, his wife, and their children. Sarah's let-ter to Edmund in 1898 indicated that she had close contact with her half-sisters Fannie and Lucy and acknowledged the "good times" they had shared. Given her status, it is unclear how much influence her mother had on her early life. When she was fifteen months, old her father, Edmund, selected a spouse for her mother from a nearby plantation, with whom Harriet had four children. When Sarah was between seven and nine years old, her mother died. Sarah continued to live at Evergreen, presumably with the support of her grandmother Celia Bishop, also a house slave, and, most likely, the other house slaves at Berkeley Plantation.

By 1870, the remainder of Sarah's maternal family was dispersed throughout Loudoun County. Hugh Churchman, her fifteen-year-old half-brother, worked as a farm laborer and lived with a White family in Mercer. Her twelve-year old half-sister, Julia, ten-year-old brother, Jarit, and nine-year-old half-sister, Harriet, lived with their father, Thomas (also listed as Churchwell), and stepmother, Isabella, and their new family in Gainsville, Virginia, not far from Edmund Berkeley. As she grew into adulthood, Sarah was surrounded not only by the White side of her family but also by a group of emancipated slave women "stayers" who continued to work in the homes of their former masters and mistresses.

With the ratification of three significant amendments to the US Constitution—the Thirteenth Amendment abolishing slavery in 1865, the Fourteenth Amendment granting citizenship to free slaves and protecting their civil liberties in 1868, and the Fifteenth Amendment giving the franchise to Black men in 1870—the Buchanans, like other emancipated slaves, enjoyed some protection under the law. These gains would quickly erode as Virginia and other southern states began to enact discrim-inatory legislation, known as Jim Crow laws, against Blacks. But with the window of opportunity that opened during Reconstruction, several of the Buchanans took steps to become literate by enrolling in schools set up by the Freedmen's Bureau or through the efforts of the local Black community, with financial assistance from the Quakers in Loudoun County.[21]

Even with some modest gains, there may have been more disappointments, especially among the younger Buchanans who had placed their fate in the federal government's Reconstruction plan and attempted to make a go of it in Virginia, where they had long historical and family roots. Life during the Reconstruction era (1865–77) was not easy. For many, the contract labor system the Freedmen's Bureau instituted was too close to the system they had just escaped. Noted historian A. A. Taylor writes about the tradeoffs Virginia Blacks had to contend with during the early decades of the post-bellum era.[22]

In addition to an average wage of five dollars per month, the freedmen were provided with rations and often free shelter, firewood, and small parcels of land for gardening and raising poultry. However, contracts were iffy. Some workers received written contracts, while others did not. Since most planters had financial difficulties, many failed to pay workers what they owed them. The working hours were excessively long and the weather hot, causing much sickness. Freedmen provided their own medical care and clothing. Nevertheless, in the face of all these difficulties Taylor notes that many "Negroes worked faithfully under contract and the crops were reported as generally good where the planting had been adequate."[23]

As they began to see their world crumble, some migrated to the District of Columbia and Maryland. But for the children of two brothers, Travers and Thornton (the sons of George and Leah Buchanan), and their first cousin James Fenton (the son of Fenton and Harriet Buchanan), the Northeast did not hold the promise of a future. Looking far beyond Loudoun and the Potomac River, they began to think of ways to renegotiate their lives by embracing the fervor of western migration. They set their sights on Colorado, where silver mining was booming and land was available for homesteading.

But getting to Colorado was not as easy as they had originally thought. First, they had to prepare for the trip, a costly venture. It would take several years for them to pool sufficient resources to make the journey. Second, they were leaving behind family, friends, and a community that had been their support system from slavery through their newfound freedom. Difficult as the decision must have been, they clearly understood that the economic conditions in Virginia were not readily going to change. The new agricultural labor system—sharecropping—did not provide autonomy and independence. Instead, it became a system of exploitation, economic dependency, and poverty. In the 1870s the average rural freedman in Virginia eked out only six to ten dollars a month. A small handful managed to buy their farms, but the majority were landless peasants caught up in an endless cycle of poverty and debt.[24] Slavery did not end; it just changed its shape and donned a new name. The cousins decided that their best future was on the new frontier. In the meantime, they began to consider the personal relationships they were nurturing. Marriage, therefore, became an even more important decision.

Of the three first cousins, James Fenton Buchanan, Lucile's father, would be the first to marry. For some time, the strapping six-foot-tall, twenty-year-old James had had his eye on the curvaceous and beautiful seventeen-year-old Sarah Lavina Bishop. Although oral interviews with Lucile indicated that her grandfather, Edmund Berkeley, had selected James as a suitable spouse for her, it is equally plausible that his cousin Thornton, who lived closer to Sarah, may have alerted his cousin to her presence. Besides, Sarah would have had greater access to the kinds of social networking that occurred during Reconstruction, particularly through churches, which were essential to community building.

Lucile's recollection of the role Edmund played in the selection of Sarah's spouse is key to understanding Sarah, her father (the former slave owner), and their relationship. Edmund had selected a husband for Sarah's mother, Harriet, when she was a slave on the plantation in 1854. Selecting Sarah's husband was therefore the continuation of an old master-slave habit, which included the slave owner performing the marriage ceremony on his plantation.[25] Finally, as Sarah's father and only surviving parent, it made sense that even as he would not publicly acknowledge his paternity, he might have had a desire to approve Sarah's spouse, as he did for any of his other children. But there was one more factor to consider. Sarah's grandmother, sixty-eight-year-old Celia Bishop, lived in Edmund's household from slavery through Reconstruction. Having come to Evergreen from Tennessee with Edmund's wife, she probably knew the household secrets. Therefore, having the ceremony at Evergreen followed an old tradition and paid appropriate (if quiet) deference to both Edmund and Celia.

Thus, on November 14, 1872, in Prince William County, Virginia, twenty-two-year-old James Fenton Buchanan and eighteen-year-old Sarah Lavina Bishop were married.[26] The young couple took up residence in the Bull Run Mountains, sandwiched between the village of Aldie and the town of Warrenton. Bull Run had been part of the underground railway, and a number of free Blacks founded settlements in the area, which included Bowmantown[27] in the early 1800s and Stewartown,[28] founded in 1868.

James and Sarah had their first child, a daughter named Katy, on October 15, 1873. James's father, Fenton, registered her birth at the Loudoun County Courthouse. Tragically, Katy died shortly after birth. A second daughter, Hattie, named for her maternal grandmother Harriet (aka Hattie), was born almost a year later, in October 1874. On November 9, 1875, a third daughter, Hannah, named for her paternal grandmother, arrived. She was followed by the birth of Laura, nicknamed Lolly or Loll, on March 1, 1878. And on July 26, 1880, Sarah and James had their first and only son, who was named after his paternal grandfather, Fenton Mercer.[29]

The next cousin to marry was twenty-seven-year-old Thornton Buchanan (sometimes listed as Buckhannon). In 1879 he married seventeen-year-old Mary A. Godfrey of Mercer District. Mary's father, William H. Godfrey, her mother, Mary Elizabeth, and their children were free Blacks (listed as Mulattoes in the 1860 Census) during the antebellum era. In 1860 Godfrey was a farm laborer, with his personal wealth valued at $100 (approximately $2,980 in 2016).[30] This relative wealth gave them the opportunity to own property and amass a small personal estate. By 1870 the Godfreys were one of the few financially stable, landowning Black families in Loudoun County, with $592 ($10,447 in 2016) in real estate and $280 ($4,940 in 2016) in personal property.[31] Following their marriage, the newly-weds moved in with Mary's family while Thornton worked as a laborer on his in-laws' farm. This intergenerational family structure helped the young couple care for their two young children: a one-year-old daughter named Frankie and seven-month-old Lizie.

As for Travers Buchanan, in 1870 the sixteen-year-old lived in Upperville, Fauquier County, Virginia, and worked as a farm laborer for John T. Cochran alongside thirty-year-old John Watson, also a former slave from Oatlands Plantation. The 1870 Census shows that two of John Watson's younger brothers, including Slewellew, lived with Travers's father, George, in Mercer.

In 1875 Travers returned to Mercer District in Loudoun County. Following in his father, George's, footsteps, he became a blacksmith. At about the same time, twenty-one-year-old Travers married nineteen-year-old Maryetta Chillis, daughter of Peter (a farm laborer) and Chaney Chillis of Charlottesville, Virginia. The 1880 Census shows that they were living in Mercer with their four children: five-year-old George Fenton, four-year-old Leah F., two-year-old Ann E., and one-year-old Elinora.

By 1880 all three members of this close-knit group of Buchanan males, the sons of two brothers, were married and building their new families. But 1880 was also a significant year in that the leader of the Exodusters movement, Benjamin "Pap" Singleton, was summoned to Washington, DC, and called before the US Senate Select Committee investigating the "Negro Exodus from the Southern States" to testify on the causes of the Great Exodus, in which tens of thousands of Blacks fled the post-Reconstruction South to escape violence and poverty.

Many Black migrants to the West went to Kansas, establishing several communities such as Nicodemus. It is possible that through the informal communication networks developed during slavery, free Blacks in Loudoun were well aware of Singleton's visit and the Exoduster movement. Yet again, maybe it was the romanticism of the new western frontier and its tales of adventure, great riches, and wild mustangs galloping over the vast plains that dazzled Travers, the blacksmith in the group. Was it the opportunity to own land that Fenton yearned for or the talk of silver mining that sparked an interest in Thornton? Whatever the reason, the three first cousins felt sure that whatever was ahead was far better than what was behind. The question is, why Colorado?

5

Colorado and the Promise of Freedom

The nation has not yet found peace from its sins; the freedman has not yet found in freedom his promised land.

—W.E.B. DU BOIS

Colorado attracted few Virginia-born Blacks before or after Reconstruction. Why, then, were the Buchanans attracted to Colorado? Not yet an independent territory, Colorado was part of a four-territorial (Kansas Territory, Nebraska Territory, New Mexico Territory, and Utah Territory) census in 1860. The population then was around 34,277, of which 46 were Black. A decade later Colorado's population had grown to about 39,864, of which 456 were Blacks,[1] with about 47 of those Blacks having migrated from Virginia.

STARTING TO MAKE A DIFFERENCE

The 1870 Territorial Census shows that of the territory's Black population, 237 lived in the city of Denver and were beginning to capitalize on their newfound freedom.[2] Several Blacks built businesses, and a few would amass small fortunes. On June 7, 1870, Assistant Marshal George H. Mills recorded in the census that thirty-nine-year-old Virginian-born Jackson Smith was a "farm laborer." However, Smith was a laborer on his own farm, which was valued at $2,500 (about $49,213 in 2017). Another Black entrepreneur, thirty-year-old Charles Huston, could read but not write, while his wife, Mary, could do neither. However, they established a laundry business in Denver valued at $1,500 ($29,528 in 2017).[3] To supplement their income, the Hustons took in two White female boarders, one of which was Mary L. Barber, a milliner.

The 1870 Census also showed that the vast majority of Black men were relegated to unskilled tasks as laborers, a carryover from slavery when the majority of slaves were restricted to unskilled rural tasks requiring no formal education or training. Nevertheless, there were Black laborers who showed more wealth than their White counterparts. Twenty-nine-year-old Kentucky-born James Whitsell, whose occupation is listed as laborer, lived in his own house, located between the rented homes of two White families. His property (real estate) was valued at $750 ($14,764 in 2017).[4]

Although some Black men may have been ill-equipped to handle occupations other than those on the very bottom of the labor market, the 1870 Census shows the beginning of a skilled labor force that included Black men occupying positions such as brick mason, teacher, pressman, store clerk, shoemaker, clergyman, painter, glazier, and barber. Among these early pioneers was Maryland-born Henry O. Wagoner, a restaurateur and saloon owner who by 1870 was the wealthiest Black American in Denver, with assets valued at $6,300 ($124,016 in 2017). The 1870 Census also shows the first Black teacher hired in the territory, thirty-four-year-old Rufus K. Felton, was hired in 1871 at a monthly salary of $75.00.[5] In 1870 the territory's Black female population was about 168, of whom 92 lived in Denver. In most cases the census reported women (single or married) as "keeping house," an occupation without any monetary return for services rendered. For Black women, this occupational category was particularly misleading and would continue to be problematic in subsequent censuses, since it relegated them to the private sphere and did not take into consideration any supplemental occupations and incomes these women were able to amass in and out of the home.

Black women occupied a type of fusion sphere, which blended the public and private as their personal needs required. As a result, Black women were not seen to be embracing "true womanhood," which elevated domesticity, submissiveness, piety, and purity to something approaching cult status, heavily promoted among middle- and upper-class White women in the later nineteenth century.[6] While there were Black women who for myriad reasons strived to emulate middle- and upper-middle-class values generally attributed to Whites, the majority of Black women who initially ventured into Colorado were born into slavery and thus had worked side by side with Black men in the fields, engaging in backbreaking work.

By 1870 Black women in Colorado were augmenting their family's income by taking in boarders (across the racial divide) and operating laundry businesses in and out of their homes. One of these hard-striving Black women, Rebecca Mosby, had entrepreneurial skills that placed her in a category that foretold a different level of success. First, not only did both Rebecca and her husband work, but they were what we'd call today a dual-career couple. She was a dressmaker, whose personal income was twice that of her hotel cook husband's earnings in 1870, $600 ($11,811 in 2017), while her husband's income was $250 ($4,921 in 2017).[7] Rebecca also supplemented their income by taking in two boarders: Elizabeth Smith, a White music teacher from Wisconsin, and Frigbee Hayden, a Black barber from Ohio.

Black women also owned real estate, with some amassing sizable personal wealth. In 1870 the two wealthiest women in the territory were both Kentucky-born former slaves. Sixty-year-old Clara Brown of Central City's real estate assets were valued at $6,000 ($118,111 in 2017) and her personal estate at $500. Nellie French, a Denver sex worker, owned real estate valued at $2,500 ($49,212 in 2017), while her personal estate was valued at $1,000 ($19,685 in 2017).[8]

While the middle-class Victorian ideal of women staying at home began to emerge among Blacks—particularly among the Mulatto class, who were more accepted and had more economic opportunities—two-parent households in which both parents worked outside the home were not unusual. Thus, this Victorian ideal never gained a solid foothold among the majority of Blacks in Colorado. As these women began to break into the workforce, they merely continued to work as they always had. In 1870 and 1880 the largest numbers of Black female wage earners were employed as servants and laundresses. However, by the 1880s many had begun to manage boardinghouses as proprietors or as supervisors of established dressmaking and hairdressing businesses. As Black women transitioned from slavery to freedom, they did what they had to do to survive, and given their past experiences, they were able to broaden the definition of womanhood by incorporating resourcefulness and independence—necessary survival skills for tackling the new American frontier.

On August 1, 1876, Colorado gained statehood. By 1879, with the arrival of the Union Pacific and the Denver and Rio Grande Railways, Denver's population had more than quadrupled to 194,471, of which 1,662 were Black. The 1880 Census found that Virginia-born Black migrants represented about 8 percent (132) of Colorado's total Black population, of which 58 percent were males and 42 percent were females. At this time, most Black migrants to Colorado hailed from Missouri and Kentucky, with Virginia coming in a distant third.[9]

The residency patterns among early Black migrants suggest that they settled in areas where they had the best chance to enhance their economic and social opportunities. While many stayed in the major mining towns of Aspen, Central City, Georgetown, Idaho Springs, and Leadville, the majority were concentrated in the urban center of Denver.

As with the 1870 Census, there were a number of occupational coding challenges with the 1880 Census.[10] Even so, table 5.1 provides a glimpse into Denver's employment opportunities available to Black men sixteen years of age and over, by marital status. The majority of Black men were single, and their work, concentrated in personal service occupations, fell under the category of laborer, typically the jobs associated with the antebellum years.

But the third largest classification—servant—presented the greatest number of challenges. First, the census asked the person's relationship to the head of household. For Blacks as well as a number of immigrants from Ireland, Prussia, Bavaria, Sweden, and Norway and US-born Whites, servant was the designated name of the relationship to the head of household, whether the head was Black or White. The enumerators also asked the person's occupation or trade. Sometimes, occupation was not specified beyond the label "servant." In these cases, it was difficult to understand the exact duties of Black men who were listed as servants in the labor force.

While the vast majority of the occupations were menial, in some cases they were esteemed occupations within the Black community. For example, a porter in 1880 might work as a doorkeeper at a prestigious men's club such as the Denver Club, at the state capitol, or in any one of the town's twenty-five hotels and boardinghouses, such as the Wentworth House at Fifteenth and Curtis Streets. Today, these positions would be part of the professional hospitality industry, and the jobs would still be to ensure that residents and guests receive exceptional service. Unlike today, it would not be of interest that the jobs provided daily interactions across racial lines.

Although small in number, the 1880 Census points to a number of Black males who had established themselves as entrepreneurs and self-employed artisans in Denver, Leadville, and Georgetown. For example, thirty-three-year-old Gilbert Alexander owned a lunch stand in Leadville, while thirty-four-year-old James Coles had a restaurant; Albert Tenneson (sometimes Tenison or Tennyson), from the Scott District in Fauquier, Virginia, owned and operated the Chicago Restaurant out of his Denver residence at 493½ Holladay Street (now Market Street), serving individual meals for thirty-five cents and weekly boarding for four dollars.

TABLE 5.1. 1880 employment patterns of adult Black males ages 16–60, by marital status

Occupation	Single	Married	Divorced	Widowed	Total
Agricultural (Farm work, Farmer)	5	5	0	1	11
Bank Messenger	0	1	0	0	1
Barber	21	34	0	0	55
Bartender/Saloon Employee	4	2	0	0	6
Blacksmith	0	3	0	1	4
Building Trades (Carpentry, Masonry, Painter)	5	6	0	1	12
Clerk	1	1	0	0	2
Cook	49	38	2	4	93
Engineer	1	0	0	0	1
Fireman	0	1	0	0	1
Freighter	1	0	0	0	1
Gardener	0	1	0	0	1
Herder	7	1	0	0	8
Hod Carrier	0	3	1	0	4
Hotel Industry (Hotel Keeper, Works in Hotel)	3	1	1	0	5
Janitor	2	2	0	0	4
Keeps Restaurant	1	0	0	0	1
Laborer	160	89	1	5	255
Laundry	2	2	0	0	4
Miner	34	15	0	1	50
Porter	33	18	0	1	52
Servant	48*	9	1	1	59
Dept. Sheriff	0	0	0	1	1
Shoemaker	0	2	0	0	2
Tailor	0	1	0	0	1
Teamster	9	4	0	0	13
Waiter	25	9	0	0	34
Watchman	1	0	0	0	1
TOTAL	411	232	6	16	682

Sources: 1880 US Federal Census [database online] (Provo, UT: Ancestry.com Operations, Inc., 2010); Corbett, Hoye, and Co., *Sixth Annual City Directory in the City of Denver* (Denver: Rocky Mountain News Printing Co. Printers and Binders, 1880).

* Within this category, there were four Black males working as servants who are not included in this table. Six Black males listed more than one occupation. In each case, I coded for the first occupation.

One of the most profitable occupations during this period was barbering. The 1880 Census shows that Denver boasted about forty-seven Black barbers, in a city with a Black male population of about 316. In other words, there was one barber for every seven Black men. Like ministers, Black barbers were attuned to the political and social needs of their community. Since their clientele often included Whites, many were able to leverage political clout and make invaluable connections to the power structure that ultimately benefited the Black community.

By contrast, Black women continued to work at menial occupations (table 5.2). Even though a little over 40 percent of Black women lived in Denver, most were spread across Colorado's vast landscape, living in farming, ranching, and mining communities. About 45 percent (226) of Black women were married. By 1880 the number of Black women had grown to 653, with the entire Virginian-born female population almost tripling in number, from about 49 in 1870 to 129 a decade later.

Although the 1880 Census lists most Black women as keeping house (meaning for their own family or for themselves) without any gainful occupation, many of these women were married to a gainfully employed spouse. But the census does show signs of an emerging professional entrepreneurial Black middle class, reported as occupations such as dressmaker, keeping a boarding house, and hairdresser.

THE EARLY RACIAL CLIMATE

Toward the end of the nineteenth century, Blacks were arriving in Colorado in greater numbers. As the fourth largest non-European population settling in Colorado—after Chinese immigrants, indigenous Indians, and Mexicans—Blacks were able to build their own communities and thrive without large-scale interference from the dominant White population. As Jesse T. Moore Jr. suggests, "Blacks were a curiosity, perhaps even an amusement, to Western Whites, but fears that Whites harbored of Blacks in other sections of America seemed not to have been an issue in the 'Wild West.'"[11] He attributes this lack of fear to the large foreign-born White population settling in Colorado who had not been raised with the view of Black inferiority/White superiority prevalent in the American South. By 1880 one of every four Denverites claimed foreign birth.

Historian William M. King suggests that the relative diversity of the West also minimized racial tension between Black and White settlers: "Whites viewed Blacks as superior to the Chinese and Native Americans, who were believed to be heathens or savages because of their strange languages and unfamiliar cultures. Blacks were treated less harshly than either the Italians or Chinese populations."[12]

TABLE 5.2. Black women's occupations in 1880 by Colorado cities

Occupation	Total Number	Number Living in Denver	Other Locations Black Women Lived in 1880
Keeping House	171	53	Ansle, Arkansas River, Bear Creek, Bent, Black Hawk, Canyon City, Central City, Colorado Springs, Fort Collins, Fort Lyons, Georgetown, Golden, Idaho Springs, La Porte, Las Animas, Leadville, Lincoln City, Littleton, Park, Pueblo, Silver Cliff, Trinidad, Ute Creek
In/At School	56	34	Bent, Colorado Springs, Fort Collins, Georgetown, Las Animas, Littleton
Laundress	69	21	Alamosa, Buena Vista, Colorado Springs, Fort Collins, Fort Garland, Greeley, Idaho Springs, Lake City, Las Animas, Leadville, Littleton, Tomichi, Trencherar
Servant	68	16	Bent, Breckenridge, Colorado Springs, Del Norte, Fort Collins, Golden, Idaho Springs, Lake, Las Animas, Leadville, Longmont, Pueblo, Saguache, Trinidad
Cook	29	14	Brownsville, Crookeville, Elbert, El Paso, Fairplay, Gunnison City, Lake, Leadville, Silver Cliff
Hotel Cook	5	1	Boulder, Gunnison City, Lake City, Silver Cliff
Housekeeper	7	1	Boulder, Gothic, Pueblo
Housework	8	4	Boulder, Leadville
Keeps Boardinghouse	4	1	Leadville
Prostitute*	3	—	Leadville
Dressmaking	4	1	Central City, Silver Cliff
Chambermaid	3	1	Bent, Leadville
At Service	3	—	Georgetown
Hotel Work	2	—	Colorado Springs, UT-Hotsprings, Rio Grande
Hairdresser	3	2	Leadville
Day Worker	2	2	

Source: 1880 Manuscript Census, total n = 630; total n = 467 Black women fifteen years of age and older: 226 married (312 minus 164 = 148 single women), 74 widowed, 9 divorced = 458 (9 missing)

* This number represents only those women who listed themselves as prostitutes or whom the enumerator chose to list as prostitutes. There were a number of ways in which the census or women themselves masked their occupations as sex workers.

Photographs taken in the mid- to late 1800s often show Black males in close proximity to White males, working side by side as miners, barbers, and cooks. The Colorado Works Public Administration Federal Project, which interviewed twenty-three early Black pioneers, found no unabated racism in the early days of the territory or following statehood. For example, Missouri native Mike Thomas mentioned having both Black and White friends in Denver. John Henry Lewis, who arrived in Denver in 1906 and opened a restaurant in the Five Points neighborhood, stated that at his restaurant, Blacks and Whites ate at the same table without friction.[13]

This apparent racial harmony, however, does not imply that Black Denverites were not subjected to racial bigotry or that they were not conscious of White privilege. Lucile's youngest sister, Claribel, born at the end of the nineteenth century, summed up what she had learned as a young child in an opinion piece published in the *Denver Post* in 1950: "'Free, White and 21' is a saying I've heard since childhood. For centuries, White Americans have had all the advantage and opportunities 'Our Grand America' has offered, but are all Americans free? Seemingly not, for many are chained to that insufferable monster 'Racial Prejudice.'"[14]

Emancipated slaves and free Blacks settling outside of Denver were not entirely free of the White privilege and racism that had governed their lives elsewhere. But in the new frontier, which for them offered greater hope and opportunity, they were not going to settle for second-class citizenship, and they did not have to. They came to the West with a fire in their bellies and a conviction to go forward, not backward, so they took an active role in challenging anything they felt was predicated on racial disparities.

Among those who took on leadership roles in the anti-racism battle was a small, distinguished group of mixed-race pioneering elites who identified as Black. Typically male, these leaders were economically privileged, educated, politically astute, and respected across racial lines, and they held significant social standing. They were all barbers by profession and were the first Black entrepreneurs in Denver to own their own barbershops, restaurants, and hotels.[15]

One of the more progressive local leaders was William Jefferson Hardin, a free Black man from Kentucky. A teacher, professional barber, and noted public speaker, Hardin developed a great passion for equal rights. Arriving in 1863, a year before the US Congress had given the territory permission to draft a constitution and apply for statehood, Hardin spearheaded the effort to block statehood as long as Black men were denied suffrage. Working with fellow barbers Edward J. Sanderlin and Henry O. Wagoner, Hardin organized a campaign, garnering 137 male signatures to petition the territorial legislature, as well as members of Congress, to deny Colorado statehood "until the word White be erased from her State Constitution."[16]

In a strategic move meant to bolster the campaign's strength, they brought in much-needed reinforcements. Wagoner was a personal friend of abolitionist leader, author, and statesman Frederick Douglass and was able to bring on board Douglass's two sons, twenty-seven-year-old Lewis Henry and twenty-five-year-old Frederick Jr., who fortuitously had arrived in the territory earlier to teach evening classes on government and politics as they sought work as typographers. With Douglass's sons adding prestige to the enfranchisement movement and the relentless efforts of Denver's early Black citizens, Hardin, Sanderlin, and Wagoner were able to overcome overwhelming White opposition and help "influence Congress to pass in January 1867 the Territorial Suffrage Act, which prohibited territorial restriction of suffrage based on color,"[17] eight full years before Colorado attained statehood.

But the issue of social justice did not begin and end at the borders of the territory. When the financial difficulties Black Exodusters were experiencing in Kansas came to the attention of Blacks in Denver, church leaders and Black barbers went into action. They held a public forum and initiated a multiracial Central Executive Committee to explore ways to alleviate some of the Exodusters' financial hardships. Beyond fundraising, territorial governor John Evans added, "The privilege of emigration is one of the greatest, which can be conferred on man. It has made this country; it has made individuals self-reliant and manly; it has made nations prosperous."[18] The doors for emigration opened, especially since the territory was experiencing a growth spurt and needed Blacks in both the unskilled and skilled labor markets.

Even though more jobs were available in the unskilled sector, it could be argued that pigeonholing Blacks into specific menial occupations is a direct result of the legacies of slavery and centuries of servitude. In an address to the Maine State Colonization Society in 1862, Edward W. Blyden, a Liberian educator and statesman, suggested that "as soon as the Negro is seen, the presumption at once is that he is a menial. His colour at once associates him with that class of persons, and the general feeling is to treat him as such."[19]

A similar argument was made in May 1890, when the White editor of the *Colorado Graphic* suggested that White and Colored men should step up to reduce the Chinese population in Denver. For Blacks, this meant taking over the Chinese laundry businesses. Edwin H. Hackley, the clerk at the County Clerk and Recorder Office and editor of the *Denver Weekly*, replied, "The colored man is not confined to any single channel of trade, he is an all-around man and [is] success[ful] from a boot black to a banker, from a newspaper courier to a financier, when he is give[n] an honest chance. He has washed the Caucasian's dirty duds many a year, but you will never see him washee, washee, allee somee Chinaman."[20] Clearly, Hackley's response to the assertion that Black men should not be seen solely as menial workers is the same argument Blyden made twenty-eight years earlier. But in trying to elevate Blacks and separate them from the Chinese, Hackley indulges in his own brand of racial stereotyping and mockery. Hackley's argument is limited to males, without acknowledging Black women. In 1880 only two Black men worked in the laundry business compared to forty-one Black women, who were mostly illiterate widowed mothers.

There were times, however, when Blacks simply gave up when faced with Denver's particular brand of racism. It was after much internal deliberation that the Denver-based Chamber of Commerce membership committee accepted Dr. W.H.P Westbrook, a Black medical doctor, as a member in December 1911. However, when his application came before the full chamber, the "White Southerners threatened to withdraw, and Dr. Westbrook withdrew his application."[21] A more odious situation occurred two months later, in February 1912, when Dr. Thomas E. McClain, a dentist who was building his family's home on Vine Street in one of Denver's White neighborhoods, received the following letter:

> You have doubtless lived long enough to know that the American people when aroused are not to be trifled with, and while I am not predicting violence to either yourself or [your] property, you are certainly aware that either or both might occur. Legally you might be right, but in reality, you cannot help but know that you are wrong, and unless I am badly mistaken, a particularly . . . successful man of your own race, Booker T. Washington, has made it an invariable rule to never intrude where he is not wanted, if he can possibly avoid it. Personally, I am only too glad to grant you all the privileges due an American citizen, but I do object to you enjoying those privileges in an exclusively white community.[22]

While the treatment of Dr. McClain might have been a local story, it made national news when W.E.B. Du Bois reported the incident in *The Crisis* magazine. From all evidence, Dr. McClain gave up his dream and continued to live in the Five Points neighborhood until his death in 1949.

DENVER IN THE EARLY 1880S

As "citified" as Denver considered itself, it still retained many of the characteristics of a frontier town. A report on the social statistics of cities, filed in 1886 with the US Department of the Interior by George E. Waring Jr. of the Census Division, told a different story. According to Waring, the city had 200 miles of streets, none of which were paved. The sidewalks were made of wood, cement, and stone, while the gutters were cobblestones or natural soil. Property owners planted trees at the outer edges of sidewalks (close to the gutters for irrigation). There were eight miles of horse-drawn railways, with twenty cars and fifty horses, that furnished employment for twenty-five men. Fares to ride the rails were five cents. There were no regular omnibus lines, but seven vehicles carried passengers, for fifty cents each, to any part of the city. The only municipal buildings the city owned were six fire engine houses, with plans on the way to erect a city hall and a jail. Recreation consisted of two four-acre parks; two theaters, one seating 300 and the other 500; two halls used for theatrical performances, and four beer gardens with a seating capacity of 2,000 total. Denver's dead were interred in one of five cemeteries: City Cemetery, the Hebrew Cemetery, the Catholic Cemetery, Riverside Cemetery, and the Masonic Cemetery.[23]

The city's Board of Health—consisting of the mayor, three aldermen, three citizens appointed by the common council, the city clerk, and the city physician, paid a salary of $1,200 per annum—had police powers over all matters of health and was the final authority on all things health related. In 1880 three members of the board were physicians. Under the rubric of public health came responsibilities for street cleaning, sprinkling, general sanitary measures (including anti-contagion measures in public and private schools), the inspection of defective house drainage, privy vaults, cesspools, and sources of drinking water, as well as control over the conservation and removal of garbage.[24]

Another view of Denver came from Nathaniel S. Shaler, a paleontologist and geologist from Harvard University, who took off to explore the American frontier. In a series of articles he wrote for *Atlantic Monthly* magazine, he described Denver as "on the very front of civilization . . . where there were shops that would do credit to Broadway, and houses that would fit in our oldest towns," with "people who had elevated themselves a step above the image of the frontier."[25]

Certainly, not everyone lived in the booming elegance Denver had achieved in such a short time. Poor Whites, Chinese, Mexicans, Native Americans, and many Blacks did not. For Shaler, Blacks and other non-White groups were tantamount to invisible, in part because of his own philosophical and scientific support of polygenism, a racist theory that postulated biological and intellectual inequality among the human races. He took the train out of Denver at "nine p.m." heading to Leadville, he wrote. "We first see the signs of the wilderness people in the train; the little sleeping-cars are cramped with a motley lot of humanity, supercivilized and savage in all degrees."[26]

No doubt Shaler saw what he wanted to see during his brief stay in Denver. But others who lived and worked in the early 1880s saw another side of the Queen City. William H. Bergtold, a local physician who arrived in Denver in August 1881, recalls that although some parts of the major business sectors had sandstone sidewalks, in the town's two residential business sections, sidewalks were made of either 2 × 16 wood planks or dirt. Streets were not paved, and following heavy snowmelt or rain, it was not unusual to see wagons stuck "hub deep in the mud." Street gutters were used for irrigation. Most working-class Whites and Blacks living in the downtown area north of Seventeenth Street had no domestic water supply, often relying on sporadically scattered wells. Many households used ditch water for laundry and wells only for potable water. It was quite a chore to keep a home supplied with drinking water, to say nothing of bathwater.[27]

Attorney Robert H. Latta, who arrived in 1881, a year before the Buchanans, recalls in his memoir the seedier side of Denver, where "saloons, gambling houses and houses of ill-fame were flourishing and wide open."[28] And while Edward Chase boasted that he ran a clean operation at his gambling house, the Palace Theater, located at 357 and 359 Blake Street, Latta reported "it was a common event for someone to be shot there,"[29] a claim Chase adamantly denied. Latta also reported mob violence: "One evening I heard shouts near the [Tabor] Opera House, and found that a mob had a murderer and was going to hang him. They did so, but I did not want to see it."[30]

While enjoying a silver boom in the 1880s, Denver still had its share of problems that largely affected the working poor. Into this environment the Buchanans arrived, just as another side of Denver began to emerge. An aspiring Black community—separated from the majority culture and ripe for opportunity, complete with churches, Black-owned businesses, and a network of fraternal, social, benevolent, and self-improvement organizations—had been established in the 1860s and 1870s. It was here that the first Black congregation in Colorado, Zion Baptist Church, was founded on November 15, 1865. Located at 532 Arapahoe, between Twentieth and Twenty-first Streets, the church was a "neat frame building, well-furnished within and without." Three years later, in 1868, Shorter Community African Methodist Episcopal Church (described in 1880 as the Methodist Church and in 1882 as the African M.E. Church) was established at the corner of Stout and Nineteenth Streets, with Virginia-born Rev. Robert Seymour as its pastor. Seymour, "a very intelligent and active colored man and a devoted Christian," is credited with taking the congregation from worshipping in a "half-completed building, low, dark and shabby without and uncomfortable" to a "substantial brick structure, which would do credit to a wealthier congregation." In fact, it was noted that "very few congregations in Denver are better housed and more prosperous."[31]

Also located at the corner of Stout and Nineteenth Streets was the newly established Antioch Baptist Church, led by Georgia-born Elder Samuel Shepard, who served as its first pastor from 1874 to 1878, when Rev. Charles B. Murphy assumed its leadership. Described as a "missionary enterprise," Antioch was also known as the "Foot Washing Church," since the philosophy behind the church rested on the idea that unless you wash your feet, you can't go to heaven.[32] By 1895 several other churches had been established to cater to the spiritual needs of Denver's Black population, including the Church of the Holy Redeemer, Five Points Congregational Mission, Paul Quinn A.M.E., Ward's Chapel, Central Baptist, and Pilgrim Rest Baptist.

In addition to the strength of the church, Blacks in Colorado wasted no time establishing a number of benevolent societies and fraternal lodges in their communities. On June 5, 1868, the first Black fraternal organization was established in the Territory of Colorado, the Rocky Mountain Lodge no. 1 for the Prince Hall Freemasonry with twenty members. As the population increased, so did the number of fraternal societies.[33] By 1882, there were six Black fraternal organizations in Denver, including the Household of Ruth no. 376 for the wives or women related to men in the fraternal order of Odd Fellows. Susan E. Foster, a new arrival from Chicago, organized in 1887 the Sisters of the Mysterious Ten, a women's group of the benevolent society the United Brothers of Friendship.[34]

RISKING IT ALL FOR COLORADO

It was during this period of economic growth and new opportunity that in May 1882 the Buchanans arrived in Colorado. They brought all their possessions (e.g., clothes, Sarah's wedding dress, photographs, bedding, an oak armoire, family Bible, a Morse chair, and James's tools)[35] and myriad skills learned on the plantations among the Black families of Oatlands and Evergreen. James and his cousins Traverse and Thornton brought to the new American frontier agricultural know-how, bricklaying and blacksmithing skills, and knowledge of road and ditch work. Lucile's mother, Sarah, had the delicate finesse necessary for building relationships with Whites that she had learned as a house slave in her father's home. The family also brought the belief that through hard work, temperance, thrift, and the acquisition of wealth and property, they would become full citizens and be able to assimilate into the western frontier.

Denver was the opposite of the serene life they had known for generations in Virginia. Now they had to face the hustle and bustle of a booming city, which included a constant flow of visitors, White settlers largely from the East, and second-generation immigrants from Wales, Ireland, France, Germany, Sweden, Norway, Italy, China, Prussia, Austria, Scotland, and England—all hoping to mine, farm, or ranch their way to prosperity—as well as fortune hunters arriving not only by wagon but also by train at the newly opened Union Depot at Seventeenth and Wynkoop Streets. Apart from the inflow of people and the constant "ringing of the factory whistles in the morning," the Buchanans, especially the younger children, must have been in awe of the architectural splendor and extensive real estate development that resulted in the "construction of hotels, inexpensive boardinghouses, and temporary apartments."[36]

Travers, the blacksmith, traveled with his wife, Marietta Bryant (sometimes recorded as Martha, Mary E., and Maryetta), and their daughters: four-year-old Leah Frances (Edna Frankie), who became a cook; and two-year-old Esther Pearl, who would become a teacher in Denver; and their six-year-old son, George Fenton. It is unclear whether their daughters Ann, born in 1878, and Elinore, born a year later, made the trip to Denver. Neither daughter shows up in the city's 1900 Census. In addition, the census indicates that by 1900 only nine of Marietta's eleven children were alive.

When they arrived, Travers secured work driving a team of horses and wagon for Edward J. Binford, a wholesale and retail coal dealer at Nineteenth and Wazee Streets, making him the first of the family to be listed in the 1882 Denver City Directory. His cousin James would work for the same company. As new migrants to Denver, Travers and James found lodging at 347 Delgany Street, whereas Thornton lived at 383 Fifteenth Street. From 1882 to 1899 Travers changed his residence every two to three years, always residing near the railroads and close to his work. During these years he held a variety of positions ranging from driver/teamster to yardman and foreman, mostly working for Binford Coal.

As for moral and spiritual comfort, Travers and his family took no time joining Zion Baptist Church, where in 1881 the Rev. Henry H. White served as senior pastor. Somewhere along the way, Travers felt the call to take on more of a leadership role and became an associate pastor. After establishing himself and working for others from the time he arrived in Denver, Travers exercised his agency as the head of his family and a citizen of the United States and purchased land under the Homestead Act of 1862, which provided 160 acres of underdeveloped land to anyone who had never taken up arms against the United States, including freed slaves. Thus, on April 7, 1897, almost fifteen years after arriving in Denver, Travers went from worker to rancher by purchasing 160 acres of land in Jefferson County, near the town of Critchell, Colorado, a small mining town established in 1887 that really never took off. He paid $1.25 per acre. While still maintaining a residence in Denver at 2144 Fifteenth Street, Travers moved with his family to Critchell, which required claim holders to live on the land for five years. Obtaining the land had been the easy part; developing it and eking out a living from it presented insurmountable challenges.

It was especially difficult for him without his oldest son, George Fenton, who had died three years earlier, in July 1894, from a spinal trauma. Helping him turn the land into productive use was his wife, Marietta, forty-two years of age, and their remaining children, who ranged in age from two to sixteen.

Trying hard to achieve economic prosperity through land ownership, Travers spent the next three years as a rancher. It is likely that he also dabbled in mining, since at about the same time he acquired his homestead, small amounts of gold, copper, and other minerals were found near Critchell, causing another minor mining boom in Jefferson County.[37] Unfortunately, neither ranching nor mining paid off for him. On April 13, 1900, after three years of ranching, forty-six-year-old Travers Buchanan died in Critchell. He was buried next to his twenty-one-year-old son, George Fenton, in Riverside Cemetery, Denver's oldest operating cemetery. Daughter Edna Frankie Buchanan, who had remained in Denver, residing at 2544 Lawrence Street, took care of his funeral arrangements, including four funeral coaches for a total of $62.50 ($1,690 in 2016). The senior pastor, the Rev. John Ford of Zion Baptist Church, officiated at his burial service on April 19.

Unlike his brother Travers or cousin James, each of whom worked steadily as teamsters or yardmen at coal companies, Thornton had an array of job interests that seemingly did not pay off, thereby forcing him to room with Travers at various intervals. He first worked as a janitor in Denver while residing at 363 Fifteenth Street. He is officially listed in the 1885 Colorado State Census as a widower living and working as a servant in a hotel in Clear Creek County.[38] He returned to Denver in 1894, ostensibly prompted by Clear Creek's severe economic crisis in the mining industry in 1893, causing its related businesses, including the hotel industry, to suffer a severe downturn.

For the next couple of years, Thornton was able to secure employment as a porter (gatekeeper or doorkeeper) while living at 1353 Tremont Street. He tried his hand at mining in 1896, possibly in Critchell, while residing with Travers at 1010 Converse Road. A year later he secured a job as a yardman, alongside Travers, at the Atlas Coal Company. He continued to live with Travers through 1897, residing at 2144 Fifteenth Street. When the 1900 Census was taken on June 4, forty-six-year-old Thornton was mistakenly coded as White.[39] The census showed that he was working as a coachman while boarding at 1355 Pearl Street with two White females, one a servant from Sweden and the other the head of household living with her sixteen-year-old son. When the Denver City Directory came out in late 1900, he was listed as working at the Union Depot as a porter (baggage handler.) For the next year and a half, he returned to work as a coachman while listing his residence as 1540 Lincoln Avenue.

Following Travers's death, Thornton stepped in to help his sister-in-law Marietta while she and the children moved back to Denver to live with her daughter Edna, who worked as a cook, and son William, who worked at the Trunk Brothers Drug Store. In trying to keep Travers's dream alive, Thornton filed a homestead claim on April 1, 1901, for the same 160 acres in Critchell that had belonged to Travers. Within four months, on August 17, 1901, he voluntarily gave up the property. Why Thornton relinquished the property remains a mystery. Presumably, he lacked the capital, fortitude, and support of his older brother Travers, whom he had depended upon since arriving in Colorado, and he was not able to bring Travers's homesteading dream to fruition. It is unknown what exactly precipitated his next decision, but eleven months later, on July 24, 1902, forty-nine-year-old Thornton committed suicide. Thornton's suicide was the second in the Buchanans' history in Colorado, but it would not be the last. Thornton's body would join those of his brother Travers and nephew George Fenton at Denver's Riverside Cemetery. His other nephew, William T. Buchanan, joined them in May 1913.

Although all three cousins lived together or near each other when they first arrived in Denver and worked in a similar occupation, Lucile's father, James Fenton, followed a different path. This wing of the Buchanan family seemed to have arrived in Colorado with more economic stability and a clearer vision. They wanted property but, unlike Travers and Thornton, were not willing to venture too far into the hinterlands of Colorado to secure it. Sarah's rearing, initially in the home of her father and owner and then in his sister's home, might have had a greater influence on how much of pioneering life she would be willing or able to endure.

6

From Denver's Bottoms to P. T. Barnum's Town

Freedom is never voluntarily given by the oppressor;
it must be demanded by the oppressed.
— MARTIN LUTHER KING JR.

From its earliest days, the confluence of the South Platte River and Cherry Creek played an important role in Denver's development as a boom city in the West. By the mid-nineteenth century, Colorado had attracted national prestige when small deposits of gold were discovered along the South Platte River and Cherry Creek. While minimal, the news spread quickly and fortune seekers soon converged on the settlement increasingly known by its more romantic moniker, the "Queen City of the Plains."[1]

With infrastructure not yet in place, early settlers camped beneath the cottonwood trees on the banks of the South Platte River and Cherry Creek.[2] Tents quickly dominated the landscape but soon gave way to tarpaper shacks; scattered log cabins, often built with cottonwood logs; and sod huts. With Denver's gold boom of 1858 not panning out, prospectors went further west to the mountain towns of Leadville, Cripple Creek, Gold Hill, Black Hawk, and Central City. During the Pikes Peak Gold Rush, Denver reinvented itself and became the headquarters for outfitting and supplying the state's mining communities.[3]

When the Buchanans arrived in 1882, they, too, settled along the banks of the South Platte River, locally known as the Bottoms. Bordered by the South Platte

River on the north, the Union Railway station on the south, Thirty-first Street on the east, and Walnut Street on the west. The Bottoms included a booming industrial belt, small wood-frame houses juxtaposed with numerous persons still living in tents or tarpaper shacks, and a constant flow of people and goods from the railroads. Migrants from across the nation and the second and third waves of European immigrants came to Denver full of optimism and seeking to improve their lives.[4]

The Buchanans' arrival also coincided with Denver's first trade fair, the National Mining and Industrial Exposition, which opened August 1, 1882, and ran sixty-one days before closing on September 30. As part of the spectacle, the organizers put on display a group of Ute Indians.[5] A former slave, John Taylor, accompanied the Ute and served as their translator. John spoke several Indian languages after spending his adult life riding with the Chiricahua, Southern Ute, Navajos, Hopi, and Apaches. He married 10–12 women of Mexican, Navajo, Apache, Hopi, and Ute heritage.[6] While an ideal candidate for the job, his illustrious lifestyle may have added unwittingly to the popular opinion and stereotypes of Native people and Blacks. Nevertheless, this expo may likely have been the Buchanans' first introduction to some of the original inhabitants of the State of Colorado.

LIFE AT THE BOTTOMS

Typically, males outnumbered females in the western frontier.[7] This was also true on Delgany Street, where the Buchanans' neighbors included single men from Ireland, Italy, Prussia, Denmark, and Germany. These settlers brought various skills and experiences with them. A few had families, but most shared their living quarters and often living expenses with one or two other single men.

As for women, four were listed in the 1883 Denver City Directory living around Delgany Street—the Buchanans' next-door neighbor, Mrs. Catherine Arata, and Mrs. Mollie McHugh, who lived at the corner of Delgany and Fifteenth Streets. Dressmaker Mrs. Sarah E. Arnold lived at the corner of Delgany and Twenty-second Streets, and Henry Barker's wife, Dianna, lived with him at 537 Delgany. When it came to groceries, Norwegian-born Hans T. Esbensen's store at the corner of Twenty-first and Delgany was within walking distance of the Buchanans' home, making shopping for basic groceries easy.

While the family arrived too late for James to be included in the 1882 Denver City Directory, in 1883 the directory listed him as head of household living at the rear of a home at 347 Delgany Street with his first cousin Travers. In 1887 the first Sanborn Map (created to assess fire insurance liability in urban areas) showed 347

Delgany located about 200 feet from Cherry Creek, within a cluster of five homes. Two Irish men—Michael Geary, a fifty-year-old laborer, and his twenty-five-year-old son Patrick (listed as a police officer at one time and a miner at other times) occupied the house at 347 Delgany.[8] Yet the Sanborn Map shows no dwellings at the rear of the structure. So, where did the Buchanans live? An article in the *New York Times* on July 25, 1881, suggests that "large numbers of people (lowest estimate about 3,000) were living in tents, making the collection look like a village—as well as many tents in the river bottoms."[9] These kinds of living arrangements—shared with family, friends, or even total strangers—were not unusual in a town where employment was tied to industry cycles of boom and bust, and they became common in Denver during the late nineteenth century.

In 1882 the Buchanans were the only Blacks living on Delgany. Most Blacks lived slightly southeast of Delgany, around Lawrence, Larimer, and Blake Streets. Running along the northern fringe of Denver's commercial district, Delgany Street fell within the boundaries of the Union Depot (today known as Union Station), which served a daily flow of twenty-one railroads and eighty passenger trains. Railroad maps of the late 1880s portray Delgany differently, but they all show the street near the railroad tracks. Some have the street running parallel to the tracks so that the street is indistinguishable. Others show it more separated. In either case, the houses along the street shook every time the "iron horses" arrived at the station, and poor sanitation in and around the train yards led to frequent outbreaks of diseases.

Train-yard activity kicked up dirt that permeated people's living quarters, and nearby foundries and coal companies gave off smoke and dust that polluted the air. In 1890 a resident said, "Children be dyin' down 'ere all the time . . . It all comes from these piles of dirt . . . An' nobody comes and takes it away like they do on Capitol Hill."[10] The noise of the steam engines and their plumes of white smoke were often intolerable. James and Sarah had young children and were more than likely concerned for their safety, fearing the pollution, poor living quarters, and disease as much as the many grade-crossing deaths that occurred on the tracks themselves.

While the railroad tracks presented the Buchanans and their neighbors with one set of challenges, living in close proximity to Denver's two major waterways presented yet another, with occasional flooding causing property damage and even death. Life in the Bottoms could be a double-edged sword. They were conveniently located near the center of town where they had access to shopping, banks, druggists, doctors, and dentists. The area was also where jobs, both skilled and unskilled, were located. Also, living near the confluence produced fertile ground that allowed residents to maintain family vegetable gardens, which either supplemented their food supply or provided produce to sell, with the area's Italian migrants proving quite adept at the latter.[11]

CLAIMING MY WHITE HERITAGE

Around October 1883, Sarah found herself pregnant with her sixth child. The make-shift dwelling the family shared with cousin Travers and his family could no longer sustain them. Taking the horses[12] and wagon north to a shed at 120 Platte Street, close to the South Platte River, they settled in their new home before winter.

On Friday, June 13, 1884, Sarah gave birth to a healthy daughter—her first child born in Colorado. For the family, the birth was a cause for celebration. For Sarah, the event marked a new beginning where risk taking became even more a matter of course. She saw it as an opportunity to exercise her agency far away from Virginia, where the structures of slavery and the bigotry of the culture had denied her the right to claim her White heritage. She named her daughter Lucy Berkeley Buchanan—Lucy, the name of her playmate and White half-sister, and Berkeley, the surname she could not claim as a slave or as a free person in Virginia. Lucy Berkeley unknowingly became the standard-bearer of the hidden history of the White side of Sarah's family.

Shortly after Lucile's birth, the family moved to 65 Platte Street. But the move was short-lived. The devastating flooding of the South Platte River on the evening of July 26, 1885, drove the family back to Cherry Creek and their old neighborhood. This time they moved into a wood-frame house at 1438 Delgany Street, right next door to their old residence at number 347.[13] The Buchanans' moving patterns were not unique. Many of Denver's early settlers moved several times during their first few years, never staying in any one place longer than a year. Like many of their fellow migrants, with every move the Buchanans remained in close proximity to one of Denver's two waterways: Cherry Creek or the South Platte River.

But in 1886 the river that had provided several advantages may have expedited their move to Barnum. Toward the end of August 1886, the *Rocky Mountain News* reported increased incidences of typhoid fever in Denver as a result of the sewage emptied into the Platte River near Fifteenth Street, not far from where the Buchanans lived. According to the article, "Local physicians stated, filthy alleys were also contributing to the problem as was prolonged dry weather."[14] This combination of factors may have encouraged the Buchanans to take their children out of harm's way to the land they had purchased four years ago, which had its own set of hardships but was far better than what they continued to experience in the Bottoms.

FIGURE 6.1. *Youngest Buchanan children, Laura (standing, about six years old), Fenton (about three years old), and Lucile (about eighteen months old), ca. 1886. Buchanan Archives.*

DOING THE UNEXPECTED

One of the places southwest of Denver that interested the Buchanans when they arrived was an unincorporated area that Francis S. Kinder suggested would become "White man's country soon after the Civil War."[15] The making of this "White man's country" began seven months after the Civil War ended on December 1, 1865, when Daniel Witter—an attorney specializing in land law, a member of the first territorial government in 1861, and eventually a US assessor—purchased the first tract of land in what would become Villa Park. Shortly thereafter, other Whites purchased land in the area: Alexander McChesney registered his land deal on December 10, 1867; Lawrence Welty, a boot maker and farmer who had emigrated from Germany, bought land on June 1, 1868; and Dennis J. Shaw staked his land claim on October 20, 1868. Witter, the most aggressive speculator, owned the largest amount of land. He also had a resource the others did not—financial backing from his brother-in-law Schuyler Colfax, the Seventeenth vice president of the United States.

By the late 1860s, Witter had transferred his holdings to the Denver Villa Park Association (DVPA), incorporated on February 10, 1870.[16] The DVPA was able to pay off the money owed to Colfax while securing additional loans for the purchase of more land.

As Kinder suggests, the DVPA seemed to be prospering until a number of lawsuits and bankruptcies of several members brought the association to the brink of collapse. Per a court order issued on March 11, 1874, one of the trustees sold the land to Julius J. Gorham.[17] It was during this era of uncertainty that famed circus entrepreneur and showman Phineas Taylor (P. T.) Barnum arrived.

There has been some speculation that Barnum initially bought land from the DVPA as a winter site for his circus, but this was not the case. Barnum's interest in Colorado went beyond the circus. He first visited in 1870, giving temperance speeches in Denver, Georgetown, and the Union Colony (Greeley) on "How to Be Healthy, Happy, and Rich." He obviously liked what he saw in Greeley—a temperance colony—and soon not only bought membership in the colony for $150 but also invested heavily to erect buildings (e.g., Barnum Hall and the P. T. Barnum Hotel) in an area that became known as the Barnum Block. Barnum had personal connections to Greeley as well. Originally named the Union Colony of Colorado, the town changed its name for Barnum's good friend and newspaper publisher Horace Greeley, who had a hand in establishing the colony.[18] Barnum's cousin, Edward T. Nichols, also homesteaded in the area during the late 1860s, and by the 1870s he was operating a general mercantile business on a corner of Barnum Block.[19]

In 1871 Barnum entered the cattle business with the purchase of the 15,000-acre Huerfano Ranch, with his friend David W. Sherwood, in Huerfano County in south-central Colorado. About eight years into the business, Barnum lost interest and sold his share to Sherwood.[20] Still, Barnum's time in Colorado cannot be discussed without mention of Helen Maria, one of his four daughters, whose marital infidelity was a source of anger and embarrassment for the self-styled Prince of Humbug. Helen eventually ran away to Chicago with her young physician paramour, Dr. William H. Buchtel, leaving her husband, Samuel Henry Hurd, and their three daughters behind. Adding to Barnum's shame and disappointment, Helen lived openly as William's mistress in Chicago before her divorce from Hurd was granted.[21] Soon after their marriage in South Bend, Indiana, on March 22, 1871, they moved to Greeley.[22]

The decision to settle in Greeley was no accident. Besides having access to Barnum's property, it would appear that Barnum, who may not have liked William, was looking out for his daughter's interest when suggesting that they live in a high-altitude temperance town to address Buchtel's tuberculosis and his drinking problem.[23] But things did not work out well for William in Greeley. The young doctor was accused of lacing his medicines with wine, a practice common at that time. This did not sit well with the town's leaders.[24] He was arrested[25] and not long thereafter he and Helen moved to Denver in late 1871, hoping that William would re-establish his medical practice and that his health would improve.[26]

But perhaps Barnum's most speculative, and ultimately most troublesome, real estate venture occurred in 1874. Always looking for the next money-making venture, Barnum purchased controlling interest in the struggling Villa Park Association, with an initial payment of $36,000 for 765 acres of land and the Villa Park House, a two-story hotel on "the Boulevard" (today Federal Boulevard).[27] Situated about four-and-a-half miles outside the Denver city limits, the property was bound on the north by West Sixth Avenue, on the south by West Alameda Avenue, on the east by the Boulevard, and on the west by Sheridan Avenue. Originally called the "Barnum Addition," the property seemed an ideal investment.

While there was some correspondence between Barnum and his Greeley-based attorney/property manager Silas B. Haynes about possible housing and economic development, the Villa Park House and the Barnum Subdivision never took off as he had envisioned.[28] As a result of a series of setbacks, including an inadequate water supply and a sales force that could not get its act together, Barnum decided on May 15, 1882, to unload the property, valued at about $175,000.[29] He contracted with John S. Blankman, a real estate speculator and president of the Safe Land

and Development Company, to handle the deal with his partner, son-in-law, and vice president Dr. William H. Buchtel.[30] Shortly thereafter, on July 3, 1882, Barnum announced the public sale of the land and unveiled a plat of the town showing the streets, building lots, and alleys already on it.

As part of the sales promotion, likely orchestrated by Barnum, some of the original twenty-four streets were named for people with whom he had a connection or simply admired. For example, Emerson Avenue (later First Avenue) was named for Ralph Waldo Emerson—essayist, poet, Unitarian minister, and leader of the Transcendentalist movement in the early nineteenth century. There were also streets with a circus theme; for example, Jumbo Avenue (later Hazel Court) was named after the famous African elephant in Barnum's circus. Streets were also named for family members, friends, and business associates: Helen Avenue (later Julian Street) was named to honor his daughter. In 1896 Barnum was annexed to Denver, and the original street names were changed to conform to Denver's uniform street-naming system.[31]

RELOCATING TO BARNUM

The opening of the Barnum Subdivision in 1882 came at an opportune time for the Buchanans.[32] Denver's makeshift dwellings were certainly not what Sarah had envisioned when they moved to Colorado. Furthermore, the frenetic social atmosphere in the city differed greatly from that of rural Virginia, with a proliferation of saloons, bawdy houses, and gambling establishments within walking distance of her home. As a house slave, Sarah had a different experience than her husband, who spent years toiling in the fields. Life for her in Colorado was tougher than it had been in Virginia—a sentiment she expressed in a letter she wrote to her father, Edmund Berkeley, in 1898.[33]

With all the hardships Sarah encountered, she apparently came prepared to become a property owner. About three months after Barnum and his realty agents listed lots for sale, the Buchanans became the first Black family to own property in Barnum. Sarah signed the deed on May 15, 1882, paying $100 ($2,578 in 2017) for five lots located in the most remote part of the subdivision. Very uncommon for the time, the warranty deed and title to the property was placed in Sarah's name. One explanation is that in 1874, two years before Colorado gained statehood, the territory passed the Married Women Property Rights Act, giving married women separate title to their own property and estates. According to historian Evan Roberts, the act was motivated in part by the periodic financial crises of the nineteenth century. "By securing married women's

FIGURE 6.2. *James Buchanan with his dog, Spareribs, next to the barn behind his home in Barnum, Colorado. Buchanan Archives.*

continuing title to assets they brought with them into a marriage, married women had some possibility of financial fallback if their husband were to die, desert, or divorce them."[34]

This act gave Sarah the legal means to enter into a contract with Barnum and his representatives without James. In an interview with Doris Smith, Lucile suggested that her grandfather, Edmund Berkeley, gave her mother money to help the family relocate to Colorado.[35] Whether Sarah was the more financially secure of the two or whether it was a strategic move to front Sarah, a Mulatto who could possibly pass for White, to buy the property, James and Sarah had a unique partnership for the time.

Although the Buchanans experienced hardships in the Bottoms, they faced a new set of challenges in Barnum. Namely, lack of water, finished roads, and horse/ street railway transportation to Denver. In addition, Barnum lacked many of the daily conveniences and amenities Denver offered—postal service, churches, physicians, shops, and close proximity to James's work. Most likely for these reasons, they continued to live in the Bottoms until they found ways to manage a permanent move to Barnum sometime between 1886 and 1888. By 1889 the Buchanans were listed with a Barnum address in the Denver City Directory: "Buchanan, James, col'd, teamster, r. Barnum's Add."[36]

For Sarah, living in Barnum must have been especially frustrating and emotionally taxing. It would be several years before two artesian wells were "refurbished at the corners of First Avenue and Hazel Court and Seventh Avenue and Knox Court."[37] However, these wells were still about a mile from their property, which meant Sarah, who did the washing, had to tote dirty clothes one way and clean but heavier wet ones the other way in either the blistering summer heat or the harsh Colorado winters.

Sarah, also had a new job thrust on her—helping to manage the family's farm, an enormous task that primarily fell upon James. The barren rolling hills had few trees to help hold the soil in place. Years later, the common joke around Denver was "How do you spell Barnum? Answer, 'M-U-D.'"[38] The heavy clay soil compacted easily and held in moisture for longer periods. James, who was accustomed to Virginia's rich loam soil, had to learn ways to cultivate Denver's clay soil before planting could even begin. He also had to erect a fence to prevent the family's milch cow from wandering off and to keep predatory animals at bay. However, his most ambitious task was to erect a two-story wood barn on Stuart Street in which to stable his draft horses, store the family's crops, and provide temporary shelter for the family.[39]

FROM SUBDIVISION TO BARNUM TOWN

On August 27, 1887, the Town of Barnum was incorporated. In anticipation, a constitution was adopted on November 1, 1887. Barnum's son-in-law, Dr. William Buchtel, became the first mayor. The constitution called for annual elections for the town's mayor,

> recorder, treasurer, attorney, street commissioner, marshal, police magistrate, and trustees.[40]

At the time of incorporation, Barnum was a predominately first- and second-generation European lower-middle- and middle-class community. About eight families lived within close proximity of the Buchanans' property. Six of the eight families on Stuart were of German, French, Scottish, Canadian, and Irish ancestry. The remaining residents migrated from Illinois, Indiana, Iowa, Ohio, New York, Pennsylvania, Kentucky, and Wisconsin. Overall, there were about thirty-six people living in the two blocks.

Of the eight families that lived in the Stuart/Raleigh Streets vicinity, all owned their own homes and only three of those homes were mortgaged (the Buchanans' being one). By 1900, most of Barnum's wage earners were men working in manufacturing, trade and transportation, administrative support, and civil engineering and as clerks, dairymen, or day and farm laborers; every one of them could read, write, and speak English.[41] This put the Buchanans economically and educationally on par with their neighbors, some of whom became lasting friends. Of the photographs Lucile left behind, most were studio portraits of their Barnum neighbors, especially babies and toddlers, taken during the 1890s and early 1900s. The Buchanans' experience with their White neighbors is further explained by Claribel in a *Denver Post* editorial on June 5, 1950, in which she singles out their father, James: "Speaking of the need for human relations—one grand old pioneer came to Denver in 1880. He must have been a credit to the community because he was elected street commissioner of Barnum. His political competitor was white. This Negro was so highly respected that on each Christmas the members of the community—all white—would take up a collection among themselves and purchase a Christmas gift for him. That grand, old pioneer was the late James F. Buchanan (my father)."[42] This kind of relationship between Whites and Blacks in Barnum speaks to new western historian Patricia Limerick's thesis that the American West was a meeting ground of cultures where numerical "minorities and majorities occupied common ground."[43]

As new migrants arrived in Denver and as the Bottoms became more and more industrialized, Barnum became one of many suburban communities close enough to downtown Denver to attract low-middle- and middle-income residents. In 1894 a second Black family had moved into Barnum, consisting of forty-eight-year-old George W. Willis,[44] his forty-year-old wife, Mary, and their seventeen-year-old Colorado-born daughter Margaret. Born in Canada to Kentucky-born parents, George had immigrated to the United States in 1860 and then became a naturalized citizen in 1868. His wife, Mary, was from Pennsylvania. It is possible that the Willis's move into Barnum was influenced by George's employment in 1887 as a laborer/coachman for P. T. Barnum's daughter Helen at the Villa Park House.

Living in Barnum did not isolate the Buchanans or the Willises from the larger Black community or from some of the handicaps Blacks faced in Denver. While migrating to the West was much better than remaining in the South, Blacks still had to contend with some of the same racist forces that had beset them in the places they left. An article published in the March 17, 1890, edition of the *Denver Republican* indicated that by the 1880s, Denver's Black population was increasing as migrants were arriving in large numbers from Arkansas and Mississippi and

FIGURE 6.3. *Family friends Jacob and Alice Seibert lived at 136 Quitman, a short walk from the Buchanans' home. Jacob, of German parents, migrated from Kentucky. Alice was French-born. Ca. 1900. Buchanan Archives.*

found that White homeowners "would not rent to them." This sustained act of racism led to a planned housing development scheme created by Black and White entrepreneurs. As the article reports: "It was finally decided by some of the more prominent resident Negroes, and by a few white owners to build and sell these to colored men small houses on the installment plan. It was a necessity for the colored immigrant to accept this proposition. The result is that proportionately, more colored men own their houses in Denver than in any other Northern city."[45]

Even though Denver had its share of prejudice, Edward J. Sanderlin, a friend of the Buchanans and one of Denver's well-known Black pioneers, reflected on what he considered the state of Blacks in Denver at the beginning of the 1890s: "There was a time when the colored vote controlled the election of city and county officers. They live principally now in the Fifth and Eight wards and a great many of them are getting land outside the city. I know of at least fifty prosperous Negro ranchmen. There is but one trouble. It is difficult to find openings for young Negro men in the trades. The hod-carriers [unskilled laborer in the building industry],

93

to be sure, are mingled as to color, but a Negro cannot get a chance to become a machinist or a skilled carpenter."[46] Even with the racism and other challenges Blacks faced in Denver, Sanderlin considered Blacks to be "the more prosperous than in any other Northern city" and was optimistic for the next generation, forecasting that as the old slave owners died out, "there will almost be an equality and in the next twenty years Blacks would make significant gains in education and home ownership."[47]

THE OTHER VICTORIANS

At the turn of the twentieth century, Barnum had been uniformly platted, with each plat accommodating twelve lots. The early residents were few and scattered. Most lived in eighty-six frame homes, about thirty-six of which had frame barns as well. In addition to the brick school at South King Street and West Third Avenue, there were fifteen brick homes, one of which belonged to the Buchanans.[48] Since brick homes were a major financial investment and each was constructed over a period of several years, the building of brick homes in Barnum, which had not yet been annexed by Denver, was the decision of the landowner—unlike the situation in Denver, whereby an 1863 "Brick Ordinance" required all new buildings use brick or stone. The Buchanans' home followed the prevailing construction style, with brick walls laid three bricks thick in common bond. More important, this type of construction was not uncommon in Loudoun County, Virginia, where James had most likely witnessed and/or assisted in the construction of such houses.

Whether as bystanders or participants, it was difficult for some Blacks to either ignore or escape the Victorian era (1839–1901). Indeed, once slavery had ended, Victorian ideals began to emerge in every aspect of life during Reconstruction among a small but active Black elite, including outspokenness of free Blacks, particularly in the North, dress styles, aesthetics, and home construction. This generation of Blacks—sometimes referred to as the Reconstruction generation and at other times the New Negro (a term first popularized by Booker T. Washington in 1900)—was equally active in defining their values and their place within the larger society. Because Sarah remained in the Berkeley family household until she married, she was privy to every aspect of Victorianism—from its ideas on morality to religion to the home—before migrating to Colorado. Therefore, she was, like her White Victorian counterparts, "committed to the domestic sphere, where she was wife and mother . . . managed home and attended to sundry household chores . . . and [was] a supportive and dutiful companion to her husband and a loving and nurturing mother to her children."[49]

As a dutiful wife and mother, she may have deferred to James's judgement on any number of things. Nonetheless, she was still the owner of the property on Raleigh Street, worked in the public sphere as a nurse for a White family, and like her husband placed a high value on formal education as paramount for her children. However, although she may have nurtured some aspects of Victorian culture, particularly concerning gender roles and domestic life, she also adjusted, however reluctantly, to the realities of a much harder life on the western frontier as it applied to unpredictable weather, constant water struggles, poor sanitation, and the resultant diseases.

One aspect of Victorianism that seems to have captured the imagination of all the Buchanans was the image of what home should look like, inside and out. While most Blacks were on the margins of Victorian society, archaeologists Adrian and Mary Praetzellis point out that "material culture mattered [to Victorian society] as they use these symbols as strategies to pursue their own ends."[50] Arriving in Colorado during the late Victorian era, the Buchanans made their home a symbol of Victorian tastes and gentility. It is here that they could "communicate their respectable values to their peers and nurture them in their children."[51] And it was through this vehicle that they were able to cultivate their status as members of the Black middle class.

According to Denver's city housing records, construction of the Buchanans' home began in 1903 and was completed in 1905. However, other records show that the house was completed years earlier. The Denver City Directory, printed between 1889 and 1897, records the family living in Barnum on Connecticut Avenue (in 1898 renamed Raleigh Street). Furthermore, an article published in February 1899 in the *Rocky Mountain News* discussed the death of Lucile's sister Laura in a two-story house at 227 Raleigh Street.[52] While the first construction on the property was a horse barn with living quarters above the stables, about ten years after arriving in Denver the Buchanans had built a red brick, two-story, five-bedroom, mini Queen Anne–style house on family land. Nationwide, the Queen Anne–style was popular in the United States between the 1880s and 1910. The Buchanans' home, still standing on the sloping hillside as of 2018,[53] exemplifies the Queen Anne style through its rectangular massing and steeply pitched gable-front roofs, flared eaves on the sides, Tuscan columns, and a porch that extends across the main body in front.[54]

To make the home luxurious, James contracted with two German craftsmen to create the elaborate interior woodwork, using lumber from Missouri.[55] The carpenters installed wood trim at every possible opportunity, a major feature of Victorian-era homes. Dark stained woods dominated the decor, with hardwood interior doors and frames, baseboards, window trims, and stairs, as well as wainscoting in the kitchen. A narrow cherry wood staircase led from a small vestibule with a beveled glass window up to the second level. The walls and ceilings were covered with embossed floral wallpaper in cream and tan. A hardwood door in the vestibule led to the parlor, one of two rooms in the house with two entrances.

The focal point was a Buckley mirrored coal-burning fireplace with a cast-iron front in the living room. The turquoise ceramic tile and intricate detail of the fireplace surround lent to the overall air of elegance. A large window faced the street. It was here that in her later years Lucile would sit for hours rocking as she listened to her radio.[56]

Leading off the living room was an archway to the dining room, which featured wood-trimmed bay windows that look out on the flower garden. Since the Buchanans valued education, the parlor just off the dining room housed an array of well-worn books for schooling, self-improvement, and reading pleasure. Among the books they owned were J.B.T. Marsh's *The Story of the Jubilee Singers* (1881); Joseph G. Richardson's *Medicology; Or, Home Encyclopedia of Health* (1906); H. Laurent's 10-volume *Mental Efficiency Series: Personality, How to Build It* (1916); and the family Bible.[57] Inside the Bible's front cover, the births of the nine Buchanan children and their parents were recorded.

An ornate solid wood door in the dining room opened to the kitchen where Sarah, likely with the help of her daughters, prepared the family's meals on the coal-burning stove, a popular alternative to wood-burning stoves in the nineteenth century. The two large kitchen windows, set high in the walls, provided light and ventilation. In the Victorian period, it was understood that kitchens were used only for cooking. Houses were built with separate pantries and sculleries. Adjacent to the kitchen was a small walk-in pantry with a convenient two-door entry where food and dishes were stored. The scullery was used only for washing up, scrubbing vegetables, and other messy activities that involved water. Even very small and modest Victorian houses had a separate scullery, as it was rare for sinks to be installed in kitchens before the twentieth century.[58] As Lucile aged, she succumbed to blindness and could no longer climb the stairs to her bedroom and bath, so she had a sink and toilet installed in the pantry and turned the scullery into her bedroom.

The house James built for his beloved Sarah and their children is the only surviving home built by an emancipated slave in P. T. Barnum's old town. It was an ideal Victorian-era home, a symbol of success and respectability in the public sphere. As members of Denver's rising Black middle class and possibly reflecting a desire to keep up with their more affluent neighbors, James spared no effort in his quest to replicate the dominant features of the Victorian era in the new frontier. As survivors of slavery, photographs of the Buchanans tell the story of a family empowered with a quiet dignity and disarming smiles who, while choosing to be left largely alone, still yearned to be considered as good as their White counterparts, if not better.

Within the idyllic setting of a picture-perfect Victorian home and garden, the family was not spared the stark realities of life and death. This included the grief surrounding the 1899 suicide of Lucile's third sister, Laura, in a bedroom on the second floor and the joy of the at-home birth of her youngest sister, Claribel, only twenty-three days after the family buried Laura. Years later, the eighty-one-year-old Lucile found the body of her bachelor brother, Fenton, lying peacefully amid the peonies, apple trees, and grape vines he had tended most of his life. And Lucile, the last surviving child of Sarah and James, lived here for the final forty years of her life before being unceremoniously removed under court order by the City of Denver.

The courage exhibited by these former slaves in building their life in a predominantly White community is remarkable. I often wondered whether James, born on the same Virginia plantation as his father and grandfather and now a homeowner and patriarch to children born free, had realized what South African anti-apartheid activist Stephen Biko would say many years later: "Whites must be made to realize that they are human, not superior. Same with Blacks. Blacks must be made to realize that they are also human, not inferior."[59] It would appear that neither James nor Sarah or their children felt inferior to anyone and that they did not see Whites as superior. As new citizens, they would not let the historical discrimination they had known in Virginia confine them to a residential enclave in Denver (Five Points) that many other Blacks had chosen for its familiarity, convenience, or restrictions imposed upon them. They clearly rejected the idea put forward by numerous scholars that Blacks "could almost never achieve total relaxation, but that they came closest to doing so when there were no whites around."[60] While they may have experienced fear and racism, especially in the early 1920s, when the Ku Klux Klan dominated political life in Denver, living in Barnum kept them somewhat isolated from the Klan terror, which predominantly targeted Catholics, Jews, and the foreign-born at that time in Colorado history.[61]

The Buchanans' behavior, however, raises significant questions about their attitude toward race and whether they felt the need to reconstruct their racial identity by outperforming the image Barnum's Whites may have had about Blacks. In what way did the trope of the "New Negro" work to undo the legacy of slavery? As Henry Louis Gates Jr. states, the term "New Negro" suggested education, refinement, money, assertiveness, and racial consciousness[62]—qualities that I kept seeing in the Buchanans, and especially in Lucile. Moreover, what did James and Sarah think about Denver's racially segregated Five Points neighborhood, where the majority of their girl children, with the exception of Lucile, would end up living? How did their slave experience help define their attitude and impact their future race relations in the West? Did their presence in Barnum help to close gaps created by race? Did Sarah's mixed-race ancestry, during a time when color-consciousness resulted in a strong correlation between light skin and increased opportunity, have a profound effect? How did Sarah and her children (originally listed as Mulattoes on the censuses) choose to handle the matters of class and race within their family? How did they re-present those decisions to the larger world? While their home became a symbol of Black success and equality with their White neighbors, it also served as way to counter and redefine the racist stereotypes that popular and material culture promoted amidst the racist social Darwinism and eugenics theories arising in the late nineteenth and early twentieth centuries which enshrined White superiority and Black inferiority.

It was in this all-White environment that the Buchanans decided to build their home. While we may never know why they chose Barnum, their action quite possibly struck a chord with their neighbors, which allowed them to seemingly live outside the boundaries of race and class while freeing them to negotiate for power within the boundaries of race and class. Nonetheless, they became a symbol of Black success and equality that went beyond the dominant stereotypes of the day that permeated popular and material culture.

7

Education, Politics, and Leisure

I am America. I am the part you won't recognize. But get
used to me. Black, confident, cocky: my name, not yours; my
religion, not yours; my goals, my own; get used to me.
—MUHAMMAD ALI, 1975

Like the many Blacks who ventured to the West prior to the Civil War or during
the post-Reconstruction era, the Buchanans were attracted to Colorado in search
of greater opportunity, freedom, and self-determination over their own lives. As
with their forebears, they took on every new challenge with optimism and looked
forward to carving their own destiny, with a positive view and expectations of liberty and equality.

Migrating largely from former slave states, Blacks settled in both urban and
rural environments, where they found various ways to engage with Colorado's
economic, political, and cultural landscape. Taking up the challenges and opportunities presented, the 1870 US Census shows that there were approximately 456
Blacks living in the Colorado Territory (six years before statehood) working as
barbers in Denver, Central City, and Trinidad; a teacher in Denver; teamsters in
Gilpin and Golden; cooks in Denver and Bent; porters and waiters in hotels in
Central City and Denver; laborers in Bent, Kit Carson, and Denver.[1] This small
Black population consisted of single women and men, married couples, and children born in Colorado during the late 1860s. While Blacks were dispersed across
the state, their presence was mostly felt in Colorado's urban frontiers, with the

largest population living in Denver. But as the twentieth century emerged, Black visionaries with a fierce independent streak decided to strike out on their own and created two all-Black settlements. One was established on May 5, 1910, in Dearfield, thirty miles east of Greeley, and by 1915 another in "the Dry," eight miles south of Manzanola in southern Colorado.[2]

Much earlier, Blacks who arrived in the Territory of Colorado were acutely aware they existed on the margins of power, and thus began to engage the public sphere through mass meetings at churches, at fraternal halls, and at individual members' homes (often related to women's activism). Although they saw their political actions as an in-group activity, at times they invited Whites to speak at mass meetings and lend their support and voices on Black issues. These events would be made quite public through press coverage.

Not long after Blacks began to arrive, they were able to achieve a number of the reforms they pushed for from the mid-1860s through the early 1880s. This desire to reform society and the activism it engendered would continue into the years 1890 through 1920, during which a plethora of movements aimed at promoting progress emerged to challenge the status quo. Concentrated largely within Denver's Five Points, there was rapid growth in the public sector, as Black businesses emerged to address the economic, health, legal, political, and leisurely needs of the growing community. Although many activities occurred across class divides, there was still a level of consciousness that Blacks had to present a demeanor that would demonstrate to both insiders (the Black community) and outsiders (the White community) a level of respectability in the public and private realms. Thus, the home not only became the cultural symbol of individual prosperity and the center of leisure for the Black middle class, it also functioned as the center of organizing for change, where clubwomen met to plan and conduct business, thereby creating a new fusion sphere.

As a larger and more stable population began to emerge, Blacks fostered a sense of community through their churches, fraternal organizations, women's clubs, and social clubs and by investing in their community through the growth of Black-owned businesses—such as hotels, clubs, restaurants, orchestras, and boarding-houses—or through work as tailors, dressmakers, members of bands, barbers, and hairdressers and for newspapers.

With the growth of transportation, industrialization, and a growing middle class, Blacks began taking up leisure pursuits along with the rest of the country, as popular culture, spectator sports, and other pastime activities became available during the eras known as the Gilded Age (1878–89) and the Progressive era (1890–1920).

ORGANIZING FOR CHANGE

By the mid- to late 1860s, Denver's Black population (about 46 in 1860)[3] included the first generation born in freedom and destined to be the first generation educated in public schools. With the enfranchisement of Black men in the Colorado Territory on January 31, 1867 (three years before the Fifteenth Amendment to the US Constitution was ratified, granting Black men the right to vote), Blacks took on yet another pressing issue: education in the Denver public school system. Simply put, rights denied under slavery became essential in Black national life, with education becoming a top priority following emancipation.

The most vexing issue stemmed from an act passed by the Colorado Territory (pre-statehood) Legislative Assembly during its first session in 1861, introducing a tax on Black property owners to fund public schools that Black students were excluded from attending. The law required that a list of all Whites between ages five and twenty-one be kept. It was based on this list that funds were allocated. Black learners were automatically excluded. According to historian Harmon Mothershed, if a Black child attended a school, the "district was not paid for his attendance."[4] Requests for corrective action in 1865, three years after the first public school opened, and again in 1866 produced no changes. Lewis Henry Douglass, son of the famous abolitionist Frederick Douglass, lived in the territory and challenged Colorado Republicans to either provide schooling for Black children or face the loss of Black support at the polls.

Thirty-six-year-old William Jefferson Hardin and thirty-year-old Edward J. Sanderlin, the latter a father of four, spearheaded the effort to undo these disparities. Hardin and Sanderlin went before the Denver Board of Trustees for Schools in June 1867 to demand integrated education. When the trustees failed to respond, Black parents in east Denver sent their children to the local Public School on Larimer Street (between I and K Streets) at the start of the 1867 school year.[5] Although reminiscent of school integration efforts by Black parents in the late 1950s and early 1960s, these parents' actions preceded them by almost 100 years. Incensed by the parents' action, the school's head teacher and principal, D. D. Hatch, called for the expulsion of the Black students. When unsuccessful, he tendered his resignation rather than educate them. Hatch's resignation letter stated that while "he never opposed the admission of colored children as a right, the true interest of both [Black and White students] would be served by keeping them separate temporarily."[6]

Alarmed by the level of activism from the Black community and faced with the possibility of an integrated school, the trustees reached a compromise with the Black leadership, allowing all students to access the school building as long as they were racially segregated within it, with each ethnicity occupying a separate floor. This compromise ended at the beginning of the following school year, when the trustees offered yet another solution—a separate school for Black children,[7] ushering in the beginning of "separate but equal" in Denver.

This solution resulted in Black students being shuffled from one rented space to another. The first space was in a building at Sixteenth and Market Streets. Then, in February 1869, the school moved to Zion Baptist Church on Arapahoe, between Twenty-first and Twenty-second Streets. A third move placed the school at Shorter Community A. M. E. Church at Nineteenth and Stout Streets. The separate school compromise would remain in effect until 1873, when Black students were re-integrated into the public school system despite White opposition.[8] By the 1920s segregation had returned to Denver schools, as students were once more segregated in elementary, middle, and high schools.

Some of this re-segregation is attributed to the rise of the Ku Klux Klan in Colorado in 1921, when the Klan dominated Colorado politics from the election of the governor, to the appointments made by the Denver's mayor, Benjamin Stapleton, to having control of the state legislature. While the Klan's presence was short-lived, this pattern of systematic segregation, established by the Denver School Board, would continue until the US Supreme Court decision on June 21, 1973, stipulating that Denver had "the affirmative duty" to desegregate its schools.[9]

TAKING ACTION

Between 1862, when the first school opened, and 1882, the year the Buchanans arrived, public school education in Denver remained in a contentious state of flux as a result of financial difficulties, the dearth of available space, and political wrangling regarding school integration. With two school-age children at home, eight-year-old Hannah and seven-year-old Hattie, Sarah probably enrolled her daughters at the Twenty-fourth Street School located at Holladay Street (Market Street today) at the corner of Twenty-fourth Street, in close proximity to their residence. Principal Jeannie P. Tidball and four teachers—Eva L. Barnes, Evangeline Eaton, Emma Miles, and Josephine Williams—operated the school. When the 1885 Colorado State Census was taken, the Buchanans were still living at the Platte River Bottoms. Lucile's three older sisters—eleven-year-old Hannah, ten-year-old Hattie, and seven-year-old Laura—are recorded in the 1885 Colorado State Census as attending school.[10]

When the Buchanans moved from the Bottoms to Barnum, Sarah enrolled Hannah, Hattie, Fenton, and Laura in the one-room Barnum School, erected in

FIGURE 7.1. *Louis Charles McClure, Villa Park Public School. Courtesy Western History and Genealogy Dept. Denver Public Library, ca. 1901.*

1889 at a cost of $2,125 ($58, 839 in 2017). About two years later, the Villa Park School at West Eight Avenue and Hazel Court, erected at a cost of $40,000, served the influx of new residents in Barnum and the surrounding communities (Colfax, Villa Park, and Cheltenham Heights). Later, the Villa Park School was incorporated into Denver's School District 21[11] and accommodated fifty-three students.[12] At the time of incorporation in 1895, the district voted to enlarge the school by eight rooms to include a high school at 845 Hazel Court between West Eight and Ninth Avenues.[13] Lucile and her siblings were the first Black students to attend the Villa Park Elementary school, and her sister Laura was the first to graduate from its high school.

When it came time for Lucile's graduation in June 1901, an article appearing in the *Denver Post* on the six Villa Park High School graduates reported that "a large and enthusiastic audience of friends and patrons of the school, who listened with hearty appreciation to the music and essays and orations delivered by the six graduates, after which Judge Hinsdale delivered a brief but appropriate address."[14]

Twelve days later the *Post* ran a subsequent article, "RECEPTION TO GRADUATES, Colored People Honor Young People Who Have Left School" which discussed a celebratory event held at Zion Baptist Church honoring Denver's three high school graduates: Lucile; Howard Edmund Page from East Denver High; and Zipporah Marcella Joseph, Denver's first Black valedictorian, from Manual Training High. Also included were graduates of colleges and institutions in and outside the state: Wade Anthony Jones, Denver Homeopathic; Ida M. Anderson, Mrs. Speer's Private Latin; Mary Belle Price, Denver Normal Preparatory; and Belle and Mercedes Evans, Union College, NE.[15]

Some ordinances and regulations Barnum instituted did not make life easier for the Buchanans or their neighbors. Adding to the day-to-day frustrations of a pioneering life, access to potable water continued to be a major concern for Barnum's residents. So much so that James and eight of his neighbors recognized that only their collective effort could bring about the changes necessary to improve their quality of life. On February 17, 1890, they petitioned Barnum's mayor, William H. Buchtel, and the board of trustees for water, in hopes of expanding waterways to their section of Barnum. Their petition read:

> Gentlemen:
>
> Your petitioners would respectfully request that water pipes be put in on the following route. Commencing at the corner of Emerson and Waldemere, thence west on Emerson to Richmond, thence north on Richmond, one block north to Beecher, thence one block west on Beecher to New York, thence north on New York to Collier, then west on Collyer to Connecticut, and also from the corner of German Avenue west on Tabor terminating on the west side of Waldemere, which will accommodate many property holders and tax payers and we urge your immediate action.[16]

Throughout the next several years, James's signature would appear on numerous of the town's policies and actions. For example, on April 13, 1891, James and three of his Barnum neighbors took out a $500 performance bond on Henry Beers, Barnum's new town marshal. His involvement in these actions came at the moment he was beginning to take advantage of the opportunities the western frontier offered—freedom to explore both the land itself and the economic possibilities it offered. His life began to epitomize what historian Frederick Jackson Turner spoke of when describing the frontiers of America as providing "a new field of opportunity, a gate of escape from bondage of the past; and freshness, and confidence . . . breaking the bond of custom, offering new experiences, calling out new institutions and activities, that, and more . . ."[17]

Not only were the Buchanans conquering a new geographic space, with all its untamed and aggressive character, they were also engaged in conquering the psychological restraints carried over from their days in bondage. While some Whites in Denver and, later, Barnum may have challenged their humanity, not all did; thus, they were able to understand and experience a new, larger world that allowed them the opportunity to grow, take risks, change, develop, and explore. But their success can also be measured by the fact that the family did not pose a threat to any of Barnum's White residents. As the sole Black family (to be joined several years later by another Black family) in the mid-1890s, the Buchanans seemed to understand their position as newbies in a state and, more important, in a town (Barnum) where they were a numerical minority, unlike the Virginia plantation where they greatly outnumbered the Whites. In addition, as slaves, they were unofficially schooled in the study of whiteness, which gave them an added advantage that they brought with them to Colorado.

By the end of the 1880s, James had quit his job at Binford Coal and started his own business. With his team and wagon, he hauled dirt and transported building materials throughout Barnum and the greater Denver area. When Barnum became incorporated, James worked for the town digging ditches. This work, far from insignificant, was so valued that the town's constitution spells out the importance of ditches in four sections, highlighting, among other things, where ditches were to run, bridging ditching, obstructing ditching, and the fines imposed for various infractions. Ditches were the lifeblood of the town, providing much-needed water for irrigating crops and trees. James's work was extraordinarily important, as he was a custodian of the town's survival.

According to the town minutes, the town of Barnum paid James the daily rate of $4 ($103 in 2017) for his ditch work. Receipts for this period show that he was the only non-White consistently working for the town's trustees over a long period and was often paid more than White workers.[18] In addition to Barnum, James also bid on other town contracts when available. On November 24, 1891, the board of trustees met to decide the awarding of contracts to build the new town hall at Fifth Avenue and Knox Court. It was awarded to Tomlinson and Wood for $2,288. Within that contract, bids were also received for removing dirt and excavating the cellar, which, on the motion of trustee Duncan and seconded by trustee Selleck, was awarded to James at the sum of $0.14 per yard. The motion was carried unanimously. After hauling away 105 yards of dirt, James presented his first bill to the trustees for $15 (approximately $387 in 2017) on December 15, 1891.

Ten years after arriving in Barnum, James was ready to engage further in the town's politics. On April 21, 1896, at 8:00 p.m., Mayor Oram E. Adamson, a commission

105

merchant, called the special meeting to order to address a number of financial obligations and to elect a street commissioner, who would be responsible for all work done on the streets, lands, avenues, irrigation ditches, and alleys. Trustee Somerville nominated Robert Foster, a gardener. Hazen seconded his nomination. Trustee Muckle then nominated James Buchanan. Miles seconded his nomination. The nominations were closed, and the vote was taken. Sommerville and Tuffield were appointed to count the votes. James received four of the six votes cast and was appointed street commissioner for the Town of Barnum.

In executing his duties, James had to be both decision-maker and rule enforcer of seventeen sections of Ordinance 2 when it came to "the use of streets and alleys and the condemnation of private property to be used as streets and alleys." He received $3 (approximately $90 in 2017) a day for his work as street commissioner plus $2 a day for the use of his team, as he traveled around town executing the duties of his office.

THE PURSUIT OF HAPPINESS AND LEISURE ACTIVITIES

Soon after arriving in Colorado, Blacks found ways to participate in leisure activities, which were essential to balancing a life often filled with hardship and uncertainty. This long tradition was also found in other parts of the United States, where Black churches, fraternal organizations, benevolent societies, and social and political organizations took the lead in sponsoring formal and informal recreation, which included picnics, dances, socials, house parties, concerts, card games (particularly Bid Whist), board games (chess and checkers), baseball games, visits to parks, and vacations (both in state and out of state). Even though living in Barnum physically isolated the family from the Black community in Denver's Five Points, they found ways to participate with family and friends in myriad leisure activities.

This participation was made easier in 1895, when the Denver and Southwestern Railway Company extended service to Barnum.[19] This led to family-focused activities exploring the vast territories of Colorado on day-trips to Golden organized by the railroads.[20] Family photographs from the late 1890s to mid-1900s show the Buchanan girls on mules with friends at Manitou Springs, seventy-six miles south of Denver; visiting the Garden of the Gods in Colorado Springs; as well as picnicking and wading on warm summer days along Boulder Creek, in Colorado Springs, at Rocky Mountain Lake in the Berkeley neighborhood northwest of Denver, and at Bear Creek Lake in Lakewood. They also found time to relax and socialize at Lincoln Hills-in Pine Cliff, a resort area about a two-hour drive from Denver, which was built for the recreation needs of middle-class Blacks.[21]

FIGURE 7.2. *Lucile's niece Carol Jarrett (center rear) and other Denverites at the Garden of the Gods, Colorado Springs, ca. 1921. Buchanan Archives.*

FIGURE 7.3. *Evelyn Napper (Lucile's niece) in dark dress with hat and friends Wella, Francis and her aunt Stella Parker at Bear Creek Lake, Denver, ca. 1940s. Buchanan Archives.*

The Buchanans also participated in citywide cultural activities. After an eleven-year hiatus, Lucile's mother, Sarah, and her youngest sister, Claribel, dressed as Indians, were keen to participate in Denver's Festival of Mountain and Plain, held October 15–18, 1912.[22] The annual fall festival celebrated the pioneer days of the Old West—the mining of the mountains and the husbandry of the plains. Since its first celebration in 1895, the three-day event always began with a "historic parade on the first day representing a pageant of progress in the state's history . . . [and] the second day [was] devoted to a masquerade parade, and in the evening, to a public outdoor mask ball," at which people danced until daybreak on Broadway under a canvas covering. On the third day is the "military and social parade, ending with a sham battle at City Park, and in the evening the parade of the slaves of the silver serpent.[23] Although the 1912 festival would turn out to be the final Mountain and Plain celebration, there was more excitement than ever that year because of the new electrical illumination and the fantastic artistic creations displayed on the many floats. It was also the first outdoor celebration where the city and the merchant class began to recognize the value of multi-colored (mostly red and yellow) decorative electric lighting for attracting customers at night. For the most part, cafés, saloons, restaurants, hotels, store windows, and movie theaters were already lit. Thousands of electric lamps were used, creating a canopy effect. Stringers were hung from the roofs of buildings and out over the sidewalks, forming great overhead domes of light. The Daniels and Fisher Store's tower on

FIGURE 7.4. *Sarah Buchanan and daughter Claribel, dressed as Native Americans, celebrating the Festival of Mountain and Plains, ca. 1912. Buchanan Archives.*

Sixteenth Street was outlined with red lights and at night had the appearance of a gigantic red ball suspended in midair by some unseen force.[24]

THE BLACK PRESS, POLITICAL ACTIVISM, AND SEGREGATED LEISURE

While Denver's majority press covered some news affecting the Black community, it was Denver's weekly Black presses, *Denver Star* (1882–1934) and the (*Colorado*) *Statesman* (1885–1961), that presented a home flavor supporting the cultural, religious, social, economic, and political life of the community by giving voice to organizations as well as providing a road map for action. Newspaper editors were especially astute in using their pen to bring attention to discriminatory practices, laud on the accomplishments of young people and the rising Black middle class, or to be involved in the organized efforts to improve the conditions of Denver Blacks. In 1905 Joseph D. D. Rivers, editor of the *Statesman*, used the paper to organize Blacks into a Colorado-wide organization because "Negroes should have perfect and complete organization to fight disenfranchisement." The outcome resulted in an April 20, 1915, *Rocky Mountain News* article recognizing that the editor of the *Statesman*, Joseph D. D. Rivers, was part of a Denver political league whose purpose was "working for the advancement of civil and political rights of the Denver league." However, the organizing efforts of the Black press began in 1896, when newspaper owners/editors across the West formed the Western Negro Press Association, pledging at their annual meetings to "stand for the highest in journalism and for the propagation of all things uplifting and inspiring."[25]

As the pivotal communication vehicle, the *Statesman*'s masthead read, "Labor Shall Be Free—Race, Country, Party," and highlighted births, deaths, weddings, and travel plans (who's leaving town, their itinerary, and who's arriving). Everyone benefited, especially new arrivals. In 1882 the Buchanans were made aware through the *Denver Star* that the Women's Committee at Shorter A.M.E. Church was preparing for their annual September event and would "spare no pains . . . making the event the grandest entertainment held by our people in this city."[26] The same paper notified them that the Independent Workers of Zion Baptist Church, which would eventually become their home church, would be giving a "grand festival" to which all were invited.

The *Star* also reported on Black entertainers and out-of-town performers appearing at non-race–based venues, such as Frank Heller's East Turner Hall at Larimer and Tenth Streets, which was showcasing the 1887 children's play the *Little Mountain Fairies*, written by Black dramatist and teacher Louise A. Smith from Washington, DC. Smith was part of a small group of Black playwrights[27] who toured the nation reading their plays in public halls as a means to counter the hegemonic messages of Jim Crow and the minstrel shows, which instilled a stereotypical imagery of Blacks as lazy, stupid, subhuman comics with an inborn penchant to sing, dance, and act as grinning fools.[28] Adding to the more structured leisure activities, the family could simply enjoy ice cream at the newly opened C. P. Keys's Ice Cream Parlor at 307 Nineteenth Street.

Like most early newspapers across the country, Denver's early Black press depended upon subscriptions rather than advertising for the major portion of its revenue, creating a symbiotic relationship between the press and the public. Even so, the subscription model had its downside, leaving Rivers to highlight the following announcement under its "City News" column in January 1917: "THE COLORADO STATESMAN, wants to be your helper in your JOYS, to your SUCCESS, to your BUSINESS and to your future. Make us your companion for 1917. Let us come into your home, into your shop or store or office. In laying out your new plans be sure to take this PAPER into ACCOUNT."[29]

One form of recreation that would grab the attention of entire communities, build friendships, provide avenues for networking among Blacks of varying socioeconomic standings, and at the same time generate income was baseball. As early as the 1840s, baseball became part and parcel of the fabric of African American life, when a number of clubs were established in New York City and soon spread to dozens of cities and towns.[30] In the post-slavery era and with the institution of Jim Crow laws, Blacks could not play on professional White teams and were excluded from organizing all-Black professional teams. As a result, Blacks began to organize semi-professional teams in the 1850s and early 1860s in Albany, Brooklyn, Manhattan, Chicago, New Orleans, Kansas City, Philadelphia, and St. Louis and, by the 1880s, in Colorado.

In 1884 Pueblo launched Colorado's first all-Black semi-professional baseball team, the Pueblo Blues. By the early twentieth century Blacks became enamored with baseball, and the sport would become a mainstay that popped up and down. By 1905 baseball became a major pastime, and the season sometimes opened with a grand ball prior to the first game.[31] Some of these early all-Black men's teams included the Iron Jackets, Buckingham, Colorado Giants, Five Points Boosters, the Colorado Springs Black Sox, Denver's Tyndall Graves, the Boulder Blues, and Denver's White Elephants, which played through 1935. And in Colorado Springs, the Brown Bombers, named after heavyweight boxing champion Joe Lewis's moniker, was established in the 1940s. Black women also took to the field in 1915 with their Brownskins and Darktown baseball teams. While their actions challenging

FIGURE 7.5. *The Boulder Blues, ca. 1930s. Courtesy Polly Bugros McLean.*

the status quo are historic, they still played into the colorism and racial physiog-nomy on body image through the naming practice of brown (meaning lighter) versus black.

CULTURAL POLITICS AND LEISURE

Naturally, Blacks enjoyed leisure activities. And while they were the beneficiaries of Colorado's 1895 Civil Rights Act and were finally able to enjoy leisure activities in public parks with family and friends, including the use of their facilities (tennis courts, benches, golf links),[32] they still had to contend with the challenges of rac-ism when it came to certain leisure activities, as well as the visible signs that made sure they understood their second-class status.

For instance, in the 1910s the owner of a local chili restaurant at 1727 Curtis Street established the White Peoples Chili Parlor.[33] Anthropologist Mark Hanna Watkins's insightful study on de jure segregation in Denver mentions that while Blacks were "concentrated in and adjacent to the Five Points," there was no segre-gation in "public supported hospitals, 'Jim Crow' schools are lacking and there is no segregation on the streetcars or buses."[34] However, segregation at times affected White patrons as well. The Roxy Theatre in Five Points was a de facto facility serving only a Black clientele. When Black out-of-state performers visited Denver, the Rainbow Ballroom at 38 East Fifth Avenue, a popular dance hall amongst Black promoters, had a stipulation in the contract, enforced by local police, that prevented White patrons from dancing with members of their own group. In addition, while Blacks were admitted to Elitch Gardens, the city's top entertainment facility, "they were not permitted to dance."[35]

While there were some social barriers along racial lines, Blacks embraced leisure activities popularized by the majority culture. But participating in these activities did not always turn out the way Blacks likely envisioned it.

In 1885 the management of the Tabor Grand Opera House refused to honor the prepaid tickets of James Hawkins, a highly respected Black professional, and his female companion, refusing to seat them in the audience. As soon as word of this incident spread to the Black community, Massalina M. Moss, together with her father, Henry O. Wagoner, Denver's first Black deputy sheriff and a major political force in the state created the Ladies' Legal Rights Association (LLRA). The exact membership of this organization remains unclear, as does the role Moss's very well-connected father played in helping to bring it to fruition. However, once established, the LLRA vowed to remain operational until Blacks achieved civil rights in the public sphere. Having access to large numbers of Denver's citizens through church and family connections and no doubt the Black press, the LLRA called for a public meeting on Tuesday, February 10, to address the Tabor incident.

On the podium was a multiracial group of Denver's leading citizens supporting the LLRA's efforts, including Edwin H. Hackley, Denver's only Black attorney; the Rev. J. R. Fields of Zion Baptist Church; John Milton Chivington, cleric and politician from New York and a retired US Army colonel; the Rev. Gilbert De La Matyr, pastor at the Lawrence Street Methodist Episcopal Church; and Thomas Painter, a local business owner and pattern maker.

The large audience, composed mainly of Blacks but including a few White allies, was treated to speeches addressing everything from the evils of slavery to guarantees of equality expressed in the US Constitution to a Civil Rights Bill being introduced in the Colorado State Legislature by Senator M. B. Carpenter. The last speaker to the podium was Massalina Moss:

> I speak on behalf of my sex. So keenly do we deplore the insult of one of our number—one that is deserving of our respect, both morally and intellectually—that we feel we can tolerate this state of things no longer. We have borne, for many years, insults, rapine, and injustice, and now we appeal to you, and ask you, our countrymen, to arise and demand of our oppressors redress for the repeated wrongs and

insults offered to your mothers, wives, sisters and lovers. All we ask is the right to exercise that liberty accorded us by nature, and we will give you all the aid we can in defense of these rights.[36]

Action arrived quickly. About seven weeks after that first meeting, an article in the *Denver Tribune-Republican* announced, "Colored People Happy: They Celebrate in No Uncertain Way the Passage of the Civil Rights Bill—the Republican Party Warmly Thanked."[37] The Black community was jubilant. A second meeting, chaired by Moss's father, celebrated the victory and praised the quick action of the Colorado State Legislature, especially the efforts of Senator Carpenter, for introducing and securing the passage of Senate Bill no. 161, Colorado's 1885 Civil Rights Bill, which forbade discrimination in public facilities and places such as hotels, railroads, theaters, and restaurants. In 1885 Colorado became one of a small number of states that passed legislation banning public accommodations segregation. The other states were Illinois, Indiana, Michigan, Minnesota, Nebraska, New Mexico, and New York.

Not only did the 1885 Civil Rights Bill put public establishments on notice against discrimination, it also gave Colorado citizens a legal means to challenge infractions. Fifty-eight years later this bill would be tested in the summer of 1943 when Lucile's youngest sister, Claribel, was refused service at the Chinese Rice Inn at 100 East Twentieth Avenue. In a scrapbook Claribel kept is an article with the headline "Woman Refused Service Receives Judgement," which describes the success of her civil action when she was awarded fifty dollars (the sum specified in the law for such an offense). In the same story the newspaper carried a letter of apology to Claribel from Willie Tom, the owner of the Chinese Rice Inn, expressing his displeasure concerning the incident and vowing that there would never again be discrimination based on race, color, or creed in his restaurant.

Claribel's political action was not an isolated incident. Starting in the mid-1860s, Blacks living in the Colorado Territory began to participate in a number of civic and political organizations to either challenge the racial status quo or to build parallel political structures in an effort to negotiate change. A reoccurring theme among Colorado Black Republicans was that despite their voting strength, the national Republican Party has not aided them in their fight against disfranchisement and has driven them into a position of political helplessness.[38] To address the call for political action, the "Colored Central Republican Club of Denver" began operating in the late 1880s, attempting to engage the local political system by electing Black men to political office.

In the midst of this political fervor, Black women were not simply bystanders. Toward the end of the nineteenth century, Black women began to take on more visible roles in the political and social life of the community. In response to the disenfranchisement of women, coupled with a desire to "uplift the race," Elizabeth Piper Ensley, who arrived in Denver in 1888, became the city's leading Black suffragette and a trailblazer in the women's club movement. She became treasurer of the largely White nonpartisan group, the Equal Suffrage Association of Colorado. This group helped mobilize Black men, which would have included Lucile's father and uncles, to fight for suffrage for women—a goal that was realized on November 7, 1893.[39] Immediately after this victory, Ensley, along with other Black women activists Ida DePriest and Emma Azalia Hackley, helped to establish the Women's League of Denver and the Colorado Colored Women's Republican Club, both of which were dedicated to educating Black women on their rights as new voters.[40] As a result of their mobilizing efforts, Black women across the state went to the polls, helping elect Colorado's first Black state legislator, attorney Joseph H. Stuart, in 1894, as well as the first female state legislators in US history: Clara Clessingham, Carrie Holly, and Frances Klock.

Black women had been active in reframing and improving the social conditions of the race ever since Blacks began arriving in Colorado in the 1860s. The training for community organizing and activism was originally obtained through the church and the auxiliary groups of Black fraternal organizations, such as the Daughters of Rebekah, the Order of the Eastern Star, and the Sisters of Calanthe.[41] They also learned their way around community organizing through mutual aid societies, such as the People's Aid Association of Denver, created in 1878. Although state suffrage gave Colorado women a stake in the political sphere, it was clear to the Black community that legislation was not enough. They needed a dual strategy that took into consideration the emancipation of the mind and spirit. One of the national strategies employed by Black women, which also impacted Colorado women locally, centered on the creation of women's clubs: the Phyllis Wheatley Clubs (named after a slave poet who lived from 1753 to 1784), the Colored Women's Republican Club, and the Women's Club Movement,[42] a version of the gathering of independent White women that had taken hold during the Progressive era.

With the growth of the middle class, ever-increasing leisure time, and following a national trend, Denver's Black women launched a statewide club movement with the creation of the Denver-based Pond Lily Art and Literary Club in 1901, the Dahlia Art and Literary Club in 1902, the Carnation Art Club and the Self-Improvement Club in 1903, and the Taka Arts Club in 1904. Recognizing their growing impact across the state, in 1905 Elizabeth Ensley unified the state clubs into the Colorado National Association of Colored Women's Clubs, federated under the National Association of Colored Women's Clubs in Washington, DC. By the mid-1900s women's clubs were going strong in Denver, Colorado Springs, and Pueblo, with Denver alone establishing an estimated twenty-two clubs between 1901 and 1925.[43]

Overall, these middle-class women were driven by a thirst for learning, self-improvement, and overall betterment of their community.[44] For many, education was considered a lifelong process in which individuals continued to learn outside formal academic settings, regularly practicing what W.E.B. Du Bois called, "education within and without the schoolhouse walls."[45] As historian Lynda F. Dickson notes, Denver's Black clubwomen "were aware that every Black woman who did not behave herself in a lady like manner and every child that was unruly and uncared for was a further indictment of all Black women."[46]

As young Black girls witnessed the development of women's clubs, and with help from adult leaders, they moved to create parallel clubs such as Select Six, a club for young girls that often gave "full dress" parties at the Five Points Hall. The High School Girls' Club chaperoned by Zipporah Parks and the Phyllis Wheatley YWCA club for young women to study the lives and works of Black men and women.

Committed to educating the next generation, Charles A. Franklin, editor/owner of the *Statesman*; Dr. Wade A. Jones; Benjamin W. Fields, owner/manager of O.K. Cleaning Works; Nelsina Howard; and Zipporah Marcella Joseph, a 1901 graduate of Denver's Manual High School, created the Inter-Graduate Association (IGA) with Zipporah as its president. While Zipporah and Lucile did not attend the same high school, both attended Zion Baptist Church. It was probably through this connection that Lucile became a member of the IGA. IGA not only saw its role as celebrating the intellectual accomplishments of Blacks who graduated with distinction from high school and beyond but also mentoring high school students and making them aware of the accomplishments of those who completed secondary and post-secondary education.

Also meeting the leisure and entertainment needs of the Black community were numerous moneymaking ventures, such as the Oriental, Buckingham, and Jeffersonian Clubs, where Blacks could meet, greet, eat, and have a drink. There was also Two Jims' Social Club, "Denver's Favorite Pleasure Resort," at 1859 Champa Street, where patrons could play "whist, pool, chess, checkers and other pastime games."[47] And then there was Mr. and Mrs. D. W. Lacy's Mecca Café and Chilli Parlor at 2226 Arapahoe Street, which as its newspaper ad states, was "for ladies and gentlemen at all hours."[48]

THE BUCHANANS' PRIVATE SPHERE

Lucile's parents, James and Sarah, were born during the Victorian era. In the decades following the Civil War, commonly known as the Gilded Age, they were married and began to build a family in Virginia before spending the Progressive era in Colorado, where they completed their family. These two periods reflect their family values and determined how they constructed their leisure, especially within the home.

As members of the emerging Black middle class in Colorado, the home the Buchanans built in the 1880s incorporated features of the social landscape that blended Victorian-era and Gilded-Age flavors, resulting in what is often referred to as a mini–Queen Anne. This house became the center of their leisure activities, which emphasized book collecting and family reading time (placed at high value in the post-emancipation years), scrapbooking, and art collecting, which accommodated not only the leisure activities they saw on the Virginia plantations but also those leisure activities they encountered in the West.

Home leisure became even more pronounced as new entertainment technologies developed at the turn of the twentieth century, and Blacks clamored to fit their homes with these devices. I was therefore not surprised to learn that the Buchanans had purchased a Victor talking machine[49] for which they paid three dollars in 1901 ($90 in 2017), and for which they began buying ten-inch black label records from Victor and the Columbia Phonograph Company. The collection of records in their home included a 1904 recording of the Haydn Quartet's signature barbershop song "Sweet Adeline," lyricist George V. Hobart and composer Silvio Hein's "Arab Love Song," Pale K. Kua's 1914 guitar duet of "Aloha oe!" (Farewell to Thee), Kua's 1914 guitar solo "The Rosary," baritone Charles Bennett's 1915 recording of "Oh Promise Me," the 1924 recordings of Lambert Murphy's performance of "Rose-Marie," and the Columbia University Orchestra's 1915 recording of "Shubert Serenade."[50]

Although the Progressive era brought new types of music into the home—ragtime, blues, and jazz—these musical genres, created by Black artists, were deemed too sensual and too working class and were initially rejected by educated Blacks seeking to counter negative stereotypes with more positive images and exemplary behaviors along a more classical White-approved continuum. Psychiatrist and philosopher Frantz Fanon presents a formidable explanation by suggesting that Western popular culture equates whiteness with purity and goodness and blackness with impurity and evil.[51] As a result, how did Blacks attempt to shed the negativity assigned to them? Others argued that the music created by Black America would stand on its own and eventually make its way into the most assimilated Black families. Indeed, the music that survived in Lucile's family home did not include the heritage of Black America. Does this mean, as Fanon suggested, that to elevate themselves, they had abandoned their blackness?

By the end of the 1890s the Buchanans had achieved their vision of the American dream; they worked hard and had successful lives that ensured their position on the national race/class scale. They were part of Denver's Black elite and could easily out-perform their White neighbors in Barnum in terms of the trappings of middle-class life. However, they were still haunted, as were many middle-class Blacks, by the stereotypes, images, and treatment that publicly questioned their humanity every day. Engaging in strategies of ultra-respectability designed to destroy negative Black stereotypes, they demonstrated that they understood and shared so-called White values.[52]

The music of White America became one of the doors through which the Buchanans believed they could travel to prove their humanity and demonstrate (if temporarily) their access to the privileges of whiteness, even in the face of diminishing odds. While the collection of music the Buchanans left behind failed to embrace the popular Black music of the Progressive era—I can't help but reflect on the themes of Du Bois's "double-consciousness" (always looking at oneself through the eyes of others).[53]

All in all, I would argue that the Buchanans, and all Black middle-class club-women for that matter, understood the communicative properties of their actions and knew how to put on an ostentatious performance through the music they embraced in public and showcased in private. The Buchanans did not necessarily become "whiter," nor did they renounce any of their blackness. I saw their desire to be accepted as more in line with what Du Bois suggested in *The Souls of Black Folk*, in that they simply wished "to be both a Negro and an American, without being cursed and spit upon . . . and without having the doors of Opportunity closed roughly in his face." To overcome the intense racial practices and ideologies of this period and to challenge the injustice about which Du Bois spoke, Lucile's parents seem to have followed Booker T. Washington's model for Black economic and social progress through his philosophy of racial uplift, which emphasized respectability, industrial education, temperance, thrift, gentility, and economic self-reliance. If Blacks practiced the values attached to the ideology of racial uplift and rose to middle-class status, Whites would accept them as equals, was the theory.

Despite any challenges they encountered as they migrated West, by the late nineteenth and early twentieth centuries the Buchanans had defied the old order and all obstacles. They had achieved a considerable degree of prosperity, brought about by James's dogged perseverance and skills he initially learned in his slave community in Virginia, which he was successful in parlaying into a career as an independent teamster. As the family grew, they were able to take care of educational opportunities for their children that would prepare them for middle-class status. With their social and economic advancement, brought on by industrial and technological changes, they were able to take advantage of leisure activities both inside and outside the home. In every way, the Buchanans had arrived. They wore a new public face of race. Nonetheless, they were still living in a White supremacist culture with unprecedented problems yet to deal with.

8

The Frontier in Our Souls

I don't believe an accident of birth makes people sisters or brothers.
It makes them siblings, gives them mutuality of parentage.
Sisterhood and brotherhood is a condition people have to work at.

— MAYA ANGELOU

Lucile idealized her three older sisters, Hattie (1874–1940), Hannah Elizabeth (1875–1942), and Laura (1878–99), and her brother Fenton Mercer (1880–1963), and looked to them for inspiration and leadership. I imagine that Lucile's older siblings provided her with additional nurturing and protection while their parents worked away from the home. Each sibling brought a set of unique skills and interests that set a path for Lucile to follow. Since they attended the Villa Park School in Barnum, Lucile likely benefited, scholastically and emotionally, from their experiences by the time she enrolled. One benefit was increased achievement. Much like Hannah and Laura, Lucile set her sights on post-secondary education and a career in teaching.

Her four older siblings were born in Virginia during the early years of Reconstruction. The remaining group, born in Colorado, included Sadie Bishop (1888), Edith Mae (1890), Nellie Evelyn (1893), and Claribel (1899), who came of age during the end of the Gilded Age and in the first decades of the Progressive era—a period often labeled the "Nadir" of Black history where White supremacy gained strength and race relations between Black and Whites reached their lowest point. Blacks were targets of horrendous violence, Jim Crow laws and segregation in

FIGURE 8.1. *Family portrait on front porch, 227 Raleigh Street, Denver. Back row (left to right), Nellie, Sadie, Hannah, Fenton, Edith, and Lucile. Front row, James, Claribel, and Sarah, ca. 1910. Buchanan Archives.*

southern states promulgated the lasting stereotypes of Black inferiority, and savage tendencies were forged and disseminated through popular culture (e.g., books, magazines, newspapers, cartoons, racist coon songs, minstrel characters, radio, film, and eventually television). In Denver, Blacks escaped the especially pernicious racism of the South. Their lives, seen through photographs and other visuals, letters, clothing, and newspaper clippings they left behind, tell a story of how they established themselves and molded their identities when the tide of White supremacy finally reared its ugly head.

HATTIE SETS THE STAGE

Hattie, the oldest, began her education at the Twenty-fourth Street Public School not far from the family home on Delgany Street in the Bottoms. When the family moved to Barnum, she completed the eighth grade at the neighborhood Villa Park School. As the oldest daughter, she likely assumed a great deal of responsibility in helping her mother manage the household. Likely, her leadership skills developed from a young age. Hattie also inherited her father's ambition and entrepreneurial spirit. With her innate friendliness, leadership abilities, organizational skills, and stunning beauty, Hattie soon became the dream of many a young Black man in Denver. Shattering that dream for all but one, she married twenty-two-year-old Missouri-born Elias W. Jarrett in a civil ceremony on Wednesday, December 11, 1895. The Rev. Samuel William Byrd, the pastor of Shorter Chapel AME, performed the ceremony. Hattie's eighteen-year-old sister, Laura, and Elias's co-worker from the Denver Club, William E. Rice, served as witnesses to the marriage.[1]

The wedding of the first daughter of one of Denver's well-off pioneering Black families became the talk of the Black community. The December 21, 1895, issue of the *Colorado Statesman* ran a front-page story on Hattie and Elias's wedding reception, which took place at their new home at 2454 Grant Avenue, in Denver's racially mixed Five Points neighborhood, which speaks to the social standing of both families, evoking the type of status that transcends class and racial lines.

The *Colorado Statesman* reported that because of Elias's "pleasing manner he had made many friends in this city." Not surprising, nearly all the Black men at the reception were Elias's friends and, like Elias, were either waiters or porters at a number of prominent establishments in town (the Union Depot, the Lotos Club, the Pacific Express, and the American House Hotel). The largest contingency, however, constituted his co-workers from the elite Denver Club. Several of these men were also members of the Black fraternal benevolent organization, the Grand United Order of Odd Fellows, and had held leadership positions in the organization.

Barbers, porters, and waiters were the moving drivers of the rising Black middle class in Denver. Not only did they receive higher wages than other workers, they regularly touched shoulders with Denver's White elite and would be able to parlay these contacts into some social status within the Black community, particularly in terms of material wealth and political influence. In fact, the *Colorado Statesman* made a point to include a paragraph in the article mentioning the nine "White friends" who attended the reception. While none of the Whites listed were from the Barnum community and may not have been the only Whites in attendance, these were the ones of the greatest social and political significance. They included one of Denver's most prominent jurists, the first president of the Denver Bar Association, and dean of the University of Denver law school, Albert E. Pattison, his wife, Emma, and their children, Lucia and Myron. They gifted "solid silver spoons, a butter knife and a gold bowl with sugar spoons" to the newlyweds. Dry goods merchant and state legislator the Hon. Clarence Preston Elder's gift was a set of Victor Hugo works. Mrs. Hattie (Harriet) Sporborg, the wife of real estate developer Moses W. Sporborg, along with her daughter, Myra, gave Hattie an imported bracelet and a decorative Agate knife. One White friend, Mrs. Annie

M. Sadd, traveled from San Francisco to join the celebration, gifting the couple with a "handsome set of table doyles [*sic*]."

The newspaper article provided an additional clue to one of the most popular leisure activities enjoyed by members of Denver's Black community across class, gender and age lines. As Blacks came West, they not only established parallel fraternal, benevolent, and social organizations (separate and unique from their White counterparts), they also established parallel leisure clubs. Not to be out-done by the chess, checkers, and whist clubs patronized by Denver's White social elites—the Capitol Whist Club, the Woman's Whist Club, and the Silver Whist Club—Denver's Blacks created their own whist clubs such as the Mariposa Whist Club, Rabbitville Whist Club, Columbine Whist Club, Twentieth Century Whist Club, the Bachelor Girls' Whist Club, the UAC Bell Boys Whist Club, and the East End Progressive Whist Club. The one mentioned in the article was the ONO (Or Nearest Offer) Whist Club.

Whist was popular in the eighteenth and nineteenth centuries amongst plan-tation Whites, as it taught counting skills needed for plantation life and was con-sidered acceptable for Blacks to play. There are a number of plausible explanations for how the game arrived in Denver. It is conceivable that as Blacks migrated to Colorado in the 1860s, they brought the game with them. Or possibly the Pullman porters, who are credited with helping shape the Black middle class, brought the game they played on long rail journeys back home in the late nineteenth and early twentieth centuries. During this period Black Denverites, including Hattie and Elias, engaged in whist with a passion. Fourteen members of the ONO Whist Club attended the wedding reception. Many were Elias's co-workers and their wives, while others were single women like Belle Bradley, a dressmaker at 2033 Welton Street in Five Points.

In the late 1890s, Hattie and Elias were members of the ONO (Or Nearest Offer) Whist Club of which fourteen members attended Hattie and Elias's wed-ding reception. The article covering the reception ends with the following: "The Colorado Statesman congratulates Mr. Jarrett in the selection of one of the daugh-ters of old Virginia for his helpmate, and wishes the young couple many years of happiness."

Hattie, seeing a gap in the market and likely inspired by the triumphant suc-cess of Madame C. J. Walker—America's first female self-made millionaire who in 1906 founded her hair product line in Denver—turned her kitchen at 2457 High Street into a working lab. With the help of a chemist and working under the name Madame Jarrett, she developed a cosmetics line called Adarose Exquisite Toilet Preparations. Beginning with home sales, her niece Evelyn states that the Daniels

FIGURE 8.2. *Adarose Beauty Preparations on display at Hattie's home at 2457 High Street, Denver. Buchanan Archives.*

and Fisher Store at Sixteenth and Arapahoe also sold Adarose.[2] However, this relationship with the department store was short-lived as Hattie embarked on a new career: motherhood.

After twelve years of marriage, Hattie gave birth to the couple's only child, Marjorie Carol (aka Carol) on August 29, 1906. By 1916 Hattie had reentered the workforce as a candy maker at Baur's Confectionary Company.[3] Hattie's candy-making skills and leadership qualities soon caught the attention of management just as the company was adding a restaurant to the business. In 1918 the managers appointed Hattie "head of the kitchen," a position she would hold for the next twenty years.

Hattie died on February 10, 1940, at age seventy-one. Funeral services were held at the Church of the Holy Redeemer, Colorado's oldest Black Episcopal church. She was buried in the family plot at Fairmount Cemetery beside her husband, Elias, who preceded her death in 1939.

WITH MISSIONARY ZEAL

While Hattie made great strides as an entrepreneur and restaurant manager, Lucile's next oldest sister, twenty-nine-year-old Hannah Elizabeth, packed up her belongings in 1904 and headed south to Atlanta, Georgia, to enroll in the Christian Workers

FIGURE 8.3. *Hattie Buchanan Jarret with daughter Marjorie Carol, ca. 1918. Buchanan Archives.*

FIGURE 8.4. *Hattie Jarett, head of kitchen of Baur's, ca. 1939. Courtesy Baur's Collection, Ph. 00562 (10054697), History Colorado.*

Department of Spelman Seminary (now Spelman College) for women and girls.[4] She carried with her a letter of introduction to Harriet E. Giles, the co-founder and second president of Spelman from Rev. J. E. Ford of Zion Baptist Church.[5]

Denver, Colo
Nov 17—1904
Miss Giles
Atlanta, Ga.

Dear Madam:—

The bearer Miss Hannah Buchanan is a member of Zion Baptist Church of Denver and I cordially commend her to your confidence as one who is trustworthy, conscientious, studious & desirous of improving herself and giving her services to the Cause of Christ. She has the approval & prayers of the church Missionary Society of which she is a member.

Yours very truly
J. E. Ford, Pastor—
Zion Baptist Church

Born in Loudoun County, Virginia on November 9, 1875, Hannah embraced the Christian values and moral rectitude that Spelman was founded on, and, accordingly, the college catalog reflected these values. "We train the intellect, store the mind with useful knowledge, induce habits of industry and a desire for general information, inspire a love for the true and the beautiful, and prepare the pupils for the practical duties of lie. These are the objects earnestly sought to be accomplished. Our motto is, 'Our whole school for Christ.'"[6] According to author and educator Benjamin Griffith Brawley, "The school is best known for its training of teachers and nurses, for its emphasis on domestic science and for its constant ideal of Christian womanhood. Spelman has moreover in the record of its graduates who have gone as missionaries to Africa."[7]

As for the rest of the city, Atlanta was considered more progressive than most southern cities and had become a leading industrial center in the South. By 1900 almost 90,000 people called Atlanta home, of which about 36,000 were African Americans.[8] In contrast, Denver's population around the same time was about 134, 000, of which 3,900 were Black.[9] On one hand Atlanta provided Hannah with hope and opportunity since the city was experiencing the emergence of a class of elite and educated Black professionals who were becoming more involved in the political sphere, creating social networks and launching new businesses. It was also where W.E.B. Du Bois spent his early years firing the imagination of the Black intelligencia with a roadmap for action in an effort to overcome the social, economic, and political conditions of Georgia Blacks and as well as those across the nation.[10] On the other hand, Hannah, who was raised in a predominately White community and attended a predominately White school system, had to bravely reposition herself and take the attendant risks from a Jim Crow state where there were far more racial incidences and where White supremacy and legal segregation reigned.

Hannah graduated with her missionary certificate from Spelman's Christian Workers Department on May 16, 1906.[11] She was spared the savagery of Atlanta's September 22–24 race riot of that year since she had assumed a teaching position at Florida's Baptist Academy (FBA), one of four private institutions in Jacksonville founded by Bethel Baptist Institutional Church, the oldest and wealthiest Black congregation in the city.[12] From its early beginnings, the school provided secondary educational opportunities for a number of older youths as well as trained the clergy. Unlike Spelman, which focused on educating women and girls, the FBA attracted both genders (male and female), relegating women teachers and girls to the second and third floors of the school's three-storied building. At the end of her first year of teaching in 1907, Hannah returned to Atlanta, enrolling in Spelman's

FIGURE 8.5. *Hannah Buchanan (front row, second from right) upon graduation from Spelman Seminary, ca. 1908. It is possible that her academic regalia (very different that the other graduates) was borrowed from Lucile, who graduated with this very type regalia in 1905 from the Colorado State Normal School (UNC). Buchanan Archives.*

Teachers Professional Department and earning her teaching diploma on May 10, 1908. Although she may have had her eyes set on remaining in Atlanta, she returned to her previous teaching position in Jacksonville.[13]

After a five-year absence, Hannah came home to Denver in June 1909 along with Lucile, who also returned from her teaching exploration in Little Rock.[14] This would be a temporary reunion. During the week of October 3, 1909, Hannah returned to Jacksonville, resuming her teaching at FBA. And while Jacksonville provided her with a vibrant Christian community with a large Black population (larger than Atlanta), it was still not Atlanta.

Eventually opportunity arose in 1915 when she landed a teaching position at the Storrs School (a forerunner to Atlanta University), established by the American Missionary Association (AMA) in 1867 for freed men and women in the post–Civil War. It was known throughout Atlanta as a first-rate private school that supported the employment of Black teachers and where parents clamored to get their children enrolled. The school drew mainly from Mulattoes who lived on Auburn Avenue and had owned successful businesses or were professionals such as doctors, teachers, lawyers, and civil servants and who were largely educated at Storrs. Many sent their children to Storrs.[15]

When Hannah returned to Atlanta, she settled in the low-lying, flood-prone, segregated Fourth Ward. Despite this segregation, Hannah found herself in the heart of the evolving institutions serving the needs of Blacks in higher education by supplying teachers and librarians to Black schools throughout the South. She lived in walking distance to what are now some of the oldest universities and colleges serving the Black community: Morris Brown College (closed in 2009), established in 1881 by the African Methodist Episcopalian Church; Atlanta University, founded in 1865 by the American Mission Association, and the first Black institution to offer graduate degrees; Clark College, founded in 1869 by the Freedmen's Aid Society of the Methodist Episcopal Church (later the United Methodist Church); Spelman Seminary (later Spelman College), and Morehouse College, established in 1867 as the Augusta Institute by the oldest independent Black church in the United States, the Springfield Baptist Church. This strong nucleus of Black colleges and growing economic opportunities laid the foundation for an emerging influential Black middle class, into which Hannah fit quite easily. It is likely that this educational environment may have influenced Hannah to earn a bachelor's degree in education, which she did on June 5, 1929, by taking evening classes from Morehouse College.[16]

More importantly, the Atlanta she returned to in 1915 was radically changing. New laws restricted Blacks to certain residential areas, and Atlanta had become the headquarters of the newly reconstituted Ku Klux Klan. While the Klan brought its own level of fear and frustration, it was the actions of Atlanta's Board of Education that probably disappointed her the most. According to Donald Lee Grant, the Board had eliminated the eighth grade from all its public schools in 1915, and Whites graduating from the seventh grade went directly to high school; Blacks were on their own since there were no public high schools for Blacks in Atlanta. The only option for Black students was to enroll in Atlanta's private Black colleges (known as the Atlanta University System), which offered high school courses for a small fee, preventing a large number of Black students from attending. Hannah taught in Spelman's high school while she was a student in the college.

For the next nine years Hannah continued to teach at Storrs, including serving as principal in 1922. In September 1924 the first Black public high school in

Georgia opened in Atlanta with 1,947 students. Ever since her brief high school teaching at Spelman and her leadership at Storrs, it is possible that Hannah was recruited or jumped at the opportunity to teach mathematics, eventually heading the mathematics department, at the new Booker T. Washington high school beginning in 1924 through 1940.

Hannah died on January 23, 1942, at sixty-five. She did not live to see the erection of Atlanta's second Black high school in 1947. Florence M. Read, the fourth president of Spelman, sent a note of condolences to her sisters Lucile and Edith, which read:

January 28, 1942

Dear Mrs. Jones and Mrs. Davis,

Please accept the deep sympathy of Spelman College in the loss of your sister, Miss Hannah E. Buchanan. The thoroughness with which she performed her work, her insistence upon exactness and her willingness and joy in serving others are qualities which will live on in the lives of those who came under her influence. May this be a comfort in this hour of sorrow.

Following her funeral service in Atlanta Hannah's body was brought back to Denver for burial in the family plot at Fairmount Cemetery, near her parents. Father Harry A. Rahming of the Church of the Holy Redeemer (formally St. Stephen's Episcopal Church) officiated at the funeral services.

LAURA, THE BRIGHT LIGHT

With Hattie married and Hannah biding her time before taking off to follow her dream of teaching in Atlanta, the Buchanans turned their attention to Laura, their third-oldest daughter. Laura, like Hannah, expressed an interest in teaching, which had become one of the most honorable occupations among Blacks and carried significant community and social standing.

The high school courses officially introduced at the Villa Park School around 1895 made it possible for Laura to gain a year of secondary courses before graduating with the high school's first class on June 5, 1896. With a class of only five students, the school and the community went all out to make it a memorable experience. On the evening of Friday, June 5, 1896, Laura became the first of Sarah and James's children to graduate from high school. The Barnum community turned out in record numbers to witness Villa Park high school's first commencement. The stage was decked off with peonies and carnations. An orchestra set the mood with upbeat selections. Following the opening prayer, Laura took to the stage to deliver her "first class essay, based on a quote by the English poet George Byron: I slept and dreamt that life was beauty; I woke and found that life was duty." According to an article in the *Denver Rocky Mountain News*, Laura's essay "showed meritorious care and preparation." On Saturday, June 6, the graduating class went to Mt. Vernon Canyon, west of Denver for their class picnic.[17]

After graduation, Laura's life appears to have taken two directions. First, she became involved with a number of church-based activities, some of which were highlighted in the local press. For example, because she taught Sunday school at Zion Baptist Church, the church selected her as its delegate to the multiracial Arapahoe County Sunday-School Association's annual convention, held in Denver in February 1897. As a delegate, Laura was one of three people handling public relations for the event. She also served as the press person for Denver's annual Emancipation Day observances for former slaves and their children, held at Zion on September 20, 1898. And while Laura attempted to find work as a teacher following her high school graduation in 1896, it would take two more years before Colorado hired its first Black teacher, Florence Mabel Branch, a graduate of West Denver High, who was appointed to District 15 School at Pine Ridge, near the Arapahoe and Douglas County line. According to research conducted by prominent Black leader Geraldine Lightner on the state of Black teachers in Colorado during the early twentieth century, Laura was the next in line to replace Florence, who had taken off to do missionary work in British Central Africa (today Malawi), but Laura's unexpected death in 1899 changed everything. Florence's friend Leona Troutman was appointed to the position, which she held for two years. It was not until 1918 that Colorado hired another Black teacher.[18]

About two years following her high school graduation, twenty-year-old Laura was accepted into the class of 1900 at Colorado State Normal School in Greeley, now the University of Northern Colorado (UNC), established in 1889 to train qualified teachers for the state's public schools. All students accepted into the program agreed to teach in Colorado's public schools in exchange for free tuition and the use of their textbooks. Laura's major expenses would be room and board and the cost of traveling by train to and from Greeley. Laura therefore arrived in Greeley with few expenses but a great load of family expectations placed on her. Since there were no accommodations on campus for students, Laura found accommodations in the home of forty-nine-year-old Tennessee-born Harvey English, a produce merchant; his thirty-nine-year-old wife, Sarah, and their four children: twenty-one-year-old Elbert, seventeen-year-old Clarence, twelve-year-old Myrtle, and six-year-old Ralph.

On Friday, October 28, 1898, her fourteen-year-old sister, Lucile, penned an illuminating letter[19] to Laura, known affectionately as Lolly or Loll. The letter includes some local gossip and her opinions about people they knew. Lucile also took Laura to task for embarrassing her in a recent letter, saying "you should not have put the criticisms on my writing right-in with the rest of the letter" and in future correspondence, "put it in a separate place and put, Lou, before it." Clearly, some of Lucile's character begins to emerge as she writes:

Barnum Colo.
Oct 28 1898

Dear Loll:

Shall I write vertical or slanting? Oh! I guess you will try me once more—writing slanting. We received your most welcome letter a week ago today; and were very glad to hear from you, to hear that you were well and doing well; although you never mentioned to us whether you were dead or alive, or how you were doing and I do not know where you closed up, though I search for the words "good-bye al" [sic] over the papers. You should not have put the criticisms on my writing right-in with the rest of the letter. Because I was reading so fast I did not see that until I had read it with the rest to mama. You should have put it in a separate place and put, Lou, before it.

Miss Maggie Graham is back, as I guess you know by this time, and was just, a–acting Sunday as usual, with Mr. W. A. Jones (I guess you will know who he is). Fenti [brother] says he is saving his hellos until Christmas. Don't you wish it would hurry and come? Mama has just answered a letter of Auntie's. She has written two letters, since August and mama is just answering them.

Edna Stills has a lovely new dress, though the way it is made does not become her. It is a mixed brown and black. Trimmed in plaid silk. It is made a kind of blouse and a belt, and it has a sailor collar trimmed with the silk.

Miss L. Anderson said she got a letter from you two weeks ago, she always tells me when she heard from you. Mrs. Berger [sic] is gone, so mama got through sooner this wk in her work.

I will close now because these must get to the P.O. We are all well and hope you are the same. We remain as ever,

The family
Write soon.

To get her letter to Laura mailed, Lucile walked about twelve blocks to the post office run out of a store owned by P. T. Barnum's first cousin William A. Nichols, who served as postmaster until 1900. She bought a two-cent stamp and carefully placed it on the small envelope and gave it to the postmaster. Laura received the letter about November 2. When I first saw the letter, I was taken aback by its stellar mint condition, having been carefully kept in the same envelope Laura had opened over a century ago. Although there was slight browning of the lined paper and envelope, the handwriting is bold, the ink still legible and clear. The old fold lines are still intact and can be opened without tearing. This is one of two pieces of physical memories of her sister Lucile had kept throughout the decades.

Sometime after receiving Lucile's letter and before the end of the fall semester, Laura came home to Barnum. Unbeknown to her family, Laura never actually enrolled in classes. All the family apparently knew was that her physical health had presumably been adversely affected by her "studies." At this time in history, the idea of emotional health, in all likelihood, may not have been considered. Christmas came and went. The winter term at Colorado State Normal School began on January 3, 1899, but Laura was not there. Neither family nor friends had managed to shake her out of her depression. Weeks passed as she languished about, likely despairing about her choices. She would pray and ask God for guidance. Then on the morning of February 17, 1899, she began to write:

> I think this is the last that I shall have to say. At least I hope so. I am so tired of everything. It seems strange that in this great, large world there can be no place found for me; I've tried to do what I could; more than that is impossible. I cannot carve a new way of life here and I believe God will be merciful and make room for me with Himself, where I will cease to be an incumbrance [sic].[20]

The February 18, 1899, Saturday morning edition of the *Denver Republican* read: "SOUGHT RELIEF IN DEATH: Laura Buchanan, Colored, of Barnum, Fatally Shoots Herself, Overstudy Wrecked Her Health and She Thought Herself a Burden to Parents." The accompanying article reported that in Greeley, "She studied so hard that her health broke down, and that she was obliged to return home. Ever since she had brooded over her condition." I cannot imagine the intense grief that must have beset the Buchanans, especially at a time when there was a lack of understanding surrounding mental illness and suicide. I have thought often of the aftereffects on the survivors: the parents, siblings, and extended family in Colorado and Virginia. The Buchanans surely spent time trying to understand what could have gone so terribly wrong, and likely as a means of combating the stigma associated with suicide, they attributed Laura's death to her intense studies at the Colorado State Normal School, which had caused her to be emotionally taxed. All along they had not known that she never enrolled. Either Laura had kept her secret from the family, or they needed a way to explain the unexplainable: the loss of their beloved Laura to suicide.

However, while Laura laid dying in the hospital, Denver's *Rocky Mountain News* covered the story on February 18 with surprisingly blunt honesty. The headline read, "COLOR DISCRIMINATION DROVE A GIRL TO SUICIDE." The article states: "Laura Buchanan is intelligent and well educated. She had hoped to become a schoolteacher, but found that on account of her color she had little prospect of obtaining a position. Her mother wanted her to go out and work as a domestic, but this she would not do." I was surprised that a White-owned and operated newspaper in 1899 would be so forthright in declaring that the cause of her suicide was racial inequality in employment. I was also struck by the tension between Laura's ambition to teach and Sarah's efforts to soften the disappointments Laura was experiencing. Sarah's solution was to suggest that she pursue domestic work, as many of her contemporaries had done. But Laura rejected this pathway, and while she was as qualified to teach as her White contemporaries, her race was an intractable obstacle to employment; the resulting despondency and depression must have played a significant role in her suicide. Sadly, Laura's journey was over. Her life ended.

While the *Denver Republican* article addressed her being overburdened by schoolwork, her suicide note was silent on this point. It is not addressed to anyone and includes no specific messages or references to any family member. She was clearly not ambivalent about committing suicide and took full responsibility for her actions. She chose a method that was unusual among women in the nineteenth century and remains the least chosen method of suicide by women in the early twenty-first century: a gun. Yet the note suggests a sense of loneliness, of not feeling part of the world, and just maybe not being able to achieve her ambition to be a teacher, even though she tried: "It seems strange that in this great, large world there can be no place found for me; I've tried to do what I could; more than that is impossible."

French sociologist David Émile Durkheim's seminal work *Le Suicide*, published in 1897, two years prior to Laura's death, addresses a type of suicide he describes as "egoistic suicide," which reflects an individual's inability to integrate into society—leading to a sense that life is meaningless, which in turn leads to apathy, melancholy, and depression.[21] Could this be applied to Laura's suicide?

On that fatal day her sisters, Edith, Hannah, Lucile, and Nellie, were at school; her brother, Fenton, was working in town as a day laborer; her father, James, was working in the barn; and her mother, Sarah, was at the home of Calvin T. Ward, a neighbor and friend, doing her washing where water was accessible. According to the newspaper account, Laura was alone in the house. She climbed the stairs to the room she shared with some of her sisters, laid down on her cot, and fired a .45-caliber bullet through her left breast. No one heard the shot. The *Republican* reported that when James entered the house about a half hour later, "He heard moans and murmuring upstairs, where he found his daughter lying in a pool of blood on the floor. Her hands were clasped tightly across her left breast and firmly held the weapon. She had gone into his trunk where she knew that he kept his revolver and shot herself." She was barely alive when he rushed her to the Arapahoe County Hospital on Sixth Avenue, between Evans and South Fourteenth Streets. The coroner, Robert P. Rollins, wrote in his 1899 Death Book that twenty-one-year-old Laura Buchanan died on February 19, almost two days later, as a result of suicide from a gunshot wound. Her body was turned over to the I. N. Rollins and Son Mortuary at 1531 Champa Street and was buried on Tuesday, February 21, 1899, in the section of Fairmount Cemetery in Denver that traditionally interred Whites.

Coping with Laura's death was particularly painful for the family. With front-page coverage by a local newspaper known for sensational reporting, their life became a spectacle. More salient for Lucile, Laura died when Lucile was only fifteen years old. Over the years she saved the only known photograph of herself, Laura, and Fenton, taken in or about 1885. Lucile's ultimate choice, decades later, to be buried next to Laura and not near her parents might indicate how long her bereavement process took, since this final action may have been her only way to bring closure to the horrific loss of her sister.

CHANGE IS ABOUT TO HAPPEN

At the turn of the twentieth century, the frontier life Lucile was born in to was rapidly changing. As a fifteen-year-old, she began to witness major inventions and innovations that were beginning to impact the way her family worked, played, and lived. Because her father was earning a good income as a teamster and street commissioner in Barnum in the 1890s, her family had an edge when it came to adopting the technological benefits of the new century. The family's home transitioned from gaslights to electric lights, extending the daylight hours and making it much easier for the children to do their schoolwork. By 1910, Barnum had been annexed by the City of Denver, and water became less of a problem. James closed off the outdoor privy in the side yard and converted a bedroom on the second floor into a bathroom with the addition of a tub, sink, and toilet. In 1900 the Denver City Tramway Company converted its cable cars to electricity and extended street-car service to Barnum, with at least four stops within walking distance of the Buchanans' home.

Although transportation may have been easier with the extended streetcar service, the new transportation technology that most fascinated the Buchanan children were the Brass-era cars (horseless carriages) manufactured between 1906 and 1915 at the Colburn Automobile Company at Fifteenth Street and Colfax Avenue.[22] While the children may have dreamt of their father upgrading to this new means of transportation, cars were still not competitive with horses. James did not bend to pressure and continued to depend upon his team of horses and wagon for their livelihood. After all, while in 1910 Denver had twenty-one car dealerships, it still maintained sixty-seven blacksmiths.

Following the birth of Lucile, Sarah and James welcomed their second Denver-born daughter, Sadie Bishop, on January 6, 1888. Sadie would graduate from Villa Park High School. Like her mother and several of her sisters, she worked as a housekeeper for a private family. In the late 1800s and early 1900s occupations such as butlers, coachmen, barbers, hairdressers, dressmakers, hotel cooks/chefs, waiters, and servants/housekeepers (in upscale homes) were considered professional.

On December 22, 1908, Sadie married twenty-three-year-old Roy Charles Reed, a hotel cook from Missouri, in Ogden, Utah. Within a few months of their marriage, the couple moved to 310 Brigham Street (now South Temple Street) in Salt Lake City, Utah, where they joined approximately 588 Blacks who were also working and living in the city. Roy secured a position as a hotel cook, and Sadie continued to work as a housekeeper for a private family.

By the time the 1910 US Census was taken, Salt Lake's Black population had almost doubled, to 1,144. But moving to Utah did not shelter them from the discriminatory challenges Blacks continued to face forty-three years after the abolishment of slavery. As a result, Blacks in Utah took a proactive role in creating their own public sphere by duplicating what Blacks had created throughout the United States: establishing churches, fraternal organizations, women's clubs, and newspapers;[23] creating political organizations; celebrating significant historical events (e.g., Emancipation Day); and taking on the community's recreational needs by building a community center and establishing semi-professional baseball teams.[24] While they stayed in Salt Lake City for several years, it was just a stopping-off point on their way to their final destination, California. The 1920 Census shows Sadie and Roy living at 1549½ Leavenworth Street in San Francisco, California, where they both worked as hotel cooks.[25]

Roy died in 1929 at the start of the Great Depression, and, according to the 1930 Census, forty-six-year-old Sadie moved to 1845 Scott Street in the Lower Pacific Heights District of San Francisco.[26] She lived in a community that in many ways mirrored the multiethnic flavor of Barnum, Colorado, while working as a "receiving clerk" at a hotel. In 1936 Sadie took a position as a matron for O'Conner, Moffatt and Company, a department store at Stockton and O'Farrell Streets, while still living on Scott Street. To assist her with the $32 a month rent, Sadie took in Swedish-born Hanna Olsson, who worked as a servant for a private family, as a lodger. On February 10, 1967, Sadie, now living in Riverside, California, went with her sister Nellie to San Diego's historic Mount Hope Cemetery, where her brother-in-law was interred, and bought a burial plot for $120. Two years later, on March 14, 1969, Sadie died at age eighty-one and was buried in the plot she had purchased.

Denverites had much to celebrate on Friday, July 4, 1890. Red, white, and blue buntings draped every building downtown as throngs of residents gathered to witness the Freemasons lay the cornerstone for Colorado's State Capitol. While the celebration was in full swing, Sarah went into labor and gave birth to Edith Mae. A sister, Nellie Evelyn, born on January 19, 1893, followed her. They grew up together, learning the same values, reading some of the same books, attending classes with the same teachers, working around the house, and learning their mother's culinary skills. As members of the Smart Set Clubs, they planned and executed holiday events and excursions all over the state. They learned to shoot and cared for the horses and the family dog, and they had the same independence and risk-taking streak as their older siblings.

But when twenty-two-year-old Edith and twenty-year-old Nellie decided to strike out on their own in 1913, there were limits to their risk taking, especially since Denver still had a shady side—prostitution, opium dens, and gambling establishments. To give themselves some room to explore and to begin their journey into Denver's labor market, they moved into the Five Points area, taking up residence at 1018 Twenty-fourth Avenue with their oldest sister, Hattie, her husband, Elias (who was often on the road as a Pullman porter), and their six-year-old niece, Marjorie Carol. Hattie offered them hope and sanctuary.

While living in Denver, Edith was able to secure employment at the Brevort Hotel at 1651 California Street. Similarly, Nellie found work at the Hotel Luxor at 1445 California. The hotels were about a two-minute walk from each other. Furthermore, in 1913 Nellie apparently had an air of confidence as she left home. It could have been a result of the gun she packed, a .32 Smith and Wesson five-bullet revolver with a pearl handle, which she took with her wherever she went in Denver and, later, in California.[27] Within a year of Edith and Nellie's venture into Denver

FIGURE 8.6. *Nellie Buchanan, ca. 1915. Buchanan Archives.*

in 1913, they were back at the family home on Raleigh Street, where they remained until each of them married.

Nellie was the first to marry. She had fallen in love with a former Missourian, William Robert Lenoir. Born on July 13, 1888, in Centralia, Missouri, he had migrated to Denver in 1908 with his parents, John and Mary Lenoir; his younger brothers Clay, Frank, and Leon; and his sister, Pearl. Nellie and William chose to marry on Valentine's Day, February 14, 1917, at the office of the County Clerk of Arapahoe County. Following their marriage, the couple lived in the Five Points neighborhood at 3020 Welton Street with William's father and two of his younger brothers. During the next several years they moved to various homes on Glenarm Place and Downing, Franklin, and Ogden Streets, each time living with one or more of William's siblings. William had a steady job as a porter at the Broadhurst-Young Shoe Company at 1616 Champa Street, a position he would maintain for about twenty years. A little less than four months after the wedding, the United States entered World War I, and on June 5, 1917, William registered for the draft. He was not deployed.

In the first years of their marriage, Nellie went back to work at the Hotel Luxor as a maid. In 1925 her sister Hattie went from head of kitchen to manager at Baur's Restaurant and hired Nellie as a cook, a position she maintained throughout the Depression. In the late 1930s Nellie and William left Denver for San Diego, California. Soon thereafter, William's health began to deteriorate, and he died at home on July 17, 1948. His luxurious granite headstone, which towers above those around him, reads, "At Rest My Baby." Nellie remained in California. She died on November 30, 1976, in San Diego at age eighty-three and is buried near her husband and her sister Sadie. The couple had no children.

Just ten days after Nellie's marriage, on February 27, 1917, Edith married twenty-six-year-old Charles H. Davis, a car cleaner who worked for the railroads and had migrated with his family from Missouri about six years earlier. The Rev. David E. Over of Zion Baptist Church performed the ceremony, with Hattie and their mother serving as witnesses. After living in a series of rental properties in the Five Points neighborhood, Edith bought a home at 2430 Franklin Street, which in 1930 was valued at $2,500. While Edith wore one mask in public as part of the growing Black middle class, her personal life was filled with pain and sorrow as she struggled with intimate-partner violence. As the survivor of a twenty-four-year abusive relationship, Edith filed for divorce on January 31, 1941—almost a year after Lucile had filed for divorce on similar grounds.

The divorce decree accused Charles of "causing the plaintiff to suffer great mental agony and distress, her health to become impaired and endangered . . . that the defendant has repeatedly cursed and abused the plaintiff, called her opprobrious and disrespectful names, and often to violently beat her; has often and habitually remained away from home for days at a time, spending his money at gambling games and in drinking parties with other men and women."[28] Edith ended her statement to the court by stating that she feared for her safety. The divorce was granted on December 20, 1941. She died childless on November 4, 1959, and is buried with her family at Fairmount Cemetery in Denver.

STANDING HER GROUND

Claribel Audra, Lucile's youngest sister, was born in Denver on March 12, 1899. Among Sarah and James's children, Claribel was most adept at pushing boundaries and taking on insurmountable challenges. In looking at her life, I was never sure whether the research on birth order (her being the last born) may have affected her personality when it came to risk taking. In a brazen move, the *Colorado Statesman* headline "Girl Captures Burglar" on November 2, 1912, reported that thirteen-year-old "Claribel was at home alone on Tuesday, October 29, 1912, when she found herself looking into the muzzle of a large revolver held by an unknown [White] man. He told her to throw her hands up, which she did. She thought for a moment and in a true western spirit, she quickly kicked the gun from his hand and gaining possession of it, she ordered the man to walk two blocks to the nearest phone, where she called the police." The article further states that Claribel is "about the best colored girl athlete we have and quite a favorite in the younger circles." The man was arrested and identified as Samuel Sloan of Meeker, Colorado.[29]

While the family's Bible records her first name as Clara and her middle name as Belle, she chose a different spelling, made her first and middle name one, added a different middle name, and became known as "Claribel Audra." She was the only daughter to marry before her high school graduation, at eighteen years of age. This first marriage was to Denver-born George Bowman Parker, a former miner from a well-respected Denver mining family. On May 13, 1913, Justice of the Peace Clifford W. Mills performed the marriage ceremony at the Denver Court House. Two of George's former silver mining buddies, William E. Sanderlin and Frank E. Moody, clerk of the Denver Court House, served as witnesses. The couple had one daughter, Evelyn Lucile Parker, born on July 25, 1914.

Given the ongoing changes in international finance, the repeal of the Sherman Silver Act, and the Panic of 1893, which greatly affected the mining industry, George moved on to hold a series of odd jobs—including laborer and porter—until his marriage, when he landed a job as a molder at the Mountain Iron Works in Denver. In July 1918 the *Colorado Statesman* ran a bulletin stating that "George Parker, only colored iron molder in Colorado, and accredited one of the best in the Rocky Mountain region, will be a very valuable asset to Uncle Sam's expeditious action in his shipping output."[30]

FIGURE 8.7. *Claribel and daughter Evelyn, ca. 1915. Buchanan Archives.*

George and Claribel's marriage lasted about five years. By 1920 the twenty-three-year-old Claribel was back home with her sixty-three-year-old mother, thirty-nine-year-old brother, and her five-year-old daughter, Evelyn. She would spend the next seven years living at the family's home while she worked as a waitress or cook at various Denver establishments.

FIGURE 8.8. *Hattie McDaniel (1893–1952) at her home in Los Angeles, ca. 1949. Buchanan Archives.*

Like her sisters Sadie and Nellie before her, Claribel migrated to California in the late 1920s, making Los Angeles her home. Her circle of friends included two of Hollywood's famous Black radio, film, and television stars—Hattie McDaniel, the first Black performer to earn an Oscar in 1940 (for her role as Mammy in *Gone with the Wind*), who had lived in Denver from 1900 to the 1910s, and film and television

141

actress Louise Beavers, who was one of the first Black actors to star in a television sitcom, *Beulah*.

Louise and Claribel's friendship began when a mutual friend introduced them at a dance. Shortly thereafter, Claribel and her daughter, Evelyn, moved in with Louise and her mother, Ernestine Beavers, at their home at 914 Forth-ninth Place in Los Angeles. On May 21–22, 1928, Louise performed with an all-women's minstrel group called Lady Minstrels at the Philharmonic Auditorium at 427 West Fifth Street. Claribel also appeared in the same production, performing with "Pete" (apparently a pet name for Beavers). According to a clipping from a newspaper article written by Claribel, she states, "As a result of her excellent performance, Miss Louise Beavers was offered a movie contract. And thus began her illustrious career as a film star."[31]

On July 10, 1934, thirty-six-year-old Claribel married thirty-eight-year-old Missouri-born John Ottoway Henley, a medical doctor with a practice in Kansas City. The couple met in Los Angeles sometime around 1931. This was John's third marriage and Claribel's second. The Black press in Los Angeles, Denver, and Kansas City covered the multiple engagement parties and their marriage ceremony. From all the fanfare and excitement (across three states) leading up to the wedding date, the marriage seemed all but ordained by heaven.

The July 11 morning edition of the *Call* covered the Kansas City wedding ceremony at the parsonage of the Rev. William Frank Taylor, one of two founding members of the nine-year-old Metropolitan Spiritual Church of Christ. Almost immediately, Claribel became suspicious that something was wrong with her marriage. Having been raised in Denver in a more traditional Baptist church, she may not have been aware that the Metropolitan Spiritual Church of Christ was "founded on a Four-Square Ministry of Teaching, Preaching, Healing and Prophecy and was noted for its unusual order of service."[32] The church was firmly wedded to a Black Spiritual movement noted in its formative years for not only incorporating elements of "Black Protestantism but also Roman Catholicism, and Voodoo or at least its diluted magical form, hoodoo . . . other elements some Black Spiritual churches incorporated were Islam, Judaism, New Thought, and astrology."[33] As a result, she was shocked by the marriage ceremony, which according to her consisted of Rev. Taylor "only reading the 23rd Psalm." She voiced her concerns, and John agreed to have another ceremony on July 23 at the home of Rev. A. L. Reynolds Sr. of Centennial M. E. Church. Two weeks after the ceremony she contacted her pastor, informing him that she had made a "horrible mistake." In early June 1935, a little less than a year following her well-publicized wedding, Claribel left Kansas City and headed to Dubois, Wyoming, where she had secured

FIGURE 8.9. *Claribel (left), Leroy Moore (Beaver's husband), Unknown male, and Louise Beavers, at the Derby Club Event, ca. 1955. Courtesy Burnis McCloud.*

a position as the chef at the Diamond C Ranch. Before leaving Kansas City, an article appeared in the *Call* informing John that after she left town, he could file for divorce on grounds of desertion, a solution to which he apparently agreed. The article further notes that "Mrs. Henley, a member of the prominent Buchanan family in Denver . . . lived under the most pitiable circumstances" and "neither has the time nor funds to fight the infamous lies," which is not clarified in any of Claribel's writings.

Claribel soon returned to Denver, got back to work, and started a new life. On September 15, 1938, she married forty-seven-year-old George Earl Perkins, who had migrated to Denver from Iowa in 1934. The couple lived at 2037 Franklin Street with her twenty-four-year-old daughter Evelyn and Sanford, George's twenty-three-year-old son from a previous marriage. As part of Denver's Black middle class, Claribel continued to be covered in the society page of the *Colorado Statesman*, with her lavish dancing parties at venues such as Denver's Coronado Club (aka Denver Turnverein), and at the Beverly Gardens, or having film and television actress Louise Beavers as a house guest in May 1955.[34]

While Claribel took her social standing seriously, she was also committed to racial equality. In the 1940s Claribel became a member of Denver's Committee of Racial Equality (CORE), which was established in 1942.[35] In 1945 she was listed as the program chair for a reception CORE was hosting for famed contralto Marion Anderson at St. John's Parish House on Sunday, January 21, the day before Anderson's captivating performance at Municipal Auditorium.

Claribel, no stranger to using the popular press to air grievances, began confronting issues of racial misunderstandings through the *Denver Post* in its letter to the editor column, the Open Forum. For example, on June 5, 1950, under the heading "Negroes Ask Fairness," she responded to a letter to the editor written by H. T. Bartlett of Broomfield under the heading "The Negro and Africa." Bartlett's major argument was that "Disgruntled American Negroes" should be repatriated to Africa to share in its benefits and at the same time help other members of their race.[36] In her retort Claribel asserted that "Negro citizens are interested in fuller equal opportunities" and "America is the American Negro's native land and that American Negroes were born here, have contributed towards American economic and cultural development and that their first loyalty is to the United States." Adding that since other European ethnic groups "claim America as their country, interest themselves in American developments, American Negroes, as other races, speak American, have American ideals and customs, so why should they wish to return to a foreign land from whose customs and languages they have been removed for generations." She signed the letter "MRS. CLARIBEL A. PERKINS (a Native daughter)."[37]

In a subsequent letter dated July 21, 1950,[38] Claribel responded to two previous letters to the editor. One was written by Thomas C. Westfall, titled "Negro Beats Handicaps," in which he stated that "despite prejudice, persecution, intolerance, and misunderstanding the Negro has demonstrated his ability to function as a free citizen in a free land . . . and has contributed richly to all phases of our culture for many, many years." While she lauded Westfall for his insights, she took to task a letter written by Terence C. Byrnes titled "Mann Tangled Up." Mann in this case was Earl Mann, Colorado's second Black state representative, who had contributed to passing the open-occupancy bill that aided Blacks in Denver with housing opportunities. In the same letter she responded to Byrnes by asserting that racism is real for Blacks, and even though Whites have all the advantages, not all of them are "free" since many are "chained to that insufferable monster Racial Prejudice." She then challenged those who referred to Mann's philosophy as "peculiar" and "curious," reminding them that "there is a tendency of uninformed persons to term 'curious' things that they do not wish to understand." She chastised Byrnes, who suggested that Blacks needed to return to Booker T. Washington's philosophy, with a warning that "all things purely social can be considered separate is unthinkable in our present times. America and Americans can no longer afford to think, act or exist separately, socially or any other way. Aviation and science have dissolved all boundaries. We are now living in a world community and as such it is impossible to set up social barriers for any group of individuals and continue to exist according to Mr. Washington's 'Separate as the fingers, yet one as the hand.'" Claribel died on July 9, 1974, and is interred with her natal family at Fairmount Cemetery.

SOLID AS A ROCK

Fenton Mercer, the Buchanans' only male child, was born in Prince William County, Virginia, on July 26, 1880. Like many of his sisters, Fenton altered his birth name by changing his middle name from Mercer to Morris. He also attended Villa Park High School but earned only one year of high school credit before venturing into the labor force. As a child, he worked side by side with his father, absorbing his father's skills with horses, his work ethic, and his entrepreneurial outlook. Fenton always worked. In 1899 he struck out on his own, working as a laborer for Ward Auction Company, owned by Barnum resident and family friend Calvin T. Ward. The following year Fenton took on a variety of odd jobs, including as a waiter for the Overland Park Club, a day laborer, and a gardener. Nonetheless, his main occupation remained that of a teamster. In 1903 he joined the International Brotherhood of Teamsters and remained an active member until the mid-1940s.[39]

In 1918 Denver's City and County Highway Department hired him as a teamster. By now, technological advances were such that motorized trucks were replacing horse-drawn wagons for construction, repair, and maintenance of roads,

FIGURE 8.10. *Fenton Buchanan, ca. 1940s. Buchanan Archives.*

highways, viaducts, and bridges. As a modern-day teamster, Fenton seems to have fit nicely into the transportation revolution, which defined the life of a teamster. Even with a steady job, he sustained the occupation and entrepreneurial instinct he had learned from his father, maintaining the horses, a plow, and a wagon in the family's barn on Stuart Street to be used in his second job digging basements for new homeowners.

Of all the Buchanan children, he seemed to have most strongly internalized the frontier spirit. He lived a frugal and self-sufficient life, reminiscent of his family's early days in Barnum. When his sister Hannah wrote him a letter from Atlanta in 1921, she pointed out, "You certainly have vegetables enough, along with the chickens, eggs and cow; you all have very little to buy, so you can afford to stay in [in] bad weather." Indeed, Fenton grew beans, tomatoes, squash, turnips, onions, carrots, cabbage, and cucumbers, as well as two fields of corn, potatoes, watermelon, and cantaloupe. He also raised hogs and geese. Hannah, who remained single and childless, understood Fenton's paternal instincts and reminded him: "Nobody knows what is inside of you until you are put to it. You are an ideal father. You really ought to have a house full of kids so that you might have occasion to show every day the stuff of which you are made."[40]

As Lucile and several of her sisters moved away from Colorado, Fenton had the responsibility for maintaining the family's home, which he lived in most of his life. Donna Teviotdale, who was born in 1929 and lived on Stuart Street at the back of the Buchanans' home, recalls: "He lived by himself. Occasionally, two sisters [Edith and Claribel] visited him. He told me that he came to Colorado with his parents in a wagon. We were always so taken [a]back as to how clean he kept the barn. It was so clean you could eat off the floor; everything was clean and shiny, and the linoleum in the kitchen sparkled." But there was more to Fenton than keeping a clean house. Donna recalls the generosity of this kind man:

It was a hard time [the Depression] and he had apple trees in his yard and would always give bushels of apples to my family—my mom and dad and my five sisters. My mom was always grateful. I even think he supplied apples to a woman who had at least eight children down the street from where we lived. That act of kindness helped so much. As I got older my sister and I would pick cherries to sell and we'd always stop at Buck's place. And he'd always buy them from us. Buck was a nice old gentleman. Very kind. I must say the family did keep to themselves. I was never all over the house. Just in the kitchen.[41]

The idea of "keeping to themselves" must be understood on several levels. Fenton was a single Black male, middle class by all standards, living in a large home by himself in a predominantly White neighborhood. He appeared prosperous. As part of the first generation born after slavery, he was acutely aware of the unstated but clear boundaries between him and his White neighbors.

Although Fenton could not tell me his story, he was thought of fondly by his Barnum neighbors and was very much a part of the Black landscape in Denver. Fenton retired from the highway department in 1945. He then took a job as a night watchman (something many of his contemporaries did), at which he worked for an additional five years. He was eighty-three when he succumbed to a heart attack on August 26, 1963, while working in the garden of the family home he shared with Lucile. Sisters Sadie and Nellie, both widows, came in from Los Angeles, where they had been living together, to attend the funeral. The youngest sister, Claribel, also widowed, lived in Denver.

Lucile, who was named the executrix of Fenton's estate, took charge of the funeral details and arrangements. She arranged for the Rev. Wendel T. Liggins of Zion Baptist Church to deliver the eulogy, not knowing that in twenty-one years he would be called upon to do the same for her. At Lucile's request, Fenton's open casket was covered with a blanket of white roses and placed under an apple tree in the garden that had brought him so much joy and comfort. One of Lucile's friends from Chicago wrote to her:

The death of your only brother was really picturesque lying there in the garden under that apple tree! Sure, the job of administrating and clearing earthly leavings is a most difficult problem—you are the one who can do it with ease and fairness. Just put your mental ability to it and say to yourself, "This cross is heavy but I'll stand up with it."

Another letter Lucile received was from classmates Mary and Margaret Gavin, first-generation Irish who lived within walking distance of the Buchanans.

Dear Lucy,

A few days ago, I was glancing over an old paper and came across an article announcing your brother Fenton's death. It brought to mind our school days when we all were in High School [Villa Park] together. We mentioned the names of so many of our schoolmates and you and Fenton were kindly remembered. We want to extend to you and your sisters our sincere sympathy.

Mae [Mary] and Margaret Gavin

Many in the Barnum community, where Fenton had lived for seventy-two years, came to pay homage, as did many Denverites. Attendance at his funeral cut across racial, ethnic, and class lines, with his pallbearers including the famed jazz conductor and musician George Morrison, retired firefighter Logan Brown, and a Barnum neighbor and friend Herman Dick, who would later take on the role of Lucile's driver/aide as she aged. Fenton was laid to rest near his parents and his sister Hannah who, after their mother's death in 1921, had written to him saying, "I know you want to meet our mother someday. I am praying for you and we have a savior who is pleading for us all. Lovingly, Sister Hannah."[42]

EXTENDING THE HORIZONS

Lucile, her sisters, and her brother were among the first generation of Blacks to reach adulthood after slavery and to embrace education as both a civil rights strategy and a means to economic success. At the same time, they adopted their parents' aspiration and desire for a better life and the willingness to excel through hard work, perseverance, and determination. They also represented a small but growing Black middle class who did not know what it was to be poor and illiterate and were not bound by the forced deference that governed their parents' generation. They were the "elites" of the race and as such had certain expectations placed on them regarding articulating a positive Black identity galvanized by Du Bois's ideology of racial uplift and an ethos of self-help.

Fenton followed his father's occupation as a teamster and managed to maintain a level of success as the country transitioned from horsepower to motorized vehicles. When he wasn't working at his primary job, he used his horse-drawn freight wagon to haul rocks and dirt from excavations as a secondary income. As for Lucile and her sisters, they carved multiple distinct paths as they took on positions that were not only unique but also brazen for women in the 1890s and early 1900s. Some carved out careers in teaching (Hannah and Lucile) and management (Hattie and Sadie), while others found work where women were typically employed, in the food and hotel service industries (Claribel, Edith, and Nellie).

Clearly, Lucile and most of her sisters were not afraid to take on new challenges and territories as they left Denver and pushed further west, living in cities such as Los Angeles, Salt Lake City, and San Francisco, or in the urban North in the south side of Chicago. They also ventured south into Jim Crow country, living in Atlanta, Hot Springs, Jacksonville, Little Rock, and St. Louis (Hannah and Lucile). They appear to have continually pushed and redefined their role as women through their lived practices, with their family duties negotiated and renegotiated time and time again. Sometimes they were the heads of household (Lucile and Hannah), other times the primary wage earners (as in Edith's case, who purchased the house in which she and her husband, Charles, lived), and other times co-providers (Claribel, Edith, Nellie, and Sadie). But what seemed to matter most was a strong determination and belief in the promises that they could rise in status and be able to gain equality.

One substantial advantage Colorado offered was that the state did not have the culture of violent racism that was prevalent in the South.[43] Certainly, there were racial boundaries—institutional, housing, colorism—but despite these hurdles, the Buchanans endured. It is therefore likely that most of Sarah and James's children were self-confident, independent in their thinking, and unabashed risk takers. While slavery had a deleterious effect on the Black family, as W.E.B. Du Bois points out in his studies of Black families in Philadelphia,[44] the system of slavery in which James and Sarah survived in Northern Virginia (two-parent households and a close-knit slave community) may have helped bring stability to their lives, which they were able to pass on to their children and grandchildren. An added factor is that they migrated to the West, where they and their children had access to schooling and more economic and political opportunities. I am reminded of James's election as Barnum's street commissioner over a White competitor and the family's first action when they arrived in Denver, buying land to build a home amidst the brashness and fertility of nature in the most remote part of Barnum.

Clearly, Lucile's parents laid the groundwork for their children to follow. And while Laura's untimely death hit hard, they recovered. Living in Barnum, a predominantly White middle-class community, provided opportunity for them to execute their agency, take risks, and work across racial lines. Before the turn of the twentieth century, these two emancipated slaves were able to close the racial and wealth gap in Colorado, something their children observed keenly. And as their parents had before them, they, too, pushed boundaries, sometimes stumbling but always persevering.

9

School, Community, and Love Lost

The real life of the race is an enduring monument to the school teachers and educators of the race, who have demonstrated to the world the
fact that the pen is the most useful instrument of human progress.
— G. P. HAMILTON

No time to marry, no time to settle down; I'm a young
woman, and I ain't done runnin' around.
—BESSIE SMITH, "YOUNG WOMAN'S BLUES, 1927"

I slowly began to unravel Lucile's history in Arkansas by way of an inscription, "At
Ark. Baptist College, Lucile Berkeley Buchanan 1914," which she wrote in the book
Lucy Lescom's Poems, a collection of five poems written by the English romantic
poet William Wordsworth. While the inscription provided a date and a venue, it
did not mention what she might have been doing there.

Arkansas Baptist College (ABC), in Little Rock, was founded by the Colored
Baptists of the State of Arkansas in 1884 at their annual convention in Hot Springs,
with two primary objectives: to prepare young people for the ministry and to train
primary and secondary school teachers through a "Normal," or teacher education,
school.[1] Since Lucile earned her teaching credentials in 1905, I thought her relationship with ABC in 1914 might relate to teaching in the Normal Department.
Working at a Baptist institution was appropriate, as Lucile was a staunch Baptist
herself. Many of the people I interviewed recalled her saying, "It doesn't matter
what religion you are as long as you are a Baptist."

While in Arkansas she would begin to see her pathway as a teacher unfold
under the influence of Frederick Douglass and W.E.B. Du Bois who, despite
their differences, both preached the power of education as a weapon for Black

empowerment. Although Lucile was likely well-educated, the sheltered path she walked in Colorado did little to prepare her for the brutal reality of Jim Crow laws fully sanctioned in Arkansas. Ill-prepared or not, through her independence she would put the leadership of an entire school and its school board on notice. Her duties and priorities set, she decelerated the advances of a love interest, wanting to do things in her own time and accepting responsibility for her own decisions.

GOING BACKWARD, MOVING FORWARD

Verifying that Lucile had taught at ABC was challenging. In 2006, when I thought I had finally navigated the institutional maze, an ABC staff member told me a fire had destroyed all of the school's archives, and there were no copies anywhere. At this point ABC became a back-burner item until Sunday, January 27, 2008, when I found an online encyclopedia entry written by Johnny D. Jones, the new executive vice president and chief academic officer at ABC.[2] Jones had written a brief history of ABC. I imagined that with a name so similar to that of Lucile's husband, he would be receptive to my research. My hunch paid off. After some correspondence and several phone conversations, I arrived on April 7, 2008, to meet with him.

With a semester spent teaching at Howard University in Washington, DC, one of 101 Historically Black Colleges and Universities (HBCUs) in the United States, I knew to expect a heightened level of formality, in which deference and formal titles mattered. All interpersonal technicalities aside, the deprivation and neglect that beset this once prestigious institution surprised me.

As Jones and I walked across the campus, our first stop was the one-floor library building, which appeared slated for demolition. Shelves were removed and the walls were peeling. Jones told me that as a result of water damage, most of the books had been discarded long ago. Those that remained were piled haphazardly along a wall. The floor tiles were cracked where they were not pulled up entirely. Astonishingly, two students sat at one end of the room using long-outdated computers.

As noon approached, Jones invited me to lunch in the cafeteria. Students, staff, faculty, and administrators sat around tables according to their respective roles. Jones and I next went to the student union—a room about 20 feet long by 15 feet wide, decorated in ABC's black and purple school colors. The male students were dressed mostly in white T-shirts and jeans, except for the candidate running for president of the student government, who wore a gray suit and tie. His pride in ABC and in his own accomplishments shined bright as he spoke to me.

In the midst of the neglect, there were signs that under the new president, Dr. Fritz Hill, the only Baptist HBCU west of the Mississippi was returning to its past grandeur.[3] Much to my disappointment, though, Lucile was nowhere to be found. Of the three buildings with which Lucile might have had some engagement—the Boys' Dormitory, the Alumni Cottage/President's House, and the Main Building (which also served as the Girls' Dormitory)—only the Main Building, a two-story brick structure badly in need of repair, remained. I had certainly hit a stumbling block in writing Lucile's narrative in Little Rock, especially in trying to ascertain what factors may have led her there.

Still, my visit to Little Rock was not for naught. Under the guidance of Linda McDowell, the coordinator of African American History at the Arkansas History Commission & State Archives, I found some details of Lucile's life. Lucile was not in Little Rock after all in 1914. I found her listed in the Hot Springs City Directories in 1912 and 1915, teaching at Langston High School, the only Black high school in the city and one of five public high schools for Black youth in Arkansas. Both directories listed the basic information considered standard at the time: "Buchanan Lucile B (c) tchr Langston School, b 328 E Grand av.,"[4] along with her name, the fact that she was Colored and a teacher, the school she taught at, and the address where she lived.

Langston High School began life as the School Street School in 1903. In 1908 it was renamed the Langston School after John Mercer Langston (1829–97), an educator, diplomat, and attorney and the first African American elected to the US Congress from Virginia. Misfortune hit in March 1905, when a devastating fire destroyed the school along with twenty-five blocks of the southern section of town. The school was rebuilt at a cost of $12,500, with the Black community asked to contribute $1,500. The new school—a small, two-story, red brick building with about eight classrooms on each floor—opened on School Street (today Rugg Street) in autumn of 1906, with Frank Cornelius Long as principal.[5] To accommodate the growing school-age population, the school board decided that a grade would be added each year until the school served twelve grades. By that time course offerings included Latin, English, science, history, and mathematics; and graduates were gaining entrance to top colleges.[6] In 1910 Langston graduated its first high school class, composed of ten students.[7]

LANDING ON HER FEET

By the time Lucile arrived in Hot Springs, the town boasted national notoriety for its "healing" thermal waters, earning federal recognition in 1832 as "the National

Spa" and "the National Sanitarium." Her arrival coincided with the Progressive Movement's debut in Arkansas. Lucile, a child of this movement, understood its multifaceted reform ideology. But it was as new to Arkansas as she was. While some historians, such as C. Vann Woodward, noted that the Progressive Movement, in fact, benefited White men and failed to address the fundamental problems of the Black community,[8] the evidence suggests that Blacks were not passive victims of white supremacy but rather worked to ameliorate the barriers to progress by creating parallel institutions run by and for Blacks. As Jimmie Franklin wrote, "Much like other progressives, they [Blacks] sought a better life free of debilitating ills and political proscriptions. They bequeathed to the country a legacy of self-help that remains with us as America still desperately struggles for a solution to its most difficult social problem."[9]

Like most Black progressives, Lucile came from a middle-class background with traditional Republican roots, an urban outlook, a greater sense of community steeped in service, and a strong determination to achieve based on the racial uplift ideology of two powerful race shapers, Booker T. Washington and W.E.B. Du Bois. However, as a woman of the new century, Lucile was the product of two competing ideologies—traditional Victorian middle-class values, which blended gender progressivism (witnessing her older sisters pursue careers and entrepreneurial activities), and the values of the frontier, which idealized self-sufficiency, confidence, hard work, and risk taking. Educating young Blacks was her gateway to affecting change and would be a catalyst for Black progress.

Upon her arrival in Hot Springs, Lucile took up residence at the home of Dr. James Webb Curtis, a prominent Black physician,[10] his wife, Alice May, and their three daughters at 328 East Grand Avenue. Grand Avenue, combined with Malvern and Central Avenues, formed the city's cosmopolitan hub where Whites and Blacks (within the confines of Jim Crow laws) congregated for the curative mineral waters and the cultural and economic pleasures of resort town life.

For several years, all I had was "At Arkansas Baptist College, 1914" written inside the cover of a book over 100 years ago. While my visit to ABC opened up Hot Springs, the book kept reminding me that she indeed had been there—but why? For three years my search continued, but to no avail. Then in 2012, Ancestry.com made available all US city directories (with the exception of Alaska) from 1821 to 1989, which added over 1 billion items to its database. I entered "Lucile B. Buchanan, Arkansas, USA," and to my delight, three hits returned. Of the three, two gave me information I already had—her teaching at Langston High School in Hot Springs in 1912 and 1915—but one was new, showing that Lucile's relationship with educating the young people of Arkansas began in 1907, in Little Rock. Two years after her teaching obligations in Colorado ended, twenty-three-year-old Lucile traveled to Little Rock to assume a position as a teacher in the Normal Department at ABC. With this new information, I began to understand the informal community network of support she had in Hot Springs almost five years later.

Lucile's devotion to education appears to have been acknowledged and supported by those around her. One person who recognized her contributions was the Rev. Joseph Albert Booker, who served as president and treasurer of ABC from 1887 to 1926. In 1911 G. P. Hamilton, the principal of Kortrecht High School in Memphis, Tennessee, referred to Booker as "the most influential educator of the race in the State of Arkansas."[11] Then there was the Rev. Elias Camp Morris, president of the National Baptist Convention, one of the most recognized religious leaders not only in Arkansas but in the nation. As a founding member of ABC and a member of the board of trustees, he would have had to have approved Lucile's hiring. But the connection between the two went deeper. She taught his son, Elias A. Morris, a member of the 1907 graduating class, who, in addition, had an interest in the Silver Wave Mining Company in Park County, Colorado. Thus, the father would have been familiar with her home community. Lucile, a devoted Baptist and teacher, quickly made a name for herself among leaders of the Baptist and education communities. Therefore, Booker, Morris, or both likely had a hand in helping Lucile secure employment and find suitable accommodations in Hot Springs.

James Webb Curtis commanded enormous respect in Hot Springs, and the connection would have helped Lucile find her place in the community. His pedigree went back to his father, Alexander H. Curtis, who was born a slave and later became a merchant and served six years in the Alabama State Senate. James Webb Curtis earned national recognition of his own when Booker T. Washington profiled him in his book *A New Negro for a New Century*, published in 1900.[12] His academic and professional credentials made him a local hero and provided Lucile with the opportunity to rub shoulders with some of the leading citizens straddling the racial divide in Hot Springs.

Over time, Lucile and the Curtis's oldest daughter, Mabel, became friends. Born in May 1884, slightly a month before Lucile, Mabel also taught public school. In addition, Curtis's wife originated from Richmond, Virginia, and thus provided Lucile with a connection to her parents' home state. The Curtises, like Lucile, were deeply religious and members of the Roanoke Baptist Church in Hot Springs, making it likely that Lucile attended there as well.

There were other similarities. Both families rose up through the ranks of the Black middle class in which membership is determined by certain characteristics including "color, family background, occupation, income, property, urban or rural residence, religious affiliation and education."[13] Historian Fon Louise Gordon sums up the Black middle class as "primarily urban and less dependent on Whites for their livelihood, and therefore . . . more insulated from the more humiliating and degrading aspects of Jim Crow." They were dedicated to the "elevation and uplift of the race" ideology within the Black community and "were accorded respect and deference"; as such, they set the standards for "material success, morality, behavior and etiquette, leadership and organizational skills, church and secular benevolence, language proficiency, and marital stability" to which the rest of the Black community aspired.[14]

Despite the benefits engendered by her status within the Black community, the Curtises' support for Lucile was crucial since she still had to contend with the Jim Crowism she had first experienced in Little Rock five years earlier—for example, Arkansas's 1903 Streetcar Segregation Act, which assigned Black and White passengers to separate but equal sections of streetcars. In both cities, Lucile lived and worked largely within the confines of the Black community, which afforded her some level of protection in a world of de jure segregation. In Hot Springs, she lived near a thriving Black business district along a three-block strip off Bathhouse Row.[15] On Malvern Avenue between Church and Garden Streets, there were several grocery stores, a furniture store, a realty and employment agency, barbershops, hotels, lawyers, shoemakers, tailors and dressmakers, butchers, restaurants and saloons, dry cleaners, boardinghouses, churches, the office of the Black weekly newspaper the *Arkansas Review*, two chiropodists (today podiatrist), and four physicians, including physician and surgeon James Webb Curtis.

RACE AND SCHOOLING

When Lucile arrived in Hot Springs, she faced her first job teaching in a public school at a time when the state-mandated segregation education system, enforced with the passage of Act 52 of 1868, fostered indifference toward Black children. This institutionalized indifference meant a lack of adequate teaching materials, lower salaries for Black teachers, inequalities in state appropriations for Black public schools, limited provisions for high school education, ill-prepared teachers, inferior facilities, and inadequate classroom space, leading to overcrowding. Public school teachers in Arkansas's sixty-three counties received $3,043,400 in salaries in 1912–13. Of this sum, $2,587,462 was paid to the teachers of 199,717 White children and $455,938 to the teachers of 99,310 Black children. On a per capita basis, this works out to $12.95 for each White child and $4.59 for each Black child. In Garland County (Hot Springs), where 25 percent of the population was Black, per capita expenditures based on salaries for teachers of White children were $13.22; teachers of Black children received $8.32. Naturally, Langston was affected by all these factors and would present Lucile with many unique challenges in educating the Black children of Hot Springs.[16]

In March 1914, during Lucile's second year, Langston's high school enrollment consisted of 21 females and 18 males, for a total student population of 39. Enrollment in the elementary school, grades one through eight, stood at 405. There were four teachers at the high school: three women (including Lucile) and one man. The coursework consisted of English, which Lucile taught, geometry, algebra, history, physics, biology, civics, and half-year courses on agriculture, physiology, and physical geography.[17]

THE BREAKUP AND THE MAKEUP

Lucile, a statuesque single woman who came well prepared to teach the children and was personable enough to win the hearts of their parents and the community, left Hot Springs after two years amid a storm of controversy. While little is known as to what triggered her premature departure, it is clear that once she decided to leave, there were numerous attempts to lure her back.

In June 1914, prior to the end of the school term, Lucile submitted her letter of resignation and moved to Little Rock, taking up residence at the home of friends and fellow teachers Alfred and Jeney Reeves. On June 18, 1914, Lucile received a letter from Milton Lewis Calloway, the science teacher at Langston and her good friend. It was one of four letters from Hot Springs that Lucile kept, storing them in a steamer trunk for seventy-five years. Taken together, these Hot Springs letters offer valuable insight into Lucile's early adult life. The pages of the letters were neatly folded and carefully re-folded each time she read them before being placed back into envelopes that eventually turned yellow with age. Calloway's letter was a blend of affection, instructions, and, most important, gossip that demonstrated a deep friendship.

He told Lucile that the town was abuzz about her resignation: "Say, the City is in a stir because they have heard that you were not going to return." He wrote that Matt Rose, the White superintendent of Hot Springs Public High School, thought a salary increase would entice her to return: "Mr. Rose is put out over the matter. I suppose you have a letter from him by now because he was trying to get your address. He thinks that you are dissatisfied about something and has been wondering whether or not an increase of salary would bring you back." He continued: "Mr. Tom Shelton wants you to write him just what the trouble is to get you to come back." Thomas Shelton was the treasurer of the Warren Undertaking Company, established by John T.T. Warren about 1908. Among the professional class in the Black community, undertakers were held in high esteem, and his interest in the matter says a lot about the circle in which Lucile likely traveled and how aware community leaders were about her work as a teacher.

During Lucile's tenure at Langston, there was one state institution for the training of Black teachers, Branch Normal College of the University of Arkansas in Pine Bluff (today, the University of Arkansas at Pine Bluff). ABC's "Normal" school served as an additional training facility. In his letter, Calloway included a clear warning that if she visited ABC, she would be asked to teach there. Lucile may likely have received additional pressure to help ABC because she was living in the home of its former vice president (Alfred Reeves). Lucile did not heed Calloway's warning. The inscription she left told a different story—"At Ark [Arkansas] Baptist College, Lucile Berkeley Buchanan, 1914" implies that she taught a course at the college during her stay in Little Rock.

At the end of the letter, Calloway reminds Lucile that he was planning to give his final biology exams on Saturday, June 20, and would administer her English exam right after that. It also appears that Lucile had written an article for the local newspaper, as he mentions that it would not be published for a week because the paper had to be sent to Little Rock for printing and that as soon as it came out, he would send a copy to her Denver address. He ends his letter asking her to follow the advice she had often given him regarding the family she was staying with, especially Mrs. Reeves, which was to always be sociable even when it is difficult. Unswayed, Lucile boarded a train on June 23, 1914, at the Rock Island Argenta Depot at Fourth and Hazel Streets and headed home to Denver.

THE COMPOUNDING EMOTIONAL STRESS

Almost two months after arriving in Denver, Lucile received a special delivery handwritten four-page letter dated August 22, 1914, from Frank Cornelius Long, principal of Langston High School. He was most apologetic about her departure, stressing her invaluable service and the years it would take for the school to recover from her departure. Long eloquently sought to understand whether Lucile left on his account. The entire text of his letter reads:

Box 453
Hot Springs, Ark
Aug 22, 1914
Miss Lucile Buchanan
Denver, Col.

Dear Miss Buchanan –

I am attempting to write you under difficulties this morning as I am confined to my bedroom and have been for nearly two weeks.

I have been very much worried and chagrined all of the summer over your sudden "breaking off" from our school work here, since I have been given reason to believe that your real reason for resigning has been kept from me.

It appears, from what I understand that you have some personal grievance against me as the main cause of your leaving us. If so, out of justice to me, especially, and to others concerned and interested in you, you should have mentioned your grievance to me and "squared" matters before leaving, even tho' you resigned at any rate. My feelings have been mortally wounded by the rumors afloat that we had some misunderstanding, "words," and that you left or quit on my account.

There's no man or principal easier, anywhere else easier to get along with me than I am, and it would cause me untold repentance to hurt a woman's feelings, especially one like yourself whose services in our school have been invaluable. The teachers seem to be in possession of the facts of your leaving.

Your going first at this juncture has done or will do us untold harm and give the work a set back from which it will take several years to recover. In the first place, the Supt has public[ly] led it, that it came to him, you and the principal had some words, and I think he has impressed certain members of the Board that way—at any rate, the Board is not willing to fill the vacancy, and has informed me that Mr. Calloway will have to take your work and the sciences will be dropped—you can see what that means to the school. First, it means that an entire course of subjects must be eliminated from the high school, and another entire course poorly taught, as I do not think that Mr. C. can handle your subjects *well*. Secondly, it means, the parents will eventually take their children away, and send them where they can receive proper training.

I want you to think carefully over the fact [that] my seven years [*sic*] work of hard, unselfish, sacrificing effort, must go to the wall under present outlook.

If you have been mistreated I want to beg you to forget and forgive, however I do not know of anything on my part that I have done to cause this break.

The place has not been filled and I am exceedingly anxious to have you return to us—the teachers and other friends are waiting for you to reconsider your resignation and return to us. I am quite certain the Board will be happy to know of your reconsideration of your resignation.

Now come on back to us and help us out of the lurch.

Everything is moving on well. The new building is being "rushed." Several things of interest about which I could write, but I am nervous and am going back to bed. Kindly let me hear from you. Hope you have had a pleasant vacation[.]

—Your Friend, F. C. Long[18]

Long's letter acknowledges Lucile's invaluable service to the Hot Springs community, especially at the only Black high school in town. Almost sixty-one years later that same service to the community again took center stage. Local historian Dorothy Logan had a particular interest in the history of the Langston School. In an interview granted prior to her death in 2008, she told me she began interviewing elderly alumni of Langston during the mid-1970s, sometimes venturing into the countryside to find them. Several of those interviewed remembered Lucile. In her 1976 article "History of Black Education in Hot Springs Prior to Integration," Logan mentions Lucile as one of fifty-seven Black educators in Hot Springs.[19] In a subsequent article about Langston High School, written in 1980, Logan states that Langston had nineteen teachers in 1914 (previously having noted that four of the nineteen, including Lucile, taught in the high school). She went on to report that six of the nineteen teachers "left a lasting impression on the community during this period." They were "Mattie Dover Young, Lucy McAdoo, Nellie Eden, Rosetta Graham, Milton Calloway and Lucille [sic] Buchannan."[20] The memory of Langston's alumni, who were in their seventies when interviewed, says a lot about Lucile's effectiveness and her connection to her former students, especially since her tenure there was less than three years.

It remains unclear what spurred Lucile to leave Langston so abruptly. However, there were other challenges that may have tested her faith and endurance outside the school. First, on June 19, 1913, a mob lynched William Norman in Hot Springs after he allegedly raped and murdered Garland L. Huff, the fourteen-year-old daughter of his employer, Judge C. Floyd Huff.[21] He was just one of fifty-one Black men lynched in Arkansas that year.[22] Newspaper accounts said Norman was lynched at one of the busiest intersections in the city, much to the horror of hundreds of health-seeking tourists. He was stripped of his clothing, hanged from a telephone pole, and shot to death before a crowd of about 5,000 cheering onlookers. His body remained on display for more than an hour before it was cut down and burned.[23] A mother who witnessed the horror mailed a picture postcard to her children, depicting the utility pole at the junction of Central and Ouachita Avenues with an "X" where the hanging occurred. She included this message: "Dear Carl and Pearl—the cross marks the electric pole where they so shamelessly hung and shot the Negro. His crime was unspeakable but the crime of an excited and angry populace was worse. Even the women were bloodthirsty and cried out for bloodshed."[24] This would be the first time Lucile had come face to face with the carnivalesque spectacle of this savage ritual and the terror faced regularly by Black communities living outside Denver.

On Saturday, September 5, 1913, less than three months after William Norman's lynching, Lucile, then in her second year of teaching, survived the most disastrous fire in Arkansas history. The fire started on Church Street—a few blocks southeast of Bathhouse Row and about six blocks from where she lived on East Grand Avenue. High winds shifted the fire west, sparing Grand Avenue but destroying sixty city blocks and causing an estimated $10 million in property damage. About 2,500 people were left homeless. With the power plant destroyed by fire, it would take at least thirty days to re-light the city. Some of those left homeless slept on the streets to protect what little they had left. The city sent out a plea to neighboring communities: "Thousands of people have been rendered penniless and homeless. The destitution is acute and the need of assistance is imperative and immediate." Governor George Washington Hays requested the militia (today the National Guard), fearing that Blacks, greatly affected by the fire and "having nothing [and] with no place to go, . . . would start trouble."[25]

Large sections of the affluent Black community on Malvern Avenue, including businesses and churches, were destroyed. The Pythian Sanitarium and Bathhouse burned, as did Langston and Hot Springs High School (the White high school). Accounts of the fire in the mainstream White press (even in the *New York Times*) mention only the loss of the White high school. No newspaper coverage mentions the Black high school. For the rest of the school year, Langston operated in temporary headquarters in the basement of the Visitors Chapel in the A.M.E. Church, at the northeast corner of Church and Laurel Streets, and in the nearby Grand United Order of Odd Fellows Hall (called the Auditorium) on the southeast corner of Gulpha and Laurel Streets.[26]

When it came time to rebuild the Black high school, controversy arose. According to Stanley Gordon, a local history buff, "Students were told that they were going to be transferred from town to a school out-of-town, which didn't sit too well with the Black students. When time came for the change to come there were name calling etc., a terrible fight ensued—Black and White students were hurt."[27] With the two high schools' close proximity to each other and the racial tensions that at times escalated to physical altercations, the White school board adamantly and judiciously wrote: "It has been deemed wise and prudent . . . to change the site of the high school for negro students, because of the frequent clashes with white pupils at Hot Springs High School."[28] In the end, both schools were rebuilt a mile apart. In 1914 a fourteen-room building for Black high school students was constructed at 315 Silver Street, at a cost of approximately $35,000. A much larger and more visually impressive multi-story Gothic Revival structure was built at a high elevation, visible from multiple locations in the area, to house the White high school. Separate and unequal continued to reign.

AND THEN THERE WAS LOVE, MAYBE?

The letters Lucile saved reveal a lot about her values. Of the four Hot Springs letters, two were love letters, in their original envelopes, from a suitor whom Lucile requested "curb his emotions, bridle his enthusiasm and keep careful check upon his affectionate inclinations." It appears she felt it necessary to hide the true nature of their relationship, an action he found more difficult than she did. As his letters describe, he was struggling to "make believe" that they are "only acquaintances— not even fond friends." While he acknowledges that the pretense is "essential" for her "welfare" and his, he clearly wanted the pretense to end so he could shower her with the affection he obviously felt.[29]

The pages of the letter I hold gingerly in my hand are folded into tiny rectangles with neat handwriting traversing the pages both horizontally and vertically. The first letter arrived on April 14, 1914, mailed from Little Rock. Some words are underlined, and a poem is intricately woven into the text with Xs (a universal symbol for kisses) scattered throughout:

My Very Highly Esteemed Friend:—

Would that I might say *more* than "Esteemed Friend." But I must, at least partially, abide by your wish and desire that I curb my emotions, bridle my enthusiasm and keep careful check upon my affectionate inclinations. You may adjudge it a decided mark of weakness for me to admit that it's a strenuous battle I'm fighting to "make believe" that we are only acquaintances—not even fond friends. And yet, it's necessary and essential to your welfare and mine. And here and now I choose to assert that the sacrifice is none too great.

Indeed, you are worthy of more sacrifices than I'm able to make. Still, my very kind friend, there would be some small degree of solace if I could only have the positive assurance that there is, even now, some hope held out by *you* for *me*. May I have such delightful and soul-satisfying intelligence from you *real soon*? Furthermore, will you pardon my seeming persistence? If you will permit me to become better known to you, it will be speedily ascertained by you that my admiration, regards and esteem for you are of the most honorable and sincere nature. Truly this accompanying poem very eloquently and adequately expresses my innermost feelings—and more.

In the letter, he went on to quote the second and sixth (last) stanzas of Scottish poet and journalist William Duncan Latto's "Conjugal Felicity" (Marital Happiness):

> When I first beheld thy face
> And pressed in mine thy gentle hand,
> Thy blooming cheek and modest grace
> Waved o'er my soul a magic wand;
> Thy kindly tone, thy playful smile,
> Bespeaking innocence and love,
> The luster of thine eyes the while
> That beamed like angel orbs above—
> All joined upon my heart to pour
> A joyance never felt before!
> _____ ____ x x x_____ ____ x x x____
> Life is a changeful scene, and we
> May scarce have felt its sorrows yet,
> But still, what'er the prospects be,
> The path how'er with thorns beset
> Still true to thee and Heaven above,
> I'll seek no other one for mine
> For solace, but hold fast the love
> That never guides my soul to thine;
> Still shall I to thy heart repair
> And find my consolation there!
> x x x x x x x x x x x x x x x x x

And yet! And yet! Ah, that "yet"! It bars my deeper emotions for you said that I must defer full expression. Hope you will successfully read between the lines until you release me and permit me to fully express myself. And now, I again crave your pardon for having broken across the "dead-line." Am I forgiven? Have you any compassion for me who is in earnest and will not give up until you dictate it? O, let me have the assurance!

With sincerity and highest regards and—,

I am, as ever, your admirer,
Pythias

Unlike the rest of the letter, which is written in clean, formalized penmanship, clearly expressing an outpouring of love and begging for acceptance, the signature "Pythias" is extremely small and hard to read. Clearly, it is a code, as the real name of the author would not be signed to such a letter. Why Pythias, I wondered? What meaning did it have for Lucile or the writer?

While not common, Pythias (aka Pythers, Pithian) is associated with the given naming practices among some Blacks in the early 1900s.[30] Therefore, the name Pythias should come as no surprise. However, in Arkansas and among African Americans throughout the country, the Pythias also symbolized the Fraternal Order of the Knights of Pythias, launched in 1880 as one of the more prestigious and wealthy secret Black fraternal orders in the early twentieth century. The Pythians attracted thousands of members across the country, providing a sense of community and national connection, with civic and social activities as well as business opportunities, especially in real estate. In Hot Springs, the Pythians purchased the Crystal Bathhouse for the exclusive use of Blacks (Jim Crow laws prevented them from sharing such a space with White patrons). When the 1913 fire destroyed the building, the group spared no expenses when rebuilding. The new seventy-room three-story Pythian Sanitarium and Bathhouse on Malvern Avenue continued to cater to Blacks eager to "take the waters" of the healing therapeutic springs.[31]

Less than a month later, on May 4, 1914, Lucile received a second letter from the same suitor, this time mailed from Hot Springs:

Saturday a.m. 5/4/—1914

My Beloved Friend:—

As you will note, I wrote the preceding pages last night—about the mid-night hour. And, at an early hour this morning I was awakened by that same "something" that has kept company with me for the past several months. Immediately, I began to argue with myself as to whether or not my innate pride could survive a rude, unwelcome rebuff.

There being the possibility and probability that my sincere and honorable affection for you would soon receiver its death-blow, I wondered if, after all, my fond dreams would ever come true. For, doubt and pessimism had me in a firm grasp. And I had to arise from my couch and bestir myself before my good angel spiritually appeared.

No, no, no! So noble and sweet a character could do no ruthless act to him who continuously worships at her shrine of loveliness. For I realize that though we both are yet young and youthful, yet we have lived out those days of spasmodic infatuation and its kindred attributes. Mine took the wings of the morning quite a decade ago never to return. During that empty, lonely season, I endeavored to drown constant pessimistic and very discouraging events in the sea of *enforced* levity. And for that I have suffered much misrepresentation and was periodically harassed. However, I thank my Master that He kept me from the depths. And when you came into my darkened life I believed it to be an answer to my prayers and a reward (heavenly) for my faith in Him to make all things right. And to be chosen by the Master to inject new life into a miserable creature to lift up his bowed-down head; to apply the balm of love to his wounded heart; and, in return, for you to receive his unalloyed, undying love and devotion; surely, an office of an angel of light being filled by you. Would you reject so great an offer? I implore you that you act slowly if you have an inclination to reject all this. For, while I feel *certain* that you have many admirers and that others have begged this same privilege, yet I *know* of a truth that no one of them felt so deeply as I for mine is of divine origin. Whether accepted or rejected, I shall *always* be

Your ever devoted,

J

Like Lucile, the letter writer seemed to be well educated. His letters are absurdly romantic, gushing with poetry, florid appeals, flowery language, flirtation, and sensuousness. He is not afraid to admit to having experienced a previous heartbreak followed by a period of mourning and to being misunderstood by those around him, causing the "misrepresentation and harassment" that so painfully affected him. This admission followed a healing period (evoking a religious awakening), after which Lucile arrived as the answer to his "prayers." He was cautious never to use her name but instead penned endearments such as "My Beloved Friend" and "My Very Highly Esteemed Friend." He was also cautious enough to identify himself by the coded signatures "Pythias" and "J," the meanings known only to him and Lucile. As for the choice of "Pythias," Lucile likely came into contact with several members of the fraternal order, including John E. Knox, principal of the Normal Department at Arkansas Baptist College, where she taught in 1907;

Frank Cornelius Long, principal of Langston High School; Dr. James Webb Curtis, prominent physician and head of the household where she lived; Thomas Shelton, the treasurer of the Black funeral home; and the widower John T.T. Warren, undertaker and manager of the Pythian Sanitarium and Bathhouse. What is known about the letter writer is that he was a Pythian and that one of his names may have begun with the letter "J."

I often thought that Lucile, as a woman of the Progressive era, actively sought employment away from Denver to create a new life on her own, separate from her family. Teaching provided her with a means for social and economic advancement as well as a set of ideals that would continue to motivate her for the remainder of her professional career. She demonstrated her autonomy by resigning from a position at a school where she excelled and was clearly well-liked and respected by students, administrators, and fellow teachers. While dedicated to the racial uplift pedagogy, she never hesitated to take a stand regarding some injustice or perceived slight she encountered in Hot Springs. In the same vein, she exercised her own agency by not responding to the first love letter, leading her suitor to write another a month later. She clearly represents the "new woman" of the Progressive era—earning a salary on her own power and achieving financial security, breaking from the confines of male dominance, and carving out her own autonomy within a romantic situation, secure in the knowledge that she had the choice to accept or reject her suitor's advances.

In her brief time in Hot Springs, Lucile experienced disappointments and hardships, but she also had tremendous accomplishments, which in the eyes of the community should have outweighed the hardships, the details of which they likely did not know. It is possible that Long's letter praising her accomplishments triggered her strong work ethic, resulting in her return to Langston. But I could also envision that Calloway's letter indicating that her departure was the "talk of the town" and that prominent citizens, both White and Black, wanted to redress whatever wrong she perceived may have played a small role. Whatever the reason, when Lucile returned to Hot Springs, she did so under her terms: to fulfill her teaching obligations at Langston in the fall of 1914.

EARLY DETOUR INTO CHICAGO

In the summer of 1915, after Lucile had satisfied her teaching obligation at Langston High School, she moved to Chicago, a city that held a number of attractions for the adventurous Lucile. Among them, the University of Chicago (UChicago), a top private university that had welcomed women and Blacks since 1870.[32] Chicago also had "the Stroll," a vibrant center of economic and entertainment activity along State Street between Twenty-sixth and Thirty-ninth. Most important, leaving Arkansas and the Jim Crow laws for Chicago's anti-discrimination legislation, the most progressive in the country, was assuredly a breath of fresh air. Having banned school segregation in 1874 and the segregation of public accommodations in 1885, Chicago became a mecca for Blacks, who gravitated to the city as part of the first Great Migration (from 1910 to 1930), during which over 1 million Blacks left the South for greater opportunities up north, in cities such as New York City, Detroit, Cleveland, Washington, DC, Philadelphia, and Chicago.

However, Lucile's stay in Chicago during the summer of 1915 was meant to be temporary so she could enroll in courses at UChicago in elementary German and elementary Greek, as well as a course on the British poets Robert Browning and Alfred Tennyson. Lucile also gravitated to Chicago because of the distribution of Chicago's progressive newspaper, the *Chicago Defender*, throughout the nation, including in Denver. The *Defender* often discussed Chicago's Black social, political, economic, and cultural life. Furthermore, the *Chicago Defender* served as a point of agitation and mobilization for Black equality. As early as 1910, the *Colorado Statesman* carried a front-page column called "Race News," which highlighted significant accomplishments and concerns of Blacks throughout the United States and the world. The *Chicago Defender* used an aggressive approach to encourage southern Blacks to migrate north by showcasing articles that lauded the economic opportunities, cultural freedom, educational benefits, and lack of Jim Crow laws in cities like Chicago. In both newspapers, Chicago was often described as a place of increased opportunity where Blacks could live the American dream and forge a stake in the city's social, cultural, and political life. Black southerners took notice and headed north in record numbers with Chicago as a major destination. This migration expanded the city's population by 148 percent (over 65,000) between 1920 and 1932.[33] And while Chicago surely offered a number of enticements for the adventurous Lucile, the city was far from her mind as she took her next steps.

10

A Fly in the Buttermilk

COLORADO AND THE WORLD OF HIGHER EDUCATION

Living as a fly in the buttermilk [the only Black among
Whites] was not comfortable, but it enabled me bit by bit to
build a method for surviving and eventually thriving.

—CECIL A. REED

As a child of the first post-slavery generation, Lucile aspired to rise above the typical menial work associated with Black women. As a young girl, she watched her
father overcome the adversities of racism by utilizing a set of values that stressed
the importance of hard work, self-improvement, and self-respect as a way to
achieve the American dream. At the same time, Lucile witnessed her mother
negotiating and reconciling the double burden of her employment as a nurse for
a White family with the domestic work inside her own home. Although raised in
a middle-class family and exposed to the success of her entrepreneurial father and
older sister Hattie, Lucile grew painfully aware that the majority of Black women
in Denver (and across America) lacked higher education and occupied unskilled
service jobs. Higher education, therefore, became her ticket to independence and
upward mobility.

Once Lucile made her decision to venture into higher education, she had several
choices, each with a unique set of challenges: (1) attend either of two Black institutions of higher education (out of approximately eighty-three) capable of offering college-level work—Howard University (Washington, DC) or Fisk University
(Nashville, Tennessee); (2) follow the Hampton-Tuskegee model of pursuing an

industrial education, a trajectory supported by Booker T. Washington and the White philanthropic community that funded Black colleges; (3) pursue a liberal arts education, as advocated by W.E.B. Du Bois; (4) follow her sister Hannah's lead and attend Spelman College for Black women in Atlanta, or (5) venture outside the box and attend any state or private institutions opened to Black students.

CHOOSING RESPONSIBLY

In June 1901, just shy of her seventeenth birthday, Lucile graduated from Villa Park High School, where she would briefly work as a substitute teacher. Soon thereafter, she entered employment of the American Publishing Company of New York as an agent in Niagara Falls, NY, for one year. Returning to Denver in 1902, she became a bookkeeper for Paris City Cleaning Works.[1] Bent on becoming a teacher, on September 8, 1903, she enrolled at the University of Northern Colorado (UNC) in Greeley.[2] The same school her sister Laura meant to attend three years earlier, before coming home and tragically committing suicide—a loss from which Lucile and the entire Buchanan household were likely still suffering. T. J. Wray's work on surviving the death of a sibling suggests that not only must siblings "deal with their own grief; they must also help their parents cope with losing a child."[3] Therefore, attending the same school with the same goal as her sister and walking the same grounds surely saddened Lucile while reinforcing her determination not only to complete Laura's legacy but also to make it her own.

Several days before the start of the semester, nineteen-year-old Lucile packed up her college accoutrements and loaded them into the back of her father's wagon for the ride to the Union Depot in Denver. She boarded the one-car passenger Union Pacific and Colorado and Southern Railway train and headed to the one-story stone railroad depot in Greeley, fifty-four miles away, where classes would begin on Tuesday, September 8, 1903.

At this time, the school consisted of one building, Cranford Hall, which served both administrative and academic purposes. Without housing or boarding facilities on campus, students had to room and board with private families, who charged from $3.50 to $4.50 per week. Lucile found housing at 1115 Ninth Avenue with Edward Moore Nusbaum, a local brick contractor from Ohio; his Canadian-born wife, Agnes Strickland; and their sixteen-year-old son, Jesse.[4] Back in 1886, when Edward served as the chief of the Greeley Fire Department, he donated $25 ($692 in 2017) to the building of UNC. The Nusbaums, staunch Republicans and abolitionists, were part of the settler class that arrived in Greeley during the post–Civil War era. While economic factors might have played into their decision to

FIGURE 10.1. *Lucile's State Normal School (today UNC) graduation portrait, 1905. Buchanan Archives.*

host Lucile, the strength of their moral conviction as abolitionists may have also contributed to their decision to bring a Black woman into their household.

Lucile had worked diligently in high school and took great pride in her acceptance into UNC. Her transcript demonstrates that she applied the same academic rigor to the eighteen-week Normal School semester, which required her to attend

FIGURE 10.2. *University of Northern Colorado 1905 Class Photo. Lucile depicted left. Courtesy, UNC Archives and Special Collections.*

twenty-five recitations per week. A year of schooling added up to a total of fifty term hours or 900 recitations.[5] During her two years (four semesters) at Greeley, she took all the required courses—arithmetic, English, psychology, physical education, pedagogy, music, geography, reading, manual training, and practice in teaching—for a total of ninety-six credits. Her only elective, taken in her senior year, was German.[6]

She was the only Black student in her 1905 graduating class, which consisted of 115 females and 14 males. To celebrate her success in Greeley, the *Statesman* reported on Saturday, June 10, in its City News section, "Mrs. S. L. Buchanan and a few of her friends left for Greeley this week to attend the commencement exercises at the State Normal School of which her daughter, Lucile, will graduate."[7] Lucile became the first Black student to earn a normal degree at UNC.[8]

Commencement exercises were held on Thursday, June 8, at the Greeley Opera House.[9] The program began with Mendelssohn's "Fair Tinted Primrose" by the Ladies' Chorus, followed by the invocation. Math teacher Mary Kendel sang Luigi Luzzi's "Ave Marie" [*sic*]. Remarks by Katherine L. Craig, the state superintendent of public instruction and president of the State Board of Education, to the graduates were "received with much enthusiasm." Richard Broad Jr., former mayor of Golden, chair of the State Silver Republican Central Committee, and trustee of the State Normal School, presented the diplomas to the graduates, at the conclusion of which the Ladies' Chorus sang Macrirone's "A Farewell." Dr. Richard W. Corwin, a physician and member of the board of trustees gave the commencement address, followed the benediction.[10]

RETURNING HOME

Once Lucile returned home, she and fellow members of the Inter-Graduate Student Association were honored at a reception for members who graduated from high school and institutions of higher education that year: Misses Beatrice Thrunabley and Lillian Hawkins of East Denver High School, Spencer Smithea of Manual High School, Miss Lucy Buchanan from the State Normal at Greeley, and Miss Carrie Barnes from Columbia College, New York.[11]

Having committed to teach in a public school after completing her two-year degree, Lucile applied to the public school in Maitland, a coal mining camp and company town in Huerfano County, south-central Colorado. Poet and writer Carl Sandburg said it best when he described a mining camp/company town as follows: "You go to a company school. You work for this company according to company rules. You all drink company water and all use company lights. The company preacher teaches us what is right."[12]

I often wondered why the Maitland school was her only choice or one that she sought out? But having ventured across the United States to Niagara Falls in 1901 for employment, conquering a coal mining town would have been an easy transition for a woman coming of age during the Progressive era (marked by risk-taking behaviors and activism among both Black and White women). But this era was also marked by what historian Rayford W. Logan refers to as the "nadir" of African American history, where racism was tragically at its very worse.[13] Racism, covert or overt, did not escape Colorado. Therefore, how did Lucile fare in this period of American history? To begin, she had a number of things going for herself: excellent academic qualifications and good role models growing up, and she was raised by a prominent Black family in a predominately White community. Even with such credentials, I wondered whether her standing at the intersection of gender, class, and race impacted hiring decisions either at the school board level or in Maitland.

On July 25, 1905, an article in the *Walsenburg World* with the headline "Colored Teacher Applicant" stated that "among applicants as teacher in the school at Maitland is, Lucile B. Buchanan, who holds the distinction of being the first colored graduate of the Colorado State Normal school. The young lady was born and raised in Denver where she received her high school education and did some work as substitute teacher. The probabilities are that the former Maitland teachers will be retained, but the young lady will no doubt find a remunerative school without any trouble."[14] The journalist's faith that Lucile's credentials would make her employable did not pan out.

Apparently not getting any headway in securing her first regular teaching job in Colorado, she found employment at a historically black school in Little Rock in 1905.[15] With almost three years of teaching credentials under her belt, Lucile returned to Denver in 1908, assuming that her qualifications would finally earn her a teaching position in Denver's public schools. This was not the case. The editor/owner of the *Statesman*, Joseph D. D. Rivers, responded in a blistering editorial titled "We Shall Try Again," written on June 13, 1908, which speaks to the issues of race, education, and equality:

The school board of Denver has taken no action upon the application of Miss Lucy Buchanan for a position as a teacher in the city schools. It has neither refused her a position, nor has it granted one. In some respects, it is a gain to know that a Colored applicant, could have such evident fitness that it would be rank injustice and race proscription to turn her down, yet it is a sad blow a disheartening decision for them to remain silent and withhold the reward of merit. Having qualified herself in the city schools and in the State Normal, the Colored people had hoped that the five members of the school board would measure up to the best there is in American statecraft and appoint her. All this is apart from any rights which we have as citizens to equal consideration, because of our citizenship or tax-paying. The spirit of the American schools is against castes of any kind. Therefore, it was not too much to ask of the school board that it set an example of freedom from taste distinctions. In the discussions of this appointment, various members of the board said that they had no personal objections to Colored teachers in mixed schools but feared the objections of white parents. In rebuttal city after city was cited to show, that no ill feeling developed elsewhere, and they were urged to give our own girl a Chance, as other cities have done. They have failed to do so, and we are While we construe their silence as some gain over a refusal, it is a sorry handicap to put upon our struggles to withhold reward for the cultured and striving Negro, over his shiftless and illiterate brother. The men composing the school board have risen in life from lower stations. They are Americans and cannot believe that anyone should be circumscribed by the conditions of his birth. They cannot overlook the ever-increasing number of tax payers among us. And when Negroes buy property out of wages that do not average over SGO per month, when they look up under the hard conditions that surround them, and strive to be good citizens, it is unbelievable that the school board will fall below the traditions of Americans schools and tell us we fight in vain. Let Omaha speak in behalf of Miss Buchanan. Chicago, Cleveland, New York, Philadelphia, all pay tribute to the Negro woman who qualifies herself to teach. Denver is silent, but another year we shall ask again and we hope with better success.[16]

Petitioning Denver's School Board three years later yielded the same result. Lucile, described in a 1905 *Rocky Mountain News* article as "One of the Best Educated Colored Girls in the West," continued to be denied even the opportunity to compete for open positions based solely on her race. This bigotry she suffered in 1905 and in 1908 in Colorado would not be her last.

SETTLING FOR BOULDER

On September 5, 1877, with forty-four students, the University of Colorado opened for business with Joseph A. Sewall, a medical doctor and professor of chemistry, as its president and Justin E. Dow, former principal of Boulder's State Preparatory School (today Boulder High School), as the only instructor of its Preparatory and Normal departments. Thirty-nine years later, a now thirty-two-year-old Lucile, defined by the university as a "mature student" (meaning twenty-one years of age or older), walked onto the campus to attend her first class in September 1916. While the only Black female student on campus, she was not the only Black student. The Colorado *Statesman* reported in their column "Boulder Notes" that nineteen-year-old Alexander Jesse Brickler (1897–1957) of Denver would join her.[17] A third student, Earle Hugo DeFrantz, also enrolled, but chose to drop out before the semester ended.

However, university records indicate that in 1912, Charles Durham Campbell, born on May 19, 1885, in Georgetown, Colorado, became the first African American to graduate from the university. In September 1907 the university admitted twenty-two-year-old Campbell into the College of Engineering. Midway through his junior year, Campbell unexpectedly transferred to the College of Liberal Arts, where he went on to earn his degree in mathematics. The comment Campbell likely submitted to appear under his photo in the 1912 *Coloradoan* yearbook speaks to this change: "Engineering is easy—so I'm taking college."[18] Though I can never be certain, I wondered whether his tongue-in-cheek statement was an attempt to publically shame the College of Engineering by sending a clear message regarding his abilities.[19] Nonetheless, Campbell had the distinction of being the first Black undergraduate student to graduate from the university, when Lucile graduated in 1918, she was the second and notably, the first Black woman.

Although Lucile took courses to bolster her career prospects at UChicago in 1915, she spent only a short time there before choosing to pursue a bachelor's degree at the University of Colorado a year later. Prior to 1916, there were twenty-seven Black colleges in the South. Many of these institutions were initially founded as non-degree-granting schools, focusing primarily on preparing students for agricultural, mechanical, and industrial careers. None of these schools offered Lucile the liberal arts education she wanted, and only two provided four-year degree programs.[20] While these institutions would have provided her with the cultural experiences and networking benefits of attending a Black school, she chose Colorado.

During her two-year teaching assignment in Hot Springs, Arkansas, she earned sufficient funds to attend the school of her choice. This was especially important since the University of Colorado required entering students to have "enough money to pay a reasonable part of the first semester expenses."[21] Another factor in her move from Chicago to Boulder may have simply been practicality. Tuition fees were much lower at the University of Colorado, as were room and board.

As the 1916 school year approached, finding suitable accommodations in a city of about 12,000 presented some of the same challenges she had faced in Greeley—namely, no resident halls for women students.[22] While Woodbury Hall provided male students with accommodations since 1890, women would not get dedicated on-campus housing until 1934, when Sewell Hall opened. Even so, these accommodations would not have benefited Lucile, since residence halls were not integrated until the 1950s. Her options in 1916 were the same as those available to White women: seek accommodations in private homes and rooming houses approved by the university and accredited by the Dean of Women S. Antoinette Bigelow.[23]

Most private rooms for rent were located within walking distance of the University on Pine, Bluff, Grove, and Pleasant Streets; many more were in the downtown area, from Twelfth to Fifteenth Streets, with the majority on Pearl Street, the hub of activity in Boulder. Another option for Brickler and Lucile, though in short supply, was to rent a room in the "Little Rectangle," a four-block neighborhood between Nineteenth and Twenty-third Streets and Goss and Water Streets (previously Railroad Street and presently Canyon Boulevard), where approximately 71 percent (about eighty) of the 120 Blacks residing in Boulder lived.[24] The other forty or so individuals lived either where they worked as servants, house girls, or cooks with White families; at the Boulder, Colorado Sanitarium and Hospital at the corner of Fourth and Mapleton; or as lodgers in private White or Black households.

Accommodations in the "Little Rectangle" were stretched to their limit. This was particularly problematic in the summer, when Black teachers came to the university to upgrade their qualifications from states that denied them access. As a result of the increase in the number of Black teachers during the summer and the growing interest in higher education amongst Colorado's Blacks, Dr. Paul Edward Spratlin,[25] former chief medical inspector for Denver and a leading Black public figure, suggested at the Boulder Ministerial Union's annual meeting in 1916 that a large rooming house should be built to accommodate Black students who wished to attend the university.

Even though many of Boulder's White citizens were accommodating of the small Black population and the city had no official segregation policy, there were still racial boundaries. Reflecting on the racial dynamics in Boulder, Helen McVey Washington, who was about eight years old when Lucile enrolled at the university, said, "We went to school with them [Whites] and they followed us home sometimes but for us to go to their home, no, no, that was a horse of a different color . . . I guess it really and truly had segregation those days and we just didn't know it . . . we stayed where Blacks usually stayed on their side of the street and Whites stayed on their side. We did have some friends who were White who were very nice to us and they'd come by, but as far as we going to their homes that was a no, no."[26]

Despite the barriers, Lucile found accommodations in a newly built house at 821 Mapleton Avenue owned by Harold U. Wallace, a civil engineer from Illinois and manager of Boulder's Western Light and Power Company.[27] Wallace, his wife, Lura Dean Wycoff, and their four children, lived in a very spacious Edwardian Vernacular-style home. Prior to and after Lucile roomed with them, they took single boarders (male or female) who likely occupied the enclosed back sleeping porch, which had its own entry. This would have cost Lucile about three dollars a week, an amount that could have been greatly reduced by her doing light housekeeping. While Lucile had been welcomed in the Wallace's home, she faced a series of obstacles that likely precipitated her move the next semester: namely, snow. In November 1916 Boulder experienced 17.4 inches of snow, followed by 13.6 inches in December. Even though one of the train lines circled around Mapleton, she had a six-block jaunt to reach the train depot to catch Boulder's Street Railway, with its dark green and gold Birney cars.

The next academic year Lucile moved to 1304 Pine Street at the corner of Thirteenth Street, less than two blocks from the train depot. Frank Tyler, a prominent farmer and citizen, and his wife, Rowena, owned the house and rented out several rooms. As with her previous residence, Lucile was the only Black person in the house, a familiar position for her.

Living in Boulder was not a hardship for Lucile. When she arrived in 1916, the Black community had coalesced around two churches that helped maintain community stability—Second Baptist, founded in 1884 and located at Twenty-

FIGURE 10.3. *Lucile's accommodations in Boulder, 1916–18. Left 821 Mapleton Avenue (still standing) and 1304 Pine Street (parking lot of the Hotel Boulderado). Courtesy, Boulder Public Library, Carnegie Library for Local History.*

fourth and Pearl Streets, and Allen Chapel AME, founded in 1908 and located at 2014 Eighteenth Street, at the corner of Eighteenth and Pearl. Although small congregations, these churches created benevolent societies to serve the financial and spiritual needs of the community while providing both secular and religious opportunities for adults and youths.[28]

Boulder also had the advantage of being close to her family in Denver. Each day eighteen Denver and Interurban electric trains traveled the fifty-one-mile "kite route" to Boulder.[29] With its hub at Union Station, nine trains traveled a northern route through Louisville in an hour and fifteen minutes, and nine took a southern route through Superior and Marshall in an hour and eight minutes. The fare was 70 cents one way and $1.20 for a round trip.[30]

Soon enough, Boulder's small Black community knew of Lucile Berkeley Buchanan. At the beginning of her second semester, an article in the *Boulder Notes* column in the *Statesman* said, "Miss Buchanan and Mr. Brickler of the university made all credits the past semester."[31] It is evident that the Black communities in Boulder and Denver were being informed of the academic achievements of both Lucile and Brickler through the Colorado *Statesman*.

Equally beneficial to Lucile's quick transition to Boulder is that she grew up in a majority White neighborhood in Denver and spent much of her education in predominantly White institutions, adding to her quick and comfortable transition. In addition, her parents succeeded in instilling in her a sense of equality, no matter the legal or social efforts, which attempted to discourage that feeling. As the first and only Black woman pursuing higher education at the University of Colorado in the fall of 1916, things might have been different if she hadn't overcome some of the adversity of race, class, and gender and already felt comfortable being the proverbial "fly in the buttermilk."

A FLY IN THE BUTTERMILK

S. Antoinette Bigelow, the university's fourth dean of women (serving from 1910 to 1928) and assistant professor of English literature, attended to the welfare of women students. Women's colleges and coeducational institutions commonly employed a dean of women. These early deans were typically quite progressive, politically astute, and members of a wide constellation of social and political organizations. For example, Bigelow was president of the Woman's International League for Peace and Freedom, a member of the National Association of Deans of Women, and a member of the Socialist Party of America. Once hired, Bigelow discovered that the university's philosophy encouraged plain living as good for high thinking. As a result, conditions were rather spartan for both the dean and the students. Eventually, Bigelow won over the university president (James H. Baker) and the board sufficiently to secure basic amenities and perhaps even a few luxuries for her women students.[32]

When Lucile arrived, things were pretty much set for White students. Bigelow's responsibilities included all aspects of the lives of women students under age twenty-one, including their health and personal hygiene; in fact, she regulated social activities for both men and women. She also oversaw the availability of a women's physician and supervised the houses in which women roomed and boarded off campus. In these endeavors, she received much-needed support from the few women faculty members and the wives of the male faculty.

The center of activity was the Women's Building (today the Hazel Gates Cottage), which by 1916 functioned as a clubroom for women. It was equipped with a library, chairs, tables, a hall for meetings and entertainment, and other conveniences.[33] The building also housed Bigelow's office and the offices of both the Women's League and the Young Women's Christian Association (YWCA).[34] The Women's League was open to undergraduate women, alumni, and the wives of members of the faculty. Its purpose was to bring women together to get to know one another and to add to their social lives. It also offered loans to women, who were often unable to obtain them through traditional banks. The university also supported the league's role in promoting the intellectual and social welfare of women.[35] For example, in 1916 Bigelow and the league joined forces to create a more shared governing structure among students and to enhance communication between university students and the women in whose homes they lived to create more rigid enforcement of rules and more satisfactory living conditions for all.

On Friday afternoons and Saturday evenings, the Women's Building opened to gatherings of female students in an effort to build camaraderie and relationships among them.[36] On Friday nights it was not unusual to find the league sponsoring

Vaudeville shows with women-only audiences, in which female students would sometimes don drag and blackface, a form of entertainment popularized in the nineteenth century in which White performers painted their faces in burned cork or black grease, often outlining their lips with red or white to make them look grotesquely larger, and in a very crude way performed an imitation or caricature of Black life for the entertainment of their peers. One such event was reported in the semi-weekly student-run newspaper *Silver and Gold*: "As negroes, Winified Castle and Lucille Morrison changed the atmosphere from the sublime to the ridiculous in their skit: 'Over the Back-Yard Fence.' In the negro wedding, Miss Castle acted two parts, minister and bridegroom changing her costume each time."[37]

The YWCA and the YMCA were among the many other religious associations housed at the university. Each held Bible classes, discussions on its worldwide missions, and Vesper services in the chapel at Old Main.[38] But there was a vast difference between the services provided for men and those available for women. The men's association had a permanent employment and information bureau for male students, whereas the women's association had a book exchange and a self-help bureau, which was open only at the beginning of each school year.[39] Lucile continued to attend religious services with her family at the Zion Baptist Church in Denver or at Boulder's Second Baptist Church, under the leadership of the Rev. A. C. Jackson.

Before registering for classes on September 8, Lucile, like all her classmates, reported to the Registrar's Office in Macky Auditorium to present her credentials. Since she sought advanced standing because of her prior coursework at the State Normal School of Colorado, Lucile had to present an official record of her work, a marked catalog, and a letter of honorable dismissal from the last institution she attended. She presented her transcript for fifteen courses: biology, sociology, English, psychology pedagogy, practical teaching, Latin, history, algebra, chemistry, physics, botany, physical geography, zoology, gym, Browning and Tennyson, and German. Since one of her math grades did not transfer, she was admitted on September 18, 1916, on a provisional basis. However, on November 20, after presenting evidence that she had passed plane geometry, the university lifted her provisional status. After completing her first year, she would have to register first with Fred R. B. Hellems, dean of the College of Liberal Arts, and then with the Registrar's Office.

Higher education in Colorado was not as severely affected by the direct prejudice and discrimination that existed in other states, particularly in the Jim Crow South. Racial integration existed in the classrooms. Lucile attended classes taught predominantly by Whites males.[40] She went to classes with all White students.

Every Tuesday from 11:00 to 12:00 a.m., she and her classmates and teachers were required to attend a student assembly where the faculty or an invited guest addressed the students. Though part of the community, as a mature Black student she stood out.

While the scripts we construct and play out in our heads guide our actions, they also frame and stereotype our relationships with the "Other." Did Lucile's classmates and teachers otherize her? I wondered how often, or if, others mistook her for one of the many Black women employed in service occupations such as servants, laundresses, or cooks for university presidents, or in fraternities and sororities on campus that were close to her classes in the College of Liberal Arts (Old Main). Did she experience any intentional or unintentional microaggressions, in and out of the classroom? Was her voice heard when asking or answering a question in all of her classes?

Apart from academic life, most extracurricular activities catered to the vast majority of students who were young and White.[41] These included the sixteen literary societies and clubs, which catered to religious groups, language study groups, specific majors (engineering), or special interests such as debating, drama, arts, writing, or politics.[42] Given Lucile's age, gender, and race, she would have either been excluded from most campus social activities or chosen not to participate. The one campus activity Lucile may have participated in was the *Deutscher Verein*, which was exclusively composed of students and instructors in the Department of Germanic Languages, and promoted interest in the language, music, and customs of Germany. The *Verein* met twice a month on Thursday evenings, and participants only spoke German at the meetings.

The kind of support available for incoming first-year female students included a greeting committee, in which a member of the Big Sister Committee greeted new arrivals at the Boulder Railroad Depot to help newcomers make friends, get situated, and become registered.[43] As students became acclimated to campus life, Bigelow, the Women's League, and each sorority and fraternity planned social events, including dances, relay races, and Vaudeville shows. Students also attended off-campus events at Chautauqua Auditorium where the Williams Original Dixie Jubilee Singers, a Black a cappella ensemble, and operatic performances introduced them to the likes of soprano Marie Rappold of the Metropolitan Opera and contralto Frances Ingram, as well as silent films.

It is difficult to say whether Bigelow, whose social and political leanings were more progressive, or any of the established support systems for women reached out to Lucile. None of Bigelow's writings mention her. Nothing about her appears in the campus's *Silver and Gold* or in the *Coloradoan* yearbooks. What is known

179

is that Bigelow created a number of activities to reach out to female students. In November 1917, for example, Bigelow decided that she wanted to get to know every female student on campus. To accomplish this, she held a series of teas in her study in the Women's Building. Bigelow's teas became a mainstay of women's social life on campus until she determined that she had reached every female. It is difficult to say whether an older, nontraditional student would have been invited to participate in Bigelow's teas."[44]

In March 1918 Bigelow decided that students needed more self-governance and greater say in their accommodations. Together with the Women's League, she created a committee that included a representative of each house in Boulder in which three or more women students were living and arranged for it to meet once a month to facilitate better cooperation between the university and its female students.[45] Lucile's living accommodations did not fit Bigelow's or the league's criteria. No one from her home received an invitation.

As Lucile was coming to the end of her second term, President Woodrow Wilson, arguing that "the world must be safe for democracy," asked the US Congress on April 2, 1917, to declare war on Germany. Four days later, the United States joined the fight. The university's students, faculty, and staff went all out to support the war effort, with a strong commitment to national service or participating in government service as soldiers and staff for the Department of War (e.g., doing library work at a US Army camp or serving in a medical capacity or as the military secretary for the YMCA). Leading by example, the president of the university, Livingston Farrand, requested a leave of absence in July 1917 to serve as director of the Commission for Prevention of Tuberculosis in France for the Rockefeller Foundation. Women students and faculty wives joined forces with the American Red Cross in knitting socks and sweaters, making bandages, wrapping surgical dressing, providing farm labor, and teaching methods of preserving food. Khaki became the compelling color for uniforms as the faculty voted in October 1917, to establish a Reserve Officers' Training Corps (ROTC) and hundreds of men drilled.[46]

The continuing militarization of the campus accelerated in April 1918, when the Department of War Committee on Education and Special Training contracted with the university to house, feed, and train 250 (eventually 308) student soldiers by establishing a Student Army Training Corps (SATC) program. The physical structure of the university also changed as a mess hall and barracks (primarily tents) went up to meet the SATC's needs.[47] *Silver and Gold* vigilantly reported war news, such as the deployment of troops, the creation of new war-related courses, multiple student drives to raise money, reduction of social activities, and the rise of patriotic events.

Although the war presented a number of challenges for students, the vast majority found ways to engage the patriotic fervor. But what about Lucile? A couple of options can be considered. With the university focus primarily on getting male students battle-ready and the female student body occupied in a supportive role, Lucile likely continued to suffer the consequences of institutional invisibility. As Africana philosopher Lewis R. Gordon postulated, "The black body lives in an anti-Black world as a form of absence of human presence."[48]

After living under Jim Crow laws in the South, Lucile also appears to have come to understand how to use the public sphere in ways that cloaked her visibility and how to negotiate the sometimes intolerance of her presence. But her invisibility does not suggest that the war did not impact her in significant ways. Even though they never saw combat, her brother, first cousin, and two of her sisters' husbands had to register for the draft in anticipation of being called to fight. Boulder's Black community supported a number of war-related activities that could have sparked her interest, including benefits for the Red Cross Fund or attending a lecture on Universal Military Training sponsored the Mutual Literary Society. Another option is that she may have sided with a small but vocal number of Blacks who thought it hypocritical to promote democracy and freedom in Europe while denying Blacks civil rights at home.[49]

It would not be far-fetched to say that Lucile refused to stay in her place. As a member of the first generation out of slavery, Lucile understood that constraining Black education was used as a potent weapon to quell Black agency—a fact that probably intensified her desire for higher education. She came to the university uniquely focused and knew what she wanted to get out of her studies. Her initial choice of UChicago and subsequent move to the University of Colorado are demonstrative of her character. At a time when most of her contemporaries were studying at Historically Black Colleges and Universities (HBCUs), Lucile chose not to take this traditional pathway and instead picked a coeducational White institution where she would obtain a more thorough liberal arts education and where she could major in German, following up on some of the coursework she began at UNC and UChicago.

THE BLACK-GERMAN BOND, WORLD WAR I, AND ITS CHALLENGES

What could possibly have driven Lucile to study German literature, history, and language? In the mid-nineteenth century, while not yet a unified nation, Germany came onto the radar in the United States among abolitionists and freed people as the University of Heidelberg awarded in 1849 an honorary doctoral degree to renowned author, orator, minister, and fugitive slave, Jesse W. C. Pennington.[50] By the end of the nineteenth century and into the early decades of the twentieth century, the Black intelligentsia viewed Germany and Germans as their "spiritual kin."[51] Some of this could be attributed to the limited role of Germany during the Trans-Atlantic slave trade relative to other European nations. Additionally, many leading intellectuals such as sociologist, civil rights activist, historian, Pan-Africanist, writer, editor, and scholar W.E.B. Du Bois; civil rights leader and first president of the National Association of Colored Women, Mary Church Terrell; bishop of the African Methodist Episcopal Church, editor of the *Christian Recorder*, and president of Wilberforce University Richard R. Wright Jr.; philosopher and President of Wilberforce University, Gilbert Haven Jones; the first African American to receive a PhD in Germany in 1909 and writer, philosopher, and educator Alain LeRoy Locke studied at universities in Germany.[52] Almost universally, their experiences were rewarding and transformative as they encountered a Germany that was more racially tolerant than the white supremacist country they left behind.

With this history, along with the influence that Germany had on the development of America's universities, many segregated Black private and public colleges that opened following the Civil War institutionalized formal instruction in the German language, especially at the two premier Black institutions, Fisk and Wilberforce Universities.[53]

In addition to a prevailing interest in Germany and the German language among the Black educated class, Lucile's interest could have come from two additional sources. First, there was a sizable population of Germans in Loudoun and Prince William Counties, where her parents were enslaved, and they may have passed on to their children Germans' almost unanimous anti-slavery position, support for the Union, and opposition to the Kansas-Nebraska Bill of 1854 that would have extended slavery in Nebraska and Kansas.[54] As far as many Blacks were concerned, prior to World War I, Germans were on the right side of justice, humanity, and national union.[55] Second, German immigrants made up the largest foreign-born population in the Barnum community. Lucile went to elementary and high school with children of German ancestry and knew many of their customs. It is possible that Lucile was not as isolated majoring in German as she would have been in other disciplines. For example, four of the five faculty members were women: the chair of the Department of Germanic Languages, Grace Fleming van Sweringen (the first woman hired with a doctorate degree), a member of the Kappa Kappa Gamma sorority who was known to have a "love for all her students."[56] The other women faculty were Ruth M. Shellely, Florence Farrington, and Frieda Meents. Also teaching in the department was Assistant Professor William F. Baur, Grace's husband, whom she outranked. Given the gender composition of the department; the twenty-one undergraduate courses it offered (all conducted in German), of which Lucile took ten; and the Black intelligentsia who studied in Germany, on many levels majoring in German was a natural pathway for her.

However, her interest in Germany could prove troublesome, as on April 6, 1917, when the United States declared war on the German-led central powers. Lucile, like many Blacks, was privy to the ensuing debate in the Black press and among Black intellectuals and leaders (e.g., A. Phillip Randolph, William Monroe Trotter, Arthur Shaw, Kelly Miller, and Chandler Owens) over the hypocrisy of fighting and dying for democracy in Europe while Blacks in the United States often faced horrendous inequality and violence. A possible solution to the segregated inequality and abuse Blacks suffered was to show unquestioned patriotism to the war effort, in hopes it would pay off in the postwar years in improved race relations and equal opportunity. Plus, showing anything other than loyalty placed her at risk because of the June 1917 Espionage Act and the May 1918 Sedition Act, aimed on cracking down on dissent.[57] Lucile seemed to have maintained her silence quite possibly due to the barrage of anti-German sentiment that gripped the nation and Colorado in particular from the spring of 1917 to the fall of 1918.

A *Denver Post* article on March 4, 1918, describes an employee at a bus and cab company who had an altercation with a fellow employee over disparaging remarks against Wilhelm II (last German Emperor). He was then severely beaten and required to kiss the American flag. When he refused, a rope was placed around his neck and he was dragged behind a truck to the *Denver Post* headquarters, where he collapsed and was rushed to the hospital. In Boulder, all businesses tied anti-German sentiment into their advertising in an effort to boost the sales of Liberty bonds and to show patriotism. On April 4, 1918, the *Daily Camera* carried a Boulder Flour Mills ad which began with "Boost the Bonds that Buy the Bombs to Bust the Beast of Berlin. We'll put the Kaiser on the Run and add the letter G to Hun." Tensions also rose between newspapers. When a *Rocky Mountain News* and *Denver Times* cartoonist refused on November 10, 1918, to stand at a restaurant when the house band struck up the national anthem, the *Denver Post* took his actions to task with an editorial on November 14, accusing the newspapers he worked for to be Hun-loving newspapers, openly pro-German, and serving the Kaiser while posing as American institutions.[58] The university had a public book-burning rally "to throw in books written in German as well as those in English that made favorable comments about Germans or Germany."[59] At times, the war-fueled anti-German sentiment spilled over into entertainment, which included blackface Minstrels. Like most of the Black middle class in the early twentieth century, Lucile would have seen this type of entertainment as demonizing Blacks while she and others were fighting to uplift the race. Thus, during her final semester at the university she read in the *Silver and Gold*, "Black-Faces to Play Jazz Music for Soph Dance." The dance, billed as an "anti-German dance," took place on Friday, March 8, in the Armory building and featured Jackson's orchestra of Denver and the six singing "nigger minstrels."[60]

After stoking anti-German sentiment on campus, the university administration sought not to let mass hysteria govern its academic mission while staying committed to its patriotic duty. In blending these two missions, the university moved quickly to include a number of war-related subjects such as military explosives and military mapping and sketching in appropriate courses and to install new courses. On January 11, 1918, the *Silver and Gold* published a news story under the headline "New German Classes Installed to Help Future War Workers," such as Colorado and the War, the United States and the War, the European Origins of the War, Governments and Ideals of the States at War, Military Hygiene and Sanitation, and Automobile Construction and Maintenance.[61]

There was also a large push to study the German language for practical reasons. These classes demonstrated the need for military officers to speak German and the desirability of knowing German for members of the secret service and other government agencies. Again the university leadership took a strong and practical position by saying that "despite the war and its prejudices, the university has determined to keep up the department of German knowing its value as a weapon with which to fight the Kaiser."[62]

SAVING THE RACE

By the time Lucile arrived in Boulder, she had been well schooled in the opposing philosophies of Booker T. Washington and W.E.B. Du Bois on the best ways to fight White supremacy and advance self-sufficiency. Washington's accommodation philosophy advised Blacks to trust the paternalism of southern Whites, accept the fact of White supremacy, and help themselves through parallel institutions. Du Bois placed his faith in legal and political action, which required education, particularly in the liberal arts.[63]

While Lucile's parents stressed more of the self-help economic program that Washington propagated, she leaned more toward Du Bois's model of the Talented Tenth:

Can the masses of the Negro people be in any possible way more quickly raised than by the effort and example of this aristocracy of talent and character? ... [I]t is, ever was, and ever will be from the top downward that culture filters. The Talented Tenth rises and pulls all that are worth the saving up ... This is the history of human progress ... How then shall the leaders of a struggling people be trained and the hands of the risen few strengthened? There can be but one answer: the best and most capable of their youth must be schooled in the colleges and universities of the land.[64]

In other words, Du Bois recommended a classic liberal arts education for elite Blacks, who would then use their superior intellect, knowledge, and reasoning to battle racial inequities while educating their own poor masses. In an attempt to help her farther understand Du Bois's thinking, she purchased a copy of *The Souls of Black Folk* and gave it to her father as a birthday gift in December 1909. The fact that she gave her father this particular book, in which Du Bois turned every historical tenet that excluded Blacks from the political and civil life of mainstream society upside down, reinforced what he accomplished in the Barnum community.

Clearly, her father did not frown on his children having a liberal arts college education; two of his children pursued a college education. But her father also knew how much his hard work had paid off and how through that work he had gained a level of respectability in mainstream society. Through it he overcame, albeit modestly, the stigma of being Black in the growing community of Barnum, and through his business skills he earned the respect of many Whites. Lucile witnessed Washington's philosophy pay off in her own home, yet she lived with the hope of Du Bois's dream for the entire race.

DISAPPOINTMENT AND TRIUMPH

Lucile entered the University of Colorado as student number 2464. The Registrar's Office scheduled her to graduate with the class of 1919. Lucile was not preoccupied with campus social life, and she was disciplined and hardworking in her courses. Thus, after completing four semesters of coursework, she was ready to graduate by 1918.

Her transcript shows that she took the basic requirements of science, math, language, and the classics. Majoring in German, she had a choice of minoring in history, Latin, or French; she chose history, concentrating on European history. Since the university curriculum changed once the US entered World War I, Lucile registered for a popular course called "The United States and the War," which counted towards her minor in history. Of the thirty-three courses she took during her junior and senior years, sixteen were in her major or were relevant electives.

As the spring semester of 1918 came to a close and Lucile finished her final exams, she turned her attention to commencement: her excitement in her grand achievement and the joy and pride of her family in celebrating her accomplishments. Sadly, the excitement was overshadowed by the emotional turmoil following the untimely death of her father six months earlier. In spite of his physical absence, her mother (dressed in full mourning attire), two of her sisters, and a niece came to the university to support her and to witness the joyous event.

With the war taking center stage, the administration went all out to normalize the commencement ceremony. The day before the awarding of the degrees, the university held class-day exercises that went into the night, with the campus decorated with electric lights and a large American flag hoisted on the top of Old Main, lit by the rays of a strong searchlight. Class-day activities began at 10 a.m., with the faculty and graduates' baseball game at Gamble Field (presently the University Memorial Center). This was followed by the senior class farewell exercises, which began with the readings of the class prophecy at the library entrance (today the University Theater Building), the class history at the Hale Science Building, and the class oration at the Guggenheim Law Building. In the evening, Boulder's city band played several selections on the law school lawn. The festivities ended with an alumnus-sponsored event for the graduates at Macky Auditorium. There is no evidence to suggest that Lucile attended or participated in any of these events. What is known is that on the day of commencement the *Boulder Daily Camera* listed the names of all the graduates, including Lucile Berkeley Buchanan.[65]

On Wednesday, June 5, 1918, at 10 a.m., about 168 students, including Lucile, entered Macky Auditorium to begin their commencement exercises. The ceremony was simple. As the faculty and students entered the building, twenty members of the Denver Symphony Orchestra, led by George M. Chadwick, professor of music, played "Minuetto" from the first *L'Arlessienne* Suite by Georges Bizet. An alumnus and current university professor, Rev. David Loren, gave the invocation, followed by a musical interlude consisting of "Sous lestilleuls" by Massenet. President Livingston Farrand returned briefly from France to deliver the commencement address and confer the degrees on the graduates.[66] After the awarding of degrees, the audience joined the graduates in singing "America" and then listened to the benediction offered by Robert A. Schell, pastor at the Christian Church of Boulder.

Of the graduating class, about 43 percent, or seventy-three individuals, were women. Sixty-four of those seventy-three earned their Bachelor of Arts degree. Of the rest, four received training in nursing, one earned her bachelor's degree in pharmacy, two earned doctorates in medicine, and two received Master of Arts degrees. Lucile's name was tenth in the commencement program's list of those receiving their Bachelor of Arts degree.

However, something went wrong. The joy of this momentous occasion quickly turned to grief as a cruel twist of irony compounded the recent loss of her father. Her niece, Evelyn Napper, describes what happened next: "I recall that she told me about her experiences at CU. She said that CU officials did not want her to appear onstage with her graduation class. Thus, they sent a woman 'classmate' to Aunt Lucy while she was sitting and waiting for her name to be called. The woman gave her the following message . . . 'I'll be your partner, Lucy.' Then she placed Aunt Lucy's diploma in her hand and 'disappeared.' Aunt Lucy never did go onstage."[67]

As Evelyn explains, they cruelly denied Lucile the opportunity to participate in her own commencement, depriving her of the privilege rightfully expected of all graduates, to hear her name called out and to walk across the stage to receive her diploma. As the only one of Sarah and James's children to earn a bachelor's degree, and with her mother proudly watching this momentous occasion, the event had turned sour. I can only surmise that the phrase, "I'll be your partner, Lucy" implied that when Lucile's name was called, if it was called at all, she, the White classmate, would be her stand-in onstage. Lucile left the University of Colorado on June 5, 1918, vowing never to return. She kept her promise.

But the university's actions did not diminish the pride Lucile felt regarding her accomplishments. She had completed her degree. She had her diploma. The question was, how could she get the word out about her accomplishments? Beginning in July 1914, The Crisis magazine, the official organ of the NAACP, began to record the names of Blacks who had degrees confirmed upon them by universities and colleges throughout the country, including the Ivy League schools, northern private institutions, state universities, and the leading Black colleges and universities. How were Du Bois and the NAACP able to pull off this feat, and did they capture all the graduates?

Under the headings "Our Graduates" and "the Year in Negro Education," the magazine listed those who earned bachelor, master's, doctoral, and professional degrees, including any special commendations awarded to members of graduating classes, certainly a major undertaking by a national magazine to showcase the most educated young Black Americans. But then again, it speaks to the value placed on higher education within the Black community.

The year Lucile earned her bachelor's degree, The Crisis devoted many column inches to higher education. The July 1918 issue began with this report: "The war has made serious inroads on Negro education, but the harvest is still commendable. Twelve students take higher degrees in arts (masters and doctorate); 384

FIGURE 10.4. *Lucile (center) holding her diploma poses with her mother Sarah (far right), her sisters Hattie Jarrett and Edith Davis and niece Carol Jarrett (far left), outside the family's home on Raleigh Street, Denver, on June 5, 1918. Buchanan Archives.*

Bachelors in Arts and Sciences; and 475 in learned professions (e.g., law, medicine, dentistry, theology, pharmacy, veterinary medicine, teacher training and nursing), and partial reports give nearly 2,000 graduated from the high schools."[68]

The article went on to discuss the 31 Black students who received Bachelor of Arts and Science degrees from renowned private colleges and universities such as Brown, Carnegie, Colgate, Cornell, Dartmouth, Radcliffe, and Smith; the 209 degrees conferred on Black students from the thirty-one Historically Black Colleges and Universities, including Atlanta University, Fisk, Florida A&M, Howard, Lincoln, Morehouse, Spelman, and Wilberforce; and the fifteen state universities, including Colorado, Illinois, Kansas, Michigan, Ohio State, and Pittsburgh, who conferred Bachelor of Arts and Science degrees on 29 students.

In a rare occurrence, Lucile is listed twice in the article. She is first listed among the 29 graduates from the state universities: "Lucile Buchanan, *University of Colorado*," and later she is one of nineteen students among the 871 graduates that Du Bois chose to profile with a photograph and the caption, "MISS L. B. BUCHANAN, Colorado."[69]

It is still unclear as to how Lucile or any other student became featured in *The Crisis* since I could not find any announcements for graduates to submit their information. However, the information traveled to Du Bois, and *The Crisis* let it be known that Lucile earned her bachelor's degree at the University of Colorado, that she was proud of her accomplishment, and that she was now a newly minted female member of the "Talented Tenth."

Education and self-determination were at the top of Lucile's agenda at the turn of the twentieth century as she mastered the skills needed for success from all-White institutions in Colorado, adding to what she had learned from her parents (survivors of chattel slavery) and from informal education channels such as Denver's Black press, the *Statesman*, which gave her a wide perspective on local, national, and international news as well as the perils of racism and discrimination. The discrimination that she faced from the Denver school board in 1905 and her being denied to walk across a stage to receive in hand her diploma from the University of Colorado in 1918 led her to devote a lifetime of service to race advancement.

11

"Goin' to Kansas City"

EDUCATION AND BASEBALL

I'm coming to do a job and that's what I'm going to do.
— CHARLEY PRIDE

In July 2008, a quick hour-and-a-half plane ride took me from Denver to Kansas City, Missouri. Almost a hundred years ago, Lucile took the same trip in the fall of 1919 for a teaching position at that city's all-Black Lincoln High School. There were some significant differences in our trips, of course. In the fall of 1919, Lucile spent about thirteen-and-a-half hours in a segregated railroad car. And while I stayed downtown at the lavish Art Deco–style Phillips Hotel, Jim Crow segregation laws, race restrictive covenants,[1] and local customs required that Lucile find lodging within the confines of the Black community.

WALKING THE WALK AS A COMMUNITY STRIKES BACK

After spending several days searching through Kansas City's archival repositories, I set out on Saturday, July 19, 2008, to find the historic Washington Wheatley neighborhood where Lucile had lived eighty-nine years ago. I came prepared to walk where she walked, to see what she saw, to feel what she might have felt. Yet in every field research endeavor there are challenges and restrictions, some of which I was about to discover.

Aja, my Albanian-born cab driver, seemed uneasy when I gave him Lucile's old address at 2444 Montgall Avenue. At about 7:00 a.m, with the morning dew still wet on the streets and the sun barely over the horizon, I felt an unnatural quiet in the air. Armed only with a disposable camera, a researcher's curiosity, and a passion to uncover Lucile's past, I was driven through streets still empty of human and vehicular traffic. As we neared Montgall Avenue, it struck me that the neighborhood was especially hit hard by the US housing bubble of the early twenty-first century. Many businesses and homes were boarded up and dilapidated. I knew that a similar picture had existed when Lucile arrived. I couldn't help but think of the French expression, "plus ça change, plus c'est la même chose"—the more things change, the more they stay the same.

Aja and I slowly drove through the neighborhood in search of Lucile's home. I busied myself snapping photos through the window from the right passenger side. Without warning, a red pickup truck sped by us and just as quickly swerved around, forcing Aja to make a quick stop. We sat startled, confused, and a bit in fear as a middle-aged Black man just as quickly jumped out of the truck and appeared at the driver's-side window, demanding to know where we were going, why we were in his neighborhood, and, after noticing my camera, why I was taking pictures. Quickly working to head off the storm brewing, I exited the cab and graciously introduced myself, displayed my university faculty ID, and told the stranger about my journey to find Lucile and the house she lived in during the 1920s. To my surprise, he not only knew the exact house on Montgall, he happily volunteered to lead us there. Breathing a sigh of relief, we followed. Once there, he parked his truck and beckoned us to join him.

There we were on an early Saturday morning, listening to a history lesson about the house on the corner of East Twenty-fifth Street and Montgall Avenue. I learned about the community's efforts to preserve the house, its importance to Missouri's Black history, and its last known occupant, Lucile Bluford. At this point, I did not know who Lucile Bluford was and whether a relationship between her and Lucile Buchanan existed.

About twenty minutes into my impromptu history lesson, another car driven by a younger Black male passed by. The man yelled out his window, "What's going on here?" After again explaining my search for Lucile and the relevance of the house on Montgall, he, too, joined the conversation. So here I am, meeting community historians gleefully sharing the oral history of their neighborhood. Equally fascinating is witnessing the kind of watchdog role individuals played, especially during the era of de jure segregation, when Lucile lived here some eighty-nine years earlier and how it's being played out by a new generation. I am beginning to see through Lucile's eyes.

HEAR ME, SEE ME

In August 1919, about a year after completing her bachelor's degree at the University of Colorado, Lucile arrived in Kansas City to teach English at Lincoln High School (Kansas City's first Black public school).[2] She had declined a teaching position a year earlier at Slater Industrial and State Normal School in Winston-Salem, North Carolina. This would be Lucile's third teaching position in a racially segregated school system. Lincoln also had the distinction of being one of two schools in the Kansas City tri-county area (Jackson, Clay, and Platte Counties) that provided post-elementary education to Black children.[3] And while segregation speaks of racial injustices and unimaginable disparities, because of the superbly qualified teachers at Lincoln and the impact the school had within the community, I could not help but think about what Du Bois described in his 1922 landmark study on the role of Blacks during Reconstruction: "Had it not been for the Negro school, the Negro would, to all intents and purposes, have been driven back to slavery."[4]

Lucile had several advantages in Kansas City. A number of Denver's middle-class Blacks had moved there in the early 1900s, where there was a larger Black population, more businesses, more career opportunities, and a thriving cultural scene. In 1920 Kansas City's Black population numbered about 14,405 (14.2% of the total population of approximately 101,177) whereas Denver's Black population was 6,075 (2.4% of the total population of approximately 256,491).[5] One renowned Denverite, Chester Arthur Franklin, former editor and publisher of Denver's the *Statesman* and the *Denver Star*, migrated to Kansas City in 1913.

In May 1919, three months prior to Lucile's arrival, Franklin launched the *Kansas City Call*, which would become one of the six largest Black weekly newspapers in the country.[6] Lucile and Franklin were no strangers. In 1899 Franklin helped create Denver's Inter-Graduate Student Association, which celebrated Lucile's educational accomplishments in 1901 and 1905. Prior to her arrival, the block on Montgall Avenue had been a favorite dwelling place for teachers at Lincoln and other local schools with several of these teachers hailing from Denver.

Soon after arriving in Kansas City, Lucile wasted no time getting in step with the freedom that symbolized the "new woman" of the 1920s. She moved easily from being a Gibson Girl of the 1910s into a fashionable flapper of the 1920s. She even bobbed her hair in the flapper style. Her dresses were shorter and her necklines lower than those of other Black women teachers in Kansas City's only Black high school.[7] All across the country the old restrictions on dress and behavior were being overthrown. Lucile's education and progressive home life instilled in her the flexibility and strong self-confidence necessary to believe that she, a woman, could make choices for herself in her education, jobs, marital status, and career.

New popular forms of entertainment and artistic expression took center stage. A short walk from her residence along the Vine Street corridor brought her to the commercial and cultural center of the Black community. The historic Eighteenth and Vine, referred to as the "Paris of the Plains," was known for its rambunctious nightlife; jazz and blues clubs were the center of commerce, entertainment, and economic development for the district's growing African American community. It is here that she was able to experience the rich jazz and blues legacy of Bennie Moten's Orchestra and the blues women Lottie Beaman and Ada Brown.

Not surprisingly, living in a majority Black community had advantages as well as disadvantages. The state legislature in 1889 actively promoted separation and segregation, making it unlawful for "any colored child to attend a white school or any white child to attend a colored school."[8] By the time Lucile arrived, Kansas City had adopted Jim Crow laws, which erected barriers to all levels of socioeconomic development, including separate schools for Black and White children. To counteract intolerance and discrimination, a number of Black organizations took care of the social, political, health, educational, recreational, and economic needs of the community. These organizations included the Kansas City branch of the NAACP, of which Lucile and many of her fellow teachers were active members, and also the Urban League, the National Negro Business League, the Wheatley-Provident Hospital, the Paseo YMCA, and the Kansas City Colored Women's League.

A number of theaters were also located within the historic Eighteenth and Vine corridor. Built mainly by White entrepreneurs, they sought to capitalize by offering an alternative to the racial humiliation commensurate with the segregation of downtown theaters. A newspaper advertisement in the *Kansas City Sun* on February 22, 1920, described their patrons as representing "the social life of that large and ever-increasing number of our racial group who bitterly resent the discrimination and Jim-Crowism practiced at down-town theaters and who from a standpoint of refinement, culture and intelligence deserve an amusement place in keeping with the advancement of the race." While some of the theaters, like the Gem, the New Rialto, and Love's, primarily featured B-rated movies, the Lincoln and the Eblon—the city's only Black-owned and operated theaters—featured nationally known talent, variety and dramatic shows, Vaudeville performances, and local jazz orchestras, such as the Dave Lewis Jazz Boys, the George E. Lee Singing Novelty Orchestra, the Paul Banks Orchestra, and Bennie Moten's Kansas City Orchestra.

For Lucile, Kansas City was remarkable for another reason—baseball. In 1925 Vernithia Weddington, a member of the Lincoln High School's yearbook committee, asked each of the school's forty-six teachers about their hobbies. Thirty-three teachers (twenty males and thirteen females) responded. Looking at the role of gender, male teachers reported hobbies that were either sports-related or work-centered, turning the subject they taught into a hobby—"composing romances" from the music teacher, "gathering flowers" from the science teacher, "working in the school's bank" from the business teacher, and "looking up aged history books" from a history teacher. Among the thirteen female teachers, twelve stated either an activity associated with women in the private sphere—"creating hat fashions," "making up recipes," "making over foods"—or a nurturing hobby—"looking after the seniors" or "giving the girls good advice." Lucile, true to her cosmopolitan nature, answered "Going to Baseball Games."

In Kansas City, attending baseball games became a major cultural activity for Blacks. Some say that the birth of the Negro National League in February 1920 implanted baseball into the DNA of the city's Black citizens. Lucile particularly favored the team that would have the longest-running franchise in the history of the Negro League: the Kansas City Monarchs. Monarch games featured an additional showcase that probably sparked her interest. The Lincoln High School Marching Band often participated in the opening-game parades, and Lincoln's High School Cadets raised the American flag before home games at Muehlbach Field less than a mile from the school.

For fans across gender and socioeconomic strata, Monarch games became the ultimate social and glamor event of the week, with opening games styled as a "Fashion Parade." Janet Bruce's book on the Kansas City Monarchs notes, "Most fans did not attend in casual clothes . . . men dressed up in straw hats, patent leather shoes, and suits. Women had their hair done, their fur stoles on and their hats on—just like they left church." In fact, some churches ended their service early in order to accommodate the Sunday afternoon games.[9] Monarch games gave women the opportunity to dress in their Sunday's finest, whether at the popular Sunday afternoon games or the "free ladies' night games" during the week.[10]

Even though baseball took on a special role in Lucile's social and community life, education remained her major priority. The 1925 yearbook staff asked teachers about their favorite sayings. Most responded whimsically, "we will now hear an inspirational talk," or "such lovely ornaments," or came across as disciplinarians, "I mean business," or "shut your mouths." However, Lucile spoke to the students' learning as she emphatically said, "Few Minutes for Study." These four words reveal a lot about her commitment to education and the ethic of excellence she passed on to her students.

NO STEPS BACKWARD

While Kansas City offered Lucile a plethora of options to explore life in the Black community, Lincoln High School offered her some of the same challenges she had experienced in the state-segregated school systems in Hot Springs and Little Rock, Arkansas. Officially established as a high school in 1890 at the corner of Nineteenth Street and Tracey Avenue, Lincoln lacked equipment, had inadequate facilities, and was severely overcrowded. According to Roy Wilkins,[11] a reporter and managing editor of the *Kansas City Call*, Lincoln was "in a high-crime neighborhood bounded by 'Murder Street' on one side and rows of bootlegging joints and vice dens on the other."[12]

As Henrietta Rix Wood states, "overcrowding was such that six to eight classes were held on the stairs each day; seventeen teachers lacked desks; the minuscule lunchroom forced students to eat lunch in the halls and adjoining classrooms; windows in the science classrooms remained open year-round because of a leaky gas line; and there was no library, study hall, art department, or gymnasium."[13] What the school did have was a plethora of talented teachers[14] and a community willing to challenge the inequities of Lincoln's situation before the all-White Kansas City School Board through the political efforts of individual citizens, highly recognized Black organizations,[15] and assistance from the two local Black newspapers, the *Kansas City Sun*,[16] and the *Kansas City Call*.[17] Even with all the efforts of the Black community, it took eleven years to address the overcrowding with the construction of a new high school. In the meantime, students and teachers at Lincoln had to settle for minor changes, including the addition of an auditorium, and a free lending library, which was open to any resident of the city for the 1922–23 school term.[18] With a library, Lucile, the English teacher, was in her element, as she knew that books opened opportunities for her students and herself.

Unlike Langston High School in Hot Springs, with its academic instability, by the time Lucile arrived at Lincoln, it ranked as one of the leading high schools for Black students in the country. While certain expectations and decorum were part of student life, for this second generation born after slavery who came of age in the Progressive era, school was their world (academic, vocational, and social). Preparing a generation to survive and to lead in the face of overarching racism became the school's mission.

Although Lincoln had history classes—American and European—Black history was not part of the curriculum. However, in 1924, when Lincoln established the Negro History Club, students' interest was so profound that the school leadership took notice and instituted a regular class in Negro History, for which students received full history credits. Apart from receiving traditional academics, students at Lincoln also obtained vocational training. Boys took classes in gas engine repair, stationary engineering, painting, and building trades. Girls were offered sewing, millinery, cooking, nursing, and home economics. Both genders took classes in bookkeeping and shorthand.[19]

Twice a month, John Robert Edward Lee, the principal of Lincoln (1915–21), held "Community Meetings" with the intention of "showing the people this is their school for their own interest and uplift."[20] Held in the high school auditorium, the first meeting of the month provided an opportunity for school and community groups to demonstrate their musical talents. The second meeting was a strategic move on Lee's part, designed to bring together prominent community leaders, renowned philanthropists, school board members and presidents, local activist groups, such as the Woman's Christian Temperance Union, and principals and teachers from the "Colored" ward schools around Lincoln.

Continuing its community service tradition, Lincoln's vocational training program gave students valuable experience by servicing schools and community institutions. The Master Painter's Club used its talents to improve the furniture and buildings of the Niles Home for Negro Children and the Crittenden Home for Colored Girls. The boys of the 1919 Freshman Club built a two-room annex onto the Attucks School, the closest Black elementary. Students further extended their community outreach by participating in Kansas City's Liberty Memorial Campaign, a subscription endeavor to raise money for charity and to erect a memorial for Kansas Citians who had fought in World War I.

Lincoln played a major role in the social and cultural lives of its students. During the 1920s, a team of teachers planned bi-monthly school socials on Friday nights, from 8:00 to 11:00 p.m. The Dramatic and Arts Clubs, the Girls' Glee Club, the popular Lincoln Orchestra (mixed genders), the male-only Lincoln High School Band, and athletics became unifying forces between the school and the community.

TEACHING BEYOND THE CLASSROOM

As usual, Lucile's involvement with students outside the classroom began upon her arrival. She became one of five advisers for the local Junior Branch of the National Association for the Advancement of Colored People (NAACP), which

FIGURE 11.1. *World Affairs Club members, Lucile Buchanan, third row, left, ca. 1925. Buchanan Archives.*

had a membership of about 400 students. A reporter for the 1925 yearbook said, "Gradually, it is being instilled into the minds of our young people that one of the best ways to help ourselves is to help others, and as we realize that fact, we bent our back to the yoke willingly."[21]

Because of the sheer size of the incoming class in 1924, the administration divided the students into four groups, with each group having elected student officers and a supervising teacher. Lucile supervised Group 2 with Juanita Mills as president; Alberta V. Bean, secretary; Katie Rogers, treasurer; Dorothy Breach, chair of the program committee; and Woody Lee Walder as sergeant-of-arms.[22] The purpose was to engender a sense of camaraderie within the class, maintain school spirit, and help with the transition to high school.

In her third-hour English class, Lucile created the World News Club, which in a subtle and subversive way internationalized the curriculum. Her upbringing in Barnum, Colorado, among a plethora of first- and second-generation European immigrants, the impact of her liberal arts education—which included majoring in German—and her habit of staying informed about the activities Black leaders were beginning to engage in (pan-Africanism, for example), helped her see the world through a more global lens than did most of her colleagues, and she passed this approach on to her students at every opportunity. The World News Club, which in 1925 consisted of twenty-five students, was created with the purpose of "realizing that education means far more than obtaining knowledge from their text." One period each week was devoted to discussing world news and according to the yearbook, students "subscribed to an excellent weekly, which helped them with their learning."[23]

In the fall of 1925, Lucile initiated a project with the first-year students in her English class to create the school's first newspaper, the *Observer*.[24] The monthly newspaper was intended to "stimulate a desire for better English, written as well as spoken, and to make possible a certain ease in writing on matters of importance, which interest the students. A high standard of conduct for Lincoln is one of the main planks in its platform." To offset the cost, the four-page publication sold for three cents at first and eventually for five cents per copy. Selling the school paper for five cents was a brazen move, in that the local commercial Black newspaper, the *Call*, sold for the same price. Nonetheless, Lucile was able to garner sufficient support. The third issue included advertising for a local grocery store, movie theater, and purchasing sanitary (paper) cups, which are "guaranteed to cure all kinds of stomach and other ills," suggesting that the paper's demographics went beyond students and included teachers and possibly parents from Lincoln's very active parent-teacher association.

As for the staff, there was an editor, a business manager, four associate editors, and four reporters. The paper's content included local entertainment, letters to the editor, editorials, school happenings at Lincoln and the other all-Black schools in Kansas City, club activities, sports, alumni news, and poetry.[25]

One of the young reporters on staff, fourteen-year-old Lucile Bluford, began what would become a lifelong career in journalism at the *Observer*. However, there was much more to the story of Lucile Bluford and her English teacher, Lucile Buchanan. A year before Lucile's arrival in Kansas City, Bluford's father, John Henry, a graduate of Howard and Cornell Universities, became the chemistry teacher at Lincoln. A recent widower, John Henry, his new wife, Ada, and his three children—six-year-old Lucile, four-year-old John Jr., and two-year-old Guyon—moved into a large, two-story house at 2444 Montgall Avenue, a predominately White community in which middle-class Blacks were slowly buying property. Lucile lived with the Blufords from 1919 through the end of the 1925 school year, giving her and the younger Lucile six years to get to know one another. In 1924 Bluford entered Lincoln High School. It was at this crucial moment in Bluford's young life that she was first introduced to journalism. The third issue of the *Observer* included articles by her on sports and entertainment, which exhibited her curiosity, penchant for detail, and strong writing skills.[26]

In 1925, at the end of Bluford's freshman year, her mentor, Lucile, left for Chicago to assume a position at an all-Black elementary school. The *Observer* was taken over by another English teacher, Trussie Smothers, who began teaching at Lincoln in 1924. She soon changed the name of the paper to the *Lincolnite*. Bluford continued to work for both the newspaper and the yearbook, the *Lincolnian*. With the changing of the guard, Lucile's contribution to young Bluford's life and career was wiped from the annals of history.

Bluford would go on to become one of the most recognized and respected journalists in Missouri's history. Following her graduation from Lincoln, she attended the University of Kansas, where she studied journalism and worked on the school's newspaper, the *Daily Kansan*. After graduating, Bluford worked at the Georgia-based newspaper the *Daily World*. Returning to Kansas City, she worked at the *Kansas City American* and at the *Kansas City Call*.

Bluford's fiery spirit and determination to fight the inequities of Jim Crow would take her all the way to Missouri's State Supreme Court after the University of Missouri School of Journalism denied her graduate application in 1939. As a result of her persistence, rather than allow her to attend, the school shut down its journalism program. While the State Supreme Court finally ruled in her favor in 1941, Bluford never attended the University of Missouri. She continued her climb in the journalism profession at the *Call*, where she advanced from reporter to city editor to managing editor and eventually editor and publisher. All along the way, she used the written word to become a leading voice in the civil rights movement in Kansas City. No wonder the community historians I met on the streets of Kansas City were so moved to tell a stranger her story on a random Saturday morning.

Over time, I began to understand Lucile's use of newspapers in her personal and professional life. I remembered the letter to the editor she wrote when she got tired of being silent about conditions in Hot Springs, Arkansas. I understood the importance she placed on newspapers as an effective tool in teaching all sorts of valuable skills to the students in her English classes. And I saw that her desire to help students realize their full potential as global citizens through co-curricular activities in her World News Club was of equal importance to her.

In the 1925 Lincolnian yearbook, the last in which Lucile was included, the graduating class wrote a column titled "Ten Years from Now On" about their hopes for their teachers. Their hopes for the woman born in a shed in Denver's Platte River Bottoms were lofty but indicative of her strengths and their admiration for her as they wrote, "Miss Buchanan will be teaching English at Harvard University."[27]

12

It's Mister Jones, If You Please

It's a long old road, but I know I'm gonna find the end.

—BESSIE SMITH

Lucile fiercely guarded the details of her marriage and her husband. Details of his life are shrouded in secrecy. After much prodding from inquiring neighbors in Barnum, she would only divulge the name "Mister Jones." Her silence also extended to family members. In our correspondence, Lucile's niece Evelyn also referred to him as "Mister Jones" and did not know his given name. While Lucile turned a deaf ear when pressed for details, she did not hesitate to say that he "died in a duel."[1]

SEARCHING FOR HER SILENCE

At first, I interpreted Lucile's lack of disclosure through the lens of communicative properties that are indicative of the Black community, especially among elders.[2] One of these properties concerns what is shared, and not shared, regarding relationships and relationship development. A number of researchers suggest that when it comes to self-disclosure, Whites tend to reveal more information about themselves than do Blacks.[3] Therefore, cultural mistrust may have guided Lucile's behavior. Throughout her life, and even more so at age 103, she chose to determine what would or would not be disclosed about her personal life. But overall, referring to one's husband as "Mister" was not unusual. Because of the legacy of discrimination and disrespect Blacks endured from the days of chattel slavery, titles became more important, as they are the one symbol used across socioeconomic status and education levels that ensured respect within the Black community, even when that respect was denied them by the larger White population.

Lucile was also raised in an era when it was not uncommon for husbands and wives to address each other formally—as Mr. or Mrs.—in both private and public spheres. Lucile referred to most adult males with this level of formality, even those related to her by marriage. When she sent holiday greeting cards to her sister Hattie in Denver, the inscription read, "To Hattie and Mr. Jarrett" or "My regards to Mr. J., Lovingly Lucile." Although Lucile used the formal title to show deference to her sister and her brother-in-law, she also used formal titles as a way to exercise her autonomy and agency, negotiating a fate no longer under her control. Vi Garlington, a former administrator at Stovall Care Center in Denver, where Lucile spent her final years, agrees: "The staff had this habit of calling the elders by their first name and she would correct them. 'I've taught children older than your mother, you call me Mrs. Jones,' she would say. The staff complained, but [they] did end up calling her Mrs. Jones upon my insistence. She is probably the only one they called that way."[4]

From the beginning of my journey, Lucile became the name attached to her. But as I began to interview those who knew her, I was introduced to her as Mrs. Jones. How did this come about? As Doris Smith, who bought Lucile's house, said:

> Mrs. Jones is what Lucy called herself and expected everyone to call her. I know
> she'd set us straight right from the beginning that she was to be called Mrs. Jones
> and not Lucy. For her it was the respectful thing to do. As for me, I thought that
> it distanced her from other people. "Can we just be Doris and Lucy?" I would ask.
> "No," she would say. "How old are you, young lady? You can be Doris as long as I am
> Mrs. Jones." Even people at Stovall called her Mrs. Jones, I am sure at her insistence.[5]

Lucile lived in a world where societal practices, even the seemingly innocuous practice of calling Black women by their first names or "girl," rendered them inferior. Especially as an elder Black woman, a centenarian at that, deference mattered to her. She was after all, "Mrs. Jones."

Still, the secrecy surrounding Mr. Jones piqued my curiosity. However, finding Mr. Jones, even with a first name, is akin to squeezing an elephant through the eye of a needle—next to impossible. This is largely because the name Jones, according to the 2010 US Census, is the fifth most popular surname in the United States.[6]

As to the story of his death, I quickly debunked the notion that it resulted from a duel. By the time of Lucile's birth in 1884, the sport of honor had lost favor as a means to settle personal grievances among men of distinction, as democratic processes became more entrenched. Besides, American dueling was largely an upper-class White tradition in the South during the eighteenth and nineteenth centuries, and it held no significance among Blacks or poor Whites. Thus, by the end of the Civil War in 1865, dueling had gone out of vogue as "modern warfare, with its wholesale slaughter, redefined the meaning of personal honor for the southern gentleman and dueling became a romantic historical event."[7]

Why, then, the dueling story? Did her age impact her memory? Did she adopt this story as a way to deflect discussing her personal disappointments? Was she saving face? From the beginning, I felt this story may have been anchored in any number of rhetorical devices used by African Americans, such as indirection (meandering around a point), improvisation, or inventiveness.[8] The more I talked to Doris, the more I became convinced that Lucile likely employed a discourse pattern she had used over time. Nonetheless, I still attempted to pursue the dueling angle, since it was her reality.

THE FIRST STRETCH

Lucile spent a major portion of her adult life working in Chicago. Given her attachment to that city, if there was a Mr. Jones in her life who died so tragically, I thought it likely that they had met there. A search of the Chicago Police Department's Homicide Record Index for 1877–1930, the Illinois Statewide Death Index for 1916–50, and the local press, including the *Chicago Defender*, turned up not one story about a duel or a Black male named Jones dying in a duel. I thought I had hit a brick wall.

About two years later, in September 2007, I found my first clue of the real identity of Mr. Jones in the contents of Lucile's steamer trunk: a well-kept 1925 *Maroon and Gold* yearbook from Columbian Heights High School in Winston-Salem, North Carolina. On the first page of the yearbook is a photo of a well-dressed Black male with intense gray eyes. The dedication below the photo reads: "To our beloved Principal John D. Jones who has worked so earnestly and efficiently in the interest of the students of Columbian Heights High School, we, the Class of '25, respectfully dedicate this book." The trunk also contained a framed version of the same picture. Had I found the "Mister Jones" in Lucile's life? I began at Winston-Salem State University, where the archives for Columbian Heights High School were stored. Little did I know then that my trek to discover Mister Jones and his relationship to Lucile would take me as far north as New York City and as far south as Tuskegee, Alabama, before ending right back in Chicago.

The Columbian Heights High School yearbook contained a listing of the eighteen teachers and their degree qualifications—thirteen held bachelor degrees, with four from predominantly White institutions. The remainder of the faculty had teaching qualifications from historically Black teacher training schools (Hampton and Tuskegee). One of the four with a degree from a largely White institution was Principal John D. Jones. He earned his A.B. degree from my alma mater, Columbia University in New York City. That would be my next stop.

Columbia's alumni archive revealed a John D. Jones who graduated during the first decade of the twentieth century. I learned that his middle initial "D" stood for "Dotha." Over the next several years, my journey began to feel like I was piecing together a human quilt filled with jarring experiences, emotional highs and lows, memories, and deep secrets. Who was John Dotha Jones? How was his life shaped? What was his narrative? And if he was Lucile's husband, what had attracted them to each other? What was the outcome of their relationship?

EARLY LIFE

On Tuesday, November 22, 1888, Minerva (Minnie) Hughes from Charlottesville, Virginia, and Early Jones of Petersburg, Virginia, welcomed their second son, John Dotha, in Philadelphia, Pennsylvania. The couple had moved in the mid-1880s from Petersburg/Dinwiddie, Virginia, to Philadelphia, as the country was beginning to experience the onset of the Great Migration. They lived in severely overcrowded and unsanitary conditions in a small wood house they shared with twelve other people. Working conditions were not much better. Early was illiterate. Minerva could only read. For Early, leaving Petersburg probably meant better employment opportunities, as well as freedom from the onslaught of lynching and other forms of racial violence and White supremacy that took hold in Virginia after Reconstruction fell apart in 1877.

After arriving in Philadelphia, Early took the only job in high demand and available to the majority of Black men: laborer.[9] Shortly after John's birth, the family moved to New York City, where Early worked carting goods and equipment throughout the city on a wheeled hand-powered vehicle. The family settled in a tenement building at 130 West Twenty-seventh Street, within the old Tenderloin district stretching from about Twenty-fifth to Fifty-fifth Streets and from Fifth to Seventh Avenues. They were the only Blacks living in a building that was home to immigrants from Ireland, Russia, and Italy. While the Tenderloin was home to a large segment of New York City's Black population, they lived largely along Sixth Avenue. An 1889 *New York Times* article about the Tenderloin reported that Blacks were hemmed in by "prejudice" in the "meanest tenement district" and the worst housing in New York City.[10] The area was often referred to as Black Bohemia. Author Robert M. Dowling writes, "This region catered to African American musicians, gamblers, stage performers, and prostitutes, as well as white 'slummers,' and frequenters of the 'blacks and tans' (racially integrated bars that often provided interracial assignations and drew a great deal of public scorn)."[11]

After living in the city for almost three years, Early Jones took ill on March 7, 1891, and died on July 26 from kidney failure. Minerva, now widowed, did housework to support herself and her two sons. For a while she continued to live in the Tenderloin, even as Blacks began to move further north to San Juan Hill. Several years later, Minerva and her two sons took up residence in another tenement in the now historic Turtle Bay district. Both John and his brother, George, completed high school, with John entering Columbia College on September 27, 1906. He focused his studies on German and Latin, which formed the bedrock of a liberal arts education at the time. Brady Sloan, the associate registrar at Columbia University in 2007, said, "He had seven German courses and five Latin courses, which, when taken in the context of total courses taken, seems significant."[12]

COLUMBIA UNIVERSITY

Much like Lucile, John appears to have kept a low profile while at the university, though not necessarily by choice. The few Black students on campus "were often excluded . . . from the events opened to White students."[13] During the Progressive era, many major social reform organizations were headquartered in New York City, such as the NAACP, which opened in 1909, and the National Urban League, which opened in 1911. Therefore, Blacks had far more options to engage in the major issues of the day than Lucile would have had in Colorado.

In John's case, the only campus activity it appears he participated in was Phi Beta Kappa, the oldest and most prestigious undergraduate honor society in the United States, into which he was inducted in May 30, 1910. John was one of twelve Columbia graduates inducted into the society and one of only four graduates to earn "Highest Final General Honors."[14] He was also the only Black student inducted nationally that year and the only Black elected to the honor society in the first half of the twentieth century (1901–51).[15] Columbia's records indicated that John completed his coursework for his Bachelor of Arts degree on February 7, 1910, and graduated with the class of 1910 in June.

In 1948 Columbia's alumni office contacted George William Artway Scott, a friend and classmate, to ask about John's whereabouts.[16] In addition to the date of graduation and degree awarded, the alumni card indicated that John's mail had been returned and his address at Slater State Normal College, Winston-Salem, NC, crossed out. Penciled in the box were the words "Deceased. Q [question] to friend G.W.A. Scott at Tuskegee Inst. Ala. 3-19-48." I admit that I assumed John had died.

Nonetheless, I left Columbia that day walking five feet off the ground. After six years of searching, I had finally found Mr. Jones at, of all places, my alma mater. But who was John Dotha Jones? I wasn't sure of my next step until a few months later, when I received this email.

Dear Professor McLean:

I have some information on, and would like to talk to you about, John Dotha Jones. If you have the opportunity, I would love to speak or correspond with you.

All best wishes.
Jeffrey B. Perry

JONES, THE SCHOLAR ACTIVIST

Perry, like me, was on a mission to bring back into prominence, a Black intellectual history had forgotten, Hubert Harrison—writer, pubic speaker, labor organizer, intellectual genius, socialist, critic, activist—whom many labeled, "The father of Harlem Black radicalism." Harrison and John were close friends and Perry was searching for details of their relationship. Our path's crossed when he discovered a *Denver Post* article about Lucile, my journey and her marriage to John.[17] While at Columbia, John spent most of his free time with a circle of New York City's leading Black intellectuals and community activists, such as George Young, former Pullman porter and bibliophile; Cleveland G. Allen, journalist; Irene L. Moorman, president of the Negro Women Business League, Williana Jones, teacher and political activist, and finally Hubert Harrison.[18]

John and Harrison became fast friends and took delight in intellectual sparring. They often met at the St. Mark's Lyceum of St. Mark's Methodist Episcopal Church at 231 W. 53rd Street,[19] the largest Black church in New York City,[20] located in the Tenderloin district, and within walking distance of where John lived with his mother and brother. In the early 1900s, the district was flourishing as the city's southern-born Black population blended with the newly arriving Caribbean immigrants. As the district expanded, non-secular institutions servicing the needs of the Black community increased. These institutions included the Colored Business Men's Republican Club, the Colored Women's Republican Club, the White Rose Home for Colored Working Girls and fraternal and benevolent societies such as the Grand United Order of Odd Fellows, the United Brothers of Friendship, Sisters of the Mysterious Ten, the Colored Freemasons, and the Negro Elks.[21]

The Lyceum appears to have been an ideal public sphere for John in that its longevity and purpose likely matched his interest. In a July 7, 1907, *New York Times* letter to the editor John E. Robinson, the editor of the Lyceum's monthly paper, the *Mirror* states "The St. Mark's Lyceum has been in existence for nearly twenty-eight years and is the literary organization for many of the best and most representative colored men and women in greater New York"[22] as they discussed and debated major topics of the day and their impact on Black life both in the US and abroad.

Jones was certainly an active participant in the Lyceum and someone whom Harrison admired. As Perry notes, Harrison wrote in his diary in1908 that he had searched "for seven years" to surround himself with a group of equals who would strengthen his mind and was unable to find any, "except "in the person of Jones."[23]

For the next two years they continued to challenge each other through intellectual competition while John completed his third and final year at Columbia. On November 19, 1908, the younger John debated Harrison, journalist Cleveland G. Allen, and bookseller George Young on whether voter qualification should be a federal or state rights issue. Remarkably, John claimed first prize. Harrison took second prize wrote in his diary that while his loss took him and several members of the audience by surprise, he graciously acknowledges that John "spoke very, very well although neither his history nor his political science was very good."[24] With bolstered confidence, John soon challenge Harrison for the Lyceum critic's position. This time John was defeated, and Harrison was elected on December 10, 1908.[25]

This brief competition did not dampen their relationship. Harrison and John's friendship blossomed so much so that John was one of two witnesses at Harrison's wedding on April 17, 1909.[26] Later that year, Harrison and John were installed as judges of the "Y" Literary Society. John's presence at the "Y" led him to be labeled as "one of the popular Y.M.C.A. fellows."[27]

Up until this point, I thought I had uncovered all of John's activities both within and outside of Columbia. However, on August 24, 2009, I received yet another email. This one was from Fred Baptiste, a member of the Alpha Phi Alpha Fraternity, Inc., in New York City.

Dear Prof. McLean,

I recently saw an article on your research of Lucile Berkeley Buchanan, the first African-American graduate of the University of Colorado. In the article, it mentioned that Ms. Buchanan had married a John Dotha Jones. John Dotha Jones was a Columbia University graduate and a founder of the Eta Chapter of Alpha Phi Alpha Fraternity, Inc., which just celebrated its centennial anniversary this past June. I have been trying to research the lives of the chapter founders and I wanted to know if you had any additional information regarding Bro. Jones? Any and all assistance with this is greatly appreciated. My contact information is listed below.

Thanks and best regards,
Fred

Alpha Phi Alpha Fraternity, Inc., the first intercollegiate Black Greek letter fraternity, was founded on December 4, 1906, at Cornell University in Ithaca, New York. Its mission was to support Black men who faced myriad challenges, including financing their education, the rigors of academic programs, attrition, and racial isolation at Cornell.[28] Facing similar challenges, seven students—five from Columbia University and two from New York University—formed the Columbia Organization and petitioned the founders (aka the Jewels) at Cornell on May 1, 1909, to establish a chapter in New York City. Under Scott's leadership, the men at Columbia wrote to the "Jewels" at Cornell:

Dear Sirs:

We, the Negro students of Col. Un., realizing the need of a stronger bond, both socially and intellectually, do hereby present our application for membership. Hoping that this application will be favorably receive[d], we are

Yours truly
The Columbia Org.[29]

The vice president of the General Organization and president of the Alpha Chapter at Cornell, Henry Arthur Callis, approved the request and dispatched Roscoe Conkling Giles, treasurer of the General Organization, and Lewuel E. Graves, secretary of the Alpha Chapter, to initiate the Columbia men. Giles took the lead and on Saturday, June 5, 1909, he initiated the first members of the Eta Chapter, making it the seventh chapter of the General Organization and the first chapter of an African American collegiate fraternal organization to be established in the New York metropolitan area.[30] As a founding member of the New York chapter, John appears to have supported the camaraderie of a group of university-educated and exceptional Black men who executed their own kind of activism to counter the hegemonic force of the racial edifice that underpinned discrimination in higher education in New York City and around the nation in the post-Reconstruction era.

LIFE AFTER COLUMBIA

In 1910 John and his family moved from midtown Manhattan to an apartment building in Harlem, as many residents of the Tenderloin were being displaced during the construction of the Pennsylvania Railroad Station (1906–10), adding to the intensity of the first Black migration to Harlem.[31] Harlem was originally built as a suburb of New York City for Whites, but real estate developers were unable to find sufficient White tenants; therefore, it became an economic necessity to sell or rent to Blacks. As the population began to shift, Harlem became the epicenter of Black life in New York City as churches, clubs, and educational, fraternal, and political organizations began to grow.

While most of his fraternity brothers left New York City to carve their futures elsewhere, John decided to stay, working as a clerk there through 1914. The minutes from the chapter meeting held on Saturday, April 9, 1910, at Columbia's Hamilton Hall may tell us why. Following the reading of the minutes by Scott and a discussion about a June 3 reception for the 1910 class, with which John and Clayton T. A. French would be graduating, Scott adds, "Committee write letter of congratulations to Bro. Jones for birth of child." Since at that time there were no Joneses in the chapter, this one notation suggested that perhaps John's new parental duties might have been the motivating factor for his stay in New York City for four years after graduating from Columbia.

Although parental duties may have kept John busy, he still found time to re-engage with his Alpha brothers following a chastisement from the General Organization for his disengagement and allowing the New York City Chapter to go adrift. Several of the Jewels from Cornell, including founding members of the New York City Eta Chapter and honorary members Assistant District Attorney Cornelius V. McDougall and W.E.B. Du Bois spearheaded a reorganization. Getting Du Bois on board was a major accomplishment for the Alpha men, who found a kindred spirit in the Harvard-educated intellectual. They saw themselves as Du Bois's Talented Tenth. They were the elites of the community who were considered by Du Bois as the engine of social change on whose shoulders rested the progress of the race.

Martin Kilson, Professor of Government Emeritus at Harvard University, makes an important point when he says that central to the Du Boisian "leadership paradigm was the advancement of core agencies of African American civil society. And among these societal and institutional forging agencies were the fraternal associations among men and sororities among women."[32]

FROM POLITICAL IDEOLOGUE TO RELIGIOUS SCHOLAR

In 1915 John left New York City to take up an appointment as instructor of classics at Lincoln University, an HBCU established in 1854 in Chester County, Pennsylvania. John team-taught courses with the president of Lincoln, Rev. John B. Rendall. Under John and Rendall's guidance, students were introduced to the social, historical, political, and literary cultures of the Roman Republic through the classic texts of Virgil, Cicero, Ovid, Tacitus, and Juvenal.

While at Lincoln, John decided to pursue a second bachelor's degree at the school's Theological Seminary. Having already earned a degree at one of the nation's most prestigious institutions, it is unclear as to the factors that drove him to make the shift from a Latin and Greek scholar and political and social debater to religious scholar and eventually religious worker. Naturally, he went from Phi Beta Kappa at Columbia University to being an honor student at Lincoln, garnering theological honors and several prizes along the way. On April 17, 1917, the BA of Sacred Theology was conferred on John.

Shortly thereafter, John left Lincoln for Denmark, South Carolina, where he took a position as a Sunday school missionary at the Voorhees Industrial School (now Voorhees College) for the American Sunday School Union (ASSU).[33] The newly published *Negro Year Book* states that the ASSU "is deeply interested in the religious welfare of the Negroes of the South and is seeking to cooperate with every agency looking towards their moral and religious betterment,"[34] and it had "inaugurated a policy of placing a missionary in connection with an industrial school, which teaches the Bible and Sunday School normal class work on two days each week and assists with organizing the work in the adjacent territory."[35]

As he took off for South Carolina, surely John saw himself once again fulfilling one of Du Bois's pronouncements, "The Negro race in the South needs teachers to-day above all else."[36] In his first teaching post in the South, he reports, "I have fallen in clover. A large school, with an enrollment of 650, a splendid plant and situation, and a faculty of thirty-four, who have shown themselves extremely cordial. Surely the Lord prepared this place and gave this good beginning, and I am determined to bring about, by His help, an equal good ending." Soon after he arrived in Denmark, the United States Congress passed the Selective Service Act, drafted May 18, 1917—the nation's first conscription—which authorized the president to draft men into military service and allowed Blacks to register on equal terms with Whites. The first draft, on June 5, 1917, registered single men without dependents between twenty-one and thirty-one years old. Jones was one of the 66,902 Blacks registered in South Carolina. His registration card describes him as tall, medium build, with gray eyes and black hair.[37]

Just four months following his registration, John was ordered to report for active duty, but a number of issues had to be worked out before he could be deployed. First, the 371st Infantry Regiment, 93rd Division (Colored), would not be organized until August 31, 1917. Second, the War Department had to organize the large number of Black draftees from the South. African American leader and special assistant to the secretary of war Emmett J. Scott stated that the unwritten custom was to assign men to the camps near where they were drafted. This would have had John assigned to Camp Jackson, South Carolina. Because of the immense Black population and to "prevent the concentration of Blacks in any one camp, Black draftees found their way North in the fall of 1917, being stationed at Camps Grants, Illinois; Funston, Kansas; Doge, Iowa; Dix, New Jersey; Upton, New York; and Devens, Massachusetts."[38] On October 5, 1917, John reported for active duty at Camp Jackson. By November 5, he and 500 of the 3,380 Black recruits at Camp Jackson were assigned to the 15th Company, 152nd Depot Brigade, at Camp Upton, New York, where he was promoted to battalion sergeant major and deployed to France.

John's entry into the military found him and his fellow Black soldiers in a racial quandary that was little different from their daily reality in civilian life. Racism abounded and showed its ugly head, for example, from ridicule in newspapers to fellow military personnel that made Black soldiers the butt of company jokes. "Rastus" and "Festus" (pernicious stereotypes) were honorary titles bestowed upon many Black soldiers. Draft boards openly favored Whites in service exemptions, such as dependency deferments, while Black enlisted men were assigned to the worst details and had the slowest rate of promotion.[39] Perhaps the most blatant attempt to humiliate and degrade Black troops came in an official order from General Pershing's office to the French High Command on August 7, 1918. Alarmed at the fair treatment of Black soldiers by the French and fearful of its effect on future race relations in America, the secret memorandum urged the French (1) to prevent the rise of any pronounced degree of intimacy between French officers and Black officers; (2) not to eat with Blacks, shake hands, or seek to meet with them outside military life; and (3) not to commend Black troops too highly in the presence of White Americans. Military discrimination against Blacks ran the gamut, from name calling to the worst features of Jim Crow practice in the South. In Brest, France, for instance, the American commander of Zone Five ordered Black officers to eat breakfast an hour earlier than usual to accommodate White officers but stipulated that Blacks dine after Whites at the other two meals. Finally, officers ordered Black troops to use the open latrines, even during rainy weather, thereby reserving sheltered latrines for Whites.[40]

FROM ARMY TO CIVILIAN LIFE AND A FATEFUL FIRST MEETING

Once John separated from the army on March 19, 1919, he took no time in getting back to what he loved best: teaching. In 1919 he accepted a teaching position at Slater Industrial and State Normal School in Winston-Salem, North Carolina (currently Winston-Salem State University), joining twenty-three other teachers educating the 623 students enrolled in the school.

In a September 2, 1919, report by Principal Simon G. Atkins to the board of trustees, Atkins points to the need for more teachers, since the school had to increase its high school graduation requirements to be in compliance with the State Board of Examiners. According to Atkins, the state's requirement for Normal colored high schools was two to three years of coursework. In 1919 the state required four years of coursework, which impacted student enrollment, getting former graduates to return to complete the new requirements, and securing teachers. It was during this 1919–20 school year that John and Lucile were offered teaching positions at Slater.[41]

Upon graduating from the University of Colorado, Lucile interviewed for a position at Slater teaching English and Latin. She initially accepted the position, which was to begin in fall 1919. Confident that she would take the position, she listed her new address in the University of Colorado's 1877–1927 *Directory of Officers and Graduates* as Slater State Normal School. John had interviewed at the same time and, like Lucile, tentatively accepted the position. However, Atkins's report to the board of trustees on September 2, 1919, states: "Miss Buchanan, although she had accepted work on the basis indicated, later resigned to accept appointment in a high school in Kansas City . . . I have engaged Prof. Fred D. Morton to fill Miss Buchanan's place at a salary of $900.00 a year which I trust will meet the approval of the Board."[42]

Although Morton's salary was set at $900 for ten months of work, it is unclear whether Lucile was offered the same salary. What is clear is that the position she took in Kansas City at Lincoln High School was for $1,200—$300 more than she might have been offered at Slater. It was during this brief juncture in 1919 in Winston-Salem that Lucile Berkeley Buchanan and John Dotha Jones first became acquainted. Soon thereafter, they began their seven-year long-distance relation-ship—he living in Winston-Salem, North Carolina, and she in Kansas City, Missouri.

THE LASTING IMPACT OF A GOOD TEACHER

Hired to teach history, English, and pedagogy at $80.00 a month for ten months' work, John was one of thirteen teachers (seven women and six men) working at Slater during the 1919–20 school year. In 1923 John transitioned from Slater to another of Atkins's educational endeavors, the Columbian Heights High School, where he assumed the position of principal with Atkins as advisory principal. One of the few surviving documents about the Columbian Heights High School was written by John and published in the 1923 yearbook:

> The Columbian Heights High School is proud to belong to the most progressive
> school system in the State of North Carolina. Occupying a splendid building
> completed in 1922, modern in construction and well equipped, its boys and girls
> are equally fortunate in enjoying the most expert professional guidance. In par-
> ticular, we have profited by a new program offering three distinct courses, which
> has more fully met the special needs of the individual students. Further, accurate
> and usable knowledge concerning our peculiar problems has resulted from the
> thorough testing program conducted by the office of the City Superintendent of
> Schools. Many are our advantages in being part and parcel of the school system of
> Winston-Salem.[43]

The 1925 graduating class was the third under Jones's stewardship. Of the 119 graduates, 75 percent (89) were females. I thought the number of women grad-uates was quite remarkable[44] until I spoke to Deborah Haith Caple, the daughter of Hampton DeFontaine Haith, a graduate of the class of 1925, who said, "Parents were very conscious of educating their daughters so that they would not end up working in someone's kitchen." Although Haith reported in the 1925 yearbook that he wanted to be a dentist, his education was "cut short so that his sister Ella Drucilla Haith could attend college."[45] In addition, the Black community con-sciously placed a high value on education, particularly along gender lines, because one of the few occupations available to women as a way to rise up the social ladder was teaching.

But what was also remarkable about the class of 1925 was their ambition to break out of the traditional occupations of low-paying menial service jobs where Blacks were too often relegated. Despite living in North Carolina—a state that in

1908 prohibited Black and White children from attending the same school, mandated in 1919 that public and private hospitals that admitted Blacks must employ Blacks to take care of their own race, declared miscegenation a felony in 1921, and in the year of their graduation declared that the seats on all buses must be segregated by race—these graduates were determined not to let the conditions of their times deter their aspirations and dreams. The eighty-nine young women graduates steeped in Jim Crow were well aware of the paucity of jobs available to Black women, but they still aspired to careers not only as teachers but as nurses, violinists, singers, artists, seamstresses, orators, rhetoricians, pharmacists, dentists, and stenographers. The young men who graduated with them also imagined themselves breaking down the barriers of segregation to become doctors, dentists, tailors, businessmen, chemists, lawyers, pharmacists, musicians, teachers, stenographers, and mechanics. And while a total community invested in these students excelling, their principal, Mr. Jones, was at the center of their lives.

The yearbook closed with the class of 1925's "Last Will and Testimony," which included instructions to their principal. "*First,* we give and devise to our beloved Principal our earnest wishes and prayers for the guidance of those following us. We further will him success in all his undertakings, with an abundance of much-needed patience and a touch of humor (grano salis) that make life worthwhile." And finally, "We hereby appoint our principal, Mr. J. D. Jones, guardian of the youthful persons and estate of such our heirs as may be minors at the time of our demise."

Though he left early, Jones served as principal of Columbian Heights for three years, until spring of 1926. The senior class still gave him a proper sendoff in the 1926 yearbook: "We give our beloved Principal, Mr. J. D. Jones, our earnest desires and prayers for the faithful and tender guidance of those following in our footsteps."[46] It was an old steamer trunk filled with sentimental memories that held the secret of Mister Jones, the husband who allegedly died in a duel. I could not help but think that there was something peculiar about a relationship someone never spoke of and would go to such extremes to protect. I was, therefore, adamant about continuing my quest to try to put together the pieces of the puzzle with a 1925 yearbook, a single framed picture of John, and a notation in a 1932 book with the name "Lucy B. Jones, University of Chicago, 1937."

13

Chicago, Take Two

The bare name of educating the coloured people,
scares our cruel oppressors.
—DAVID WALKER

Lucile apparently enjoyed her visit to Chicago during the summer of 1915 so much that ten years later she decided to settle there. I often wondered whether her movements outside of Colorado, which began in Niagara Falls, New York, in 1901 and brought her to settle in Chicago by 1925, had to do with inner curiosity, her response to the disappointment and racism she faced in 1905 when denied a public school teaching job in Denver, or with the small-town flavor of Denver's Black community. In 1920 Denver's Black population, concentrated largely in the Five Points neighborhood, numbered 6,075, whereas Chicago's "Black Belt," a thriving "city-within-a-city," had a population estimated at 109,548.[1] As the second largest US city in 1910, second only to New York City, Chicago was home to a booming industrial sector, a progressive public culture, a thriving newspaper industry, and a lively political culture. Denver simply didn't compare.

A 1915 article by W.E.B. Du Bois provides yet another view as to why Chicago might have caught the attention of Lucile and many others:

> Chicago has usually treated its colored citizens more liberally than most large cities [and when compared] with other cities colored Chicago is noted for its push and independence, its political aggressiveness and its large number of middle-class

214

working people who are doing well. As teachers in the public schools, and public officials, the Chicago colored people have more than maintained their proportionate quota. Out of the mass of colored folk in Chicago have risen members of distinguished people who have made their mark in city life and even the life of the nation quite independent of their race or color.[2]

In the early 1900s, Blacks benefited from Chicago's progressive anti-racism laws, as well as a job market in which they were "gaining unprecedented access to city jobs, expanding their professional class and even winning elective office in local and state government."[3] Even so, there were still racial barriers. One of the primary blockages, a racially restrictive housing covenant, forced Lucile to live near Chicago's South Side in the Bronzeville neighborhood. This narrow, forty-two-block-long, overcrowded chain of neighborhoods stretched from Thirty-first to Sixty-third Streets, between State Street and Cottage Grove Avenue. Lucile would spend twenty-four years here before returning to Denver in 1949.[4]

TIME TRAVEL

Within a year of Lucile's arrival, John closed shop on their seven-year long-distance courtship and joined her in Chicago. They filed for a marriage license on September 26, 1926, at Chicago's Cook County Clerk's Office. John was about two months shy of his thirty-eighth birthday, and Lucile had turned forty-two in June. After a careful review of their marriage certificate, I noticed that the clerk recorded Lucile's age as thirty-four, slicing eight years off her actual age. Lucile, a teacher with a careful eye for detail, had to have seen this error. Even so, I wondered whether the age gap had been a clerk's oversight that Lucile and John simply turned a blind eye on. Age gap in marriages, beginning with the flapper generation in the 1920s through the 1930s, was a well-covered topic in the national media. One of the most prolific authors and journalists on the topic, Kathleen Norris, suggested that "if a woman likes a man, and if they have similar tastes in books, amusements, and friends, and especially if in ambitions and interests their tastes agree, they are apt to make a successful match if he is 50 and she is 25, or if she is 40 and he is 28."[5] From all appearances, Lucile and John fit the criteria Norris suggests.

One month later, on Wednesday, October 27, sixty-three-year-old Rev. Eli T. Martin of the Bethesda Baptist Church performed the marriage ceremony. Choosing Rev. Martin was in line with Lucile's and John's religious background and class status, in that by 1922 the Bethesda congregation numbered in the thousands and included "several of Chicago's richest Negroes," including "Anthony

FIGURE 13.1. *Lucile's husband, John Dotha Jones (1888–1965), ca. 1923. Buchanan Archives.*

Overton of Overton Hygienic Manufacturing Company and Mrs. Jesse Binga, wife of Chicago's most prominent Black banker."[6]

John moved into Lucile's apartment at 4931 Grand Boulevard, the hub of the Bronzeville community (aka Black metropolis). Bronzeville was composed of a racially segregated group of neighborhoods, cut off from the economic and social milieu of greater (White) Chicago. Despite toiling under the yoke of racism, the citizens of this Black metropolis created a vibrant self-help tradition. Displaying incredible fortitude, they simultaneously built thriving businesses and political organizations that wrested political control of the community from Whites while developing a rich literary and cultural movement, rivaling Harlem's Black Renaissance of the 1920s.[7]

Lucile and John's marriage brought together the children of emancipated Virginia slaves: highly educated, multilingual, and steadfastly committed to Du Bois's political ideology of racial justice through liberal arts education. They epitomized the college elite Du Bois envisioned in his Talented Tenth leadership ideology. Both entered the field of education. Being a graduate of Columbia University immediately placed John at the top of the class structure for educated Black men, and both he and Lucile matured during the Progressive era and were part of the New Negro Movement of the 1920s. They also had the proper pedigrees to be granted immediate acceptance into Bronzeville's upper class, which in the 1920s and 1930s was not based solely on income but on education and professional status as well. By all measures, their marriage seemed ideal.

A few days following their wedding, John enrolled in the graduate program at the University of Chicago's Divinity School, taking evening courses from October 1 through December 21, 1926. Lucile, no stranger to Chicago, secured a teaching position, while John balanced his studies at one of the few places where college-educated Black men could find both steady work and job security, the US Postal Service (USPS). In the 1930s the post office "seemed to be the largest employer of Blacks . . . with few moving up the ranks to a supervisory position," according to Monte Posey.[8]

On December 9, 1926, the USPS hired John for two weeks as a temporary clerk in the letter section of Chicago's main post office at a starting salary of sixty-five cents an hour, where he remained until becoming a permanent employee on January 6, 1927.[9] Interestingly, in John's record of employment, which he completed, he only listed his previous occupation as self-employed in the laundry business and omitted his position as a high school principal.

At the post office, John joined a young aspiring Black novelist, Richard N. Wright (eventually a prominent novelist, essayist, and social critic of modern

America), who took a temporary clerk's position in the summer of 1928. While Wright became a substitute clerk and mail sorter in 1929, the stock market crash that same year led to a major decrease in the volume of mail, and within a few months Wright lost his job. He continued working occasionally on a temporary basis until 1937, when the USPS offered him a permanent position, which he declined.[10] John, in contrast, maintained full-time position, because of his status as a veteran.

In 1930 Wright began to work on his first novel, *Cesspool* (published posthumously in 1963 as *Lawd Today!*), which draws on his experiences at the Chicago Post Office, where he and John worked together. Ironically, Wright's protagonist, Jake Jackson, and John Jones share the same initials. Wright's Jake, a petit-bourgeoisie postal employee caught in a quagmire of unpleasant and meaningless work who takes out his frustration on his wife,[11] was possibly modeled after John's life, as some of his demons—such as drunkenness and domestic violence—were the ones John began to exhibit, which eventually led Lucile to file for divorce.

Both Lucile and John faced a series of unjust obstacles in their careers, brought on by gender and race discrimination. Lucile, who had previous experience as a high school teacher and took additional college courses at the University of Chicago (UChicago) to bolster her credentials, could not get a job in a Chicago high school, as those jobs were the preserve of White men. Women were permitted to teach at the elementary level. Black women were further confined to "underfunded and overcrowded segregated [elementary] schools that restricted their promotion opportunities."[12]

Despite John's experience as a teacher and furthermore his experience in school administration, he too was victimized by a Chicago school system that reserved such positions of power exclusively for White men. Furthermore, Chicago identified teaching as women's work, thereby devaluing male teachers overall. Partly because of the feminization of teaching and general economic trends, Chicago males' salaries steadily declined over the years, and by the time John arrived, high school salaries were almost on par with those at elementary schools.

Kept from his chosen profession by structural racism, John's pride, self-worth, and dignity suffered what seemed like an irreversible diminishment. Despite all his accomplishments—two bachelor's degrees, the only African American Phi Beta Kappa in the United States in 1910, a founding member of the first Alpha Phi Alpha chapter in New York City, a senior noncommissioned officer appointed battalion sergeant major in the US Army during World War I, a former high school teacher and principal, a college instructor assigned to co-teach courses on the classics with a college president, and a young activist in New York City—John had to settle for a job at the post office where he faced a life, like Jake's, of "dull routines, economic difficulties, and racial discrimination."[13]

Lucile and John's marriage began in the Roaring Twenties, a period marked by experimentation, excess, risk, and modernity. As the Great Depression hit in 1929, the next decade would find their relationship, like the country itself, in turmoil. While they were employed during this devastating economic crisis, their marriage began to fall apart. Without notice, John walked out on Lucile on December 1, 1935. Lucile struggled to understand what role she had played in his decision. She felt she had always conducted herself as a "kind, true, loving and faithful wife."[14] Her pleas for him to return were of no avail. Women of her mother's generation, her generation, and those to follow lived by the credo "you get a man you keep a man." But Lucile was her own person. She thought long and hard about the pain and difficulties she had endured, and on January 3, 1940, five years after her abandonment, she hired Georgia Huston Jones Ellis,[15] a partner at a prominent Black Chicago law firm, and filed for divorce. In her testimony to the court she described John as "very erratic and indifferent towards her." Eva Bell Hawkins provided corroborating evidence, stating that she knew both Lucile and John and that while Lucile had treated John "very nice," he "didn't treat her so nice."[16]

The decree for divorce dated April 18, 1940, states that John had committed "adultery" and "had been guilty of extreme and repeated cruelty" towards Lucile. Furthermore, he had "willfully deserted, and absented himself . . . without any reasonable cause for the space of over one year" and "been guilty of habitual drunkenness for the space of two successive years prior to the filing of the complaint." The reasons given by Lucile for their failed marriage and subsequent divorce are similar to the legal grounds for divorce in the United States in 1930. Among the 191,591 divorces that year, cruelty was the major reason (81,921), followed by desertion or abandonment (59,068), neglect or non-support (23,489), and adultery (15,992).[17] Lucile's only request was for John to pay the fifty-dollar legal fee to her attorney, which the court ordered.

WAS IT A BROKEBACK MARRIAGE?

I, too, began to search for the reasons that may have contributed to John's behavior toward Lucile. During a subsequent research journey to Chicago, I managed to secure John's death certificate, which included the last address at which he lived, 335 West Fifty-eighth Street. This led me to the Recorder of Deeds Office for a chain of title searches. Amid the large tract of index books scattered around the basement title room, I discovered in a subdivision book that John and a man named Rozine Penny (or Pennie) had owned a 750-square foot, one-bedroom, one-bath, single-family house on West Fifty-eighth Street, which they purchased together in July 1957 when John was sixty-nine and Rozine was thirty-three.

Along with information on the tenancy and mortgage holder, the subdivision book indicated a probate on the property in 1966, a year following John's death. Within two weeks of my visit, I received a copy of the fifty-one-page probate document, which included John's Last Will and Testament, dated September 1, 1959, naming Rozine Penny as his executor; two depositions, including one from Rozine on the veracity of the will; and a bill from A. A. Rayner and Sons for his funeral expenses, which were paid by Rozine. Who was Rozine Penny? What was his relationship to John?

Rozine was born in Marks, Mississippi, on July 28, 1924. He had just turned eighteen when he applied for a Social Security card in February 1942. He stated that he had previously worked in a grocery store but was presently unemployed.[18] He probably came to Chicago during the second phase of the Great Migration (1940–70) for the same reasons other southern Blacks migrated north during the first wave: to escape the abject poverty and racism that flourished under Jim Crow. Somewhere between 1942 and 1944, Rozine arrived in Chicago, where he ultimately met John. In his testimony to the court, Rozine stated that "he knew the deceased intimately" and "had resided with John for 22 years," a cohabitation that would have begun around 1944, four years following John's divorce from Lucile. Rozine also testified that he knew about John's marriage to Lucile and that they had no children and had not adopted any and that he did not know Lucile's whereabouts.[19]

While John's death on February 21, 1965, proved uneventful, his final resting place took me by surprise in that John, a staunch Baptist, was interred on February 24 at St. Mary Catholic Cemetery and Mausoleums in Evergreen Park, Illinois. While the church expects that only Catholics will be buried in a Catholic cemetery, there are exceptions for non-Catholic members of Catholic families. As John and Rozine were clearly not family, how did Rozine skirt this restriction? I went in search of an answer from the cemetery staff. While Rozine, a Catholic, testified truthfully under oath at John's probate hearing that they were not related, at St. Mary, Rozine claimed to be John's nephew so he could have John buried in a plot he bought, with a simple lawn-level veteran's headstone to mark his grave.

Lifting the veil on Lucile and John's nine-year marriage has not been easy. While Lucile charged intimate-partner violence and adultery, she provided few details. What I discovered is that following his divorce, John had an enduring twenty-two-year relationship with a young man named Rozine Penny, a relationship Rozine described as "intimate." Is Rozine the paramour Lucile spoke of? According to historian Chad Heap, the Great Migration spawned a thriving lesbian and gay enclave in the Bronzeville community,[20] a commercial district offering freedom from sexual boundaries in gay nightclubs.[21] Adding to the cabaret scene were "popular Halloween drag balls, sponsored by Alfred Finnie, a Black gay hustler, in semi-safe venues such as the Wabash YMCA, the First Church of Deliverance, Washington Park, and Jackson Park."[22]

Lucile's behavior during the marriage and subsequent divorce can be viewed from multiple perspectives. First, she had to contend with the cultural stigma attached to battered women who remained in abusive relationships. When Lucile filed for divorce, psychologists claimed that battered women remained in abusive relationships because they were masochists.[23] In addition, social mores frowned heavily on divorce, especially when the proceedings were initiated by women. Yet she was the only one who took the initiative to file for divorce. Lucile's behavior was nothing but a show of strength, a counterpoint to the norm, demonstrating once again that she refused to be or to remain a victim.

Even at age 103 the dissolution of her marriage remained a sensitive issue. It did not matter how hard people pressed for information about her husband; Lucile maintained a wall of personal dignity and pride. The one thing for certain is that being Mrs. Jones, a married woman, carried a mark of distinction. Although she fiercely guarded the details of the pain and hardship she had endured with John or information about the end of their marriage, she still insisted, forty-six years after their divorce, on being called "Mrs. Jones."

With Lucile's personal life in shambles, she found solace in three things: continuing her education by taking graduate courses at UChicago, membership at Ebenezer Baptist Church, and teaching the next generation of Black students, which she did until her retirement in 1949.

SHAPING THE NEXT GENERATION

Lucile spent most of her career teaching at the Stephen A. Douglas School, located at 3200 South Calumet Avenue in the Douglas/Grand Boulevard community, part of the "Black Metropolis" created from land once owned by Stephen A. Douglas, the famed Illinois politician noted for the Lincoln-Douglas debates of 1858. The school was built in 1889 to educate the growing number of White children whose families had moved into the Douglas community. By 1900, a small number of Black children had begun attending. Two decades later there were about 76,703 residents in the Douglas/Grand Boulevard community, of which 32 percent were

African American.[24] By 1930 African Americans comprised about 95 percent of the total population of 87,003.[25] When Lucile arrived in 1925, Douglas was already an all-Black K–12 school. It consisted of twenty rooms, with twelve designated as classrooms (including art, music, home economics, and industrial arts).

Lucile experienced some of the same challenges she had faced in Hot Springs and Kansas City: segregation, overcrowding, dilapidated buildings, and double and triple shifts. In 1938, "13 of 15 schools running on double shifts [in Chicago] were in Black neighborhoods. Students spent half a day in school and were on the streets for the rest of the day."[26] By the 1920s the overcrowding situation at Douglas had become so intense that the seventh and eighth grades were temporarily moved to John B. Drake Elementary. By 1941 Douglas had "a student body of 2,800, although the school was built for only 1,800 students."[27]

Many of these challenges are attributed to the racial intolerance that arose during the influx of Black southern migrants during the first wave of the Great Migration in the 1910s and 1920s. As Blacks moved in, discriminatory practices by unscrupulous real estate brokers and land speculators led to de facto segregation of Blacks to the South Side and the hardening of racist attitudes among Whites. This racial separation came to exemplify Chicago public schools. Throughout the 1920s and 1930s, the Chicago School Board's hiring policies resulted in Black teachers being hired for substitute positions rather than full-time positions and no longer being appointed to teach at racially mixed schools, as well as a cessation in advocating for Black teachers who met resistance from White pupils and parents. Final employment decisions were left to the discretion of each individual school's principal. The school board could send a potential candidate, but the principal had the final word on who got hired.[28] As a result, the Chicago Board of Education's service record shows Lucile as a permanent employee only since 1935; even though she taught since 1926, she likely worked as a substitute teacher for many years before securing a permanent position. With a quasi-patronage system governing the hiring of teachers and a segregated school system with discriminatory hiring practices, it is no surprise that by 1930 only 2.3 percent (452) of all teachers in the public schools were Black.[29]

After John moved out, Lucile packed up her life and rented a small apartment in the home of Dr. Ulysses Grant Dailey, an internationally prominent African American surgeon, at 4758 South Park Way (now Martin Luther King Drive). Dailey served as president of the National Medical Association, co-founded the International College of Surgeons, operated his own hospital in the 1920s and 1930s, was a leader at Chicago's Provident Hospital, and helped educate surgeons in Africa, Asia, and Latin America. As had been the case in Hot Springs, renting a room from a prominent physician gave Lucile access to the Black upper middle class. However, unlike Arkansas, the class system in Bronzeville was so powerful that the Daileys would not have opened their home to her if she had not been seen as a social equal. In their landmark study on Chicago's *Black Metropolis*, St. Clair Drake and Horace R. Cayton Jr. state, "At the top of the social pyramid is a scant five percent of the population—an articulate social world of doctors, lawyers, schoolteachers, executives, and successful business people."[30] As a schoolteacher, Lucile was at the top of the social pyramid and more than likely discussed shared discriminatory experiences with Dailey.

The 1940 Census shows that of the eighty-two residents living in the 4700 block of South Park Way, forty-eight were employed between eight and fifty-two weeks of the year, earning an average yearly salary of $729 in 1939.[31] Lucile reported the second highest salary, earning $1,800 ($32,313 in 2017) for thirty-nine weeks' work.[32] Monthly rents in the neighborhood ranged from $22 to $45. Lucile lived with the Daileys for about five years, paying them $40 a month in rent.

To enhance her teaching skills, Lucile began taking courses at UChicago, which also helped to give her the financial security she desperately needed, since she was able to parlay her coursework into salary increases.[33] In March 1937, two years after John walked out on her and at age fifty-three, Lucile entered the Graduate Division at UChicago to study English Literature, 1660–1800. At the end of the school year in May 1937, while in the midst of her marital difficulties, she spent the summer in Denver as a graduate student at the University of Denver College of Liberal Arts Summer School, where she took Principles of Reading and Literature in Kindergarten and Primary, Principles of Social Studies in Kindergarten and Primary, and Interpretation of Shakespeare, earning two-and-a-half credit hours for each class. Of course, she passed them all.

After returning to Chicago in the fall of 1937, she enrolled at UChicago for both the spring and winter quarters, taking courses on Ben Jonson (English poet, essayist, and playwright) and Supplemental Arithmetic, Spelling, and Writing. She enrolled in Educational Psychology and Critique of Educational Literature in 1939, and in 1940 she took a class on American Secondary Schools. Her final graduate courses in 1941, at age fifty-seven, was Construction of Tests and American Educational Systems. Over the course of her studies at the University of Chicago and the University of Denver, her teaching records indicate that her salary was "adjusted" several times, since she had "produced evidence of experience and scholastic preparation which would entitle [her] to this salary."

On June 24, 1949, Lucile retired. She was sixty-five, the mandatory retirement age for Chicago teachers. She headed back to Denver, where she would spend the next forty years. But the Stephen A. Douglas School remained close to Lucile's heart. Some of her teacher friends from there remained in contact as she transitioned to retirement in Denver. Fourteen years after her retirement, she still kept up with student activities as well as local gossip. Following an inquiry about Christmas happenings, one teacher wrote to her:

> Yes, Xmas carols are still being sung thru the halls at Douglas, directed by Vivian Bealey. She works very hard with these teenagers and as the carolers stroll slowly thru the halls singing, every classroom door is opened. Inside the pupils listen quietly and with a feeling of reverence—It's touching—We love it.

There were also times when the information she received about Douglas would have undoubtedly been a disappointment. One teacher wrote, "I'm still teaching third grade, but getting tired. The children bring themselves up [no home support], which makes it very hard to teach them." Another wrote:

> As to Douglas—It's not all the same old school—problems, dropouts, teachers with poor abilities, or they don't care along with the head administrator who is not ready etc. makes for a frustrated atmosphere among everyone there. In 1949 [when Lucile last taught at Douglas] we had enrolled 4000 pupils—today [1963] we are down to 1200. Miss Walls had to go back into a classroom. All adjustment work is on me. I am struggling and making many mistakes.

Lucile adhered to an ideology of professionalism both in and out of the classroom. A letter written to me by her niece Evelyn Napper states:

> Aunt Lucy was a strict "disciplinarian" as an aunt and a teacher. She believed that all children, including Black children should – dress neatly, be polite and well behaved. She trained the children in her class to brush their hair down with their hands when visitors entered the classroom. When other teachers at Douglas had difficulty maintaining quiet in their classroom, they would ask Aunt Lucy to restore order. She wanted Black children to be successful and well-liked.[34]

Evelyn's description shows that discipline and classroom management were part of Lucile's teaching strengths. Even though her education in the early 1900s was devoid of behavior management courses or procedures, she maintained order in the classroom through the example of her own strict self-discipline and her insistence on nothing less from those in her care.

Chicago gave Lucile the opportunity to meet like-minded teachers who considered Black history an important subject, worthy of being added to their regular teaching load. Spurred on by the Chicago Renaissance, a literary and artistic movement that emerged in the 1930s and lasted through the 1950s, Lucile spent a good portion of her time immersed in invigorating her black consciousness, influenced by the novels, poems, and short stories of Richard Wright, Langston Hughes, Arna Bontemps, Margaret Walker, and Gwendolyn Brooks; the artistic brilliance of William Edouard Scott, Charles White, Archibald John Motley Jr., and Eldzier Cortor; and the music of famed jazz cornet player and bandleader Joe "King" Oliver and his protégé Louis Armstrong, who brought a unique Chicago-style jazz to the city and the nation.

But Lucile may have been moved most by the work of Thomas Andrew Dorsey, considered the father of gospel music, and author of such popular songs as "Peace in the Valley," "Search Me Lord," "Highway to Heaven," and "Take My Hand, Precious Lord." Dorsey created the first gospel choir in 1931 at Lucile's longtime church, the Ebenezer Missionary Baptist Church in Bronzeville. Dorsey went on to establish the National Convention of Gospel Choirs and Choruses (NCGCC) on August 17, 1932. Lucile, with her deep Baptist roots, became the organization's first recording secretary. From August 30 to September 1, 1933, the NCGCC held its first convention at the Pilgrim Baptist Church in Chicago.[35]

In addition to the cultural advances resulting from the renaissance, which energized Lucile and her teacher friends, there was also the American Negro Exposition (considered the first Negro World's Fair), held at the Chicago Coliseum from July 4 through September 2, 1941. The expo was designed to cover seventy-five years of "Negro progress" (1863–1940) and was very much in line with what St. Clair Drake and Horace R. Cayton discuss as "Advancing the Race." The expo was therefore a demonstration of "individual achievement," which "reflects credit on the race and [is] designed to raise the status of the group as a whole."[36] One of the publications that Lucile purchased was a twenty-five-cent copy of the *Chicago Defender's* publication *KYRA Booklet* (*Know Your Race Achievers*), which aimed "to perpetuate the memory of the great men and women of the Race whose achievement should serve as an inspiration to Negroes everywhere." The expo also inspired a number of Black teachers, culminating in the creation of grade-specific units for teaching Black history in Bronzeville's public schools.[37]

Lucile's class position in Chicago's Black society impacted her teachings and her aspirations for "race advancement." As her niece Evelyn reminisced, "She wanted Black children to be successful and well-liked."[38] In Bronzeville, success was tied firmly to class position, which in turn was tied to having sufficient education "to avoid grammatical blunders" and to be able "to converse intelligently." Education could help propel someone to the top, whereas lack of education could permanently handicap and relegate one to the bottom. As Drake and Cayton note,

"Education is an important measure of the man [or woman=. Because it reflects earning power, and more importantly because it denotes a broadening of intellectual horizons and tastes . . . securing an education is the most effective shortcut to the top of the Negro pyramid."[39] Whether instructing students on dressing neatly, being polite and well-behaved, brushing down their hair to give guests a good impression, maintaining discipline, or teaching race pride, Lucile saw herself as providing essential life skills to the next generation of Black America.

14

"Lincoln Was a Republican, That's All I Need to Know"

So I'm in the Republican Party for the same reason I was in the Democratic
Party: to make sure blacks are included, along with everyone else.
— CHARLES EVERS

In 1893 the United States and its territories experienced a severe economic crisis
in the wake of the US Congress's repeal of the Silver Purchase Act, which dropped
the price of silver. As a result, mines and smelters closed, the banking industry collapsed, railroads went into receivership, unemployment soared, farmers plunged
into debt, and discontent intensified. These realities forced Lucile's second cousin,
Thornton Buchanan, to return to Denver from the mining town of Clear Creek,
where he had worked in the hotel industry.

At home, belt-tightening became a matter of course. But even in this doom and
gloom economy, women had hope, as Colorado became the second state to pass
women's suffrage through popular referendum on November 7, 1893.[1] The following June, Sarah, Hannah, and Hattie Buchanan cast a ballot for the first time.
In that election, three women were elected to serve in the 1895 Colorado State
Legislature.[2] Nine-year-old Lucile would have to wait until her twenty-first birthday in 1905 to vote in Colorado state elections and fifteen more years to vote in a
federal election.

As the daughter of emancipated slaves and an educated woman, Lucile knew
that the Republican Party had formed in 1854 on a platform based mainly on the

227

abolition of slavery and that in its early decades it had promoted Black equality. She also knew of the unprecedented legal victories for Blacks that Radical Republicans,[3] like Charles Summer and Thaddeus Stevens, helped secure by amending the US Constitution to limit state power over personal liberties and civil rights—eventually leading to the passage of the Thirteenth, Fourteenth, and Fifteenth Amendments to the US Constitution, ending slavery and giving Black men full citizenship and the right to vote.

The role Radical Republicans played in enfranchising Black men in the post-bellum era was the idea of President Abraham Lincoln as the "Great Emancipator" who freed the slaves. Together, they formed an irresistible force, leading Blacks to become staunch allies and members of the Republican Party. Lucile's parents, as most Blacks, were therefore Republicans, and their political position significantly impacted her political socialization, resulting in a decades-long partisan preference for the Republican Party. "Lincoln was a Republican, that's all I need to know" became her mantra when asked about why she was a loyal Republican. Even in the 1930s, when the Republican Party began to lose favor within the African American community during the dark days of the Great Depression, Lucile's loyalty never wavered.

JOURNALING AND THE 1964 PRESIDENTIAL ELECTION

While unwavering, her loyalty did not go unquestioned. Entries penned in her dark brown journal bought for a quarter at a Denver Woolworth's provide insight into her thoughts at age eighty, a sense of her political engagement, and her acute awareness of the political climate of the day.

Following the July 2 enactment of the Civil Rights Act of 1964, the November presidential election that year certainly sparked Lucile's interest. She listened to her radio and critically analyzed the pre-election debates between the incumbent Democratic president Lyndon B. Johnson and the conservative Republican candidate, Senator Barry Goldwater of Arizona.

Five months before the general election on November 3, Lucile made her first entry in her journal:

June 26, 1964
My prediction
Barry Goldwater our next President

Her prediction that Goldwater would be the next president certainly didn't pan out. On June 19, just days before this entry, Goldwater was one of 27 Republicans that had voted against the Civil Rights Act.[4] This action along with his position on states' rights made Black Republicans shiver when he became the party's presidential nominee. For many Blacks, the party's inability to support civil rights was tantamount to betrayal of its founding ideals. They showed their disappointment by abandoning the party en masse, casting their votes to Democrat Lyndon Johnson, supporting alternative candidates, or creating splinter organizations to help redefine the party's position relative to Black Republicans, such as the National Negro Republican Assembly and the Negro Republican Organization.

While Lucile remained affiliated with the party, she began having second thoughts about her prediction of a Goldwater win, as well as whether America was ready to elect a Jewish president. Lucile left both questions open as she wrote on three separate lines:

Read!
Ponder!
No Comment!

Followed by two questions.

1. Are Republicans doing this to replace the Negro vote with the vote of the Jews?

And in an eerie prediction she wrote . . .

2. Will the Democratic Party become the party of minorities and the Republican Party the lily-white party? Adding to the bottom of this question "Self-preservation of races."

In an entry dated July 13, 1964, at 8 a.m., Lucile wrote, "Today will be a day of great excitement in San Francisco and in many other places throughout the nation. Hundreds of reporters will be converging in San Francisco to cover the Republican National Convention." She continued:

Already we have heard of great demonstrations planned by Negro organizations in protest against the nomination of Sen. Barry Goldwater, because of his vote against the Civil Rights Bill. He explained his stand on the grounds of constitutionality and is entitled to his opinions. With some of them I agree. However, since the bill has become law, he also said, if elected he will enforce it. The whole picture looks like a jigsaw puzzle. From my vantage point I think the whole situation has been carefully planned by the *King Makers* of whom we have been hearing and reading more and more recently.

In her writings, Lucile thought a lot about the racial and religious issues in the election, as well as the role Dr. Martin Luther King, Jr. and the civil rights movement had played in positioning Black civil rights as a major American issue, culminating with the passage of the Civil Rights Act of 1964. As for Goldwater, she understood his strict constitutionalist position, which led him to oppose the Civil Rights Act as a violation of each state's right to self-governance. Yet she qualified her support, stating that Goldwater was "entitled to his opinion," and indicated some areas of common ground by noting "with some of them I agree," leaving the door open perhaps for her continued Republican support and party membership.

She was also acutely aware of Goldwater's Jewish heritage on his father's side and tried to analyze the 1964 election in parallel to the election of America's first Catholic president, John F. Kennedy, writing:

> In other words, I believe the boat is rigged for the Republican National Convention just as former president Truman said the Democratic convention was when John F. Kennedy was nominated on the first ballot in the very same city and the Democrats gave the country its first Catholic for president. Will the Republicans be able to do a similar act with a Jew? If so then America can say with pride, "We have blotted out the Disgrace of Democracy."

Lucile was referring to "The Disgrace of Democracy, an Open Letter to President Woodrow Wilson" that Kelly Miller, an African American educator and one of the leading intellectuals of the early twentieth century, wrote on August 4, 1917, four months after America declared war on Germany and its allies. The letter states:

> You are the accepted spokesman of world democracy . . . but a chain is no stronger than its weakest link. A doctrine that breaks down at home is not fit to be propagated abroad. One is reminded of the pious slaveholder who became so deeply impressed with the plea for foreign mission that he sold one of his slaves to contribute liberally to the cause . . . Why democratize the nations of the earth if it leads them to delight in the burning of human beings after the manner of Springfield, Waco, Memphis, and East St. Louis, while the nation looks helplessly on? . . . The outrages complained of against the Belgians become mercifully performances of gruesome comparisons. Our frantic wail[s] against the barbarity of Turk against Armenian, German upon Belgium, Russian upon Jews are made of no effect . . .

Miller challenged Wilson to walk the talk by comparing the plight of Blacks in the United States to other oppressed nationalities in Europe. He contended that if the United States was to be the pillar of democracy for the world, it could not propagate the ideas of democracy abroad while engaging in segregation and lynching at home. A little over four decades after Miller's letter, Lucile had reinterpreted it by asking whether America was ready to elect a person of Jewish ancestry as president and stating that it must be ready to do so if it was to continue to see itself as the guardian of world democracy.

AN AMERICAN PRESIDENT AND THE ONE-DROP RULE

Continuing in her diary, Lucile began to identify presidents and presidential candidates of non-European and non-Protestant backgrounds, including Goldwater. She wrote, "We have had for president a Negro [Harding], Catholic [Kennedy] to Jew [Goldwater]. Time will tell." While she may have supported Goldwater because of party affiliation, it was also a matter of extending democracy across all aspects of American society. She clearly believed that electing someone of Jewish ancestry would be a sign of progress, indicating that the nation had finally achieved the democratic principles Miller had pointed out as missing at home. Lucile appears to have been an early proponent of diversity and inclusion, demanding it of her country's leaders long before it became chic to do so in the twenty-first century.

What was most captivating to me was Lucile's buy-in regarding the ethnic identity of the twenty-ninth US president, Warren G. Harding.[5] Given miscegenation during slavery coupled with the one-drop rule (which holds that a person with any trace of African ancestry, no matter how small, cannot be considered White), over the years many within the African American community had raised questions about the ethnic makeup of several American presidents, including Harding.[6] While these assertions have been fraught with speculation and pseudo-scientific evidence, Lucile appears to have agreed with the prevailing notion among some Blacks that if one adhered to the racist one-drop rule, Harding was indeed Black. Most of the assertions about Harding's blackness came from William Estabrook Chancellor, a professor at Wooster College in Ohio. At a time when scientific racism was still fashionable and Eugenics was the talk of the pseudo-scientific community, Chancellor, a proponent of such race-based ideology and a Democrat, attempted to discredit Harding's candidacy by introducing the one-drop rule, assuming that the American public would never elect a Black man.[7]

With speculation regarding Harding's racial identity as a backdrop, Lucile ventured to the polls in Kansas City on November 2, 1920, to cast her first vote in a presidential election. In this case, an election that pitted two Ohioans against each other: the Republican candidate Senator Warren G. Harding and the Democratic Party's nominee, Governor James M. Cox. This was an important milestone in light of her belief that freedom and voting were synonymous. But it also said something about her understanding of the racial, ethnic, and religious dimensions of US electoral politics, which she chronicled in her diary. Lucile was acutely aware of the debate within and without the Black community regarding Harding's alleged Black ancestry and the attempts to discredit his candidacy based on his supposed blackness. Most of her understanding probably came as the result of America's race categorization, which defined the social, economic, and political order in complex and nuanced ways, leading to a clear difference in the way individuals were treated based on skin color.

The reality that white skin alone conferred certain privileges led to a practice in the Black community known as "passing," in which a light-skinned Black person would live as a White person to obtain access to the rights and privileges of "being" White. Law professor Randall Kennedy explains, "Passing is a deception that enables a person to adopt certain roles or identities from which he would be barred by prevailing social standards in the absence of his misleading conduct." Discussing the classic racial passer who would have corresponded to Lucile's thinking at the time, Kennedy described him as the white Negro, "the individual whose physical appearance allows him to present himself as 'white' but whose 'black' lineage (typically only a very partial black lineage) makes him a Negro according to dominant racial rules."[8] Lucile probably didn't think much of the one-drop rule and its consequences. All that apparently mattered to her was that she considered herself a witness to history—to her, Harding's alleged blackness resulted in him being the nation's first Black president. While Harding apparently refused to comment on the rumormongering, he allegedly stated privately that for all he knew, one of his ancestors might have "jumped the fence."[9]

The politics of 1920 might have also fired Lucile's imagination and her penchant for voting. As an educated woman, she was acutely aware of the eight years of Democratic leadership entrenchment as well as the party's history on policies that mattered to her: Reconstruction and the racial ideology the Democrats spurred in the South. But additional factors could have added to her strong Republican stance beyond Black loyalties going back to the Civil War but also the party's political stance on issues that mattered to Lucile as a new voter and the new community in which she lived in Kansas City.

In addition to discussions about voting the Republican Party line, there was lots of excitement in Kansas City—in the local Black press as well as among the educated class—about Harding's candidacy. On June 19, 1920, J. Silas Harris, president of the Negro National Educational Congress, wrote a column in the *Kansas City Sun*, one of the city's two Black newspapers stating that Harding was "one of the most forceful characters in American life, a statesman of ripe experience, unquestioned ability, and of highest character."[10] Drawing a connection to Lincoln, he said, "Harding is a humanitarian with a heart full of sympathy for the struggling masses—the friendless and poor." And "in him every TRUE American, 'white' and 'black' will find a friend."[11] Two years later, Harris had a change of heart. Writing to US senator Arthur Capper (R-Kansas) he said, "In common with the great mass of my people I have been sorely disappointed in President Harding and realize that we are not going to have an easy task next fall in electing a congress that will be favorable to him."[12]

Given the history and struggle for African American and women's enfranchisement, as well as the direct disenfranchisement of Blacks in the southern states between 1880 and 1965, Lucile remained adamant that voting and freedom were two sides of the same coin. While her sight and physical health began to deteriorate, she never lost her passion for voting. In 1988 Mark Wolf, a reporter with the *Rocky Mountain News*, interviewed Lucile as one of Denver's two oldest registered voters for a story he wrote titled "Centenarians Say Freedom Linked to Vote."[13] Lucile, a lifelong Republican, acknowledged that Franklin D. Roosevelt was the only Democrat she might have supported because "over the years as I look back, there were many things he did good for the people." Her thinking about Roosevelt coincides with the beginning of the shift of Blacks from the Republican Party to the Democratic Party.

Beyond the intellectual, Lucile, 104 years of age, still regarded voting as inextricably tied to freedom. "Your freedom and my freedom are the most important things," she told Wolf. She clearly felt it was her duty to go to the ballot box to celebrate the freedom her parents had received but had been denied to her forebears who suffered and died as slaves.

Lucile's sense of civic duty had been implanted early in her life. Voting therefore remained a right and a celebration. She went to the polls for every election and in every state in which she resided, ultimately voting in fourteen presidential elections and doing her part to elect eight Republican presidents.

With the 1988 presidential election between the incumbent Republican vice president George H.W. Bush and the Democratic nominee, Massachusetts governor Michael Dukakis, less than a month away, Lucile filed her absentee ballot on October 13. As a staunch Republican, there is no doubt that she voted for Bush—it is not likely that she changed parties in what would be her last election, her final exercise of freedom. According to Wolf, as he left her room following the conclusion of the interview, she asked if he would set her radio dial to KOA so she could hear the previous night's debate.

15

Coming Home and Going Home

We are not Makers of History. We are made of History.

—REV. MARTIN LUTHER KING JR.

As Lucile began life as a centenarian, she often asked, "What does God have against me? Why wouldn't he take me?" Lucile outlived all eight of her sisters, her only brother, two nieces, and all of her contemporaries. As she aged, her only regular visitor was Herman Dick, a neighbor and friend of her late brother, Fenton. After Fenton's death in 1963, thirty-seven-year-old Herman, who in his spare time did odd jobs around the Barnum neighborhood, began assisting seventy-nine-year-old Lucile in her daily affairs and the upkeep of her home. She paid him to paint her weather-beaten gray porch, to do lawn care, and to drive her to the doctor, dentist, her attorney, and, most important, to vote.

Herman picked the grapes off Lucile's backyard vines so she could continue to make her annual batch of grape juice. He cut the light pink and white peonies Fenton had diligently cared for so she could decorate the house and take flowers to Fairmount Cemetery every Memorial Day to place on her parents' graves. He did her weekly grocery shopping with the list she gave him. Now that she was visually impaired, she designed a foolproof method to store food in her pantry by having Herman place items in alphabetical order. She not only alphabetized her food; according to Herman's daughter Audrey Theisen, she had Herman place the one- and five-dollar bills in her wallet by putting the ones in the front and the fives in the back. She even continued to pay her bills by signing checks with a piece of cardboard guiding her signature."[1] Frugal yet creative, when it came to telling time, she bought a large men's watch and had Herman remove the crystal so she could use her fingers to feel the time.

Over the years, while maintaining a level of formality, Herman and Lucile developed a profound friendship that Lucile dictated and Herman respected. He was always "Mr. Dick" and she "Mrs. Jones." Their relationship resembled the one depicted in the 1989 motion picture *Driving Miss Daisy*, but with a

FIGURE 15.1. *Herman Dick, Lucile's Driver/ Aide, ca. late 1940s. Courtesy the Dick family.*

spin. Lucile was Black; Herman was White. She was Baptist; he was Catholic. She was divorced and childless; he was married with four children. She was the progeny of slaves and the granddaughter of a White slaveholder. He was the son of Volga Germans. The one thing they shared in common was the German language they both spoke. Yet as in the movie, she remained the strong-willed lady and he was her equal, steadfast supporter.

COMING HOME

In 1949, a sixty-five-year-old Lucile retired from the Chicago Public School system after teaching for twenty-four years and came home to Denver, where she would spend the remaining forty years of her life. She joined her sixty-nine-year-old brother Fenton in the house their father had built in the 1890s. Initially, her support circle included her sisters Edith Davis and Claribel Perkins and her niece, Evelyn Napper, Claribel's daughter.[2] Sadie and Nellie lived in Los Angeles, as did Hattie's daughter Carol Roberts. Lucile focused the early years of her retirement on resolving personal and family issues.

Her first adventurous undertaking began four years after her arrival, when she decided to pre-plan her funeral by purchasing a cemetery plot at Denver's Fairmount Cemetery. While there were available plots near her oldest sister

FIGURE 15.2. *Granite headstone Lucile bought that was placed next to her sister's grave, ca. 1953. Courtesy Doris Smith and Larry Harris.*

Hattie and close to her parents, she purchased a plot next to her sister, Laura, whose tragic suicide in 1899 had deeply impacted and shaped her life. Thus, on Tuesday, December 8, 1953, Lucile, along with her niece Evelyn, drove Fenton's 1947 black two-door Chevy sedan about nine miles to Fairmount Cemetery, where Lucile paid $100 for a small plot designated for cremains next to Laura's final resting place. By choosing cremation, Lucile elected to break one of the major taboos when it came to death rituals among Blacks, who regardless of class maintained the tradition of open-casket funerals. She also bought from a local monument store and had delivered to Fairmount a small gray raised-top flat granite headstone with her name and date of birth engraved on it.

The question is, after being in Denver for four years, why did Lucile choose this particular day to exercise her agency? What news was trending? Lucile, a consummate newsaholic, spent hours listening to her radio. It is likely she knew that on December 8 the head of the NAACP's Legal Defense Fund, Thurgood Marshall (who in 1967 became the US Supreme Court's first Black justice), was appearing before the US Supreme Court rearguing the landmark desegregation case *Brown v. Board of Education of Topeka*.[3] The case aimed to strike down "separate but equal" doctrine of *Plessy v. Ferguson* (1896)[4] as it related to the desegregation of public schools across America—a segregation with which, as a teacher in all-Black public schools, she had been far too familiar. On this very important day when "separate but equal" was receiving national attention, a non-press event was occurring in Denver when a Black woman chose to buy an empty cremains plot besides that of her sister, who was interred about one-third of a mile away from the rest of the family in a largely White area adjacent to Millionaires Row. Although her sister's internment had secretly desegregated a section of the cemetery, Lucile's deliberate choice would quietly and firmly continue the process.

Was this Lucile's secret pleasure? Or was it a small revenge against the segregation she had fought all her life? As she planned her end-of-life decisions with Fairmount's staff in 1953, none of them would have known that in 1899, a young Black woman had been interred in a predominately White section.[5] This secret only the Buchanans knew. By the time I arrived at Fairmount in 2006, a line had been drawn through the racial designation of "W" for White on Laura's original internment card and replaced by "C" for Colored. Lucile's arrival fifty-three years later, seeking to buy a plot next to her Black sister, certainly prompted the cemetery staff to correct their error. The fact that Lucile picked this particular day to make her own stand against separate but equal on the grounds of a cemetery while Marshall made his stand in Washington, DC, is striking and too good to be merely coincidence.

The next chapter in Lucile's homecoming concerned her late sister Edith's estate. Over the years, Edith and Lucile shared a secret shame. They were both survivors of intimate-partner violence. For Lucile, two years after the abuse began, her husband abandoned her; on January 3, 1940, she filed for divorce. Edith, likely inspired by Lucile, gathered the strength to file for divorce on June 19, 1941, from her husband and abuser, Charles H. Davis, after twenty-four years of physical, psychological, and emotional cruelty that "greatly endangered her health and well-being to her irreparable injury."[6] But divorce did not end the relationship. Staying away from her abuser proved difficult for Edith, and in an age where there were no financial or emotional support services or laws to protect women from abuse, Charles conned his way back into Edith's life.

When Edith died, the Denver County Court appointed Lucile as administratrix of her estate, which was valued at $17,000 (approximately $145,324 in 2017). Charles contested Lucile's appointment and petitioned for her removal, claiming that her appointment was "procured under false pretense and representation" and that while they were divorced, he and Edith continued to live as common-law husband and wife, making him the sole heir at law.[7]

As Lucile prepared to defend herself, she wrote a few lines in a notebook laying out her strategy: "Reply to petition: The heirs of EBD (Edith Bishop Davis) estate represented by LBJ (Lucile Berkeley Jones) enter this reply to petitioner CD (Charles Davis) for removal of LBJ as an executer. We declare that CD is not [the] sole heir and has no legal right as spouse because (1) ED divorced him in 1941 [and] at that time [the] property was put in her name, and since then his (2) irresponsibility and incompetency of C's 10 years [sic] illness of drunkenness and ulcers."

After laying out her arguments, she hired local attorney Theodore H. Chrysler to challenge Charles's assertions in court. While the court considered Charles's demands, Lucile continued to administer her charge, and on December 20, 1960, the court accepted and approved Lucile's final report and closed the case. After deducting all of Edith's final expenses and legal fees, Charles received $93.81, the household furnishings (valued at $50) of the home at 2430 Franklin Street in Denver, one-half interest in a 1952 Chevrolet (valued at $200), and Edith's diamond ring (valued at $200). Lucile and the rest of the family members were each awarded $15.64.[8] When it came to Edith's real estate property, Charles prevailed. The court awarded him the house, which upon his death on June 6, 1965, went to his brother Lenoir Davis.

Lucile, now eighty years old, initiated a final corrective action on November 13, 1964, motioning in the District Court for the City and County of Denver to change the deed for the property and land on Raleigh Street, which had remained in her mother's name since 1882. On December 5, 1966, the court awarded Lucile, her three surviving sisters, and one of her two nieces equal (one-fifth) interests of 2.5 lots in question, including any existing structures. Eventually, Lucile would outlive her siblings and her niece Carol.[9]

On August 5, 1971, at age eighty-seven, and after living in Denver for almost twenty-two years, Lucile directed her attorney, Anthony V. Zarlengo, to prepare her Last Will and Testament. Her living relatives included her sisters Claribel and Nellie, nieces Evelyn and Carol, and two great-nieces, Lisa Claire and Veda Anne, Evelyn's daughters. Her will tells us a lot about what Lucile valued. She named her Denver-based niece, Evelyn, as the executrix, leaving the bulk of her estate (property and house) to the Denver Baptist Bible College[10] "solely for Christian activities," directing that the college "shall not rent or transfer title except by the condemnation by the City and County of Denver, the State of Colorado, or the United States of America under sovereign right of Eminent Domain." If for some reason the deal with the college did not work out, she bequeathed her property to her "niece Evelyn L. Napper, or to the descendants of her niece, in equal shares." If this failed, her estate was to be given to Denver's Zion Baptist Church, with Zarlengo stepping in as executor. She also directed "funeral services to be conducted by the Fairmount Cemetery Association" and that her "burial policy with Capitol Cooperative Plan of 1350 Lincoln Street, Denver, Colorado, be transferred to the Fairmount Cemetery Association for her funeral services and burial at Fairmount."

Over the next several years, relations between Lucile and her niece Evelyn appear to have deteriorated so badly that on January 25, 1977, she had Zarlengo prepare a codicil to her 1971 will. In it she made two important changes. She removed Evelyn as her executrix and directed all references to "Executer or Executrix" to mean "Personal Representative as denoted by the Colorado Probate Code." And she required that if twenty years after her death the Baptist Bible College had failed to use her residence for Christian activities, her property would be given to Zion Baptist Church, effectively excluding Evelyn or her heirs from the possibility of inheritance.

FIGHTING TO STAY AT HOME

As Lucile aged, she found walking increasingly difficult. Degenerative arthritis riddled her body with pain, and she developed a dowager's hump, which caused her to develop a stooped posture. She also had severe visual impairment. In addition, the pigmentation of her skin began to change, becoming noticeably darker in some spots, and the requisite lines and wrinkles appeared more pronounced as the years advanced. And most deleterious to an elderly woman's pride, she suffered from female-pattern baldness to such an extent that at home she wrapped her head in a scarf and in public donned a short wig or a hat. Audrey Theisen, who occasionally visited Lucile with her father, Herman Dick, remembered that Lucile "always wore clean clothes with an apron, light brown support hose, shoes and a head wrap, which she tied herself."[11] In anticipation of more disabilities to come, she turned the scullery room on the first floor into her bedroom and installed a new toilet.

By the end of the 1970s, Lucile was living more frugal. With the help of an antique dealer, she began to sell some of her furnishings. Years later, an appraisal by Denver-based Rosvall Auction (a registered court appraiser) declared her entire home furnishings to have a fair market value of $678.[12] Besides her radio, one of her most valuable possessions included three wooden bookcases with glass doors, which were appraised at $90, and over a hundred of her beloved books, which were valued at $20.

Despite her debilitating physical ailments, Lucile experienced little cognitive decline and memory loss. She found solace sitting on her wooden rocker in the living room near the large picture window she could no longer see out of, listening to religious programs and news on her Magnavox radio and record player.[13] She was ninety-two when Nellie, her last living sibling, died in 1976 at her Los Angeles home. Except for an occasional visit from Evelyn and Herman's household help, Lucile was more alone than ever. The one activity that continued to excite her was voting. Debbie Heglin, a notary who was then in her early twenties, remembers:

> Back in the 1970s I used to go to the home of an elderly, blind, Black lady named "Mrs. Jones" and notarize her absentee ballot during the elections. I believe the first time I notarized her absentee ballot, she had someone drive her to the law office at that time on Knox Court. After that first time, either she asked or I offered to drive to her home from work to notarize her absentee ballot. I did that a few times. I remember because I always felt bad. While I never ventured beyond her front room in any of my visits, I remember her home being sparsely and shabbily furnished. She

was obviously very, very poor, and she was always terribly, terribly appreciative and grateful—and always offered to pay me. I always declined saying it was really no big deal . . . and was happy to stop in for such a small thing. One time I do remember that she gave me a box of chocolates. She indicated that she wanted to give me something since I'd never let her pay me. It absolutely broke my heart because I knew that she couldn't afford that box of chocolates. Yet, I knew that I could not refuse it. My general impression of Mrs. Jones in the 70s was one of abject poverty.[14]

A troubling piece of information I kept hearing from those who knew the aging Lucile was that she claimed to hear voices and unfamiliar noises around the house, causing them to conclude that her mental capacity had diminished—Robert L. Steenrod even suggested to the court that she had "delusional thought content."[15] While it is certain that Lucile heard noises and unfamiliar voices around her home, it is not clear that they were imaginary or that she was delusional. According to Doris Smith, when she took possession of Lucile's home in 1987, neighbors on either side of the house had older children whose boisterous play often spilled over into Lucile's yard. She indicated that one of these neighbors had "rowdy teenagers and that the parents were equally rowdy when they drank. And if someone stood at a certain area of the backyard of Lucile's home and talked loudly, the voices were picked up in the home."[16] Based on this information, it is well within reason that the voices Lucile heard came from her neighbors' day-to-day living, and it is not unreasonable to imagine some taunting by neighborhood children directed at the elderly blind woman who lived by herself. Often, Lucile's reaction was to call the emergency number 911.

While sporadic phone calls were taken in stride, Audrey recalls that in early 1986 her father, Herman Dick, mentioned that Lucile woke up one morning and began to smell gas coming from her vintage 1930 Prosperity gas stove. She began calling 911. Following multiple house calls, where first responders once again witnessed her deteriorating physical condition and were unaware of the arrangements Lucile had created for herself, she was taken from her home by ambulance to Colorado's Mental Health Institute at Fort Logan (CMHIFL) for a seventy-two-hour hold. Removing Lucile from her home was not an easy task. She vigorously defended her right to independence and apparently put up quite a fight. Eyewitnesses allege that she was forcibly dragged out of the house. But Lucile's fighting spirit was not doused. She signed herself out of the CMHIFL and contacted Herman Dick, who picked her up and drove her home to Raleigh Street.[17] Not long thereafter, she was placed under the jurisdiction of Colorado's Department of Human Services. Ultimately, on March 3, 1986, at 10:15 a.m., she was physically restrained,[18] removed from her home, and taken to Stovall Care Center, a thirty-bed facility sponsored by Zion Baptist Church in the Park Hill section of Denver. Lucile would spend the rest of her life there.[19]

On June 20, 1986, Maxine Fitzgerald of the Denver Department of Social Services filed a petition in the probate court to appoint attorney Robert L. Steenrod Jr., the public administrator for the City and County of Denver, as Lucile's conservator, which was officially granted on September 9, 1986. What must be pointed out is that the public administrator is a misleading term in that the person is a private attorney (not publicly elected or an employee of the State or the judicial districts) appointed by district courts to act as fiduciaries for a protected person. According to the court document, Lucile had no guardian and only one living relative, her niece Evelyn, and thus was in need of a conservator as she was "totally blind and does not have the mental capacity to manage her financial affairs and her residence must either be sold or transferred in order for her to remain eligible for Medicaid financial assistance. Current income must be secured to meet the cost of the nursing home care."[20] This legal arrangement empowered Steenrod to enter into contracts, pay bills, invest assets, and perform other financial functions for Lucile, as necessary. He routinely had to report to the probate court on what money came in and how it was spent. This gave him great latitude to bill Lucile's estate for his professional and legal fees and also for fees paid to members of his staff (everything from phone calls to letters they drafted) or consultants he hired.

At the time the petition was filed, the value of her property on Raleigh Street was unknown. Her liquid assets were assessed at $2,389, which included $89.09 in a checking account, $683.39 in savings, a $256.88 monthly teacher's retirement benefit, and a $1,457.44 burial savings account with her niece Carol J. Roberts, who lived in Los Angeles. This assessment would change once Steenrod submitted to the court an Inventory of Real and Personal Property on December 13, 1986, valuing her real estate at $70,000 and her liquid assets at $28,001. These assets did not include her $80 monthly annuity from the Chicago Board of Education or her monthly pension of $363.80.

STILL STANDING

Lucile's interpersonal skills, instincts, and the strong positive influence she had on people served her extremely well in life. She would now take her talents one step further. By luck, the new owners of her home on Raleigh Street (Doris and Larry Harris) learned from Herman that Lucile was living at Stovall Care Center. Given Lucile's history and that of the house, Doris, who had a particular interest in learning about Lucile, began to visit her on Sundays, and soon a friendship developed.

According to Doris, Lucile was not pleased to be living at Stovall and wanted out. Viola Garlington, the former director of the Stovall Care Center, echoed that sentiment: "Mrs. Jones was particularly upset leaving her family's home in 1986; a home that she often spoke about helping her father build as a young child."[21] Adding to her emotional distress were the occasional physical restraints and the frequent denial of privileges. For example, self-conscious about going bald, Lucile used olive oil, a cheap natural conditioning treatment and moisturizer popular with Black women as a method of promoting healthy hair growth. Stovall apparently denied her this small pleasure. Not easily bested, Doris sneaked a bottle in at Lucile's behest. At some point, Lucile was placed on a salt-free diet. This didn't sit well with her or Doris, who felt that if she wanted salt at 103 years of age, she should have it! The simple solution delighted Lucile: sneak in a saltshaker.

Lucile employed any number of strategies to break out of what she likely considered her prison. Garlington remembers a Sunday when Lucile asked to go to services at Zion Baptist Church. The staff accommodated her request. When the service ended, Lucile decided to take direct action in the form of a simple act of grassroots civil disobedience: a sit-in. The congregants and the minister were gone, leaving only the four church deacons.[22] When the bus arrived to take Lucile back to Stovall, she refused to board it. She considered her removal from her home an affront to her personal liberty and agreed to leave the church only if they took her home to Raleigh Street. Garlington, also a long-standing member of Zion, came to negotiate. She even offered to drive her back to Stoval in her own car. It was futile. Lucile wouldn't bend. The four deacons decided that enough was enough. They physically picked her up (limb by limb) and carried her screaming and crying onto the bus.[23] Garlington states that she "became emotionally upset while witnessing Lucile's situation." But one more bitter disappointment would not deter Lucile Berkeley Buchanan Jones. She was about to dramatically change her strategy—appeal to sympathetic friends.

In my discussion with Larry Harris, he claimed that Lucile did not like "Black people" and often said, "Get me out of here [Stovall Care Center]. This place is full of Black people!"[24] Doris Smith also recalled that "Lucile clearly articulated her dislike for Blacks and didn't want to be around them."[25] As a way of assessing Lucile's alleged animosity toward Blacks, I turned to Suzanne Lipsky's work on internalized racism. Lipsky argued that despite Lucile's exceptional accomplishments, the fact that she was a product of a White supremacist society greatly influenced the way she was perceived. This set in motion "distress patterns," or side effects, not outwardly directed toward the oppressor but rather internalized and re-directed to other Blacks. According to Lipsky, distress patterns can cause Blacks to develop a defensive modus operandi of "fear, mistrust, withdrawal and isola-tion from other Blacks." They can also cause Blacks to "dramatize [and misdirect] feelings of rage, fear, indignation, frustration, and powerlessness at each other."[26]

Lucile's forceful removal from her home and her perception of being held pris-oner at Stovall may have created a distress pattern in her thinking. Garlington remembers that night in 1986 when Lucile arrived in "restraints to Stovall, for her own safety because of her strong objections to being removed unwillingly from her home."[27] In addition, Lucile was blind and likely had difficulties adjusting to the new surroundings, new voices, and unfamiliar routines.

Understandably, her relationship with Stovall's staff was often strained. Earnestine Gavin, who was in charge of medical records, pointed out that "Lucile was too demanding. The minute she came out of her door, she'd raise hell. Her main concern was that we were all taking her money. I had to remind her that it was the attorney [Steenrod] taking all her money. But, if you didn't jump she would raise all kinds of sand."[28] Gavin added, "Mrs. Jones didn't take no stuff." Whether reasserting her rights as an elder, questioning her financial solvency, being unhappy about her confinement in a nursing home, or running a game on sympathetic Whites to get out of her confinement, Lucile was very deliberative in her actions with the staff and those who cared for her as she was facing the inevi-table: the end of her life. Even so, she was optimistic, assertive, and just as adept at getting her own way.

Living at Stovall further strained Lucile's already tenuous relationship with her only living relatives in Denver, her niece, Evelyn, and her great-nieces, Lisa Claire and Veda Anne. Furthermore, she could no longer call out to her next-door neigh-bor to ask about the American elm tree on the sidewalk, and Herman Dick, her longtime driver and helper, apparently did not visit.

While a number of factors could explain her statements about Blacks, it is important to examine the extent to which the conditions of her birth—the daugh-ter of the first post-slavery generation, born and raised in the American West—shaped her ideas and responsibilities towards those less fortunate.

Kevin K. Gaines, professor of history at the University of Michigan, adds: "Against pervasive claims of black immorality and pathology, educated blacks waged a battle over the representation of their people, a strategy with ambiguous implications and results. They referred to themselves as a 'better class' of blacks, and demanded recognition of their respectability and privileged status as agents of Western progress and civilization." And while racism affects all class divisions, the middle and upper classes were thought of as having a noble calling and were therefore tasked in the first half of the twentieth century by W.E.B. Du Bois's

"Talented Tenth" ideology and the National Association of Black Women's club "Lifting as We Climb" to facilitate Black upward mobility by helping those less privileged. Lucile clearly saw herself as part of this ideology and movement.

In other words, Lucile's struggle with the nursing home staff was based on class, not race. Especially since her social identity and beliefs followed Du Bois's racial uplift ideology, which placed the burden for the welfare of the majority Black community on the most successful 10 percent of Blacks such as Lucile. Du Bois's ideology did not always resonate well with the larger Black community. As a result, a struggle emerged that divided the community along the lines of income, social class, and cultural values.[29] This class struggle impacted Evelyn's attitude toward her Aunt Lucile (who thought she was "too bossy") and the nursing home staff, which found her too assertive. But in the areas of the country where she spent most of her working life, the South and urban Chicago, Blacks were more direct and assertive in their communication style.[30] In Denver, she may have faced difficulties readjusting to the different cultural norms and expectations of the West.

Lucile was a product of two Americas. One "proclaimed the moral, mental and physical depravity and inferiority of Blacks from the press, pulpit and university."[31] The other challenged the prevailing stereotypes and "negative images by demonstrating exemplary behavior, marked respectability and intellectual supremacy within the Black community as well as within the majority culture."[32] The former separated her and other very accomplished Blacks from the majority community, while the latter also separated her from the Black underclass, as it found her critical of behaviors that did not match her expectations of excellence.

Though it could be argued that many factors drove her to make anti-Black statements, I suggest that Lucile, with her mental state minimally impaired, if at all, knew exactly which buttons to push and deliberately conveyed her dislike for Blacks to sympathetic Whites like Doris Smith and Larry Harris, whom she had embraced and whom she knew had embraced her. Lucile clearly hated Stovall and knew what would cause a reaction, especially from Doris, who she probably hoped could relieve her of her misery.

According to Doris, "Even by May of 1987, when I first met her, she was plotting to get out of Stovall. She had me call the public administrator, Steenrod, to discuss her personal needs [Steenrod's court records shows that he billed Lucile's estate twenty dollars for accepting Doris's call], and her attorney, Tony Zarlengo, to try to help her. But when I talked to him [Zarlengo], he was very familiar and friendly toward her and had already heard from her many times but couldn't do anything about the situation. But Lucy fought her imprisonment for months. I called anyone I thought would be able to help her. But even if she was able to get out, she had nowhere to go."[33] It was during one of Doris's visits that Lucile told her about her niece Evelyn. Doris hoped a living relative might be the answer to Lucile's dilemma. While Lucile did not remember the address where Evelyn lived, even at 103 years of age she was able to describe the block and what the house looked like with such specificity that Doris located 2765 West Wesley Avenue in Denver without difficulty.

Doris knocked on the door and Evelyn's husband, Herschel, answered. "The reception was cold," she said. She was not invited in. "He seemed completely uninterested in what happened to Lucy." As for Evelyn, Doris said her response was that Lucile was "too bossy and that she didn't want to see her in the nursing home. She had no use for her."[34]

When I first heard this story from Doris, I could hardly imagine what Lucile could possibly have done to warrant such a response from Evelyn. How do I read the subtext of Doris's reception? Was Evelyn having a bad day? Did the family view Doris's visit as an invasion of their private space? Was Doris's cold reception a result of her being White and a stranger interfering in family business? After consideration, I also realized that this is where Black and White perspectives regarding individual feelings and sensibilities come into play. According to communications professor Marlene G. Fine, "Sensibilities have to do with matters of taste, decorum and refinement; feelings have to do with emotion. Individual sensibilities are protected in White culture, while individual feelings are protected in Black culture. Thus, Blacks believe that they have a right to express their feelings even if that expression offends the sensibilities of another person. Whites, on the other hand, will suppress their feelings in order not to offend the sensibilities of others, or even themselves."[35]

After hearing Doris's report, finding Evelyn became my new focus. The little white frame house on West Wesley where she had lived had been sold to a church and appeared abandoned. Through the internet I found information confirming that Evelyn and Herschel had bought property in Las Vegas on December 14, 1989, about a month after Lucile's death. Herschel died on February 27, 2005, and the property was transferred to Evelyn on June 8, 2006. The question was, how would I get her attention? Given Evelyn's age of ninety-three, finding her and arranging a face-to-face meeting became a matter of urgency. I decided on a whim to go to Las Vegas in hopes that our shared gender and race would trump her misgivings and that I would be granted an interview. As a researcher, I had a good sense of the social and cultural context in which I was working, but in this case my assumptions were proven incorrect.

WHAT HAPPENS IN VEGAS STAYS IN VEGAS?

I arrived at McCarran International Airport early Friday afternoon, March 16, 2007, picked up my rented car, and went in search of the University of Nevada–Las Vegas (UNLV). My Vegas guide and host was Ardyth Sohn, a former colleague at the University of Colorado and director of the Hank Greenspun School of Journalism and Media Studies. Ardyth, a former journalist, had a nose for investigative research and the inculcated aggressiveness necessary to track down a story. Lucile's story and my search for Evelyn piqued her curiosity. Our first attempt to find Evelyn occurred the afternoon I arrived.

Ardyth and I drove to the north Las Vegas address where I was confident Evelyn still lived. The house we found, a one-story wood-frame detached ranch style with a small open porch, showed signs of neglect in addition to the wear and tear of the heat and desert sand. The yard looked thirsty for water, with irregular patches of dry grasses dotting the landscape. A huge tree, its leaves browning, stood in the middle of the lawn. At any rate, the yard looked out of place in an area where desert palms and carefully planned xeriscape yards dominated. In comparison to the other neighborhood homes, this house with its chipped and faded facade seemed clouded in mystery.

A large recreational vehicle was parked on the right side of the house inside a gated driveway. I noticed that the blinds on one of the street-facing windows near the door of the house were raised. This allowed me to see the light formed by a television playing in the room. I rang the doorbell. No one answered. I could see the hunched shape of an elderly woman watching television. I called out, "Mrs. Napper, Ms. Evelyn. Hello. Hello." She either ignored my pleas or was unaware of them. I watched through the window as she got up and walked slowly into another room. I went back to the car where Ardyth was sitting. We decided to walk across the street, where a neighbor had just come out of her house. Introducing ourselves, we asked if she knew the people in the house across the street. She said a couple of elderly women and a man were living there. She clearly knew little about them, since the elderly man, Herschel, had died at least two years earlier. I crossed back and left a handwritten note on the door with my name, title, and several contact phone numbers. That little note would later play a pivotal role in the completion of this book.

Ardyth and I returned the next morning to try again. There was a car in the enclosed driveway. My note was gone. With a new, typewritten note in hand, I rang the doorbell. Again, no one answered. This time, all the blinds were closed. I rang again. Again, no one answered. I taped the new note to the door and we drove around the neighborhood, hoping to find someone out on a Saturday morning. No one was out. We returned a few hours later and the note was gone. We were confident we had made contact. We waited the rest of Saturday and Sunday morning until my scheduled departure for Colorado, hoping that I would hear from Evelyn or one of her daughters, Lisa Claire or Veda Anne. I left Las Vegas disappointed, only to be reinvigorated a week later by the first of several letters from Evelyn. For the next several years, we maintained a relationship through phone calls and correspondence.

GOING HOME AND ITS AFTERMATH

Lucile often called out to God to take her home. For Lucile, the idea of death as going home was deeply rooted in the religious and cultural practices of Africans on the continent and in the diaspora, which have shaped the belief in an afterlife among African Americans. For Lucile, calling out to God to take her home was in essence a request to be taken to dwell in heaven with the many family members who had preceded her. In the fall of 1989, she got her wish.

After a fall at Stovall on August 2, 1989, Lucile began her long journey home. Her health deteriorating, she was taken to Mercy Hospital on September 13, 1989, at 2:15 p.m. Six days later, on September 19, she returned to Stovall, where at 4:00 a.m. on Friday, November 10, 1989, at age 105, Lucile completed her earthly stay and was taken home.[36]

While her soul was ostensibly settled to greet her long-lost kin, her earthly body had one more trial to endure. It would take nineteen days to bury her. I found this surprising since Steenrod was well aware of her end of life arrangements. Since his appointment as her conservator in November 1986, which included her prepaid cremation plot at Fairmount Cemetery and a burial savings account in joint tenancy with her niece Carol Roberts in the amount of $1,457.44. However, court documents indicate that her end of life discussion began in earnest on February 9, 1988, when Steenrod reported to the court conversations and correspondences that he and his paralegal were having with Fairmount's staff regarding Lucile's burial plans. Almost two weeks later, Steenrod reviews and signs a letter disposing of Lucile's cremation plot. His actions reported to the court in March 14 and 31, 1988 stated that the "cemetery plot was unneeded" especially since there was a "family plot space." The family plot he refers to was owned by Lucile's deceased sister, Hattie, and was where her brother-in-law Elias, her niece Carol, and her youngest sister, Claribel, were buried.

Since Carol's cremated remains were buried in a regular-sized plot, there was sufficient space for Lucile's casket. But it was this action that ticked off her niece Evelyn, who contested Lucile's burial in the family's plot where her mother, Claribel, is also buried. My correspondence with Evelyn indicated that she remembered accompanying Lucile to Fairmount in the 1950s when she bought a plot next to her sister Laura and requested cremation. Lucile's actions, therefore, provided Evelyn with enough ammunition to argue against burial in the Jarrett's plot. After all, Lucile had her own plot. Whatever the reason, the tension between Evelyn and Lucile was so great that Lucile completely disinherited Evelyn in her final Last Will and Testament that was prepared by her lawyer and notarized by two of Barnum's residents on January 26, 1977. My review of this document did not find what Steenrod reported to the court on November 15, 1989, that Lucile's will, lodged at the Probate Court, city and county of Denver, on January 26, 1977, states, "The person nominated in the Will as Personal Representative is Evelyn L. Napper." And while Evelyn was a blood relative, Steenrod clearly misread Lucile's 1977 will, which disinherited Evelyn and her heirs. In fact, Evelyn's name does not appear in Lucile's final will. Evelyn, aware of her banishment, wanted to distance herself from Lucile and the one punishment would be to deny Lucile's burial in the family's plot that she controlled—so much so that on August 17, 1989 (about seven weeks prior to Lucile's death), Steenrod received a phone call from Fairmount regarding "family dispute over burial plot."

In an interview with Jim Cavoto, then vice president of sales and marketing at Fairmount Cemetery, said, "It usually takes two to four days before the deceased can be buried. When family is not involved we have to deal with a public administrator that can slow down the process, and with cremation cases "they make you do weird things," but nineteen days is historically slow." Cavoto, who remembered Lucile's case, added, "She dies. Steenrod refused to sign cremation authorization because he would not take the legal responsibility. So, we took back the plot in trade and found somewhere else [for her resting place]." Steenrod's report, filed in Denver's probate court on October 7, 1988, shows the "Repurchase of Section 9, Lot 57, Block 17" in the amount of $41.75 on August 22, 1988. Yet Lucile's internment card states that by August 3, 1988, Fairmount already owned the burial plot. When questioning Cavoto about Steenrod's repurchasing figures, he said "$41.75 repurchase does not make sense—weird figure. Generally we would pay 70% of the original purchase price, but in a case like this we would have given 100% back."

Tragically, Lucile's carefully planned and pre-paid decisions in 1953 on her final resting place and method of burial were ignored at each step of the process. The law mandated her estate to pay Steenrod and his staff for doing what she had clearly done years ago. The day following the repurchase, the cremains of Michael D. Corely, associate executive director of the Association of Operating Room

Nurses, who had died nearly three months earlier on May 4, 1988, was buried in her plot.

Once the family plot became an option, Fairmount and Steenrod negotiated a pre-need burial contract that included a funeral service agreement (casket and service) of $1,358.50 and a cemetery service contract (opening and closing the grave) of $847.50. However, Fairmount records indicate that her actual casket, a Bates Primrose, cost slightly more ($1,555) than what Steenrod reported to the court.[37]

On the day of her home-going service, Lucile's casket was placed in Fairmont's mortuary chapel, where promptly at 10 a.m., the Rev. Dr. Wendell T. Liggins of Zion Baptist Church began the service (the same minister who had buried her brother, Fenton, twenty-six years earlier). Organist Jim Ewart and singer Leo Frazier performed funeral music. According to Audrey Theisen, "The day was cold and dreary." Besides Audrey, there were four other people in attendance—Maxine Fitzgerald from the Denver Department of Social Services; Audrey's parents, Herman and Mary Dick; and her brother, Allen. Audrey stated, "It was an open casket . . . white tin with pink flowers . . . and we were all surprised how well she looked even though she was still very thin."

A CEMETERY'S MEANDERINGS

In the spring of 2004, I paid the first of many visits to Fairmount Cemetery. Built in 1890 on 280 acres, Fairmount is Denver's second oldest cemetery and the final resting place of a plethora of Denver's early pioneers. With a map in hand I went in search of Block 52, Lot 28, Section 8. Once there, I kept walking from headstone to headstone desperately searching for Lucile's name, to no avail. It wasn't easy walking across the uneven dirt of the final resting places of so many people; I felt like an intruder. However, I kept reminding myself that cemeteries are the keepers of time, continuously holding what we once held dear. I could see that for some, the memory remained; for others, the memory had faded. But in a very personal and quiet way, I began to recognize that I was walking through Colorado's early Black history—these early pioneers who had lived in all their richness and mystery.

After a while I discovered a small, pink, upright granite headstone engraved with the names of Lucile's third cousin, Travis N. Buchanan, and his wife, Clarabell. But still no Lucile. I was just about at my wits end when I spotted a large gray granite headstone with the name Jarrett featured prominently on the top in large block letters and the name of Lucile's sister, Hattie, and her brother-in-law Elias below. It was the largest headstone in the area, clearly reflecting the wealth and prominence of those whose final resting places it marked. I recalled that Lucile was interred in the Jarretts' plot. But I was still thinking about traditional markings, which would be on the front of the headstone. Clearly, Lucile was not there. As I circled the headstone, I noticed an engraving at the bottom right corner of the back of the headstone. In bold caps were the words "LUCILE B. JONES, JUNE 13, 1884–NOV. 10 1989–FIRST BLACK WOMAN GRADUATE UNIVERSITY OF COLORADO."

Getting Lucile's name engraved on the tombstone had been the work of Frederick "Fred" John Walsen, the grandson of early pioneer Fred Walsen, who in 1873 founded the town of Walsenburg, Colorado. Born almost a year prior to Lucile's graduation from the University of Colorado, on June 9, 1917, Fred, a fellow alumnus and journalism major, was an avid history buff. After Robert Jackson's story about Lucile's burial in an unmarked grave broke in the *Rocky Mountain News*, Fred immediately went into action. He contacted Fairmount to correct what he considered an injustice and to properly memorialize a piece of history, and the cemetery staff negotiated the deal with Lucile's niece, Evelyn, who by now had accepted the idea of Lucile's internment in the family plot.

During a quiet afternoon at Fairmount Cemetery, I began to think of the need to remember and honor the past. The lives of Lucile's family and of those interred around them and the granite headstones that mark their silent history. But what Fred did is remarkable.

As the last living relative in the Walsen line, his final resting place is in Fairmount's historic Millionaires Row in a large and impressive mausoleum, with his father and the WALSEN name prominently featured. As a final altruistic act, he made sure that Lucile's name and contribution to the university and to Colorado history will live on for generations to come.

IT'S A WRAP

Lucile Berkeley Buchanan Jones was a woman of strong constitution and substance, the daughter of pioneering emancipated slaves who traveled west to Colorado in order to forge a new life in the mile-high city. Her parents brought a few customs from Virginia, including the tradition of naming their children after a family member. Sarah and James's first child born in the new frontier was named after her mother's father, Edmund Berkeley, and her half-sister, Lucy. Through the years, Lucy (Lucile) Berkeley Buchanan would never forget to remind people who her grandfather was.

Lucile's life straddled two centuries. Over the course of ten-and-a-half decades, she bore witness to many historic events, which would shape not just Colorado and US history but world history as well. She lived through the Progressive era, the Roaring Twenties, the Great Depression, Roosevelt's New Deal, Johnson's Great Society, the Vietnam War, the rise of the silent majority that propelled Richard Nixon into the presidency, and the Watergate scandal that brought him down. When crayons were invented in 1903, she was a high school senior in Denver. She became a flapper in the 1920s by first bobbing her hair in Kansas City. She lived through thirty-four major wars and conflicts in which the United States was directly involved. She was there for the birth of Coca Cola, Lifesavers, drinking straw, frozen foods, Scotch tape, freeze-dried coffee, and so much more.

She saw the onset of the counterculture in the 1960s, which gave way to the New Left, feminism, civil rights, environmental activism, gay liberation, and the Black Power movement. She listened on her radio when James Brown belted out "Say It Loud! I'm Black and I'm Proud," Sam Cooke's "A Change is Gonna Come," and Nina Simone's "Mississippi Goddamn." She was mindful of the rise of Dr. Martin Luther King, Malcolm X, and Robert F. Kennedy, and sadly their deaths through an assassin's bullet. She experienced travel by wagon and rail, and saw the invention of the automobile and the airplane. She grew and matured along with the radio, the phonograph, photographic film, motion pictures, and television, as well as the technologies that would create the internet. She survived the brutal influenza pandemic of the twentieth century, which killed more than forty million people. She saw twenty presidents take office and lived through the assassination of two—William McKinley in 1901 and John F. Kennedy in 1963. A staunch Republican, she got to see that after women received the right to vote in 1920, seven Republicans she voted for were elected president.

She lived in areas of the South where Blacks were brutally lynched, and she followed the writings of journalist and anti-lynching crusader Ida B. Wells-Barnett, who lived close to Lucile in Chicago and worked for the *Chicago Defender* when Lucile settled there in 1925. She observed the development of every key Black civil rights organization: the National Association for the Advancement of Colored People in 1909 (of which she was a member); the Brotherhood of Sleeping Car Porters in 1925, an organization to which her brother-in-law, Elias Jarrett, belonged; the Congress of Racial Equality in 1942; the Southern Christian Leadership Conference in 1957, and the Student Nonviolent Coordinating Committee in 1960.

As a student attending the University of Colorado during World War I, she witnessed the significant impact the war had on the academic life and how administrators, faculty, staff, and students contributed to the war effort. On the other hand, as a more mature student who had lived in the Jim Crow South, she was more skilled in battling the racial infringements she faced on the campus, in the classroom, and in the Boulder community. Back home in Denver, she read in the local Black newspaper, the *Colorado Statesman*, about the rise of Marcus Garvey's Black Nationalist organization, the Universal Negro Improvement Association in 1916 and its commitment to racial pride and economic autonomy.

Lucile left an indelible imprint philosophically, professionally, and personally on the lives of the students she taught in segregated public schools in Hot Springs and Little Rock, Arkansas, Kansas City, Missouri, and Chicago, Illinois. Most surprising is that at the sixteenth-class reunion, celebrating the 114 years of existence of the Langston High School in Hot Springs where Lucile taught, the local newspaper, the *Sentinel-Record*, covered the story by reflecting on the six teachers who "left a lasting impression on the community." Lucile Buchanan was one of the six.[38]

Though remaining within the boundaries of race, gender, and class of her time, she embarked on a life of adventure, achievement, and risk-taking, marked by innovation, self-reliance, and independence—qualities that were the hallmark of the West. As Viola Garlington, who first met Lucile when Lucile was 103 years old, states, "She knew how to make it work."

Lucile was a daughter of the state of Colorado whose triumphs and failures went unnoticed, leaving me the opportunity to fill a void in the chronicles of Black history—from Virginia to Colorado and beyond. As I began the search for Lucile I discovered that there was something magical about her story that had a way of touching and staying with people. In many ways, her story became the story of the people I met along the way and the web of relationships my research cultivated. At times, I thought it might have had something to do with her being "first": the first Black woman to graduate from two of Colorado's prestigious institutions of higher education (University of Northern Colorado and the University of Colorado), the first recording secretary of the National Convention of Gospel Choirs and Conventions in 1932. But Lucile's story was more than being the "first."

As I examined what she left behind (photos, postcards, her academic regalia, and other memorabilia) while walking through her house with its Victorian touches; examined the books she read, studied, and scribbled in; read the letters written to her over a hundred years ago; reviewed the choices she made in her personal and professional life; visited the plantations where her parents were enslaved and where they were able to forge a strong and durable family life, which they brought with them to Colorado, I discovered that I was not writing an ordinary biography. I was exploring her life through the complexities and meanings she left behind and through the communities she was part of. I was looking into the lives of those she influenced (e.g., pioneering Black journalist Lucile Bluford) and those who influenced her (e.g., W.E.B. Du Bois, Ida B. Wells and Luise Mühlbach) and, in an odd way, those who touched her also touched me. I was blending biography, life, and social history, coming to know and understand her story within the historical framework of the very difficult periods of US history through which she lived and the one in which I am presently living in 2018.

Wherever Lucile's family lived in and whomever they touched in eighteenth, nineteenth, or twentieth century America, they affected and were affected by the collective consciousness of people across racial, class, and gender divides. Lucile and her siblings were therefore shaped by the histories of her parents (as slaves and free people); by the Whites they toiled and toyed with (the plantation overlords); by a shared family history with their enslavers (the case of Lucile's mother and her White slave-holding father); the White middle-class communities as well as the racially restricted communities they called home; the White teachers who inspired her through formal education; the Black press that provided an informal, Black-centered, thought-provoking education on local, national, and international occurrences; Black organizations that lauded the educational achievements of Denver's Black youth (e.g., Inter-Graduate Student Association); and the Black church that provided comfort, hope, connections across state lines, and spiritual, moral, and practical needs for the community but became the epicenter of activism.

In an unassuming way the Buchanans were able to achieve economic mobility to earn middle-class status within a decade of their arrival in Denver. But that achievement came with a price for their daughters who choose teaching as a career. In Lucile's case, due to the historical racism in the professional labor market in Denver, she was not welcomed and left Denver taking her passion to serve, spent forty-three years (1905–48) serving Blacks in the Jim Crow South close the opportunity gap.

I began my search for Lucile by questioning who validates the history makers, especially at a university. At the same time, I was intrigued by memory—whether individual, group, family, or public in historical thinking. But Lucile's story sharpened my understanding of the extent to which historical memory is forged and forgotten, whether as the result of the acceptance of local mythology, incomplete research, or the prejudices of those who decide who or what constitutes history.

I needed people's memory to help reconstruct Lucile's life journeys. I needed the mistress's plantation diary to understand how she reacted to the defiance of slave and freed women during the end of the Civil War and in Reconstruction. I needed Lucile's notes about the Republican party to understand her support of the party even in the midst of Black abandonment. I needed to understand her insistance on being called Mrs. Jones even after she walked away from an abusive relationship. I needed to understand how our lives intersected in the face of overt

FIGURE 15.3. *Lucile at 103 years of age, Courtesy Doris Smith and Larry Harris, ca. 1986.*

and polite racism in an elite and privileged city and in an institution of higher learning bearing the same. I needed to understand the communicative practices she employed to maintain her dignity across racial boundaries.

Lucile made history and changed history not through headlines and not on a national stage, but through her quiet, sometimes firm, unassuming ways, and always, always, on her own terms. And as I look back on my journey through her life, I am reminded of the words of writer and editor Philip Elmer-DeWitt, who said, "some people make headlines while others make history." Lucile made history.

Epilogue

The End of the Living Line

There is no refuge from confession but suicide;
and suicide is confession.

— DANIEL WEBSTER

Well over a decade has passed since I began writing Lucile's story. Giving voice
to her and her family's history became an unrelenting passion, taking me across
ten states and through fifteen cities. I was driven, literally and rhetorically, by a
compulsion with no boundaries and a compelling aura of mystery that fired my
imagination. I wandered into people's lives as much as they wandered into mine.
No matter where I traveled, Lucile's story and that of her family energized people's
curiosity, sometimes challenging their prevailing racial dynamics, and opening
doors that had previously been closed.

There were times when the racial barriers of a lifetime rose and disappeared. I
spoke to a captivating southern White woman in Leesburg, Virginia, who initially
rejected my research on Edmund Berkeley and his philandering with slave women
but continued to listen and evaluate until the barrier broke and, to my amazement,
she invited me to her home, a historic house on Cornwall Street, built by John
Janney (circa 1780). Once there, in an interior laced with features of the antebellum era (1830–60), she shared hundreds of photos of an era long past and gave me
a copy of a letter written about 1900 by Mary Lewis Berkeley Cox, Lucile's great-
aunt and a relative of hers by marriage.[1]

255

More and more, the most poignant aspects of my journey came from encounters with people who were filled with boundless joy and willing to share their own historical adventuring. There was the library assistant at Thomas Balch Library who invited me to her home to share her husband's hobby of charting the slave history in Loudoun County. Through his research efforts, I uncovered additional information on Lucile's father.

Total strangers also warned me about places best not to go. I will never forget the alert and kind Black hotel clerk in Chicago who, upon hearing my desire to visit the neighborhood where Lucile's husband lived until his death, told me to stay away from that neighborhood because "you might not make it out alive." At times, I was overwhelmed by personal sadness and loss. In 2006 I met up with an old and dear friend whom I had not seen in twenty years, Malachi Thompson, an avant-garde jazz trumpet player. He drove me around the Chicago neighborhood where Lucile once lived, never letting on that his body was riddled with cancer. We shared a delightful reunion. Malachi died two months later.

After hours and sometimes days spent wandering through archives in dimly lit basements or brightly lit rooms, from neo-classical Revival-style buildings to completely modern facilities, I thought my decade-long research journey had come to an end. I couldn't be more wrong.

At 6:45 p.m. on Thursday, September 23, 2010, I answered a call. The woman on the other end said, "This is the Las Vegas Police Department, looking for Polly McLean."

Whoa, I thought. "Who?"

She repeated herself, and I asked her for her name. I was expecting officer this or detective that, but she responded "Brenda."

"What's this about?" I asked.

"We need to know if she is a family member of the Nappers and whether they had any health conditions," she replied.

"And whom am I speaking to?" I asked again.

"Brenda."

Suspicious of just a first name and thinking about the Las Vegas tourism tagline "what happens in Vegas stays in Vegas," I pondered for a moment, then said, "Polly McLean is not at home."

Early the next morning, I called the Las Vegas Police Department. After explaining the call I had received the previous night, I was directed to John J. Cahill, the

Clark County public administrator. What Cahill told me shook me to my core. There had been a double suicide of sisters Lisa and Veda Napper, and my phone number had been the only one found in the house.

After gathering myself, I explained to Cahill my relationship with the Nappers, Lisa Claire, fifty-nine, and Veda Anne, fifty-eight, with whom I had been corresponding in the course of my research on the life of their great-aunt but whom I had never met face to face. Cahill asked pertinent questions regarding my work and immediately understood the historical value of safeguarding any archival materials that might otherwise be discarded. Cahill decided to allow Catrice Montgomery (the Buchanan genealogist in Virginia) and me to have access to the house for four hours under police supervision. We would not be allowed to remove any materials but were permitted to place anything we deemed of historical significance in a box, which Cahill would review later and have the final say on its distribution. My previous visit to North Las Vegas in 2007, during which I had hoped to gain a face-to-face interview with the Nappers, had proved unsuccessful. Yet now, on October 19, 2010, I was about to enter their home without them or their consent. This was the scene of a double suicide, the house sealed immediately after Lisa's and Veda's bodies were removed and where the atmosphere of death still lingered. As Catrice and I walked to the front door toward the waiting police officer, the only change I noticed to the worn exterior, with its dying trees and shrubs, was a pot of brightly colored plastic flowers a neighbor had placed on the front banister as a memorial to the sisters after their deaths.

RETRO, CLUTTER, AND MEMORIES

The interior of the house presented itself as a throwback to the 1960s, when colors were pumped up to vibrant hues of yellow, green, bright blue, orange, and an entire room of razzleberry. The living room was fairly neat and eclectically furnished with a menagerie of curios, plastic flowers, bowls of artificial fruit, and old and new pieces of furniture from varying eras but nothing that matched. A life-size dark brown teddy bear wearing a western straw hat sat on a faded yellow vintage-style sofa. In the far corner, near the sliding door to the patio, stood a floor lamp and a small, compact computer desk with a hutch. On top of the desk sat a monitor and its corresponding hard drive. Among the numerous computer manuals and programs strewn on the desk were two printers. Nearby, the battery-operated clock on the wall continued to keep time.

On the fireplace mantle were framed photographs. One was of their father, Herschel, in his World War II US Army uniform. There was also a three-photos-in-

FIGURE 16.1. *Lisa Claire and Veda Anne Napper as children, ca. 1954. Buchanan Archives.*

a-frame arrangement. The middle photograph was of their mother, Evelyn (circa 1940s), and was inscribed to her mother, Claribel: "With Love to My Own Muz, Your daughter Evelyn." On either side of her were photos of Lisa and Veda as toddlers, dressed in matching outfits. Asian figurines and small brass animals were scattered across the mantel and floor. Dog, cow, and bird figurines dominated the collection on the walls.

Adjacent to the living room, the disheveled dining room appeared to have been used for everything but eating. Apart from a Bible given to Veda as a Christmas gift by her Aunt Nellie (Lucile's sister) in 1962, three things stood out immediately: ten twelve-packs of soft drinks; three extra-large Ziploc bags filled with empty pill bottles, some several years old; and multiple groupings of red cupid figurines, heart cutouts, containers of red rose petals, and other love memorabilia inspired by their parents' marriage on Valentine's Day.

The kitchen was lived in. There were four opened thirty-six-ounce soft drink bottles on either side of the sink. On the countertop next to the sink were numerous opened bags of chips and other food items stored in Ziploc bags. A rather filthy white toaster oven, a box of oatmeal, and some cookies shared space on the crowded countertop. There was a second freezer in the garage, also stocked with food. The sisters had not been starving.

Although there was much clutter in the house, it did not seem to rise to the level associated with pathological hoarding. Closets contained varying sizes of plastic bags and small boxes in which were their important papers: household statements, paid bills, multiple handwritten and notarized Last Wills and Testaments, which their mother, Evelyn, consistently revised.[2] There were other valuables around which I could easily navigate.

Two of the three bedrooms had clearly been used as storage facilities. One contained the arts and crafts projects Veda made, including hundreds of large beaded hair combs and dozens of twenty-four-inch teddy bears, as well as multiple numbered containers of craft materials and many VHS tapes.

TWO BODIES, ONE LIFE

Lisa and Veda seemed not to have developed the type of power struggle and healthy competition that often occurs between siblings seeking their own identity. When they were young, their family seemed especially sensitive in treating them as much alike as possible. When their grandmother, Claribel Perkins, sent the older, a bracelet, she immediately sent one to Veda, who in her thank you note wrote, "Dear Nannie, Thank you so very much for the lovely card and beautiful bracelet! I am glad I have one like Lisa's."

They appeared to have developed a very unhealthy co-dependency early on. The house showed no evidence that these two women led separate lives within it. In a letter written to me by their mother, Evelyn, in November 2007, she stated, "My two daughters, Lisa and Veda, and I are very 'close'! They go everywhere and do everything *together*. And, I wouldn't have it any other way." Originally, this statement confused me, since it was out of context with the rest of the letter. In hindsight, it serves as a foreshadowing of what I came to discover in North Las Vegas regarding the isolated lifestyle and the extreme control their mother exerted on the lives of these women well into their late fifties.

Even though there were two unoccupied bedrooms in the house, Lisa and Veda shared the third bedroom with their dog, Flit. There were two single beds with a two-drawer nightstand and a lamp dividing them. The beds were up against a large picture window with two layers of window coverings. On the right wall was a single shared dresser. The room was cold, dark, and cluttered, with clear storage bins stacked three to five feet tall along every wall space. Across the ceiling hung a huge hammock filled with hundreds of stuffed animals—reminiscent of what one might find in a child's bedroom but on a much grander scale.

Apart from grocery shopping at Albertsons or WinCo Foods, cremating their parents, making trips to the vet with their dog Flit, and Lisa's occasional visit to the Sunset Station Casino in Henderson, it was clear that the Nappers had little to no life outside their home. I could not find any references to friends, church, volunteer experiences, work, membership in a group or association, or any of the things one expects to find in the homes of people half a century into their lives.[3]

In addition to Lisa's sewing and Veda's crafts, their lives seem to have consisted of taking care of their aging parents and pets, watching old VCR tapes, browsing the internet, and playing a plethora of simple online games. It was a plain and sober life centered on their home. As spinster sisters who had grown up and aged together, it seemed that they not only lacked individual self-identities but that they never matured out of defining themselves first and foremost as the children of their parents. They were not two individuals—they were one, each other's best friends and confidants.

From all appearances, they were financially dependent on their parents. Although they bought the book *Starting an Etsy Business for Dummies*, there were no signs that they had opened an Etsy shop. No boxes, labels, or packing tape; and a search on Etsy in North Las Vegas for the types of crafts in the house also proved unsuccessful. The only checkbooks in the house had all four family members' names on them—mother, father, and two daughters. A search through a decade of Internal Revenue Service statements revealed that their parents claimed Lisa and Veda as dependents on their annual income taxes until both parents died. After their father's death in 2005, their mother continued to claim them until her death in 2009.

Another shared loved was for their dogs, which were also their mother's favorite pets. Not only did they immortalize their dogs when they died through large displays of dog hair on white boards, they also wrote numerous poems about them. One poem titled "Our Master Flit" reads:

> We have a darling snow-white Cairn
> Flit Napper is his name
> And he's so precious and so dear to us
> Completely free of blame
> Doing little things worthwhile
> Or things that are so funny,
> That he causes us to smile.
> And when we are feeling sad, quite low

Flit is always there for us,

To lick our tear stained face and hands

To show he cares and understands.

This poem certainly illustrates that they had a strong bond with Flit. Flit was a major focus of attention and a confidant whom the sisters placed in high esteem and considered an equal member of the household. There were also numerous holiday cards the sisters or their mother had made that attached human qualities to Flit. One such card from Evelyn was addressed "To Tweetie, Dolly and Flit" with the interior message, "You are my Valentines, One, Two and Three, My Dearest of Hearts You forever will be. And grow more precious with each coming year, Darling Veda, Lisa and Flit so dear! Love, Mama." Flit was, in essence, another sibling.

THE FINAL DAYS

Lisa and Veda had begun arranging for their suicides well in advance of their chosen date, which occurred one year and one month after their mother's death. In preparing to take their own lives, they placed their mail on hold for a month. They also bought a copy of Hemlock Society founder Derek Humphry's book, *Final Exit: The Practicalities of Self-Deliverance and Assisted Suicide*, which was on the dresser in their bedroom when I arrived.[4] The book provided information on who should know of their deaths, how to write their suicide note, and, perhaps most important, how to die together.

The illustrations in chapter 23, "A Speedier Way: Inert Gases," offered all they needed to perform auto-euthanasia, which assured a quick and pain-free death. To accomplish this, they went to the local party store and rented five fifty-cubic-foot tanks of helium.[5] As part of their pre-planning activities, they also wrote and signed a joint Last Will and Testament, leaving their entire estate to the Nevada Society for the Prevention of Cruelty to Animals. Each attached a handwritten note to her headboard making their intentions clear: "I am not to be resuscitate [*sic*] or put on any life support to prolong my life." This note was another suggestion from Humphry's book.

On Thursday, September 23, 2010, Lisa and Veda woke up to a pleasantly warm and sunny North Las Vegas day. They placed a worn red wraparound dog bed between their own beds and set their iPod Nano to a continuous shuffle among "Angel" by Sarah McLachian, "Beautiful" by Christine Aguilera, and "Note to God" by Charice.[6]

Before they executed their suicide pact, they participated in what psychiatrist Brian K. Cooke refers to as "extended suicide" by including their beloved Flit.[7] Although non-human, Flit was family, and as his family members prepared to end their lives, they believed he would willingly share the same desire they had to die with them.[8] Certainly, the sisters had a strong relationship with Flit and found meaning in their lives through the bonds they had developed with him, which may have grown stronger since their mother's death. Through the same technique they would soon use on themselves, inert gas asphyxia, Flit was rendered unconscious after one to two minutes and died painlessly a few minutes later. With Flit's death, there was no turning back.

As they prepared to die, it would appear that they took large doses of over-the-counter sleeping pills. When I entered the room a month later, the empty pill bottles were still on their nightstand. According to the Clark County coroner's report, lying on their beds with Flit's dead body on the floor between them, each sister inserted two clear plastic tubes attached to the helium canisters into a large black plastic bag, with which they then covered their heads. Each sister secured her bag with duct tape and tied it with a material that also secured the tubing inside the bag.[9] Within moments, they were rendered unconscious. Death followed soon after. Humphry's book also provided direction regarding what is referred to as the last letter, more commonly known as the suicide note. It suggested a handwritten note, signed and dated, with some suggested text. Lisa and Veda ignored this recommendation and instead crafted their own note, which they emailed to the American Civil Liberties Union (ACLU) of Nevada at 9:59 a.m. on the day they had chosen to die. The email read:

From: Fournaps@aol.com
Subject: Please Notify North Las Vegas Police

To Whom It May Concern:

We'd like to THANK YOU for taking time to read our e-mail . . . and we would like to say we're sorry (please forgive us) but we didn't know who else to email. We have no friends, neighbors or family that we could trust to do what we feel needs to be done . . . the added stress because of our failing eyesight due to complications from diabetes (as well as other ailments) has made this our only choice. Our Mommy and Daddy are already in heaven and since we had to put our Baby Flit (our puppy) to death . . . his death finally broke our already breaking hearts . . . we just got tired of trying—without any monetary encouragement (which unfortunately seems to be the only thing in this life that has any worth)—we hope you will help two stranger[s] . . . who are very sorry for adding any stress to your life . . . to get cremated.

Thanks again for helping us.

Sincerely,
Lisa C. Napper and Veda A. Napper

P.S. Please notify the North Las Vegas Police that hopefully we have died and our bodies (and wills) our [sic] in our home at 4524 Pony Express Street, North Las Vegas, NV 89031 (We would have sent our e-mail directly to the Police but it would have gone instantly to them).

Their decision to send their suicide note to the ACLU office, combined with the P.S. stating that if they had sent it to the police it would have gone "instantly" to them, left me to surmise that they wanted to avoid the possibility of any life-saving intervention. When ACLU's general counsel Allen Lichtenstein read the note, he immediately contacted the police in hopes that they or paramedics would arrive in time to intervene. According to an article written by *Las Vegas Sun* reporter Joe Schoenmann, the police "arrived at the house at 10:19 a.m., knocked on the door, and not finding any open door or window left with the idea to return later in the day when neighbors would be home to provide information on the sisters." The police also indicated to Schoenmann that the suicide note did not establish "enough probable cause to force their way in." A little after 6:00 p.m. the police returned, and learning from the neighbors that the Nappers' car was in the driveway, signifying that the sisters were at home, the police felt they now had probable cause to break in, unfortunately much too late. Schoenmann's article goes on to note that the police department's spokesperson, Sergeant Tim Bedwell, said, "It's very sad. And clearly in hindsight, we wish we would have opened that door."[10]

As I looked at their dying declaration and their desire for self-vindication, I could not help but explore the text of their suicide note for answers. As their note says, they had no friends or neighbors they felt they could trust. The few neighbors I spoke to agreed that they had no meaningful contact with the sisters or their parents in the twenty-one years the family lived there. One reported that if they inadvertently made eye contact, the sisters would go inside the house. This avoidance dance seems to have been a behavior they developed as teens in Denver that continued into adulthood.

Contrary to the suicide note, which states "since we had to put our Baby Flit (our puppy) to death . . . his death finally broke our already breaking hearts," while their hearts might have been broken, it was not an outsider, such as the vet, who directed Flit's death, as the note implies.[11] Finally, their note mentions their deteriorating health ("failing eyesight due to diabetes complications"), yet their behavior prior to their death shows tremendous self-neglect. The Clark County Coroner/Medical Examiner's Report states that only "one prescription medication prescribed in [Lisa's name] was found for Cardizen 360 mg [a channel blocker often used to treat hypertension] that was last filled on January 1, 2006." All the other medication containers I found were empty and had expired years ago.

With the loss of their mother's financial support and unemployed, they seemed utterly unaware of the resources that may have been available to them. When it came to their "failing eyesight," and while I recognize that any number of factors can contribute to vision loss and it is possible that one, if not both, of the sisters were developing vision problems, they had passed Nevada's vision screening test for renewal of their driver's licenses a year earlier.

Catrice, who had joined me on my research journey to Las Vegas, arranged for Lisa's and Veda's cremations to be performed by the State of Nevada. Since the disposal of their cremains was not part of the state's agreement, I paid the Valley Funeral Home to legally spread them close to their parents' graves—a desire noted in the various wills their mother had written. While I thought my journey with Lucile would end in Colorado, it was in Nevada that I found yet another layer of coincidences to add to the ongoing serendipity I first encountered in the research process in Colorado when I began my journey toward Lucile.

It was only by chance that I discovered Lucile's niece, Evelyn Lucile Parker Napper, and her two daughters, Lisa Claire and Veda Anne, in North Las Vegas. It was also by chance that a family I never met kept my phone number, I scribbled on two small pieces of paper that I had taped to their door four years earlier, and it was by chance that one of these small slips of paper caught the eyes of the police while looking for someone to contact in the hours following the sisters' deaths.

The list of coincidences doesn't stop there. For example, Evelyn died in August 2009 in North Las Vegas. She is interred, along with her husband, Herschel, at the Southern Nevada Veterans Memorial Cemetery in Boulder City, Nevada. I live in Boulder County, Colorado. The cemetery is located at 1900 Buchanan Boulevard. Buchanan is the surname of Lucile's paternal lineage. The gravesite is number 227, the same number of the house in Denver that the Buchanans built in the 1890s, where Lucile and her siblings grew up, and where Evelyn spent much of her childhood.

As I leave Lucile's story behind, I still struggle to come to terms with the culture of suicide in her family—one at the end of the nineteenth century, one at the beginning of the twentieth century, and two more at the beginning of the twenty-first century. I had always thought of suicide as a cowardly and repugnant act. I wondered, while death itself is inevitable, why would anyone orchestrate his or her own death? Reading Lisa and Veda's suicide note was emotionally challenging. Nonetheless, I was struck by the similarities between it and the suicide note left behind by Laura, Lucile's sister, 111 years earlier. All three suicides occurred in their bedrooms in their parents' homes; all three notes showed self-blame, hopelessness, distress, forgiveness, thankfulness, and the core belief in an afterlife common among most Blacks. Laura wrote about going home to the Lord, and Lisa and Veda wrote of joining family members who were already in heaven. While it took years for me to overcome the shock and reconcile their choice with my prejudice against suicide, one thing had become clear: their deaths marked the end of the living line for the 128-year journey for three branches of a family who left Virginia in 1882 for Colorado, seeking opportunity and freedom.

As for me, I am left with the haunting images of their deaths that continue to offer only questions: Is death as valuable as life? How do we know what happens after life stops? Since only the living can interpret or describe death, how does this color my interpretation of death in general or theirs in particular? While we are alive, we can choose to have a conversation with family, friends, or strangers in real time from within a body loaned to us for a finite number of years. In death, as far as we know, there is no conversation after the moment. No return policy to exchange the merchandise. Death is inevitable. There is no comeback. I am left to interpret their deaths from the perspective of the living.

At first, the evidence they left behind implied that the sisters chose to end their lives as an act of hopelessness brought on by their inability to cope with life. Philosopher Albert Camus's writings on life and death in his essay "The Myth of Sisyphus"[12] would suggest that the Napper sisters were only at home within the confines of their physical space in North Las Vegas and that once their human companions within that space had died, they were exiled more than ever and instinctively fell into an "absurdist" paradigm, which concludes that life is meaningless and therefore has no meaning. With this reasoning, suicide quickly became their only option. But who am I to judge? Even though they may have feared life, they did not fear death. They courageously accepted it by orchestrating a peaceful and painless exit from this life into what they "knew" was a better place. More and more, I have come to recognize that their suffering ended through their own actions—their decisions. Lucile, in contrast, relinquished her power to call out to the God she had worshipped all her life to "take her" as she aged. Asking for help in dying or taking one's own life did not seem like decisions I should judge. In each case, the living accepted the fact of death. They did not fear it. They faced it.

While the deaths of Lisa Claire and Veda Anne leave a sad aftertaste, I eventually had to let it go. After all, they died as they had lived, not as two lives but as one and in the company of someone they loved—their dog, Flit. Thinking of them and all those who preceded them, I recalled what existential psychiatrist Irvin D. Yalom said: "Death and life are interdependent: though the physicality of death destroys us, the idea of death may save us."[13]

Notes

PROLOGUE: HER VOICE CAN BE HEARD

1. Nancy S. Griffith, "Will Norman (Lynching of)," *The Encyclopedia of Arkansas History & Culture*, http://www.encyclopediaofarkansas.net/encyclopedia/entry-detail. aspx?entryID=9303 (accessed May 25, 2012); Guy Lancaster, "Lynchings Hidden in the History of the Hot Springs Confederate Monument," *Arkansas Times*, https://www.ark times.com/ArkansasBlog/archives/2017/08/18/lynchings-hidden-in-the-history-of-the -hot-springs-confederate-monument (accessed August 29, 2017).

2. Horace Clarence Boyer, *The Golden Age of Gospel* (Urbana: University of Illinois Press, 1995), 195.

3. Audrey Theisen in discussion with the author, January 23, 2011.

4. Robert Jackson, "She Was CU's First Black Female Grad—a Pioneer Buried without a Headstone," *Rocky Mountain News*, sec. 4A, June 14, 1993. Going even further, it was not as difficult to find Black students during the first two decades of the twentieth century. I went about this in two ways: return to the Black press to pinpoint some of the Black students that were lucky enough to get covered and looking yearbooks in which Black students were featured. With just names, at the Office of the Registrar, we were able to pinpoint the following African American graduates in the early 1900s: Charles Durham Campbell, 1912; Lucile Berkeley, 1918; Ucecil Seymore Maxwell, 1921; Alexander Jesse Brickler, 1922; Sam Nelson, 1923, Ruth Cave Flowers and Clement Sutton Jr., 1924.

5. Pierre Nora, "Between Memory and History: Les Lieux de Mémoire," *Representations* 26 (1989): 8–9.

6. I received a call from the office of President Elizabeth Hoffman as to whether my research was accurate, since Hoffman was giving a speech to Denver's Black community and wanted to acknowledge Ruth Flowers. I confirmed to the staff member that my research on Lucile was accurate. About an hour later, I received a second call from the same office querying my research.

7. Carl G. Jung, *Synchronicity: An Acausal Connecting Principle* (Princeton, NJ: Princeton University Press, 1973).

8. Audrey Theisen in discussion with the author, January 23, 2011.

9. Frederick or "Fred" John Walsen was the grandson of Fred Walsen for whom Walsenburg, Colorado, was named. In 1936, he graduated from the University of Colorado with a degree in journalism.

10. In 1908, journalism became an area of study housed in the College of Commerce under the umbrella of the College of Arts. A Denver-based journalist/author was hired as the first instructor. By 1917, journalism was taught in the English Language and Literature Department in the College of Arts. The program/area of study became a college (sometimes referred to as a school) in 1922 (see *The Coloradan* [1927]). In 2014 the University of Colorado Board of Regents dissolved the SJMC and approved the creation of the College of Media, Communication, and Information.

11. NAACP, https://www.naacp.org/naacp-history-carter-g-woodson/ (accessed April 24, 2017).

12. Nancy A. Naples and Carolyn Sachs, "Standpoint Epistemology and the Uses of Self-Reflection in Feminist Ethnology: Lessons for Rural Sociology," *Rural Sociology* 65, no. 2 (2000): 194–214.

13. bell hooks, *Teaching to Transgress: Education as the Practice of Freedom* (New York: Routledge, 1994), 186.

14. Sarah Nuttall, "Writing Biography: An Interview with Jon Hyslop, John Matshikiza, and Mark Gevisser," *Social Dynamics* 30, no. 1 (2004): 105–13 (quote from page 107).

15. The public administrator for the City and County of Denver is a private lawyer appointed by the Probate Court. The administrator is required to file annual reports on his or her activities with the court. While these reports are public records, the administrator maintains the records.

16. Erving Goffman, "On Fieldwork," *Journal of Contemporary Ethnography* 18, no. 2 (1989): 123–32.

17. Raphael Samuel, "What Is Social History?," *History Today* 35, no. 4 (1985), http://www.historytoday.com/print/7311 (accessed January 5, 2018).

18. Shirley A. Leckie, "Biography Matters: Why Historians Need Well-Crafted Biographies More than Ever," in *Writing Biography: Historians and Their Craft*, ed. Lloyd E. Ambrosias (Lincoln: University of Nebraska Press, 2004), 1–26 (quote from page 1).

19. Doris Smith in discussion with the author, June 13, 2010.

CHAPTER 1: INQUIRY AND EPIPHANY

1. Audrey Theisen remembers that her father, Herman Dick, erected the "Beware of Dog" sign shortly after the 1965 Denver flood as a crime deterrent.

2. John G. Laut, "Dutch Elm Disease Control in Colorado," *Journal of Arboriculture* 6, no. 10 (1980): 274–75; see also Laura Pottorff, "How Dutch Elm Disease Got to Colorado," *Colorado State University Extension* (2010), http://www.coopext.colostate.edu /4dmg/Garden/Amazing/howdutch.htm (accessed February 2, 2003).

3. By 2010 Rodriquez was disabled, leaving the tree to fend for itself. As of 2017, the American elm still survives.

4. US Census Bureau, "Census 2000 Data for the State of Colorado," last modified October 6, 2011, https://www.census.gov/census2000/states/co.html (accessed December 20, 2016). By the 2010 Census, Kiowa's population had increased to 714, including ten African Americans.

5. After closer scrutiny, I discovered the barely legible words "Sarah Buchanan" written on the back of the plywood dust cover in ink that had faded with time. I was looking at Lucile's mother.

6. "Paul Laurence Dunbar's Denver Days," *Denver Post*, February 15, 2010.

7. In 1864, William B. Daniels and William G. Fisher opened a five-story department store at Sixteenth and Lawrence in Denver. The Daniels and Fisher Department Store was Denver's largest and most prestigious wholesale and retail store during the first half of the twentieth century.

8. Edward F. Arnold, "Some Personal Reminiscences of Paul Laurence Dunbar," *Journal of Negro History* 17, no. 4 (1932): 400–408.

9. Evelyn Napper, letter to author, March 5, 2005.

10. Joan L. Severa, *Dressed for the Photographer: Ordinary Americans and Fashion, 1840–1900* (Kent, OH: Kent State University Press, 1995).

11. Shirley A. Leckie, "Biography Matters: Why Historians Need Well-Crafted Biographies More than Ever," in *Writing Biography: Historians and Their Craft*, ed. Lloyd E. Ambrosias (Lincoln: University of Nebraska Press, 2004), 1–26.

12. Carolyn Ellis, "Telling Secrets, Revealing Lives: Relational Ethics in Research with Intimate Others," *Qualitative Inquiry* 13, no. 1 (2007): 3–29.

13. Marilys Guillemin and Lynn Gillam, "Ethics, Reflexivity, and 'Ethically Important Moments' in Research," *Qualitative Inquiry* 10, no. 2 (2004): 261–80.

14. Nick Couldry, "Speaking about Others and Speaking Personally: Reflections after Elspeth Probyn's 'Sexing the Self,'" *Cultural Studies* 10, no. 2 (1996): 315–33 (quote on p. 316).

CHAPTER 2: BORN IN SLAVERY: THE MASTER, THE MISTRESS, AND THEIR CHATTEL

1. Thomas Bender, *Community and Social Change in America* (Baltimore, MD: Johns Hopkins University Press, 1978), 7.

2. Following the Carter's ownership, Edith and William Corcoran Eustis purchased Oatlands in 1903. In 1964 the family donated the property to the National Trust for Historic Preservation. Today, Oatlands is a National Historic Landmark designated by the US secretary of the interior, representing an outstanding aspect of American history and culture.

3. See Oatlands Historic House and Gardens, Oatlands Trees, https://www.oatlands .org/trees/ (accessed June 29, 2016).

4. David L. Butler, "Whitewashing Plantations: The Commodification of a Slave-Free Antebellum South," *International Journal of Hospitality and Tourism Administration* 2, no. 3 (2001), 164.

5. John Michael Vlach, *The Planter's Prospect: Privilege and Slavery in Plantation Paintings* (Chapel Hill: University of North Carolina Press, 2002), 2.

6. Charles Ball, *Slavery in the United States: A Narrative of the Life and Adventures of Charles Ball, a Black Man, Who Lived Forty Years in Maryland, South Carolina and Georgia, as a Slave under Various Masters, and Was One Year in the Navy with Commodore Barney, during the Late War* (New York: John S. Taylor, 1837), iv.

7. Oatlands Historic House & Gardens, History at http://www.oatlands.org/history (accessed January 20, 2015).

8. Quoted in Andrew Levy, *The First Emancipator: Slavery, Religion, and the Quiet Revolution of Robert Carter* (New York: Random House, 2005), 159.

9. Barbara Dombrowski, *A History of Oatlands* (Leesburg, VA: Oatlands, Inc., 1999), 9–12.

10. Levy, *First Emancipator,* 151.

11. Levy, *First Emancipator,* 136–73.

12. Levy, *First Emancipator,* 53.

13. John Vogt and T. William Kethley, *Loudoun County Marriages, 1760–1850* (Athens, VA: Iberian, 1985), 52.

14. John Randolph Barden, " 'Flushed with Notions of Freedom': The Growth and Emancipation of a Virginia Slave Community, 1732–1812," PhD dissertation, Duke University, Durham, NC, 1993, 415; William Forbes to [George Carter], May 20, 1805, C.F.P. 651-1861, Sec. 52 (Mss1 C2468 a2211=2215, Richmond, Virginia Historical Society).

15. George Carter to Sophia Carter, June 20, 1816, Letterbook, 1807–19, Loudoun County Historic Division (Mss5: 2 C2455:1), VHS, p. 170.

16. See Eugene Scheel, "Timeline of Important Events in African American History in Loudoun County, Virginia," *The History of Loudon County, Virginia,* http://www.loudoun history.org/history/african-american-chronology/; Wynne Saffer, *The Largest Slaveholders of Loudoun County, 1860, Microcopy 653 of the 8th Census, 1860, Roll 1393* (Loudoun, VA: Thomas Balch Library, 1860).

17. Will of George Carter of Oatlands, Loudoun County, Leesburg, VA, 2C, LGR (COL), 187, 1841/46.

18. Philip D. Morgan, *Slave Counterpoint: Black Culture in the Eighteenth-Century* (Chapel Hill: University of North Carolina Press, 1998), 556.

19. Daniel E. Meaders, *Advertisements for Runaway Slaves in Virginia, 1801–1820* (New York: Routledge, 1997), 85.

20. Elizabeth O. Carter's Diary, 1860–72, courtesy of Oatlands Historic House and Gardens.

21. Lynn C. Bloom, "Diaries: Women," in *The Companion to Southern Literature: Themes, Genres, Places, People*, ed. Joseph M. Flora and Lucinda H. MacKethanp (Baton Rouge: Louisiana State University Press, 2002), 212–13.

22. Elizabeth's diary acknowledges a number of slave women with whom she interacted without conflict. Yet there were other women who challenged her authority. When this occurred, she sold some of these women to slave dealers. But the one woman who stands out was Fan (aka Fann, Fanny). Six of the eleven times Elizabeth mentions a woman being "insolent" in her diary are attributed to Fan. The 1870 Federal Census shows Fan (recorded as Fannie Smith, fifty-one years of age) living in Leesburg, Loudoun County, with her daughters Tena and Delia.

23. Gale S. Alder, trans., Handwritten statement by George Carter II to his brother John Tasker Carter regarding a property with land in West Virginia and the manner in which he inherited Oatlands (June 4, 1976), 1–6 (retrieve from Oatlands Research Library).

24. Alder, written statement.

25. The Rangers lived off the land among local farmers and Confederate sympathizers and became renowned for their unorthodox and daring creativity in raiding and disrupting Union activities in Loudoun, Fauquier, and Rappahannock Counties. See Robert R. Mackey, *The Uncivil War: Irregular Warfare in the Upper South, 1861–1865* (Norman: University of Oklahoma Press, 2004), 72–94.

26. Susanne Michele Lee, "Refugees during the Civil War," *Encyclopedia Virginia*, http://www.EncyclopediaVirginia.org/Refugees_During_the_Civil_War (accessed March 23, 2010).

27. Lee, "Refugees."

28. General Orders, no. 2, May 18, 1865, from Hd. Qtrs. Military Sor. District, Lynchburg, VA, by Command of Brevet, Brig. Gen'l GREGG. The text appears in the *Mirror*, June 14, 1865.

29. Marietta Minnigerode Andrews, *Memoirs of a Poor Relation: Being the Story of a Post-War Southern Girl and Her Battle with Destiny* (New York: E. P. Dutton, 1927), 203. Marietta was also the niece of Kate Powell Carter, the wife of George Carter II.

30. Alder, Handwritten statement, 9–12.

31. Year: 1860; Census Place: Southern District: Loudoun, Virginia; Roll: M653_1359; Page: 762; Family History Library Film: 553158; Year: 1870; Census Place: Southern District, Loudoun, Virginia; Roll: M593_1659; Page:214A; Family History Library Film: 553158.

32. Dombrowski, *A History of Oatlands*, 14; Oatlands, Historic House & Gardens—The Carter Era, 1798–1897, https://www.oatlands.org/carterera/ (accessed March 31, 2011).

33. Year: 1880; Census Place: Mercer, Loudoun, Virginia; Roll: 1376; Page: 477C; Enumeration District: 054.

34. Samuel J. Barrows, "What the Southern Negro Is Doing for Himself," *Atlantic Monthly*, June 1891, 805.

35. Barbara A. Huddleston-Mattal and P. Rudy Mattal, "The Sambo Mentality and the Stockholm Syndrome Revisited: Another Dimension to an Examination of the Plight of the African-American," *Journal of Black Studies* 23, no. 3 (1993): 344–57.

36. 1850 Year: 1850; Census Place: Loudoun, Virginia; Roll: M432_957; Page: 217B; Image: 117 (accessed April 21, 2015); Year: 1860; Census Place: Southern District, Loudoun, Virginia; Roll: M653_1359; Page: 762; Family History Library Film: 805359 (accessed April 21, 2015).

37. Elizabeth R. Frain and Marty Hiatt, *Loudoun County Virginia Death Registry,* 1853–1896 (Westminster: Heritage, 2007), 243; Catrice Montgomery, in discussion with the author, January 23, 2009.

38. The date of birth (DOB) is approximate for all the children. For example, in Martin's case, the various indices, including census, death records, and marriage records, lists three DOBs for Martin (1842, 1844, and 1845).

39. Catrice Montgomery Vandross, personal conversation, Virginia, September 5, 2009.

40. William W. Layton, "The Spring of 1863—a Call to Arms," Smithsonian Associates Civil War E-Mail Newsletter 3, no. 3, http://civilwarstudies.org/articles.shtm#vol.%202 (accessed March 31, 2011).

41. "An Act for Enrolling and Calling out the National Forces, and for Other Purposes," *Congressional Record,* 37th Cong. 3d sess., ch. 74, 75. March 3, 1863.

42. Eugene C. Murdock, *One Million Men: The Civil War Draft in the North* (Westport: Greenwood Press, 1980), 180.

43. Gregory J.W. Irwin, *Encyclopedia of the American Civil War: A Political, Social, and Military History,* ed. David Stephen Heidler, Jeanne T. Heidler, and David J. Coles (Santa Barbara, CA: ABC-CLIO, 2002), s.v. "United States Colored Troops."

44. Irwin, Encyclopedia of the American Civil War, 2003.

45. City of Alexandria, Virginia, "Fighting for Freedom, Black Union Soldiers of the Civil War," http://alexandriava.gov/historic/fortward/default.aspx?id=40018 (accessed March 31, 2011).

46. Retrieved History Central, "Navy History," last modified 2005, http://www.history central.com/navy/ (accessed March 31, 2011).

47. As his three-year service ended, Martin owed the US government $49.44 on his clothing account and $6.67 for arms and equipment. His muster rolls also noted that he was due a bounty of $100.

48. Andrews, *Memoirs of a Poor Relation,* 75–76.

49. Contraband was a term commonly used to describe an escaped slave during the Civil War.

50. Margaret Richardson, *Alexandria Freedmen's Cemetery Historical Overview,* abstracted and compiled by Margaret Richardson (Alexandria, VA: City of Alexandra, 2007), 2.

51. Excerpt for Julia A. Wilbur's letter from Alexandria, Virginia, November 5, 1862, to her friend Mrs. Amy Kirby Post. From the Family Papers of Isaac and Amy Kirby Post, 1817–1918, Rush Rhees Library, University of Rochester, http://www3.alexandriava.gov /freedmens/pdf/JuliaWilburLetters.pdf.

52. Wesley E. Pippenger, Alexandria, Virginia, Death Records, 1863–1868 (the Gladwin Record) and 1869–1896 (Westminster, VA: Family Line Publications, 1995).

53. John H. Russell, *The Free Negro in Virginia, 1619–1865* (Baltimore, MD: Johns Hopkins University Press, 1913), 131.

54. Information provided by Catrice Montgomery, a descendent of Lucile's great-uncle Robert Buchanan. Until I began my research, the descendants of the Buchanans in Virginia and Washington were unaware of any Buchanans who went west to Colorado in the post-Reconstruction era.

CHAPTER 3: THE BERKELEYS, A SLAVE NAMED HARRIET BISHOP, AND HER DAUGHTER, SARAH

1. For an interesting read on Edmund Berkeley and the history of Evergreen, see "A Soldier and a Gentleman: Haymarket's Col. Edmund Berkeley," http://eservice.pwcgov. org/library/digitallibrary/hsdw/E_Folder/Evergreen76-7/pdfs/Evergreen76-7FamHist A.pdf.

2. Evergreen Country Club, http://www.evergreencc.org (accessed January 12, 2007).

3. Rosanna Hertz, *Reflexivity and Voice*, ed. Rosanna Hertz (Thousand Oaks, CA: Sage, 1997), viii.

4. Christopher Phillips, *The Making of a Southerner: William Barclay Napton's Private Collection* (Columbia: University of Missouri Press, 2008), 125.

5. Morton was the leader of the Prince William corps of the Works Progress Administration's writers project, 1937. The notes that I am citing were secured from the Ruth E. Lloyd Information Center for Genealogy and Local History (RELIC), Prince William Library System, Bull Run Regional Library, Manassas, VA, Susan Rogers Morton, Papers from the "Evergreen" Collection, Haymarket, Virginia, 1837, 236.

6. The ages given are approximate. In White's case I used a runaway slave announcement. For Harriet, I used the 1870 Census data. Also, slaves often had two names, a given name and one used only within the family circle; it is unclear whether White was a given name or a nickname resulting from some other distinguishing feature.

7. John Michael Vlach, *Back of the Big House: An Architecture of Plantation Slavery* (Chapel Hill: University of North Carolina Press, 1993), 21.

8. Property history from RELIC digital library, provided by Don Wilson, http://www.pwcgov.org/government/dept/library/pages/relichistoricrepository.aspx.

9. Berkeley, Edmund. *Prince William County Virginia, Edmund Berkeley's Evergreen Farm Day Book, 1851–1855.* Transcribed by Ronald Ray Turner, Manassas, Virginia, 2003, 12. The overseer's house was not always the sole residence of Edmund's overseer. On October 17, 1851, Edmund notes in his daybook that after seeding the Stone house field, he rented the Stone house and its garden to Mr. Monroe for twenty dollars for all of 1852.

10. Berkeley, *Evergreen Farm Day Book*, 233.

11. The 1860 Slave Schedules also show that Edmund included a thirty-year-old Black male "fugitive from the state" (runaway) and that the gender and ethnic breakdown was twenty-two males, of which three were recorded as Mulatto, and thirty females, of which seven were recorded as Mulattoes.

12. Berkeley, *Evergreen Farm Day Book*. Turner has also transcribed two additional Farm Day Books of Edmund Berkeley, 1897–1905 and 1905–10. Two more Farm Day Books are in the hands of private collectors.

13. Berkeley, *Evergreen Farm Day Book*, 58.

14. Berkeley, *Evergreen Farm Day Book*, 41, 58.

15. Stephanie M.H. Camp, *Closer to Freedom: Enslaved Women and Everyday Resistance in the Plantation South* (Chapel Hill: University of North Carolina Press, 2004), 5.

16. Berkeley, *Evergreen Farm Day Book*, 99.

17. Berkeley, *Evergreen Farm Day Book*, 2.

18. Berkeley, *Evergreen Farm Day Book*, 59.

19. Frederick Douglass, *My Bondage and My Freedom: Part I—Life as a Slave. Part II—Life as a Freeman* (New York: Miller, Orton, and Mulligan, 1855), 92.

20. Berkeley, *Evergreen Farm Day Book*, 62.

21. Berkeley, *Evergreen Farm Day Book*, 88.

22. Marie Jenkins Schwartz, *Birthing a Slave: Motherhood and Medicine in the Antebellum South* (New York: Harvard University Press, 2006), 1–5.

23. Schwartz, *Birthing a Slave*, 154.

24. Berkeley, *Evergreen Farm Day Book*, 81.

25. Richard Steckel, "The Slavery Period and Its Influence on Family Change in the United States," in *Family Systems and Cultural Change*, ed. Elza Berquo and Peter Xenos (Oxford, UK: Clarendon, 1992), 156.

26. 1870 US Census, Loudoun County, Virginia, Mercer District, p. 19, dwelling 112, enumerated June 27, 1870, by John S. Baker.

27. This is the same videotape by Larry Harris at the gravesite of Lucile's parents in 1987 at Denver's Fairmount Cemetery.

28. Mechal Sobel, *The World They Made Together: Black and White Values in Eighteenth-Century Virginia* (Princeton, NJ: Princeton University Press, 1987), 154.

29. Brenda Stevenson, *Life in Black and White: Family and Community in the Slave South* (New York: Oxford University Press, 1996), 187.

30. Writers' Program (US), *The Negro in Virginia* (New York: Hastings House, 1940), 44.

31. Writers' Program, *The Negro in Virginia*, 45.

32. C. W. Harper, "Black Aristocrats: Domestic Servants on the Antebellum Plantation," *Phylon* 46, no. 2 (1985): 125.

33. Harper, "Black Aristocrats," 125.

34. Adrienne D. Dixson and Celia K. Rousseau, *Critical Race Theory in Education: All God's Children Got a Song* (New York: Routledge, 2006), 94.

35. Benjamin Quarles, *The Negro in the Making of America* (New York: Simon and Schuster, 1987).

36. Gainesville, Prince William, VA, Census, 1970; Roll: M593_1673; Page: 406B; Family History Library Film: 553172.

37. Jessica T. DeCuir-Gunby, "Proving Your Skin Is White, You Can Have Everything": Race, Racial Identity, and Property Rights in Whiteness in the Supreme Court

Case of Josephine DeCuir," in *Critical Race Theory in Education: All God's Children Got a Song*, ed. Adrienne D. Dixson and Celia K Rousseau (New York: Routledge, 2006), 94.

38. Interestingly, Sarah's request for financial assistance coincides with her daughter Laura's (Edmund's granddaughter) acceptance into Colorado State Normal School.

39. Email correspondence from Donald L. Wilson, librarian, Ruth E. Lloyd Information Center for Local History and Genealogy, Manassas, VA, January 15, 2010.

40. Leslie W. Lewis, *Secrets in African American Literature* (Chicago: University of Illinois Press, 2008).

41. Mary Boykin Chesnut, *Mary Chesnut's Civil War,* ed. C. Vann Woodward (New Haven, CT: Yale University Press, 1981), 29.

CHAPTER 4: SLAVERY'S CHAIN DONE BROKE AT LAST

1. Eugene Scheel, "Timeline of Important Events in African American History in Loudoun County, Virginia," *The History of Loudon County, Virginia*, http://www .loudounhistory.org/history/african-american-chronology.htm (accessed February 3, 2005).

2. 1870 US Census, Population Schedules, NARA microfilm publication M593, 1,761 rolls (Washington, DC: National Archives and Records Administration, n.d.).

3. Quoted in Meghan Collins Sullivan, "At Oatlands Plantation, a Union of Historic Proportions," *Washington Post*, June 3, 2004.

4. Diary of Kate Powell Carter of Oatlands, 1861–63, Thomas Balch Library, Leesburg, VA, 929.2 Carter, 20.

5. "Gen'l Brig Brevet to Hd. Qtrs. Military Sor. District," the *Mirror*, June 14, 1865, https://static1.squarespace.com/static/559ec31fe4b0550458945194/t/563e4f4be4b0d49f2 177268b/1446924107580/Letter-Lynchburg.pdf (accessed February 20, 2005).

6. Franklin Frazier, *Black Bourgeoisie* (New York: Simon and Schuster, 1957), 132.

7. 1870 US Census: Place, Southern District, Loudoun, Virginia, Roll M593_1659, 246A, image 498, Family History Library Film 553158, 193.

8. 1870 Census, Southern District, Loudoun, Virginia, Roll M593_1659, p. 165B, Family History Library Film 553158.

9. James S. Russell, "Rural Economic Progress of the Negro in Virginia," *Journal of Negro History* 11, no. 4 (1926): 556–62; Eric Foner, *Nothing but Freedom: Emancipation and Its Legacy* (Baton Rouge: Louisiana State University Press, 1983).

10. A. A. Taylor, "The Migration," *Journal of Negro History* 2, no. 2 (1926): 336.

11. "A Trip on Horseback," *New York Herald* [Fauquier County, VA], June 17, 1865, reprinted in "The Desolation of Virginia," the *Mirror*, June 29, 1865, https://static 1.squarespace.com/static/559ec31fe4b0550458945194/t/563e34bfe4b06983d4616ac1 /1446917311110/Desolation+of+Virginia.pdf (accessed June 5, 2008).

12. Mechal Sobel, *The World They Made Together: Black and White Values in Eighteenth-Century Virginia* (Princeton, NJ: Princeton University Press, 1987).

13. Phillip D. Morgan, *Slave Counterpoint* (Chapel Hill: University of North Carolina Press, 1998).

14. In 1810 William Noland, a prominent White farmer and mill owner and his wife, Catherine, named their fourth child Charles Fenton Mercer Noland in honor of their good friend the celebrity.

15. "Anti-Slave Trade Act of 1819," Statutes at Large of the United States of America, 1789–1873, 3 (New York City: Little, Brown, 1845), 532–34, http://www.fjc.gov/history/home.nsf/page/tu_amistad_doc_12.html (accessed April 3, 2004).

16. Personal conversation with Denise Oliver-Velez, December 1, 2007.

17. James Jasper, Restless Nation: Starting over in America (Chicago: University of Chicago Press, 2000), 64–65.

18. Leon Litwack, Been in the Storm So Long: The Aftermath of Slavery (New York: Random House, 1979), 247.

19. Eugene M. Scheel, "Gleedsville: Legacy of Former Slave John Gleed," in Loudoun Discovered: Communities, Corners, and Crossroads (Leesburg, VA: Friends of the Thomas Balch Library, 2002), 96–99.

20. Scheel, "Gleedsville," 130.

21. According to Eugene Scheel, "Timeline of Important Events in African American History," there were several schools the Buchanans could have attended, including the Freedmen's Bureau School in Middleburg, the African School and the Bailey School in Leesburg, and the Second Street School in Waterford, Pleasant Valley.

22. A. A. Taylor, "Freedom in a Struggle with Slavery," Journal of Negro History 11, no. 2 (1926): 250–72.

23. Taylor, "Freedom in a Struggle with Slavery," 250.

24. James T. Moore, "Black Militancy in Readjuster Virginia, 1879–1883," Journal of Southern History 41, no. 2 (1975): 168.

25. Larry Harris, videotape interview with Lucile Berkeley Buchanan Jones, Denver, 1987. Private collection.

26. Ronald Ray Turner, Prince William County, Virginia Marriages, 1854–1938 (Manassas, VA: Ronald Ray Turner, 2002), 50: Buchanan, James F., age 22, b. Loudoun County, son of Fenton and Hannah; married to Sarah Bishop, age 18, b. Prince William County, dau. of Harriet [father not identified] married 14 Nov. 1872.

27. Eugene M. Scheel, "Bowmantown: In the Flat Below the Hollow," in Loudoun Discovered: Communities, Corners, and Crossroads, vol. 4 (Leesburg: Friends of the Thomas Balch Library, 2002), 121–24.

28. Eugene M. Scheel, "Stewartown: Above the Flats up in the Hollow," in Loudoun Discovered: Communities, Corners, and Crossroads, the Hunt County and Middleburg, vol. 3 (Leesburg, VA: Friends of the Thomas Balch Library, 2002), 130.

29. Patricia B. Duncan, Loudoun County, Virginia Birth Registry, 1880–1896 (Berwyn Heights, MD: Heritage Books, 2007).

30. 1860 US Census, Population Schedules, NARA microfilm publication M653, 1,438 rolls (Washington, DC: National Archives and Records Administration, n.d.).

31. 1870 US Census, Population Schedules, NARA microfilm publication M593, 1,761 rolls (Washington, DC: National Archives and Records Administration, n.d.).

CHAPTER 5: COLORADO AND THE PROMISE OF FREEDOM

1. Claudette Bennett, "Racial Categories Used in the Decennial Censuses, 1790 to the Present," *Government Information Quarterly* 17, no. 2 (April 2000): 161–80.

2. 1870 US Census, Population Schedules.

3. The Inflation Calculator https://westegg.com/inflation/ (accessed January 15, 2017).

4. Inflation Calculator.

5. Geraldine Lightner, *Education—Yesterday*, African American clipping file, 1890–99, Denver Public Library, Western History and Genealogy, Denver, CO.

6. Anna Elaine Brown Crawford, *Hope in the Holler: A Womanist Theology* (Louisville: Westminster John Knox Press, 2002), 43.

7. Inflation Calculator.

8. Inflation Calculator.

9. Steven Ruggles and Russell R. Menard. "Occupational Coding," Public Use Microdata Sample of the 1880 US Census Population: User's Guide and Technical Documentation (Minneapolis: Social History Research Laboratory, 1994), 24–29, http://www.hist.umn.edu/~rmccaa/ipums-europe/usa/volii/88occtc.html (accessed June 29, 2008).

10. Ruggles and Menard, "Occupational Coding."

11. Jesse T. Moore Jr., "Seeking a New Life: Blacks in Post–Civil War Colorado," *Journal of Negro History* 78, no. 3 (Summer 1993): 167.

12. William M. King, *Going to Meet a Man: Denver's Last Legal Public Execution, July 27, 1886* (Niwot: University Press of Colorado, 1990), 6.

13. United States WPA, Writers' Project Colorado, Series 3, Box 8, WH 2212, File Folder 30-1936-42, Denver Public Library, Western History Collection, Denver, CO.

14. "How Many Are Free," *Denver Post*, Open Forum, July 21, 1950, 4.

15. In 1882 Edward Sanderlin owned a barbershop and a bath business at 374 Larimer Street. When Barney Ford's barbershop burned in 1863, he rebuilt the barbershop but this time went into the restaurant business by opening Ford's People's Restaurant at 1514 Blake Street and eventually the Inter-Ocean Hotel at Sixteenth and Blake Streets. By mid-1895 he was the manager of the Colorado Shirt Manufacturing Company.

16. Eugene H. Berwanger, "William J. Hardin: Colorado Spokesman for Racial Justice, 1863–1873," *Colorado Magazine* 52, no. 1 (Winter 1975): 56.

17. Glenna R. Schroeder-Lein and Richard Zuczek, *Andrew Johnson: A Biographical Companion* (Santa Barbara, CA: ABC-CLIO, 2001), 50–51.

18. "Aid for the Immigrants," *Rocky Mountain News*, May 9, 1879, vxx, 4.

19. Edward W. Blyden, "African Colonization: Rev. E. W. Blyden's Address at the Annual Meeting of the Maine Colonization Society, June 1862" (Ann Arbor, MI: University Microfilms, 1971).

20. Quoted in Lyle W. Dorsett and Michael McCarthy, *The Queen City: A History of Denver* (Boulder, CO: Pruett, 1986), 104.

21. W.E.B. Du Bois, "The Burden," *The Crisis: A Record of the Darker Races* 3, no. 2 (1911): 76.

22. Letter reprinted in W.E.B. Du Bois, "The Ghetto," *The Crisis: A Record of the Darker Races* 3, no. 4 (1912): 145.

23. George E. Waring Jr., *Report on the Social Statistics of Cities* (Washington, DC: Government Printing Office, 1887), 769–72.

24. Waring, *Report on the Social Statistics*, 771.

25. Nathaniel S. Shaler, "A Winter Journey in Colorado," *Atlantic Monthly* (January 1881): 46.

26. Shaler, "A Winter Journey in Colorado," 46.

27. William H. Bergtold, "Denver Fifty Years Ago," *Colorado Magazine* 8, no. 1 (March 1931): 68–69.

28. Robert H. Latta, "Denver in the 1880s," *Colorado Magazine* (July 1941): 134.

29. Latta, "Denver in the 1880s," 135

30. Latta, "Denver in the 1880s," 133.

31. *History of the City of Denver, Arapahoe County, and Colorado* (Chicago: O. L. Baskin & Co., 1880), 282–83; Western History/Genealogy, Denver Public Library.

32. See interview with Kate Little, Denver Public Library EAD Project, Box 8, p. 2, Denver Public Library, Western History Collection, Denver, CO.

33. *Denver Rocky Mountain News*, December 5, 1868, 4.

34. *Corbett and Ballenger's Tenth Annual Denver City Directory* (Denver: Corbett and Ballenger, 1882); W. H. Gibson Sr., *History of the United Brothers of Friendship and Sisters of the Mysterious Ten* (Louisville: Bradley and Gilbert, 1897), 72.

35. Some of the items listed here were included in the Rosvall Auction Company's inventory of the house on October 9, 1986.

36. Sarah M. Nelson, Richard F. Carillo, Bonnie J. Clark, Lori E. Rhodes, and Dean Saitta, *Denver: An Archaeological History* (Boulder: University Press of Colorado, 2008), 156.

37. "Jefferson Co. Mines: Successful Operations in Southern Section." Colorado Transcript, August 28, 1901.

38. National Archives and Records Administration, *Schedules of the Colorado State Census, 1885* (Washington, DC: National Archives and Records Administration), M158, 8 rolls.

39. Denver Census 1900, enumeration district 0082, p. 3.

CHAPTER 6: FROM DENVER'S BOTTOMS TO P. T. BARNUM'S TOWN

1. The *American Thresherman and Farm Power*, vol. 18 (August 2015), 59, ran an article written by Eugene Parsons titled "Nicknames and Slogans of American Cities," which indicates that Denver's nicknames were Queen City of the Plains, Paris of America, Mile High Town, Convention City, and City of Lights, with its slogan "Smile and Push."

2. Even before these fortune seekers converged in the area, Denver was home to the Southern Arapaho and Cheyenne Indians, who were hoodwinked into signing a new treaty (Treaty of Fort Wise) that took away most of the land that had previously belonged to them.

3. Encyclopedia Staff, "Colorado Gold Rush," *Colorado Encyclopedia*, last modified January 6, 2018, http://coloradoencyclopedia.org/article/colorado-gold-rush (accessed March 10, 2016).

4. The second wave of immigration lasted from roughly 1820 to 1870. The third wave was from 1881 to 1920 (*The World Book Encyclopedia*, vol. 10, 1 [1997], 82).

5. William Henry Jackson, *Ute Indians at the Denver Exposition*, August 1881, WHJ-10114 Denver Public Library, Western History and Genealogy Department.

6. D. B. McGee, "John Taylor—Slave Born Colorado Pioneer," *The Colorado Magazine* (1941): 161–68.

7. Laura Woodworth-Ney, *Women in the American West* (Santa Barbara, CA: ABC-CLIO, 2008), 320.

8. Corbett and Ballenger's eleventh annual Denver City Directory (Denver: Corbett and Ballenger, 1883), 283; Sanborn Map published for the Denver Board of Underwriters (Denver: Sanborn Map and Publishing Co., 1887).

9. "Living in Tents in Denver," *Denver* (CO) *Tribune*, July 20, 1881; *New York Times*, July 25, 1881.

10. David Thomas Brundage, *The Making of Western Labor Radicalism: Denver's Organized Workers, 1878–1905* (Champaign-Urbana: University of Illinois Press, 1994), 21.

11. Thomas J. Noel, "The Immigrant Saloon in Denver," *Colorado Magazine* (Summer 1997): 54.

12. In one of my visits to the Buchanans home on Raleigh Street, I was given access to an old horseshoe that the current tenant found while digging in the barn. The horseshoe belonged to a Belgium draft horse. Given the size and strength of these horses, and since James and Fenton Buchanan did large labor projects (digging basements, working on the viaduct), it is conceivable that the family owned Belgium draft horses.

13. In 1887, Denver experienced a major change in the numbering system in the downtown area where the Buchanans resided, which accounts for the change in their address.

14. Tom Sherlock, *Colorado's Healthcare Heritage: A Chronology of the Nineteenth and Twentieth Centuries*, vol. 1: *1800–1899* (Bloomington, IN: iUniverse, 2013), 307. Accordingly, the number of deaths from typhoid was fifty-nine in 1886.

15. Francis S. Kinder, "Early Days in Barnum: First Owners of the Soil," Denver Public Library, Western History and Genealogy Department Collection, Clipping Files, Denver Neighborhood, Barnum, 1.

16. "Articles of Incorporation and By-Laws of the Denver Villa Park Association, Denver, Colorado" (Denver: Denver Tribune Association, 1872).

17. While Barnum lived in Connecticut, he depended on private secretaries and lawyers to help manage his real estate dealings. Julius Gorham not only served as Barnum's private secretary, bookkeeper, and "agent" by the 1870s but was also authorized to sign Barnum's name on letters and documents. See Timothy J. Gilfoyle, "Barnum's Brothel: P. T.'s 'Last Great Humbug,'" *Journal of the History of Sexuality* 18, no. 3 (2009): 486–513.

18. David Boyd, "A History: Greeley and the Union Colony of Colorado" (Greeley: Greeley Tribune Press, 1923).

19. Boyd, "History," 85.

20. "A Great Cattle Ranch; The Huerfano and Hermosilla Stock Farms; Vanderbilt's Latest Reported Enterprise—the Exportation of Beef—Eastern Capital and Western Lands—What Eastman, 'The Cattle King,' and Barnum the Showman, Say about It," *New York Times*, April 17, 1879, https://www.nytimes.com/1879/04/17/archives/a-great-cattle-ranch-the-huerfano-and-hermosilla-stock-farms.html (accessed March 10, 2010).

21. Irving Wallace, *The Fabulous Showman: The Life and Times of P. T. Barnum* (New York: Alfred A. Knopf, 1959), 170.

22. W. B. Vickers, *History of the City of Denver, Arapahoe County, and Colorado City & County of Denver* (Chicago: O. L. Baskin & Co., Historical Publishers, 1880), 350.

23. Silas B. Haynes, Villa Park management, Dr. William Buchtel Drinking Problem, January 1, 1879, Correspondence Received, no. 77, P. T. (Phineas Taylor) Barnum Papers, WH25, Western History Collection, Denver Public Library.

24. Jan Elizabeth Murphy, *Colorado Myths and Legends: The Stories behind History's Mysteries*, 2nd ed. (Guilford, CT: TwoDot, 2017), 41.

25. Angela Alton, "Historical Hindsights: P. T. Barnum and the 'Flaming Swords of Sobriety,'" *Tribune*, August 14, 2009, https://www.greeleytribune.com/news/local/historical-hindsights-p-t-barnum-and-the-flaming-swords-of-sobriety/ (accessed November 25, 2011).

26. His health no better, they soon sought out a higher altitude by purchasing a "2,100-acre ranch on the Divide in Douglas County, where for a time he was engaged in stock raising in addition to the practice of his profession" before returning to Denver. Buchtel, William H., clipping file, Denver Public Library, Western History and Genealogy Collection.

27. A. H. Saxon, *P. T. Barnum: The Legend and the Man* (New York: Columbia University Press, 1995), 228.

28. P. T. (Phineas Taylor) Barnum Papers, WH25, FF 13/14, Western History Collection, Denver Public Library.

29. Kinder, "Early Days," 2.

30. Kinder, "Early Days," 2.

31. Phil Goodstein, *Denver Streets: Names, Numbers, Locations, Logic* (Denver: New Social Publications, 1994).

32. On June 14, 1882, July 31, 1882, and August 25, 1882, Barnum filed a subdivision name change with the City of Denver for the P. T. Barnum Subdivision. Taken from "Legal Titles of Subdivisions in Adams, Arapahoe, Boulder, Denver and Jefferson Counties," copied from original in Denver Design Engineering Division, 58.

33. Edmund Berkeley, *Evergreen Farm Day Book, 1897–1905*, translated by Ronald Ray Turner (PWA Books.com, 2003), 27.

34. Evan Roberts, "Women's Rights and Women's Labor: Married Women's Property Laws and Labor Force Participation, 1860–1900," paper (presented at the Economic History Association annual meeting, Pittsburgh, PA, September 14–16, 2006), 7.

35. Interview with Doris Smith, via phone, July 11, 2009.

36. Ballenger and Richards, seventeenth annual Denver City Directory (Denver: Ballenger and Richards Publishers, 1889), 194.

37. Sharon R. Catlett, *Farmlands, Forts, and Country Life: The Story of Southwest Denver* (Boulder: Big Earth, 2007), 63.

38. Ida Libert Uchill, "Howdy, Sucker! What P. T. Barnum Did in Colorado?" (Denver: Pioneer Peddler Press, 2001).

39. Remnants of the barn were still on the property as of 2012.

40. Town of Barnum, Certification of Incorporation (Includes Plat), Archives 9051, FFI (Denver: Colorado State Archives, 8/27/1887).

41. Year: 1900; Census Place: Denver, Arapahoe, Colorado; Page: 15; Enumeration District: 0124.

42. "Negroes Ask Fairness," *Denver Post*, June 5, 1950, 4.

43. Patricia Nelson Limerick, *The Legacy of Conquest: The Unbroken Past of the American West* (New York: W. W. Norton, 1987), 27.

44. George arrived in Denver in 1884 and worked as a nurse at St. Luke's Hospital. In 1887 he worked as a laborer/coachman for Helen Buchtel, Barnum's daughter, at the Villa Park House. Years later he worked as a laborer and janitor until finally settling in as an expressman delivering packages and letters around Denver with his wagon and team.

45. "Our Colored Citizens; The Most Prosperous Negro Community in the North Found in Denver," *Denver Republican*, March 17, 1890, 7.

46. "Quoted in "Our Colored Citizens," 7.

47. "Quoted in "Our Colored Citizens," 7.

48. William E. Baist, Baist Real Estate Atlas of Surveys of Denver, Col. (Plate 12), Barnum (Denver neighborhood), Western History and Genealogy Department, Denver Public Library (1905).

49. Shirley J. Carlson, "Black Ideals of Womanhood in the Late Victorian Era," *Journal of Negro History* 77, no. 2 (1992): 61–73.

50. Adrian Praetzellis and Mary Praetzellis, "Mangling Symbols of Gentility in the Wild West: Case Studies in Interpretive Archaeology," *American Anthropologist,* New Series 103, no. 3 (2001): 252.

51. Praetzellis and Praetzellis, "Mangling Symbols," 252.

52. *Denver Rocky Mountain News*, February 18, 1899, 10.

53. In May 2014 James Price, who purchased the house from Doris and Larry Harris, died. Shortly thereafter, the property was sold to a Denver speculator who flipped the house, removing much of the interior Victorian woodwork that I was able to document.

54. It took a decade for me to gain access to the interior of the house. After a decade of cajoling Price and playing to his conservative values through conversations, conducting multiple visits (always on the porch), taking him to lunches, and many phone calls, Price finally granted me access in July 2012.

55. Interview with Doris Smith, Kiowa, October 20, 2012.

56. Information provided by Audrey Theisen, who visited Lucile with her father, Herman Dick, throughout the 1970s and 1980s.

57. These books came from the inventory that was in Lucile's home at 227 Raleigh Street in Denver in 1986.

58. The Victorian Society, 2012, http://www.victoriansociety.org.uk/advice/kitchens/ (accessed March 3, 2012).

59. South Africa History Online, quotes by Steve Biko, http://www.sahistory.org.za /archive/quotes-steve-biko (accessed April 10, 2014).

60. Melanie Shellenbarger, "High Country Summers: The Emergence and Development of the Second Home in Colorado, 1880–1940," PhD dissertation, University of Colorado Denver, 2008, 132.

61. While the KKK was more concerned with controlling the statehouse and promoting 100 percent Americanism, the group primarily targeted Jews, Catholics, and immigrants. Blacks did have some encounters, however. In Boulder, KKK members entered a Black church. The minister, fearing a physical confrontation, gave money to the Klan and they left. See Nicola Whitfield and Polly McLean, "Unlocking the History," in *A Legacy of Missing Pieces: The Voices of Black Women of Boulder County*, ed. Polly E. McLean (Boulder: CSERA Press, 2002), 12. Robert Alan Goldberg, in *Hooded Empire: The Ku Klux Klan in Colorado* (Urbana: University of Illinois Press, 1981), details several examples of Klan terror against Denver Blacks. For example, on February 25, 1922, Ward Gash, a house janitor, received a letter on Klan stationary warning him that he is too familiar with White women and to leave town or his hide won't be worth anything. He turned it over to the district attorney and left town for a while. By 1925 Gash returned to Denver. Dr. Clarence Holmes, president of the Denver NAACP chapter, had a cross burned in front of his office and received a threatening note for initiating a drive to integrate Denver's theaters. In the 1920s, Denver Blacks attempted to integrate some neighborhoods, and several houses were bombed. But no one was injured. No one was arrested, either, so it was hard to know whether the bombings were from the Klan or just bigotry in general. Bigotry seemed to have been a key factor in May 1920, when 250 Whites marched on the home of municipal firefighter C. H. De Priest, at 2649 Gaylord street in the Clayton subdivision, demanding that the family move out of the neighborhood since their presence would depreciate the value of their property.

62. Henry Louis Gates Jr., "The Trope of a New Negro and the Reconstruction of the Image of the Black," *Representations*, no. 24 (1988): 129–55.

CHAPTER 7: EDUCATION, POLITICS, AND LEISURE

1. Campbell Gibson and Kay Jung, Population Division, Historical Census Statistics on Population Totals by Race, 1790 to 1990 (Working Paper No. 56, 38), https://www .census.gov/content/dam/Census/library/working-papers/2002/demo/POP-twps0056 .pdf (accessed October 4, 2017).

2. M. Dores Cruz, *Black Homesteading in the American Western Frontier* (Oxford African American Studies Center, 2012), http://www.oxfordaasc.com/public/features /archive/1013/essay.jsp (accessed April 12, 2014).

3. Frank Wilmot, *Look at Race and Ethnicity in Colorado (1860-2005): Census Definitions and Data* (2006), 16, http://www.coallnet.org/wp-content/uploads/2015/04/Wil motArticle.pdf (accessed March 5, 2011).

4. Harmon Mothershed, "Negro Rights in Colorado Territory, 1859–1867," *Colorado Magazine* 60, no. 3 (1963): 215.

5. In the 1866 Colorado Business Directory, two public schools were listed bearing the name, Public School. One catered to students living in west Denver on Ferry Street, with a Miss Glenn listed as the teacher; the other catered to students living in east Denver on Larimer Street, between I and K Streets, with teacher D. D. Hatch. Two other schools are listed: Colorado Seminary, E Street, between Lawrence and Arapahoe, with B. T. Vincent as principal, and St. Mary's Academy, on California Street between E and F Streets. See Leona L. Gustafson, trans., "Business Directory," *Denver, Colorado Genweb* (2014), http://www.genealogybug.net/1866_History/bussinessdir.html (accessed April 6, 2015).

6. *Rocky Mountain News*, "Mr. Hatch's Resignation," October 3, 1867, 1.

7. Eugene H. Berwanger, "Hardin and Langston: Western Black Spokesmen of the Reconstruction Era," *Journal of Negro History* 64, no. 2 (1979): 327.

8. Berwanger, "Hardin and Langston," 327.

9. Carl Abbott, "Plural Society in Colorado: Ethnic Relations in the Twentieth Century," *Phylon* 39, no. 3 (1978): 250.

10. National Archives and Records Administration. *Schedules of the Colorado State Census*, M158, 8 rolls (Washington, DC: National Archives and Records Administration, 1885).

11. The incorporation of Barnum into the Denver public school system occurred prior to Barnum's annexation by the city of Denver in 1896. Also see the history of Denver's public schools at http://communications.dpsk12.org/history.html (accessed April 5, 2015).

12. Katherine L. Craig, "Report of the State Superintendent of Public Instruction of the State of Colorado for the Years 1907–1908" (Denver: Smith-Brooks, 1908), 10.

13. In 1929 Villa Park was renamed Eagleton School in honor of its longtime principal and educator William H. Eagleton. The school was demolished in 1975.

14. "Villa Park Pupils Have a Commencement," *Denver Post*, June 7, 1901, 3.

15. "Reception to Graduates: Colored People Honor Young People Who Have Left School," *Denver Post*, June 19, 1901, 18.

16. Town of Barnum, Colorado State Archives Public Records Archives 9015, FF8, Petitions, 2.17/1890. The signators of the petition were E. E. Tinsdale, J. F. Buchanan, P. Lang, C. Klerk, Wm. Brandenburg, S. J. Young, George Ward, Steven Liddie, and John Butler.

17. Charles Rounds, "Frederick Jackson Turner," in *Wisconsin Authors and Their Works* (Madison, WI: Parker Educational Company, 1918), 302–7.

18. For example, Barnum's town minutes show that on September 5, 1889, James was paid $74 for work performed. Only one other male made $4 more than James. The same occurred on May 26, 1890, when he was paid $54 for work performed prior to May 7. On May 21, 1890, James worked 13½ days, billing the town for $54.

19. Robert M. Ormes, *Railroads and the Rockies: A Record of Lines in and near Colorado* (Denver: Sage Books, 1963).

20. According to Doris Smith, Lucile told her that the family went to Golden on day-trips. The Golden connection could also be related James's first cousin, who owned a farm near Golden.

21. "History: A Story of Vision, Pride and Community," *Lincoln Hills* (2014), http://www.historiclincolnhills.com/history/ (accessed November 7, 2016).

22. Evelyn Napper (Claribel's daughter), personal letter to author regarding her mother's participation in the Festival of Mountain and Plain, 2009.

23. Lovette J. Davidson, "The Festival of Mountain and Plains," *Colorado Magazine* (1945): 145–57; *Portrait and Biographical Record of the State of Colorado* (Chicago: Chapman 1899), 45.

24. For a comprehensive discussion of the festival and its shift to electrical displays, see "Record of Electrical Patents," *Electrical Review and Western Electrician with Which Is Consolidated Electrocraft* 61, no. 19 (Chicago: Electrical Review Publishing Company, 1912): 894–95.

25. "Editors Issue," *Statesman*, December 30, 1911, 1.

26. "Grand Concert," *Denver Star*, May 12, 1882, 2.

27. Black playwrights included William Wells Brown, John S. La Due, and Emma G. Hatcher.

28. Paul Kuritz, *The Making of Theatre History* (Upper Saddle River, NJ: Prentice-Hall, 1987), 297.

29. "New Year's Greetings," *Colorado Statesman*, January 2, 1917, 3.

30. R. Terry Furst, *Early Professional Baseball and the Sporting Press: Shaping the Image of the Image of the Game* (Jefferson, NC: McFarland, 2014), 112.

31. Colorado teams played other Black teams, independent White teams, and other Negro League teams that were barnstorming through Colorado. In 2002 I interviewed Helen McVey Washington, who went to games in Denver and Boulder and said that Black players sometimes faced humiliation and racial slurs against White teams (especially when they were winning). Nonetheless, they played the game with dignity.

32. Mark Hanna Watkins, "Racial Situation in Denver," *The Crisis* (May 1945): 140.

33. Robert Autobee and Kristen Autobee, *Lost Restaurants of Denver* (Charleston, SC: American Palate, 2015), 54.

34. Watkins, "Racial Situation," 139.

35. Watkins, "Racial Situation," 140.

36. *Rocky Mountain News*, "The Color Line: A Meeting of Colored Citizens Called to Demand Civil Rights in Denver and Colorado," February 11, 1885, 8.

37. *Denver Tribune-Republican*, April 4, 1886, 5.

38. *Statesman*, April 23, 1910, 8.

39. Wyoming was the first state to grant women the right to vote, followed by Colorado.

40. Lynda F. Dickson, "Lifting as We Climb: African American Women's Clubs of Denver, 1880–1925," in *Writing the Range: Race, Class, and Culture in the Women's West*, ed. Elizabeth Jameson and Susan Armitage (Norman: University of Oklahoma Press, 1997), 347.

41. Daughters of Rebekah is an international service organization and a branch of the Independent Order of Odd Fellows. Order of the Eastern Star, created in 1874, is the oldest sorority-based women's organization in the United States; and the Sisters of Calanthe is the female auxiliary of the Fraternal Order of Knights of Pythias.

42. A. W. Hunton, "Women's Clubs," *The Crisis* (July 1911): 17–18.

43. Lynda F. Dickson, "Towards a Broader Angle of Vision in Uncovering Women's History: Black Women's Clubs Revisited," *Frontiers: A Journal of Women Studies* 9, no. 2 (1987): 62–68.

44. As part of their community betterment, Black clubwomen in Colorado established the Colorado Orphanage and Old Folks Home in Pueblo, Colorado, and the George Washington Carver Day Nursery and the Negro Women's Club Home in Denver.

45. W.E.B. Du Bois, "The Talented Tenth," in *The Negro Problem*, ed. Booker T. Washington (New York: James Pott, 1903), 58.

46. Dickson, "Lifting as We Climb," 347.

47. *Statesman*, September 15, 1905, 16.

48. *Statesman*, January 13, 1905, 4.

49. Among Lucile's possessions was a receipt for a Victoria Talking Machine that was purchased in Denver.

50. These records were among the inventory collected by the State of Colorado when Lucile died in 1989.

51. Frantz Fanon, *Black Skin, White Masks* (New York: Grove, 2008).

52. Willard B. Gatewood, *Aristocrats of Color: The Black Elite, 1880–1920* (Fayetteville: University of Arkansas Press, 1990); see also Evelyn Brooks, Higginbotham, *Righteous Discontent: The Women's Movement in the Black Baptist Church, 1880–1920* (Cambridge, MA: Harvard University Press, 1994).

53. W.E.B. Du Bois, *The Souls of Black Folk* (Chicago: A. C. Mc, 1903).

CHAPTER 8: THE FRONTIER IN OUR SOULS

1. Some of the information obtained was secured from the 1885 Colorado State Census found at The National Archives at Washington, D.C.; Record Group Title: *Records of the Bureau of the Census, 1790–2007*; Record Group Number: 29; Series Number: *M158*; NARA Roll Number: 1, Denver City Directories, 1922–1936, Western History/Genealogy, Denver Public Library, Colorado, County Marriage Records and State Index, 1862–2006, Film Number 001690092.

2. Evelyn Napper, letter to author, 2009.

3. Lee Jacobs Carlin, "Sweet Magic: 100 Years of Baur's Restaurant," *Colorado Heritage* (Spring 2002): 15–29.

4. On April 11, 1881, Sophia B. Packard and Harriet E. Giles of Boston, under a commission from the American Baptist Home Mission Society, established a school for the elevation of Black girls and women in the basement of Friendship Baptist Church, Atlanta. The school was originally called Atlanta Baptist College. In 1883, the name was changed to Spelman Seminary in honor of Laura Spelman Rockefeller, abolitionist, philanthropist, educator, and wife of Standard Oil co-founder John D. Rockefeller. Rockefeller was also a member of the board of trustees and had invested large numbers of funds to buildings and grounds at Spelman. For further information, see the Thirty-Third

Annual Circular of Spelman Seminary for Women and Girls in Atlanta, GA. For the Academic Year, 1913–14, Spelman Messenger Office, 1914.

5. Letter courtesy of the Spelman Archives.

6. Spelman College, "Catalog of Spelman Seminary 1891–1892," Spelman Catalogs (2018), 11, http://digitalcommons.auctr.edu/sccatalogs/11 (accessed February 23, 2018).

7. Benjamin Griffith Brawley, *A Short History of the American Negro* (New York: Macmillan Company, 1919), 138.

8. Campbell Gibson and Kay Jung, "Historical Census Statistics on Population Totals by Race 1790 to 1990, and by Hispanic Origin, 1970 to 1990, for Large Cities and other Urban Places in the United States," Population Division working paper no. 76, https://www.census.gov/population/www/documentation/twps0076/twps0076.pdf (accessed October 20, 2008).

9. Gibson and Jung, "Historical Census."

10. See Reiland Rabaka, *Du Bois's Dialetica: Black Radical Politics and the Reconstruction of Critical Social Theory* (New York: Lexington Books, 2008); David Levering Lewis, *W.E.B. Du Bois: Biography of a Race, 1868–1919* (New York: Teachers College Press, 1993); Derrick P. Alridge, *W.E.B. Du Bois in Georgia*, New Georgia Encyclopedia (accessed January, 23, 2017).

11. Spelman College, *Spelman Messenger* 22, no. 8 (May 1906): 170, http://digitalcommons.auctr.edu/scmessenger/170 (accessed January 5, 2018).

12. Spelman College, "Spelman Seminary Catalog 1908–1909," 47, http://digitalcommons.auctr.edu/sccatalogs/28 (accessed February 23, 2018)

13. "Spelman College," 49.

14. "Denver Items," *Stateman*, June 5, 1909, 12.

15. August Meier and David Lewis, "History of the Negro Upper Class in Atlanta, Georgia 1880–1958," *Journal of Negro Education* 28 (Spring 1959): 128–39.

16. Morehouse is an all-male college. But between 1929 and 1933, the college graduated thirty-three women among which Hannah graduated in 1929 with five other Black women. No women have graduated since 1933. See Add Seymour Jr., "College's Only Living Female Graduate Proud to Be a Morehouse Woman," Morehouse College, http://www.morehouse.edu/communications/archives/002366.html (accessed January 28, 2016).

17. Villa Park High School, *Denver Rocky Mountain News*, June 8, 1896, 6.

18. Geraldine Lightner, Education—Yesterday, Denver Western History and Genealogy Library, African American clipping file, 1890–1899.

19. The contents of Lucile's letter to her sister Laura can be found in the Buchanan Archives.

20. *Denver Post*, "IN DESPAIR: A Young Colored Girl Thought There was no Place for Her, The Victim of Melancholia," February 17, 1899, 11.

21. Emile Durkheim, *Suicide: A Study in Sociology*, trans. John A. Spaulding and George Simpson (Glencoe: Free Press, 1951).

22. LeRoy R. Hafen, "The Coming of the Automobile and Improved Roads of Colorado," *The Colorado Magazine*, January 1931.

23. Salt Lake City Ward 5, Salt Lake, UT, 1910 Census, Roll T624_1607, Page 11A, Enumeration District 0143, FHL microfilm 1375620.

24. Ronald G. Coleman, "Blacks in Utah History: An Unknown Legacy" (Salt Lake City: Utah State History, 1981), http://historytogo.utah.gov/people/ethnic_cultures /the_peoples_of_utah/blacksinutahhistory.html (accessed February 1, 2010).

25. San Francisco Assembly District 32, San Francisco, CA, 1920 Census, Roll T625_137, Page 7B, Enumeration District 183.

26. San Francisco, CA 1930 Census, Roll 205, Page 12B, Enumeration District 0287, FHL microfilm, 2339940.

27. In 2010, when Lucile's last living relatives committed suicide in Las Vegas, I found Nellie's gun, still intact, in their home with a written history of the gun. The city sold the gun at an auction.

28. Edith B. Davis *v.* Charles H. Davis, no. 4-29828, Div. 3, City and County of Denver, CO, June 19, 1941.

29. *Statesman*, December 1908, 13.

30. *Statesman*, July 6, 1918, 5.

31. Information from Claribel's scrapbook, Buchanan Archives. On Friday May 6, 1955, Louise Beavers came to Denver for a four-day visit with Claribel. She was showered with a host of events including a party sponsored by the Derby Club, which featured some of Denver's most prominent citizens across race.

32. Hans A. Baer, "The Metropolitan Spiritual Churches of Christ: The Socio-Religious Evolution of the Largest of the Black Spiritual Associations," *Review of Religious Research* 30, no. 2 (1988): 144.

33. Baer, "Metropolitan Spiritual Churches," 141.

34. Louise Beavers and her husband, LeRoy Moore, spent four days as houseguests of Claribel and her husband, George Perkins, at 2131 Gilpin Avenue in Denver's Five Points. She left en route to join film and stage actress Mae West in the Mae West Revue at the Sahara's Congo Room in Las Vegas on June 27, 1955.

35. Quintard Taylor, *In Search of the Racial Frontier: African Americans in the American West 1528–1990* (New York: W. W. Norton, 1998).

36. Clearly, the author of this opinion letter seems unaware that in 1950 only two of the fifty-four countries on the continent of Africa were nominally "independent"—South Africa and Ethiopia—and that repatriating US Blacks to countries under European rule would have been next to impossible or impossible. The only country in which the United States had a stake in the development was Liberia, which began as a settlement of the American Colonization Society to repatriate freed US slaves in 1822.

37. *Denver Post*, June 5, 1950, 4.

38. *Denver Post*, July 21, 1950, 11.

39. Some of the information obtained was secured from Fenton's Application for Social Security Account Number 524-18-196, his funeral service record (Buchanan Archives), Denver City Directories, 1922–1936, Western History/Genealogy, Denver Public Library, World War I Draft Registration Card, Denver County, Colorado, Roll: 1544475, Draft Board 2, and from his Last Will and Testament, City and County of Denver Court, P 31614.

40. Letter from Hannah Buchanan, 26 Parson St. Atlanta, GA, January 15, 1922. Buchanan Archives.

41. Interview with Donna Teviotdale, Denver, February 27, 2009.

42. Letters can be found in the Buchanans' Archives.

43. While miscegenation statutes barred marriages between Whites and Blacks, school segregation was barred in Colorado in 1876, and segregation in public facilities in 1885.

44. W.E.B Du Bois, *The Philadelphia Negro: A Social Study* (New York: Benjamin Blom, 1899).

CHAPTER 9: SCHOOL, COMMUNITY, AND LOVE LOST

1. Vertie L. Carter, *Arkansas Baptist College: A Historical Perspective, 1884–1982* (Houston: D. Armstrong, 1981).

2. Johnny D. Jones, s.v., "Arkansas Baptist College," *Encyclopedia of Arkansas History and Culture*, http://www.encyclopediaofarkansas.net/encyclopedia/entry-detail.aspx?search=1&entryID=2440 (accessed November 2, 2006).

3. Since Fritz Hill assumed the presidency, the ABC has increased its student population from 175 to well over 1,100, opened a GED center, partnered with Memphis Theological Seminary to offer the masters of divinity degree, secured funds to remodel Old Main (the oldest African American education building in Arkansas), and welcomed a charter high school onto its campus.

4. Polk's Southern Directory Company, Hot Springs City Directory, 1912 (Little Rock: Polk's Southern Directory Company, 1912), 99.

5. "Frank Cornelius Long, clergyman, teacher; born at New Orleans, La., Mar. 2, 1860; son of Alexander Dumas and Anna Mae (Hawkins) Long; public school educator, New Orleans; A.B., and first male grad. Leland Univ. Was first colored teacher in Bishop College, Marshall, Texas, serving as instructor of mathematics, 1881–2; principal Langston High School, Hot Springs, Ark., since 1907. Member Knights of Pythias, Knights of Honor, Mosaic Templars." Source: *Who's Who of the Colored Race: A General Biographical Dictionary of Men and Women of African Descent*, vol. 1, ed. Frank Lincoln Mather (Chicago: Memento Edition, Half-Century Anniversary of Negro Freedom in US, 1915), 179.

6. *Who's Who of the Colored Race*, 179.

7. Inez E. Cline and Wendy Richter, eds., "Hot Springs Special School District," in *The Record*, 26, no. 6 (Hot Springs, AR: Garland County Historical Society, 1985), 82–86.

8. C. Vann Woodward, "Progressivism? For Whites Only," in *Origins of the New South, 1877–1913* (Baton Rouge: Louisiana State University Press, 1951), 369–95.

9. Jimmie Franklin, "Blacks and the Progressive Movement: Emergence of a New Synthesis," *OAH Magazine of History* 13, no. 3 (1999): 20–23.

10. Before graduating from Howard University's Medical School in Washington, DC, in 1888, James Webb Curtis was the postmaster in Marion, Alabama; worked as a clerk in the pension office in Washington, DC; and was appointed special agent in the pension office in northwestern Illinois. He was an officer in the Spanish-American War and served under contract as acting assistant surgeon in the Philippines-American War from 1899 to 1901. Also

see Linda McDowell, "Dr. James Webb Curtis: An Early African American Physician to Hot Springs," in *The Record* (Hot Springs, AR: Garland County Historical Society, 2005), 81–84.

11. G. P. Hamilton, "Rev. J. A. Booker," in *Beacon Lights of the Race* (Memphis: F. H. Clarke and Brother, 1911), 166–74.

12. Booker T. Washington, *A New Negro for a New Century* (Chicago: American Publishing House, 1900), 30.

13. Fon Louise Gordon, *Caste and Class: The Black Experience in Arkansas, 1880–1920* (Athens: University of Georgia Press, 2008), xii.

14. Gordon, *Caste and Class*.

15. Cheryl Batts, "Malvern Avenue, Hot Springs, Arkansas Was 'Black Broadway,'" *Newsletter of the Historic Preservation Alliance of Arkansas* (2006): 3.

16. Department of the Interior, Bureau of Education, *Negro Education: A Study of the Private and Higher Schools for Colored People in the United States*, vol. 2 (Washington, DC: Government Printing Office, 1917), https://archive.org/details/negroeducationa02fundgoog (accessed January 9, 2010).

17. Thomas Jesse Jones, "Negro Education: A Study of the Private and Higher Schools for Colored People in the United States," *Phelps Stokes Fund, Washington, Government Printing Office* 2, no. 39 (1917): 116.

18. The letter is in the author's possession.

19. Dorothy L. Logan, "A History of Black Education in Hot Springs Prior to Integration," *Garland County Historical Review* 17 (1976): 63–66.

20. Dorothy L. Logan, "Langston High School," in *The Record*, vol. 21 (Hot Springs, AR: Garland County Historical Society, 1980), 59–61.

21. See Guy Lancaster, *Encyclopedia of Arkansas History and Culture, Hot Springs, Garland County*, http://encyclopediaofarkansas.net/encyclopedia/entry-detail.aspx?entryID=887 (accessed December 20, 2014).

22. Booker T. Washington, "Lynchings during 1913," *Journal of the American Institute of Criminal Law and Criminology* 4, no. 6 (1914): 927–30.

23. "Lynch Negro in Hot Springs Street," *Reading (PA) Eagle*, June 20, 1913, sec. P7, http://news.google.com/newspapers?nid=1955&dat=19130620&id=q40tAAAAIBAJ&sjid=hpoFAAAAIBAJ&pg=4833,2567649 (accessed April 12, 2009).

24. Ray Hanley and Steven G. Hanley, *Hot Springs Arkansas in Vintage Postcards* (Charleston, SC: Arcadia, 1998), 11.

25. "Keep Arkansas Resort in Darkness at Night for a Month," *New York Times*, September 7, 1913, Special to the *New York Times*.

26. Other researchers have noted that Langston School opened in an auditorium on Gulpha Street called the "Casino." The 1912 Hot Spring City Directory indicates that the only facility on Gulpha Street catering to African Americans was a hall that belonged to the Grand United Order of Odd Fellows, a fraternal organization founded in 1843. It is likely that the hall was called the Casino.

27. Stanley Gordon, letter to author, June 15, 2008.

28. Edmund Andrews, "Langston High School: Still a Place in Their Hearts," *Sentinel Record* (Hot Springs), July 5, 1980.

29. The letters are in the author's possession.

30. Some of the states identified in Census documents in which the name Pythias shows up as a given name are Arkansas, Louisiana, Mississippi, North Carolina, South Carolina, Texas, and Virginia.

31. Booker T. Washington, Fannie B. Barrier, and Norman B. Wood, *A New Negro for a New Century: An Accurate and Up-to-Date Record of the Upward Struggles of the Negro Race* (Chicago: American Publishing House, 1900), 39.

32. Amy Braverman Puma, "Color Lines," *University of Chicago Magazine* (January–February 2009), http://magazine.uchicago.edu/0902/features/color_lines.shtml (accessed June 20, 2009).

33. US Bureau of the Census, *Negroes in the United States, 1920–1932* (Washington, DC: Government Printing Office, 1935; reprint New York: Greenwood, 1969), 55.

CHAPTER 10: A FLY IN THE BUTTERMILK: COLORADO AND THE WORLD OF HIGHER EDUCATION

1. "Denver Girl the First Colored Graduate of State Normal School," *Rocky Mountain News*, July 23, 1905, 15.

2. On April 1, 1889, Governor Job A. Cooper of Colorado signed the bill creating the State Normal School to train qualified teachers for the state's public schools. Greeley citizens raised the necessary money for the first building, and the cornerstone was laid on June 13, 1890. The school opened its doors on October 6, with a staff of four instructors and ninety-six students. Certificates were granted upon the completion of a two-year course.

3. T. J. Wray, Surviving the Death of a Sibling: Living through Grief when an Adult Brother or Sister Dies (New York: Three Rivers, 2003), 5.

4. Jesse Logan Nusbaum was born in Greeley, Colorado, on September 3, 1887, to Edward Moore and Agnes Strickland Nusbaum. His parents and grandparents were among the original settlers of Greeley, organized by Horace Greeley.

5. State Normal School Bulletin, Series 111, no, 1, published quarterly by the Trustees of the State Normal School of Colorado, Greeley, Colorado, June 1902, 21–25.

6. Unofficial transcript, Colorado State Teachers College, Greeley, CO, 1905, no. 597.

7. "City News," *The Statesman*, June 10, 1905.

8. "Denver Girl the First Colored Graduate."

9. The Greeley Opera House, also known as the Hunter Opera House, was built in 1886 by Sam D. Hunter and was located on the southwest corner of Eight Street and Eight Avenue. See David Boyd, *A History: Greeley and the Union Colony of Colorado* (Greeley: Greeley Tribune Press, 1890), 226.

10. State Normal School, *The Crucible* 13, no. 10 (June, 1905): 276.

11. "Personal Briefs," *The Statesman*, June 9, 1905.

12. Jerry White, *Death on the Picket Line: The Story of John McCoy* (Detroit: Labor Publications, 1990), 4.

13. Rayford W. Logan, *The Negro in American Life and Thought, The Nadir 1877–1901* (New York: Dial Press, 1954).

14. *Walsenburg World,* July 25, 1905, 1.

15. *The Statesman,* October 13, 1905, 9.

16. *The Statesman,* September 4, 1908, 8.

17. According to Brickler's Draft Registration Card and the Roster of Men and Women Who Served in the World War from Colorado, 1917–18, Colorado: Adjutant General, Colorado National Guard, 1941, Brickler registered on September 12, 1918 during the third draft for men ages 18–45, in the Student Army Training Corps (SATC) in Denver. With the ending of the war in 1918, he took a job as a clerical clerk for the railroads before returning to the University in 1919 to complete his degree in mechanical engineering.

18. *The Coloradoan* (Boulder: Associated Students of the University of Colorado, 1912): 49.

19. No doubt Campbell experienced some difficulties in the College of Engineering. This became evident when I interviewed Dr. Alexander W. Brickler, the son of the first African American male to earn an undergraduate degree in mechanical engineering from the College of Engineering, Alexander Jesse Brickler. According to Brinkler, his father was discouraged from continuing his degree. It is possible that Campbell also experienced some of the same treatment. For further information on personal mediated racism see J. M. Jones, *Prejudice and Racism,* 2nd ed. (New York: McGraw-Hill, 1997). Of special note: Campbell went on to be a chemist, working at the US Naval Torpedo Station in Newport, Rhode Island. Upon his return to Denver, he opened his own chemical business, eventually securing a position as an engineer for the US Forest Service.

20. Frank Hamilton Bowles and Frank A. De Costa, *Between Two Worlds: A Profile of Negro Higher Education* (New York: McGraw-Hill, 1971), 37.

21. *University of Colorado Bulletin,* 17, no. 3, General Series 111, Catalog 1916–17 (Boulder: Regents of the University of Colorado, March 1, 1917), 37.

22. It is possible that Lucile, a mature student over twenty-one years of age, would not have been held to the same criteria as students under twenty-one who fell under Bigelow's jurisdiction.

23. *University of Colorado Bulletin,* 17, no. 3, General Series 111, Catalog 1916–17, 40.

24. This is an estimation based on the 1910 Census, which indicates that there were about 113 Blacks in Boulder, Colorado. By 1920 there were about 118. Boulder Ward 3, Boulder, Co, 1910 Census, Roll T624_113, Page 4A, Enumeration District 0043, Image 661, FHL Number 1374126; Boulder Ward 4, Boulder, CO, 1920 Census, Roll T625_156, Page 13B, Enumeration District 53, Image 547.

25. Paul Edward Spratlin was born in Alabama in 1861 and graduated from Atlanta University in 1881. He taught school in the South from 1881 to 1889 before moving to Denver, where he received a medical degree in 1892 from Denver Medical College of the University of Denver. From 1895 to 1899 he was Denver's chief medical inspector. He was active in many institutions in Denver's Black community, including the Douglas Undertaking Company, the Lincoln-Douglass Consumptive Sanitarium, the A.M.E. Church, and the YMCA. Booker T. Washington, *The Booker T. Washington Papers, vol. 5: 1899–1900,* ed. Louis R. Harlan and Raymond W. Smock (Champaign: University of Illinois Press, 1977), 427.

26. Interview with Helen McVey Washington, Denver, February 27, 2002.

27. John Moody, *Moody's Manual of Investments and Security Rating Books,* part 3: *Public Utility Investments* (New York: Moody's Investors Service, 1921), 1135. The Western Light and Power Company was incorporated in 1906 in Colorado as the Northern Colorado Power Company. In July 1914 the name was changed to the Western Light and Power Co.

28. There were a number of additional, non-church-sponsored activities that were celebrated by Boulder Blacks that would have been available to Lucile, such as lawn parties, recitals, and attending events at Chautauqua Auditorium.

29. According to Phyllis Smith's March 1984 report, *A History of Boulder's Transportation, 1858–1984, for the City of Boulder, Transportation Division* (Boulder), the route between Denver and Boulder was named the "kite route" because the route resembled the shape of a flying kite with Denver as the tail of the kite" (19).

30. Smith, *History of Boulder's Transportation,* 19.

31. "Boulder Notes," *The Statesman,* February 17, 1917, 5.

32. William E. Davis, Glory Colorado: A History of the University of Colorado, 1858–1963 (Boulder: Pruett, 1965), 25.

33. "University Notes," *Daily Camera* (Boulder), September 8, 1916, 3.

34. Directory of the Students and Faculty of the University of Colorado, 1917–18 (Boulder: Christian Associations, 1918), 39.

35. Regents of the University of Colorado, "Catalogue, 1917–1918," *University of Colorado Bulletin* 18, no. 4, General Series 125 (April 1918): 39.

36. "Women's Frolic a Big Success," *Silver and Gold* 25, no. 3 (December 12, 1916): 81.

37. See the University of Colorado Catalog, 1916–1917, p. 45, for a discussion on the YMCA/YWCA and the Newman Society. While fulfilling its religious role, the YWCA headquartered in the Women's Building also conducted a board and room register, a book exchange, and a self-help bureau for women. The YMCA, with offices in the Men's Dormitory, produced the Students' Handbook, the Student and Faculty Directory, and the Men's Employment and Information Bureau.

38. Regents of the University of Colorado, "Catalogue, 1915–1916," *University of Colorado Bulletin* 16 no. 3, General Series 33 (March 1916) 44.

39. Regents of the University, "Catalogue, 1915–1916."

40. In 1916 Lucile's home college, the College of Liberal Arts, had thirty faculty members, of which two were women: Assistant Professor of Literature S. Antoniette Bigelow and Professor of Germanic Languages Grace van Sweringen Baur, the only female full professor with a PhD at the university.

41. For example, the 1916 yearbook the *Coloradoan* shows that the junior class consisted of approximately 160 students, of which 103 were males and 57 females.

42. The sixteen clubs included the Players Club for dramatic arts, the Civic Club, the Scoop Club for newspaper reporting, the E.V.U Debating Club, the Debating Society, the Sketch Club, the Scribblers Club, the Richards Literary Society, and the Intercollegiate Socialist Society, among others. There were also clubs designed to help students master a foreign language, such as Le Cercle Français, El Círculo Español,

and the Deutscher Verein; clubs focusing on particular religious groups, such as the Intercollegiate Menorah Association for the advancement of Jewish culture and ideals; and clubs focusing on particular majors, such as for the civil, mechanical, and electrical engineers.

43. "University Notes," *Daily Camera* (Boulder) 26, no. 159 (September 8, 1916, 3.

44. "Dean Bigelow to Give Teas for All Women," *Silver and Gold* 26, no. 15 (November 19, 1917): 2.

45. "Women Plan for Self-Government," *Silver and Gold* 26, no. 40 (March 8, 1918): 4.

46. The National Defense Act of 1916 authorized the establishment of Army Reserve Officers' Training Corps (ROTC) programs to train officers on university campuses across the nation. While the university's request to establish an ROTC program was denied by the army, the faculty took the lead and established an ROTC unit in October 1917.

47. Board of Regents, Students' Army Training Corp of the University of Colorado, *University of Colorado Bulletin* 17, no. 8 (Boulder: Board of Regents, 1918); Board of Regents, *Twenty-First Biennial Report of the Regents, 1916–1918* 18, no. 12 (Boulder: Board of Regent) 21.

48. Lewis R. Gordon, "Existential Dynamics of Theorizing Black Invisibility," in *Existence in Black: An Anthology of Black Existential Philosophy*, ed. Lewis R. Gordon (New York: Routledge, 1997), 72.

49. Chad Williams, *African Americans and World War I* (New York: Africana Age: African and African Diasporan Transformation in the 20th Century, Schomburg Center for Research in Black Culture, and the New York Public Library, 2011), http://exhibitions.nypl.org/africanaage/essay-world-war-i.html (accessed June 30, 2011).

50. Herman E. Thomas, *James W. C. Pennington: African American Churchman and Abolitionist* (New York: Garland Publishing, 1995).

51. L. T. Hopkins, "Spiritual Fatherland: African-American Intellectuals and Germany, 1850–1920," *Yearbook of German-American Studies* 31 (1996): 25–36.

52. Robert Fikes Jr., "African Americans Who Teach German Language and Culture," *Journal of Blacks in Higher Education* 30 (2000–20001): 108–13.

53. As of 2017, three HBCUs offered courses in German: Howard University, North Carolina A&T State University, and Southern University and Agricultural and Mechanical College.

54. Mark Wyman, Immigrants in the Valley: Irish, Germans, and Americans in Upper Mississippi Country, 1830–1860 (Chicago: Nelson-Hall, 1984), 202–3; Eugene Scheel, "Ample Land Drew German Settlers to Loudoun County," http://www.loudounhistory.org/history/loudoun-german-settlers/ (accessed February 3, 2015).

55. Albert Bernhardt Faust, *The German Element in the United States: With Special Reference to Its Political, Moral, Social, and Educational Influence* (Boston: Houghton Mifflin, 1909).

56. "Dr. Grace Fleming van Sweringen Baur," *Colorado Alumnus* (March 1930): 6–7.

57. Large segments of the African American population opposed getting involved in World War I, a cause they saw as hypocritical given their lack of citizenship in the world's top democratic society. Even so, Blacks did engage in the war at the front lines and were

exemplary soldiers. On the home front, a small number a number of Blacks vehemently opposed the war. A. Phillip Randolph and Chandler Owens, editors of *The Messenger*, a radical publication, openly encouraged Blacks to resist military service and as a result were closely monitored by the federal intelligence agents under the 1917 Espionage Act.

58. Terrence G. Wiley, "The Imposition of World War 1 Era English-Only Policies and the Fate of German in North America," in *Language and Politics in the United States and Canada: Myths and Realities*, ed. Thomas K. Ricento and Barbara Burnaby (New York: Routledge, 2013), 221.

59. Lyle W. Dorsett, "The Ordeal of Colorado's Germans during World War I," *Colorado Magazine* 51/4 (1974): 281.

60. "Black-Faces to Play Jazz Music for Soph Dance," *Silver and Gold* 26, no. 38 (March 1, 1918): 1.

61. "To Install New War Related Courses," *Silver and Gold* 26, no. 27 (1918): 1.

62. "New German Classes Installed to Help Future War Workers," *Silver and Gold* 26, no. 28 (January 11, 1918): 1.

63. Robert A. Gibson, "Booker T. Washington and W.E.B. Du Bois: The Problem of Negro Leadership," *20th Century Afro-American Culture* 2 (1978).

64. W.E.B. Du Bois, "The Talented Tenth," in *The Negro Problem: A Series of Articles by Representative Negroes of Today*, ed. Booker T. Washington (New York: James Pott, 1903), 31–75, https://archive.org/details/negroproblemserioowashrich.

65. President Farrand, "Home from France Stirs Loyal Hearts in Great Address," *Boulder Daily Camera*, June 5, 1918, 2.

66. Davis, *Glory Colorado*, 243.

67. Evelyn Napper, letter to author, December 3, 2008.

68. W.E.B. Du Bois, ed., "The Year in Negro Education," Crisis: A Record of the Darker Races 16, no. 3 (1918): 116, http://www.modjourn.org/render.php?id=12929484385 61750&view=mjp_object.

69. Du Bois, "Year in Negro Education," 118, 121.

CHAPTER 11: "GOIN' TO KANSAS CITY": EDUCATION AND BASEBALL

1. Prior to 1900 and before the rise of the modern real estate industry, Blacks and Whites in Kansas City lived close to one another, sharing the same living spaces. Following World War I, these residentially integrated neighborhoods began to change in Kansas City and throughout the nation, leading to the rise of racially segregated communities. By the time Lucile arrived in Kansas City, Blacks were relegated to segregated living spaces.

2. Lincoln High School was organized as an elementary for Blacks in 1865, serving two hundred Black students. In 1875 the school changed its name to Lincoln High Elementary School. In 1880 the elementary and high schools were placed in separate buildings. A vocational department was added in 1915. Lucile served under two outstanding

principals—John R. Lee (1915–1921) and H. O. Cook (1921–1944). In 1986 the name was changed to Lincoln College Preparatory School. See https://www.kcpublicschools.org /Page/1016 (accessed March 20, 2017).

3. Kevin Fox Gotham, "Missed Opportunities, Enduring Legacies: School Segregation and Desegregation in Kansas City, Missouri," *American Studies* 43, no. 2 (2002): 5-42.

4. W.E.B. Du Bois, *Black Reconstruction in America 1860–1880* (New York: Atheneum, 1992), 667.

5. Campbell Gibson and Kay Jung, *Historical Census Statistics on Population Totals by Race, 1790 to 1990, and by Hispanic Origin, 1970 to 1990, for Large Cities and Other Urban Places in the United States*, Population Division Working Paper No. 76 (Washington, DC: US Census Bureau, February 2005), https://www.census.gov/population/www/documentation/twps0076/twps0076.pdf (accessed May 23, 2016).

6. "The History of the Kansas City Call," Black Archives of Mid-America Kansas City, http://blackarchives.org/articles/history-kansas-city-call.

7. This assessment of Lucile's dress style and hair vis-à-vis other teachers was found in the 1924 and 1925 yearbook pictures that she had in her steamer trunk.

8. Laws of 1889, Revised Statues (1889), 1861, State Historical Society of Missouri, Arthur A. Benson, II, box 303.

9. Janet Bruce, *Kansas City Monarchs: Champions of Black Baseball* (Lawrence: University Press of Kansas, 1985), 44.

10. Bruce, *Kansas City*, 45.

11. Following his initial career as a journalist and editor of the *Kansas City Call*, Wilkins became a prominent civil rights advocate, leading the NAACP as its executive secretary in 1955 and eventually becoming its executive director in 1964.

12. Roy Wilkins and Tom Mathews, *Standing Fast: The Autobiography of Roy Wilkins* (New York: Viking, 1982), 67.

13. Henrietta Rix Wood, *Praising Girls: The Rhetoric of Young Women, 1895–1930* (Carbondale: Southern Illinois University Press), 110; Charles E. Coulter, *Take up the Black Man's Burden: Kansas City's African American Communities, 1865–1939* (Columbia: University of Missouri Press, 2002), 185.

14. Roy Wilkins acknowledges that the successes of Black schools hinged upon the "talented teachers who would have been teaching in colleges had they been white, and partly because Negro parents and children simply refused to be licked by segregation." See Wilkins and Mathews, *Standing Fast*, 68.

15. On March 20, 1920, a memorial was signed by the leading Black organizations drawing attention to Lincoln's substandard conditions and calling for the creation of a new high school. These organizations included Lincoln's Parent Teacher Association, the Kansas City branch of the NAACP, the City Federation of Colored Women, the Black doctors of the Kansas City Medical Society, the Civil League, the Lincoln High Alumni Association, the Inter-City Lawyers Club, the Negro Business League, and the Inter-Denominational Ministerial Alliance.

16. The *Kansas City Sun* was published and edited by N. C. Crews from 1908 to 1924 and was a well-respected and influential newspaper in the Midwest. The editor purchased

the newspaper in 1911 and spent most of his career tackling issues of inequities in the African American community in Kansas City. In 1921, his editorials took on the dilapidated condition of the Black public schools, with special attention to the challenges faced by students and teachers at Lincoln High School. http://chroniclingamerica.loc.gov/lccn /sn90061556/ (accessed August 29, 2015).

17. Roy Wilkins, the managing editor of the *Call*, wrote in his autobiography, *Standing Fast*, that nothing enraged him more than the Kansas City school board's prejudice against Black schools and their lack of interest in changing the deplorable conditions. He called the schools "rat traps" or "hand-me-down facilities" abandoned by Whites with five of the twelve elementary schools without bathroom facilities. His efforts led to an organized campaign to encourage Black voters to vote down bonds for Jim Crow schools. See Wilkins and Mathews, *Standing Fast*, 67.

18. Coulter, *Take Up the Black Man's Burden*, 188.

19. *Lincolnian*, vol. 24, Buchanan Archives (Kansas City, MO: Senior Class of Lincoln High School, 1924), 51.

20. "School a Negro Center: Community Uplift Is Carried on Now at Lincoln High," *Kansas City Star* 36 (December 26, 1915): 9.

21. *Lincolnian*, vol. 25, Buchanan Archives (Kansas City, MO: Senior Class of Lincoln High School, 1925), 58.

22. Woody Lee Walder became a renowned clarinet player with the Bennie Moten Orchestra, considered Kansas City's first great jazz band. Walder's solos with the Moten band have been described as sonic art sculptures pieced together with squeals, squeaks, whinnies, whines and cries. See *Vindication of Woody Walder*, http://yestercenturypop .com/2012/07/10/woody-walder-modern-is-as-modern-does/ (accessed August 29, 2015).

23. *Lincolnian*, vol. 25, Buchanan Archives (Kansas City, MO: Senior Class of Lincoln High School, 1925), 77.

24. *Lincolnian*, vol. 25: 47.

25. The information on the school newspaper that Lucile founded and is discussed in this section was from a third copy of the *Observer* that was found in the steamer trunk she left behind.

26. Information in this section was put together from various census documents and Lincoln school yearbooks.

27. *Lincolnian* vol. 25: 37.

CHAPTER 12: IT'S MISTER JONES, IF YOU PLEASE

1. Doris Smith (who bought Lucile's house), in discussion with the author, relaying a conversation she had with Lucile about Lucile's husband and kept getting the same answer: "He died in a duel," with no first name, March, 5, 2005.

2. Michael L. Hecht, Ronald L. Jackson, and Sidney Ribeau, *African American Communication: Exploring Identity and Culture*, 2nd ed. (New York: Routledge, 2002).

3. Thomas Kochman, *Black and White Styles in Conflict* (Chicago: University of Chicago Press, 1983).

4. Vi Garlington (former administrator at Stovall Care Center) in discussion with the author, July 10, 2005.

5. Doris Smith in discussion with the author, July 10, 2005.

6. See United States Census Bureau, http://www.census.gov/topics/population /genealogy/data/2000_surnames.html, November 3, 2010.

7. Terry Isbell, "Blood and Honor: Duel on the Cane, 1839," *Old Natchitoches Parish Magazine and Mercantile Advertiser* 1 (1997): 1–7.

8. Thurmon Garner, "Understanding Oral Rhetorical Practices in African American Cultural Relationships," in *Towards Achieving Maat*, ed. V. J. Duncan (Dubuque, IA: Kendall/Hunt, 1998), 29–44.

9. Russell Frank Weigley, Philadelphia: A 300 Year History, ed. Nicholas B. Wainwright and Edwin Wolf (New York: W. W. Norton & Company, 1982), 492.

10. Frederick Binder and David M. Reimers, *All the Nations under Heaven: An Ethnic and Racial History of New York City* (New York: Columbia University Press, 1995), 100.

11. Robert M. Dowling, *Slumming in New York: From the Waterfront to Mythic Harlem* (Champaign: University of Illinois Press, 2007), 79.

12. Brady Slone (associate registrar, Columbia University), email message to author, January 22, 2007, 3:13 pm.

13. "A Betoken Honor to Brother G.W.A. Scott: An Illustrious Charter Member of the Seventh Chapter of Alpha Phi Alpha Fraternity since 1909, A Brochure Dedicated to Brother George W. A. Scott," Tuskegee Archives (1972), 9.

14. Columbia University Annual Commencement, 154–65, Columbia University in the City of New York, Tuskegee Archives, 37.

15. Caldwell Titcomb, "The Earliest Black Members of Phi Beta Kappa," *Journal of Blacks in Higher Education*, no. 33 (2001): 92–101.

16. Probably the most visible Black student on campus was George William Artway Scott. Unlike John or French, who are not pictured in the 1910 or 1911 Columbian yearbook of graduates, Scott is as prominently featured as any of his White classmates. He participated in the Economics Club and Debating Society as well as a number of varsity sports during his freshman and sophomore years. In 1910 and 1911 he came in second and first, respectively, for the Curtis Prize for excellence in public delivery of English orations. The White members of the class of 1910 wrote under his name, "His face is dark but his mind is brilliant." Columbia records indicate that Scott graduated in 1911 with a Bachelor of Science degree and headed to Tuskegee Institute in Alabama, where in fall 1911 he took a teaching position under the leadership of Booker T. Washington. Scott remained at Tuskegee for sixty-four years until his death on March 25, 1975.

17. Colleen O'Connor, "In Search of Lucile: Diligent detective work opens a new chapter on Colorado's Black History," *Denver Post*, April 3, 2007. Retrieved at: http:// www.denverpost.com/headlines/ci_5586550.

18. For an analysis of these leading Black activists, John D. Jones, and his relationship to Harrison, see: Jeffrey B. Perry's *Hubert Harrison: The Voice of Harlem Radicalism, 1883–1918* (New York: Columbia University Press, 2009).

19. David Dunlap, *From Abyssinian to Zion: A Guide to Manhattan's Houses of Worship* (New York: Columbia University Press, 2004).

20. Perry, *Hubert Harrison*, 73.

21. Marcy S. Sacks, *Before Harlem: The Black Experience in New York City Before World War I* (Philadelphia: University of Pennsylvania Press, 2006). 1–8.

22. J.E. Robinson, editor of *The Mirror* of St. Mark's Lyceum, letter to the editor, *New York Times*, February 18, 1907. Retrieved June 25, 2009, the New York Times Archives: http://query.nytimes.com/gst/abstract.html?res=9804E5DE123EE033A25751C2A9649 C946697D6CF.

23. Perry, *Hubert Harrison*, 85.

24. Perry, *Hubert Harrison*, 75.

25. Perry, *Hubert Harrison*, 76.

26. Perry, *Hubert Harrison*, 110.

27. Manhattan Y.M.C.A. *NYA*, December 10, 1908, 3.

28. Stefan Bradley, "The First and Finest: The Founders of Alpha Phi Alpha Fraternity," in *Black Greek-Letter Organizations in the Twenty-First Century: Our Fight Has Just Begun*, ed. Gregory S. Parks (Lexington: University Press of Kentucky, 2008), 19–40.

29. Tuskegee University Archives (1971), Box 9.

30. "A Betoken Honor to Brother G.W.A. Scott: An Illustrious Charter Member of the Seventh Chapter of Alpha Phi Alpha Fraternity, since 1909, A Brochure Dedicated to Brother George W. A. Scott," Tuskegee Archives (1972), 9.

31. Sudderth, "Tenderloin," 1163.

32. Martin Kilson, "Retrospective on the Washington/Du Boisian Black Leadership Paradigms: Part 1," *The Black Commentator* 172 (2006).

33. The ASSU, established in Philadelphia in 1817, was a nondenominational organization that drew its members from varying religious persuasions: Baptists, Episcopalians, Methodists, Presbyterians, Moravians, Dutch Reformers, Congregationalists, German Reformers, and the Society of Friends. Once a Sunday school was established, the parent body in Philadelphia allowed the group to determine its own denominational affiliation. Today, the ASSU has become the American Missionary Fellowship.

34. Monroe Nathan Work, *Negro Year Book: An Annual Encyclopedia of the Negro* (Tuskegee, AL: Tuskegee Institute, Negro Year Book Publishing Company, 1916), 211.

35. Monroe Nathan Work, *Negro Year Book: An Annual Encyclopedia of the Negro* (Tuskegee, AL: Tuskegee Institute, Negro Year Book Publishing Company, 1914–15), 196.

36. W.E.B. Du Bois, "The Talented Tenth," in *The Negro Problem: A Series of Articles by Representative Negroes of To-day* (New York: James Pott and Co., 1903).

37. Registration Location, Bramberg County, South Carolina; Roll: 1852494; Draft Board: 0.

38. Emmett J. Scott, "Treatment of Negro Soldiers in Camp," in *Scott's Official History of the American Negro in the World War* (Chicago: Homewood Press, 1919).

39. Theodore Hemmingway, "Prelude to Change: Black Carolinians in the War Years, 1914–1920," *Journal of Negro History* 65, no. 3 (1980): 212–27.

40. Scott, "Treatment of Negro Soldiers," 426–30; John H. Franklin, *From Slavery to Freedom* (New York: Alfred A. Knopf, 1974), 379.

41. "RG 1.2.1 Simon G. Atkins Collection," Winston-Salem State University Archives.

42. S. G. Atkins, "Report of Principal Atkins, Meeting of the Board of Trustees, Tuesday afternoon, Sept. 2nd 1919," WSSU Archives—Board of Trustees Minutes 1899–1921, 1928 (Box 1).

43. In John's report, he went on to discuss the school resources, which had "been many," and the introduction of a high school methods course, conducted by the assistant superintendent of schools. He paid particular attention to the wide range of extracurricular activities, which boosted student morale, such as "Inter-School Athletics, the Community Chest Drive, the Library Drive, the organization of a "Crown and Scepter Club," and joining the Accredited High School Debating League.

44. Report of Principal Atkins, Meeting of Board of Trustees, Tuesday afternoon, September 2, 1919," WSSU Archives—Board of Trustees Minutes 1899–1921, 1928 (Box 1).

45. Deborah Haith Caple (daughter of a graduate of class of 1925) in discussion with the author, March 30, 2008.

46. The Maroon and Gold yearbook, Winston-Salem, NC: Students of the Columbia Heights High School, 1926), 30 (published annually).

CHAPTER 13: CHICAGO, TAKE TWO

1. Timothy Samuelson, *Black Metropolis Thematic Nomination* (Cook County, IL), National Register of Historic Places Registration Form (Washington, DC: US Department of the Interior, National Park Service, 1986), 4.

2. W.E.B. Du Bois, "The Colored Chicago," *The Crisis* (September 1915): 234, 236.

3. Christopher Manning, "African Americans," in *The Electronic Encyclopedia of Chicago* (Chicago: Chicago Historical Society, 2005), http://www.encyclopedia.chicagohistory.org/pages/27.html (accessed September 9, 2014).

4. Chicago Commission on Race Relations, *The Negro in Chicago: A Study of Race Relations and a Race Riot* (Chicago: University of Chicago Press, 1922), 107–8.

5. Kathleen Norris, "Age is no Bar to Real Romance: The Character and Nature of Bride and Groom are Only Important Things," *Tacoma Daily Ledger*, January 8, 1928, p. 62.

6. Wallace D. Best, *Passionately Human, No Less Divine: Religion and Culture in Black Chicago, 1915–1952* (Princeton, NJ: Princeton University Press, 2005), 45.

7. Darlene Clark Hine, "Introduction," in *The Black Chicago Renaissance*, ed. Darlene Clark Hine and John McCluskey (Champaign: University of Illinois Press, 2012), 15–27.

8. Stacey Peterson, "Transcript of Interview with Monte Posey: Growing Up," *US Equal Employment Opportunity Commission*, http://www.eeoc.gov/eeoc/history/35th/voices/oral_history-monte_posey-stacey_petersen.wpd.html (accessed February 3, 2014).

9. John's employment records can be found at the National Archives-STL, File No. 15-859-325, Saint Louis, MO.

10. Jerry W. Ward Jr., and Robert J. Butler, eds., *The Richard Wright Encyclopedia* (Westport, CT: Greenwood, 2008), 77; see also Constance Webb, *Richard Wright: A Biography* (New York: Putnam, 1968).

11. Ward and Butler, *Richard Wright Encyclopedia*, 77.

12. John F. Lyons, *Teachers and Reform: Chicago Public Education, 1929–1970* (Champaign: University of Illinois Press, 2008), 209.

13. Ward and Butler, *Richard Wright Encyclopedia*, 71.

14. State of Illinois, County of Cook in the Superior Court of Cook County, Lucile B. Jones *v.* John D. Jones, Complaint for Divorce, no. 4OS 114, Statement Provided by Plaintiff (Lucile B. Jones), January 3, 1940.

15. Ellis had graduated from the John Marshall Law School and was admitted to the Illinois bar. After earning her degree, she became an attaché in the domestic relations branch of the municipal court. In 1941 she was admitted to practice before the United States Supreme Court. See J. Clay Smith Jr., *Emancipation: The Making of the Black Lawyer 1844–1944* (Philadelphia: University of Pennsylvania Press, 1993), 385.

16. State of Illinois, County of Cook in the Superior Court of Cook County, *Lucile B. Jones v. John D. Jones*, Gen. No, 40S114, Report of Proceedings at the Hearing of the Above Entitled Case before the Honorable Rudolph F. Desort, Judge of Said Court of the Eleventh Day of April, AD 1940.

17. US Department of Health, Education and Welfare, *100 Years of Marriage and Divorce Statistics, United States, 1867–1967* 21, no. 24 (Washington, DC: DHEW, 1973), DHEW Publication no. (HRA) 74-1902, 48.

18. Internal Revenue Service, Treasury Department, Application for Social Security Account Number, Form SS-5 (revised June 1940).

19. State of Illinois, Circuit Court of Cook County Department–Probate Division: Estate of John D. Jones, File No. 66P 3195, Docket 692, Page 223, 1966, April 28 (Chicago, IL). Following John's death, Rozine continued to live at their home in Chicago. He died on February 3, 2007 at age eighty-two.

20. Chad Heap, "Gays and Lesbians," *The Electronic Encyclopedia of Chicago* (Chicago: Chicago Historical Society, 2005), http://www.encyclopedia.chicagohistory.org /pages/509.html (accessed July 11, 2012).

21. Gay nightclubs such as the Plantation Café, the Pleasure Inn, Dreamland Cafe (Dreamland Gardens), Sunset Café, Club DeLisa, and Joe's Deluxe Club. William Howland Kenney, *Chicago Jazz: A Cultural History, 1904–1930* (New York: Oxford University Press, 1993), 25.

22. Tristan Cabello, *Queer Bronzeville: The History of African American Gays and Lesbians on Chicago's South Side* (OutHistory.org, 2008), http://outhistory.org/exhibits/show /queer-bronzeville (accessed July 11, 2012).

23. Leigh Goodmark, *A Troubled Marriage: Domestic Violence and the Legal System* (New York: New York University Press, 2012), 55.

24. Wallace Best, *Grand Boulevard*, The Electronic Encyclopedia of Chicago (Chicago: Chicago Historical Society, The Newberry Library, 2005).

25. Best, *Grand Boulevard*.

26. St. Clair Drake and Horace R. Cayton, *Black Metropolis: A Study of Negro Life in a Northern City* (Chicago: University of Chicago Press, 1993), 202.

27. Anne Meis Knupfer, *The Chicago Black Renaissance and Women's Activism* (Chicago: University of Illinois Press, 2006), 75.

28. Michele Foster, *Black Teachers on Teaching* (New York: New Press, 1997), 26–27.

29. Drake and Cayton, *Black Metropolis*, 294.

30. Drake and Cayton, *Black Metropolis*, 522.

31. Chicago, Cook, IL, 1940 Census, Roll m-t0627-00925, Page: 62A, Enumeration District 103-145.

32. Chicago, Cook, IL, 1940 Census.

33. The University of Chicago, Office of the Recorder, Records of Lucile Berkeley Buchanan Jones, Matriculation No. 54747, 1815–1941.

34. All three letters are dated Christmas 1962 and are in the Buchanan Archives.

35. Dorsey and Professor Theodore R. Frye, and singer Roberta Martin formed at Ebenezer in 1932 the first modern choir that sang gospel music. After its introduction at Ebenezer, gospel began to take off, and Dorsey and Frye performed gospel music at the Pilgrim Baptist Church at Thirty-third and Indiana. Pilgrim hired Dorsey to create a choir there, and it became his home church and gospel base for decades. While newspaper articles listed Lucile B. Jones as the recording secretary for the NCGCC, it is not clear whether she remained at Ebenezer or switched to Pilgrim with Dorsey.

36. Drake and Cayton, *Black Metropolis*, 716.

37. Knupfer, *Chicago Black Renaissance*, 81-92.

38. Correspondence with Lucile's niece Evelyn Napper, 2008.

39. Drake and Cayton, *Black Metropolis*, 516.

CHAPTER 14: "LINCOLN WAS A REPUBLICAN, THAT'S ALL I NEED TO KNOW"

1. Wyoming Territory was the first state to give women the franchise prior to the Nineteenth Amendment.

2. The three women trailblazers were Clara Cressingham, Carrie Clyde Holly, and Frances Klock.

3. Radical Republicans were members of the Republican Party who were committed to the abolition of slavery and equality of the races.

4. US National Archives and Records Administration, the Center for Legislative Archives, Roll Call Tally on Civil Rights Act 1964, June 19, 1964, https://www.archives.gov/legislative/features/civil-rights-1964/senate-roll-call.html (accessed April 12, 2018).

5. The controversy over Harding's ethnicity resurfaced in a *New York Times* article by Beverly Gage, "Reconsideration: Our First Black President?" *New York Times*, April

6, 2008, http://www.nytimes.com/2008/04/06/magazine/06wwln-essay-t.html?_r=0 (accessed February 24, 2012).

6. See, for example, J. A. Rogers, *The Five Negro Presidents: According to What White People Said They Were* (New York: Helga M. Rogers, 1965), http://www.metaphysicspirit .com/books/The%20Five%20Black%20Presidents.pdf (accessed August 5, 2013).

7. On October 29, 1920 (four days before the presidential election), the board of trustees denounced Chancellor's methods of collecting data and requested his resignation. See "College Ousts Professor Chancellor Because of Circulars on Harding; Denounces His 'Unworthy Methods,'" *New York Times*, October 30, 1920, http://query .nytimes.com/mem/archive-free/pdf?res=FA0C12F83D5411738DDDA90B94D8415B 808EF1D3 (accessed August 5, 2013).

8. Randall Kennedy, "Racial Passing," *Ohio State Law Journal* 62 (2001): 1145–94.

9. Phillip Payne, *Dead Last: The Public Memory of Warren G. Harding's Scandalous Legacy* (Athens: Ohio University Press, 2008).

10. *Kansas City Sun*, June 19, 1920, 1.

11. *Kansas City Sun*, 1.

12. Letter from J. Silas Harris to Arthur Capper, March 17, 1922, Kansas Historical Society, Topeka, KS, http://www.kshs.org/km/capper/view/217564 (accessed January 4, 2009).

13. Mark Wolf, "Centenarians Say Freedom Linked to Vote," *Rocky Mountain News*, October 14, 1988, 10.

CHAPTER 15: COMING HOME AND GOING HOME

1. Interview with Herman Dick's daughter Audrey Theisen, Lakewood, CO, June 20, 2013. Also, Robert L. Steenrod's report on Lucile's estate filed in probate court, city and county of Denver states that Herman Dick was paid $276 for lawn care for 1986.

2. In 1951 her niece Evelyn Napper gave birth to the first of two daughters, Lisa Claire. A second daughter, Veda Anne, followed in 1952. Lucile had two other sisters who chose to live in Los Angeles and never returned to Colorado (Sadie and Nellie) and a second niece, Carol, who also lived in Los Angles.

3. Board v. Board of Education of Topeka, 347 US 483 (1954).

4. Plessy v. Ferguson, 163 US (1896).

5. Interviews with the cemetery staff in 2010 yielded information on those who were interned around the same time and in the same section as Laura. They reported that beyond Laura's internment card, they found no other information on her, including who bought the plot.

6. Interlocutory Decree in Divorce, no. A-29828, Div. 3, Filed in District Court, City and County of Denver, Colorado, June 19, 1941, 2.

7. In the Matter of the Estate of Edith B. Davis, Deceased, no. P-18031, Filed in County Court, City and County of Denver, Colorado, October 17, 1960.

8. In the Matter of the Estate of Edith B. Davis, Deceased, no. P-18031, Filed in County Court in and for the City and County of Denver and State of Colorado.

9. Although her three surviving sisters, Claribel, Sadie, and Nellie, were given one-fifth interest each, Lucile also included the surviving daughter of her late sister Hattie, Carol Jarrett Roberts. She also chose not to include her other surviving niece, Evelyn Lucile, possibly because her mother was alive. I always wondered whether this action was one of several that created the rift between Lucile and Evelyn.

10. The Denver Bible Baptist College (DBBC) was founded in 1914. Faced with declining enrollment in the 1980s, the DBBC merged with the Iowa-based Faith Baptist Bible College in 1986.

11. Audrey Theisen in interview with the author, May 4, 2011.

12. Rosvall's Auctioneering report filed with the court, Steenrod states that the discrepancy between the fair market value and what the Harrises purchased is that Lucile's "niece took remaining items." Probate Court, City and County of Denver, State of Colorado. Case No. 86PR1108, April 18, 1987.

13. Audrey Theisen in discussion with the author, May 4, 2011.

14. Debbie Heglin, email message to author, April 13, 2007.

15. Probate Court, Case no. 86PR1008, City and County of Denver, State of Colorado, Filed November 13, 1986, Donald M. Snapp, clerk, 13.

16. Doris Smith in discussion with the author, September 19, 2010.

17. Audrey Theisen in discussion with the author, May 4, 2011.

18. Viola Garlington (former director of Stovall Care Center, Denver) in discussion with the author, 2007.

19. According to nursing home records, Lucile checked into Stovall at 10:55 a.m.

20. Probate Court, City and County of Denver, Case No. 86PR1108, June 20, 1986, page 1.

21. Garlington, in discussion with the author, 2007.

22. Garlington, in discussion with the author, 2007.

23. Garlington, in discussion with the author, 2008.

24. Larry Harris, in discussion with the author, 2006.

25. Doris Smith, in discussion with the author, 2006.

26. Suzanne Lipsky, *Internalized Racism* (Seattle: Rational Island Publishers, 2008).

27. Garlington, discussion with the author, 2007.

28. Earnestine Gavin (former records manager at Stovall Care Center, Denver) in discussion with the author 2007.

29. Gaines, "Racial Uplift Ideology."

30. Thomas Kochman, *Black and White Styles in Conflict* (Chicago: University of Chicago Press, 1981).

31. Gaines, "Racial Uplift Ideology."

32. Gaines, "Racial Uplift Ideology."

33. Doris Smith (buyer of Lucile's house), in discussion with the author, 2002.

34. Smith, in discussion with the author, 2002.

35. Marlene G. Fine, *Building Successful Multicultural Organizations: Challenges and Opportunities* (Westport, CT: Quorum Books, 1995), 98–99.

36. Earnestine Gavin, in discussion with the author, 2008.

37. Information included in Probate Court, City and County of Denver, Case No. 86PR 1108 and from the Fairmount Heritage Foundation, January 12, 2010.

38. Steven Mross, "Langston School to Hold 16th Reunion," *Sentenial-Record*, July 9, 2017, https://www.pressreader.com/usa/the-sentinel-record/20170709/281487866383648 (accessed August 3, 2017).

EPILOGUE: THE END OF THE LIVING LINE

1. A copy of this letter written by Mary Lewis Berkeley Cox to her grandsons, in which she discusses the Civil War and its impact on her life, her assistance to the Confederacy, and her thoughts about slaves, can be found at the Thomas Balch Library in Leesburg, Virginia.

2. While it is not uncommon for people to update Last Wills and Testaments, the wills I discovered in the home began in 1987 with the last one written in 2006, the year after Evelyn's husband died. She made two major changes. One on September 3, 1989, which ended with "Absolutely nothing is to be given to Lucile B. Jones." The feud between Lucile and her 70-year-old niece Evelyn was so intense that she added this caveat when Lucile was 105, a month before she died. The second change appeared on October 16, 2006, which stated, "In case of accident in which Veda, Lisa and Evelyn are killed, please cremate and bury us in one container in the plot of our Beloved Daddy and husband. It is located in Boulder City Veteran Cemetery plot 227."

3. The only letters located in the house were addressed to their mother in response to letters she had sent to family and friends.

4. Derek Humphry, *Final Exit: The Practicalities of Self-Deliverance and Assisted Suicide for the Dying* (New York: Dell Publishing, 2002).

5. The number of helium tanks they rented came from a suggestion in Humphry's book, which recommends two tanks for each individual, with one serving as a backup. The additional tank would be used on Flit. All tanks were still in the house when I arrived.

6. The iPod was in the bedroom when Catrice and I arrived. As a result, we were able to listen to this music.

7. Brian K. Cooke, MD, "Extended Suicide with a Pet," *Journal of the American Academy Psychiatry Law*, 41 (2013): 437–43.

8. Cooke, "Extended Suicide," 440.

9. Lisa Gavin, MD, Clark County Coroner/Medical Examiner, North Las Vegas, Report of Investigation, Coroner Case, no. 10-07935.

10. Joe Schoenmann, "North Las Vegas Police Alerted to Suicide Note, but Respond Too Late," *Las Vegas Sun*, September 29, 2010.

11. My interview with the veterinarian's office revealed that Flit was healthy and that the doctor did not put him to sleep.

12. Albert Camus. *The Myth of Sisyphus and Other Essays*, trans. Justin O'Brien (New York: Vintage Books, 1955).

13. Irvin D. Yalom, *Existential Psychotherapy* (New York: Basic Books, 1980), 40.

Index